THE LIFE IN THE
FICTION OF
Ford Madox Ford

THE LIFE IN THE FICTION OF
Ford Madox Ford

————❦————

THOMAS C. MOSER

PRINCETON UNIVERSITY PRESS

PRINCETON, NEW JERSEY

Publication of this book has been aided by a grant from
The Andrew W. Mellon Foundation

This book has been composed in VIP Palatino
Clothbound editions of Princeton University Press books
are printed on acid-free paper, and binding
materials are chosen for strength and durability
Printed in the United States of America by
Princeton University Press, Princeton, New Jersey

For T. and F.

Contents

Preface

In this book I try to answer two perhaps unanswerable questions. Why did Ford Madox Ford spend twenty-four years writing nineteen minor novels before he could, in 1913-1914, create his masterpiece, *The Good Soldier*? And why, having written that very great novel, did he give his notable subsequent works—*Parade's End*, the double novels, the lovely last memoirs and travel books—a tone and form so different from *The Good Soldier's*? What, in short, were the conditions requisite to Ford's creativity?[1] His career was unusual because *he* was.[2] Yet mostly we have had sound books about a tediously sound Ford.[3] Throughout his career he described himself, as we all know, as "mad" about literature (AL, 296; IWN, 126). He *was* mad in his admirable enthusiasms, his distressing unreliability, his fantastic fictionalizing of his own and others' lives, his eccentricities, his magnificent inconsistencies. And although he seems never to have experienced a totally debilitating psychosis, he most certainly suffered at thirty a serious, protracted, neurotic illness (diagnosed at the time as "neurasthenia"); he afterwards underwent severe recurrences and lived in sporadic fear of going insane. Indeed, he later characterized the works he wrote just after the Great War as those of a "lunatic" (IWN, 11).

My title is intended to convey several ideas. First, the personal life of this obsessive memoirist constantly reappears in his novels. Also recurrently reflected are the lives of a handful of his intimates: the women he loved, all writers or artists, Elsie Martindale Hueffer, Violet Hunt, Stella Bowen, and Janice Biala; even more importantly, his two male friends, the great novelist Joseph Conrad and the Tory gentleman Arthur Marwood. As Ford says in his last book, "once you are really saturated in the work of a writer it is legitimate to enquire into the circumstances of his life. It is human nature—and not only that, details of an author's life may cast light on passages of his work or on the nature of literature itself" (ML, 752). My title is intended to suggest its converse as well, the fiction in the life of Ford Madox Ford. Not only did his fiction constantly prophesy events in his real life, but, during the war, Ford Madox Hueffer created out of his brain "Ford Madox Ford" in much the way James Gatz created "Jay Gatsby." Above all, though, I would like the title to convey the idea of the *vitality* in Ford's fiction. Even his weakest novels have their exciting, characteristically Fordian moments, usually involving either the threat of sexual passion or some version of Ford's troubled affection for Conrad and Marwood.[4] Ezra Pound astutely says that much of Ford's "best prose was probably lost, as isolated chapters in unachieved and too-quickly-issued novels."[5] Since most criticism of Ford's novels naturally concentrates upon large matters like theme and structure and upon the works in relation to their cultural milieu, it often misses that "best prose," misses what is truly, authentically Fordian.[6]

But the title misleads if it seems to suggest that Ford confined his literary vitality exclusively to his fiction. Though his novels represent his major creative effort, some of Ford's liveliest prose is to be found elsewhere—in his fine memoir, *Ancient Lights*; in the early trilogy of sociological impressionism on London, the countryside, and the English; in the book on Conrad; and above all in the relatively unknown "Literary Portraits" and critical essays of Ford's most creative and perhaps most desperate period, 1913-1914. The existence of all this prose accounts in part for the one major, impressionistic violation of chronology in my book. I save discussions of the pre-*Good Soldier* nonfictional works and of the meaning of the 1904-1906 mental illness until the chapter on *The Good Soldier*. That novel sums up the artistry and the tortured life of Ford Madox Hueffer. It transforms into fiction personal knowledge that he had faced only in the nonfiction, if at all: that man is the suffering, cruel, helpless victim of his irrationality and his sexual passion. By concentrating on the nonfictional writings of 1913-1914 in the *Good Soldier* chapter, I hope to dramatize the unity of Ford's writing at the time and thus show that the great prose of the novel could not have come solely from the technical discovery of a first-person narrator. I hope also to indicate the relations between Ford's anxious psyche and his masterpiece by exploring the connections between his agoraphobia (the main form of his mental distress) and impressionism (his term for his peculiar artistry). In all my dealings with the life and works, my ultimate subject remains Ford's creative imagination with its characteristic tendency to shift about, in similar but ever-changing patterns, a group of familiar fictive counters closely connected to a few human beings.

Thus, this book is anything but a work of pure criticism. Nor is it biography. Arthur Mizener has masterfully chronicled Ford's outer life in all its variety and untidiness. My chief biographical contributions are two. Olive Garnett's contemporary, detailed pictures of Ford's courtship, marriage, and nervous breakdown make clearer than ever before the powerful influence those early experiences exerted upon the whole of his career. And my fuller, and I hope more balanced and sympathetic, account of Ford's intimate friendship with Conrad suggests how importantly each figured in the mind of the other. Probably my Ford is an abstraction; obviously my argument is highly speculative. It uses fiction to explain life, life to explain fiction, thus constantly violating the critical dogma of our time. Faulkner, exploring the sources of Thomas Sutpen's design in *Absalom, Absalom!*, calls his method the "best of ratiocination."[7] I would like my book to participate a little in the spirit of Faulkner's heroic enterprise. It seems to me the only way to begin to understand a figure as strange, lovable, brilliant, unhappy, jocund, generous, and altogether wonderful as Joseph Leopold Ford Hermann Madox Hueffer.

Acknowledgments

Ford Madox Ford came to life for me in an English garden one spring day in 1963; the medium was the voice—at once amused and sympathetic—of David Garnett. A few months later, reading about Ford's early years in the diary of Mr. Garnett's Aunt Olive, I first sensed the amazing consistency, the unchangeableness, even, of my subject's personality. This diary was generously provided by its owner, Olive's niece, Anne Lee-Michell. For these two Garnett cousins I feel special gratitude and friendship.

Many others, who either knew Ford personally or had close relatives or friends who knew him, have provided me, in conversation or in correspondence, with valuable information and insight. I wish to thank Henry Bouch, John Conrad, Rupert Hart-Davis, Florence Wynne Finch, Richard Garnett, Kathleen M. Hill, John Lamb, Michael Patmore, Margery Pilcher, Dame Rebecca West, and Juliet Wrightson. Several, including some who were particularly kind and helpful to me, are now deceased: Borys Conrad, Richard Curle, the ever-generous George T. Keating, and Lucy Masterman. I wish above all to remember the warmth and benevolence of the late Katharine Hueffer Lamb, who so hoped to live to see this book published. Early in my researches, certain pioneer Fordian scholars and collectors made their materials available to me: Richard J. Herndon, Richard M. Ludwig, Frank MacShane, and especially Edward Naumberg, Jr. At a later stage, I had help from Raymond Brebach, Vera Cohn, Samuel Hynes, Frederick R. Karl, Arthur Mizener, Midge O'Clair, Dale Peterson, Rex M. Ware, and Kenneth Young. The following good friends read portions, usually all, of some version of the manuscript: Paul B. Armstrong, Maclin Bocock, Albert J. Gelpi, Albert J. Guerard, David Levin, Bernard C. Meyer, Zdzisław Najder, and Ian Watt. Needless to say, they have not necessarily condoned what follows and are blameless for whatever mistakes it contains.

I wish to thank the rare book departments of the Harvard University Library, the Huntington Library, the New York Public Library, the Pennsylvania State University Library, the Princeton University Library, the University of Virginia Library, the Yale University Library, and especially the Cornell University Library. I am grateful to the Trustees of the Joseph Conrad Estate for permission to quote extensively from Conrad's letters. At home, the Art, Interlibrary Loan, Photocopying, Rare Book, and Reference departments of the Stanford University Library were endlessly helpful, as were, abroad, the British Museum and the London Library. The Stanford English Department has been patient and supportive with sabbatical leaves, stints at overseas campuses, and research and typing assistance, the last often supplemented by our Graduate Dean, Bliss Carnochan. The entire administration of Princeton University Press has provided consistently warm encouragement and support during very trying circumstances. I wish in particular to thank the literature editor, Marjorie Sherwood, my copyeditor, Judith May, and the former assistant director, Carol Orr.

A fellowship from the American Council of Learned Societies launched the project. The expert typing of Jo Guttadauro helped to finish it. Brief portions of this book have appeared in different form in *Joseph Conrad: A Commemoration, L'Epoque Conradienne, Mosaic,* and *Texas Studies in Literature and Language.* The most loyal and efficient professional help has come from my research assistant, Robyn R. Housley. Mary Churchill Moser remains essentially my collaborator. Her sociability led to the discovery of Olive Garnett; her work took us to Caroline Marwood's family. She has spent countless hours on the manuscript. Without her inspiration and that of the dedicatees, this book would never have been finished. And as to the importance of *that*, I, like John Dowell, don't know, and leave it to the reader.

Thomas C. Moser

Stanford, California

A Chronological List of
Ford's Works

All quotations come from the first English editions of Ford's works (except, obviously, for those not published in England). Pagination is supplied parenthetically in the text, with abbreviations where necessary. Ford's books are listed below in approximate order of composition rather than of publication. The information comes from David Dow Harvey's bibliography and Arthur Mizener's biography of Ford.

The Brown Owl. London: T. Fisher Unwin, 1892. Fairy tale.
The Feather. London: T. Fisher Unwin, 1892. Fairy tale.
The Shifting of the Fire. London: T. Fisher Unwin, 1892. Novel.
The Questions at the Well [Pseud. "Fenil Haig"]. London: Digby, Long, 1893. Poems.
The Queen Who Flew. London: Bliss, Sands & Foster, 1894. Fairy tale.
Ford Madox Brown. London: Longmans, Green, 1896. Biography.
Poems for Pictures. London: John MacQueen, 1900.
The Cinque Ports. London and Edinburgh: William Blackwood, 1900. History.
The Inheritors [with Joseph Conrad]. London: William Heinemann, 1901. Fantasy.
Rossetti. London: Duckworth, 1902. Art criticism.
Romance [with Joseph Conrad]. London: Smith, Elder, 1903. Historical romance.
The Face of the Night. London: John MacQueen, 1904. Poems.
The Soul of London. London: Alston Rivers, 1905. Essays.
The Benefactor. London: Brown, Langham, 1905. Novel.
Hans Holbein. London: Duckworth, 1905. Art criticism.
The Fifth Queen. London: Alston Rivers, 1906. Historical romance.
The Heart of the Country. London: Alston Rivers, 1906. Essays.
The Nature of a Crime [with Joseph Conrad]. London: Duckworth, 1924. (Written in 1906, published serially in 1909.) Novella.
Christina's Fairy Book. London: Alston Rivers, 1906. Fairy tales.

Privy Seal. London: Alston Rivers, 1907. Historical romance.

From Inland. London: Alston Rivers, 1907. Poems.

An English Girl. London: Methuen, 1907. Novel.

The "Half-Moon." London: Eveleigh Nash, 1909. Historical romance.

The Pre-Raphaelite Brotherhood. London: Duckworth, 1907. Art criticism.

The Spirit of the People. London: Alston Rivers, 1907. Essays.

The Fifth Queen Crowned. London: Eveleigh Nash, 1908. Historical romance.

Mr. Apollo. London: Methuen, 1908. Fantasy.

A Call. London: Chatto & Windus, 1910. Novel.

Songs from London. London: Elkin Mathews, 1910. Poems.

The Portrait. London: Methuen, 1910. Historical romance.

The Simple Life Limited [Pseud. "Daniel Chaucer"]. London: John Lane, 1911. Satirical novel.

Ancient Lights. London: Chapman and Hall, 1911. Reminiscences.

Ladies Whose Bright Eyes. London: Constable, 1911. Historical fantasy.

The Critical Attitude. London: Duckworth, 1911. Criticism.

Women & Men. Paris: Three Mountains Press, 1923. (Written in 1911, published serially in 1918.) Essays.

High Germany. London: Duckworth, 1912. Poems.

The Panel. London: Constable, 1912. Novel.

The New Humpty-Dumpty [Pseud. "Daniel Chaucer"]. London: John Lane, 1912. Satirical novel.

Mr. Fleight. London: Howard Latimer, 1913. Satirical novel.

The Young Lovell. London: Chatto & Windus, 1913. Historical romance.

Collected Poems. London: Max Goschen, 1913.

Henry James. London: Martin Secker, 1913. Criticism.

The Good Soldier. London: John Lane, 1915. Novel.

When Blood is Their Argument. New York and London: Hodder and Stoughton, 1915. War propaganda.

Between St. Dennis and St. George. London, New York, Toronto: Hodder and Stoughton, 1915. War propaganda.

Zeppelin Nights [with Violet Hunt]. London: John Lane, 1916. Historical sketches.

On Heaven. London: John Lane, 1918. Poems.

No Enemy. New York: Macaulay, 1929. (Written in 1919, not published in England.) Fictionalized autobiography.

A House. London: The Poetry Bookshop, 1921. Long poem.

Thus to Revisit. London: Chapman & Hall, 1921. Reminiscences and criticism.

The Marsden Case. London: Duckworth, 1923. Novel.

Mister Bosphorus and the Muses. London: Duckworth, 1923. Pantomime.

Some Do Not. London: Duckworth, 1924. Novel.

Joseph Conrad. London: Duckworth, 1924. Reminiscences and criticism.

No More Parades. London: Duckworth, 1925. Novel.

A Mirror to France. London: Duckworth, 1926. Essays.

A Man Could Stand Up. London: Duckworth, 1926. Novel.

New Poems. New York: William Edwin Rudge, 1927.

New York is Not America. London: Duckworth, 1927. Essays.

New York Essays. New York: William Edwin Rudge, 1927.

Last Post. London: Duckworth, 1928. Novel.

A Little Less Than Gods. London: Duckworth, 1928. Historical romance.

The English Novel. London: Constable, 1930. (First published in America in 1929.) Criticism.

When the Wicked Man. London: Jonathan Cape, 1932. (Written in 1929, first published in America in 1931.) Novel.

Return to Yesterday. London: Victor Gollancz, 1931. Reminiscences.

The Rash Act. London: Jonathan Cape, 1933. Novel.

It Was the Nightingale. London: William Heinemann, 1934. (First published in America in 1933.) Reminiscences.

Henry for Hugh. Philadelphia: J. B. Lippincott, 1934. (Not published in England.) Novel.

Provence. London: George Allen & Unwin, 1938. (First published in America in 1935.) Travel book.

Vive Le Roy. London: George Allen and Unwin, 1937. (First published in America in 1936.) Novel.

Collected Poems. New York: Oxford University Press, 1936. (Not published in England.)

Great Trade Route. London: George Allen & Unwin, 1937. Travel book.

Mightier Than the Sword. London: George Allen & Unwin, 1938. (First published in America in 1937 as *Portraits from Life*.) Reminiscences and criticism.

The March of Literature. London: George Allen & Unwin, 1939. (First published in America in 1938.) Criticism.

Critical Writings of Ford Madox Ford. Ed. Frank MacShane. Lincoln: Univ. of Nebraska Press, 1964.

Abbreviations

The date refers to the edition used for this book.

AL   *Ancient Lights*, 1911
CA   *The Critical Attitude*, 1911
CW   *Critical Writings of Ford Madox Ford*, 1964
FMB   *Ford Madox Brown*, 1896
FQ   *The Fifth Queen*, 1906
FQC   *The Fifth Queen Crowned*, 1908
GTR   *Great Trade Route*, 1937
H   *Hans Holbein*, 1905
HC   *The Heart of the Country*, 1906
HH   *Henry for Hugh*, 1934
HJ   *Henry James*, 1913
IWN   *It Was the Nightingale*, 1934
JC   *Joseph Conrad*, 1924
LP   *Last Post*, 1928
MCS   *A Man Could Stand Up*, 1926
MF   *A Mirror to France*, 1926
ML   *The March of Literature*, 1939
MTS   *Mightier Than the Sword*, 1938
NMP   *No More Parades*, 1925
P   *Provence*, 1938
PRB   *The Pre-Raphaelite Brotherhood*, 1907
PS   *Privy Seal*, 1907
R   *Rossetti*, 1902
RA   *The Rash Act*, 1933
RY   *Return to Yesterday*, 1931
SDN   *Some Do Not*, 1924
SL   *The Soul of London*, 1905
SP   *The Spirit of the People*, 1907
WM   *Women & Men*, 1923

THE LIFE IN THE
FICTION OF
Ford Madox Ford

"Any man . . . is any sort of man, some time or other, you know."

The New Humpty-Dumpty

OPPOSITE: Ford Madox Ford, about 1903.
BELOW LEFT: Arthur Marwood, about 1903.
BELOW RIGHT: Joseph Conrad, 1913.

Photographs courtesy of John Lamb (Ford's grandson); Henry Bouch (Caroline Marwood's nephew); Ethel Bouch (Caroline Marwood's sister).

CHAPTER ONE

Death and Love in
the First Twenty Years
1873–1894

FORD'S HERITAGE

Except for his three years in military uniform, Ford was exclusively a literary man, and any solution to the Ford "prubblum" (Pound's word)[1] will have to be found in his books. To an unusual degree, however, the world of Ford's imagination and the events of his personal life interpenetrated; and so continuing reminders of the tortured movements of that life are necessary equipment for effective exploration of the works. Although Mizener quite understandably considers art the chief motive of Ford's life, I would put passion first. Of course, in Ford's case they are inseparable. Ford's history is, like the subtitle to *The Good Soldier*, "A Tale of Passion." His fantasies about his own passionate existence inform his novels; his fiction not only reflects but often prefigures and sometimes even influences the progress of his passions.

Ford Hermann Hueffer was born December 17, 1873, in Merton, Surrey (now a part of London). His heritage was remorselessly artistic and scholarly. The principal traumas of his early years must have been the premature deaths of two male members of his family and the births of two strikingly attractive siblings. The main artistic influence came from his grandfather, Ford Madox Brown (1821-1893), the immensely industrious, rather eccentric Pre-Raphaelite painter. As Ford and Conrad say in *Romance*, "Suffering is the lot of man," and Madox Brown's life was no exception.

His first wife died in 1846, only six years after their marriage, leaving him with a daughter. Although his second wife (who, at fifteen, had eloped with him) bore him a son and a daughter, the son, a "genius," died young. Despite his originality and his hard work, Madox Brown never achieved the recognition he believed he merited, and never made much money.

Both daughters were beautiful and talented artists. Both married men with literary and artistic interests. Lucy Madox Brown, the older, married at thirty-one, in 1874, William Michael Rossetti, the brother of her father's best friend, Dante Gabriel Rossetti. Catherine Madox Brown had married at twenty-two, in 1872, Francis Hueffer (formerly Franz Carl Christoph Johannes Hüffer), a German journalist with a doctorate in philology from Göttingen. During the twenty years after his arrival in England in 1869, he published a dozen books as well as many articles and reviews. He became the regular music critic for the *Times* and correspondent for several papers on the Continent. His intellectual passions were Schopenhauer, Wagner, and Provençal poetry. Unlike the Madox Browns and the Rossettis, however, the Hüffer family consisted chiefly of prosperous businessmen.

Lucy had three daughters and a son (a second son died very young). Catherine had two sons and a daughter. Because of mutual interests and the close friendship the husbands felt for each other and for each other's wives, the families grew up together. But the half-sisters, Lucy Rossetti and Catherine Hueffer, disliked each other. Although their children apparently got along well enough at first, they ultimately detested one another, especially for political reasons. The Rossetti children were anarchists and atheists, the Hueffers conservatives with Papist sympathies.

The Madox Brown-Hueffer-Rossetti circle was twice shaken by utterly unexpected deaths. Ford Madox Brown's son, Oliver Madox Brown, died of blood poisoning November 5, 1874, at the age of nineteen, when Ford was not quite a year old. "Nolly" was the youngest child, the only son, and explicitly, overwhelmingly his father's favorite. He was a lovable boy and precocious. At ten he produced his first painting; at fifteen he began a novel and published it at eighteen. His death broke his father's heart; Madox Brown said it turned his own "life . . . into a mockery and illusion" (FMB, 295). Ford grew up among funereal reminders of his departed uncle. Wherever Ford's grandfather moved, he kept one room exclusively for his dead son's belongings. Ford's father and his uncle William Michael Rossetti edited Nolly's unpublished writings. Ford's Aunt Lucy named her firstborn Olive Madox Rossetti; Ford's mother named her second child Oliver Madox Hueffer. That Ford Hermann Hueffer should begin writing seriously at sixteen, that Ford Madox Brown should illustrate the first book, insist on its publication, and broadcast the event, and that Ford should call himself on the title page Ford H. Madox Hueffer are impressive evidence of Nolly's posthumous inspiration; they suggest, too, the heavy burden of responsibility that fell upon the precocious nephew and grandson.

Francis Hueffer died on January 19, 1889. The disastrous impact of his untimely death, by a heart attack, at the age of forty-three, has been often commented upon. The most obvious effect was financial. Although Ford's father had apparently had a decent income, he left nothing. The Hueffer boys immediately had to leave the Praetorius boarding school in Folkestone, which they had enjoyed and which had allowed them to exploit their gifts for foreign languages. Ford and Oliver returned to London to live with their mother and widowed grandfather in his house and to attend, as day students, for less than a year, Uncle Nolly's old school, University College. Expectations of a university education were, of course, at an end. These deaths must have had other less tangible but equally damaging effects upon the psyche of young Ford.

Two births also importantly marked his childhood. At two, Ford acquired a baby brother, Oliver (born January 9,

1876), and at seven, a baby sister, Juliet (born November 4, 1880).[2] Both proved to be physically very attractive, as Ford was not. Juliet and Mrs. Hueffer, Olive Garnett records in her diary, "quite took my breath away, they were so good looking" (February 27, 1892).[3] At ten o'clock one evening Oliver showed up to ask his twenty-year-old friend Olive Garnett for her picture:

> I wonder what he will be like when he is a grown up young man & whether he will feel able to ask young ladies for their photographs then, & whether if he does, they will give them. I expect he will break a number of hearts one each time he gives away a button-hole which he does very often. Finally he turned out the gas & told me to go to bed. At sixteen! (May 18, 1892)

Although Olive Garnett doted on Ford, she never talked about him in those terms. Ford was later to say that he grew up feeling like the ugly duckling. Soon after Francis Hueffer's death, William Michael Rossetti tried to interest a Hueffer relative in hiring Ford. But after a preliminary meeting, Rossetti wrote to Catherine Hueffer that Ford's uncle Alexis preferred to help Oliver because of the latter's more Huefferian type of face.[4] Ford's profile, with the hooked nose, parted lips, and receding chin, recalls more than anyone's that of Uncle Nolly as depicted in Ford Madox Brown's deathbed sketch, reproduced in Ford's biography of his grandfather. Ford's feelings of rejection included the memory that his father called him a "patient but extremely stupid donkey," a phrase that Ford never ceased repeating, and the recollection that both parents favored Oliver (AL, ix). For a child to suffer, in his early teens, the death of a parent is always traumatic. When the parent is of the same sex and when the relationship has apparently included strong hostility, the effects are likely to be long-lived and damaging. Yet Ford's electing to join the Roman Catholic Church on November 7, 1892, under the auspices of his German relatives, suggests a touching desire for reconciliation with his father. And almost as significant as his forgetting the date of Marwood's death is Ford's ultimate belief that he was twelve at the time of his father's death, rather than the less pitiable age of fifteen.

OLIVE, FORD, AND ELSIE

Ugly duckling or not,[5] Ford was from his youth extremely appealing to women. By the age of eighteen, he had secured from pretty, apparently wealthy Elsie Martindale the promise to make him eternally happy. Although Mizener's account of this important courtship and marriage is meticulously detailed, it lacks any contemporary portraits of the lovers. These the diary of Olive Garnett beautifully provides. Moreover, since Olive liked Ford very much, her eyewitness reports convey the complexity of Ford's appeal.

The Garnetts had long known the Madox Brown-Rossetti-Hueffer clan. By the fifties Olive's father Richard Garnett was friendly with Dante Gabriel Rossetti and his mentor Ford Madox Brown. It was in the Garnett drawing room that, according to Ford, Francis Hueffer courted Catherine Madox Brown (RY, 173). Olive Garnett was born August 21, 1871, two years and four months before Ford. They must have been aware of each other as young children since, in the seventies, the Richard Garnetts of No. 3 St. Edmund's Terrace and the Madox Browns across Regent's Park at 37 Fitzroy Square frequently called upon one another. Ford Madox Brown, after an hiatus of eight years spent painting frescoes in Manchester, moved in 1888 to No. 1 St. Edmund's Terrace, two doors from the Garnetts. A year later his widowed daughter Catherine and her two boys moved in with him, Juliet lodging with the William Michael Rossettis. Olive's diary begins in June 1890, just after her father became Keeper of Printed Books and the family moved to the British Museum. The diary completely confirms Ford's recollection that he had long enjoyed the Garnetts' "boundless" hospitality at their Museum house (RY, 11).

Olive Garnett was, in short, perfectly situated to observe the opening of Ford's literary career. Moreover, her ambitions and temperament combined to make her an ideal chronicler. She was determined to be a writer. Her diary begins when she is about to publish her first short story in the *Torch*, the Rossetti children's anarchist magazine. During the nineties Olive wrote drafts of several novels, published a book of short stories, and worshipped two novelists, Stepniak, the Russian revolutionary, and, from a distance, Henry James. Olive Garnett composed her diary with the care of a budding author. At the same time, writing a private document, she could be as honest as her temperament would allow. As a Garnett, she brought to the diary that plainness of speech and directness we associate with her older brother Edward, the brilliant publisher's reader, and his son David, novelist and man of letters.

Although Olive would scarcely have consciously remembered Oliver Madox Brown's death and although her diary begins a year and a half after Francis Hueffer died, she nevertheless refers to both. Clearly those unexpected deaths caused much concern over Ford. Olive, and all the Garnetts, as well as Ford's mother and grandfather, worried about his physical state: "I was . . . rather on the look out for signs of ill health in Ford," notes Olive. "His hands have a very dangerous look . . ." (March 16, 1893). Ford's cousin Olive Rossetti, however, "made light of Ford's condition. His father died of heartdisease, & so everyone was frightened about him" (March 24, 1893). Olive Rossetti's offhand remark proved accurate: Ford survived for sixty-five years. Within himself the worry over his health would have exerted contrary pulls—toward timorous self-pity and toward the impulse to seize the day. To women, his recurrent ill health and obvious vulnerability constituted a powerful appeal.

But he had other attractions. Indeed, at eighteen he was

a charmer. Chiefly, it was his talk, the brilliant, witty, sympathetic, inexhaustible outpouring that would continue to enchant until he died. Never one to spoil a story, he was already famous as a boy for his tall tales, told to please and not to deceive: "Papa asked him about his music & he said 'I am writing a pot-boiler which I want Antoinette Stirling to sing; if she will, I should get some thousands of pounds.' This may be a Huefferism but it's delightful any way" (February 29, 1892). Olive Garnett was from the first well aware that Ford was a very complicated being; she saw that his Huefferisms sometimes had unfortunate effects upon others and that they included feelings both of great superiority and of profound self-doubt. Olive's mother once reported that Ford was "immensely . . . amused" that "people who did not know what to say" about his grandfather's new painting would praise the gilt Japanese paper covering the frame. Ford, it appears, "stood like an iceberg in the middle of the room & behaved with great ceremony" (February 26, 1892). On another occasion, "Ford told Mamma that Ellen Terry had fallen in love with him & he didn't like it. Altogether he seems to have been more than usually lordly" (December 5, 1892). Olive recognized that underneath Ford's bravado lurked insecurity, even timidity; more than once she refers to his "pessimism" (March 6, 1892). A long delightful letter from Ford to Olive, February 13, 1892, announced a journal of international pessimism to rival the Rossettis' optimistic, anarchistic *Torch*. Ford intended to call his *Extinguisher*.

In two remarkable entries from the spring of 1892, when Ford was only eighteen, Olive reveals not only Ford's attractiveness to her but also his own amazing prescience about what would prove to be his permanent interests. The entertaining stories he tells to Olive have all the Fordian hallmarks: concrete details, wit, personal triumph, and even his identification with a literary figure out of history. To Olive, the show that Ford puts on is simply "refreshing"; his "lordly air" is caviar to her. Beyond this, the entries dramatize Ford's enduring fascination with the sensuous side of Catholicism. Equally important, Ford was even then quite conscious of his extremely divided, paradoxical nature, and determined to accept it rather than to compromise and sink into torpor.

Friday, March 25 [1892]

Ford was in excellent spirits, after his grandfather returned from Manchester he left No. 1 & went for a walking tour by himself in Sussex, to Rye, Appledore etc. I think he said he had walked 120 miles. One night he walked on the line for about five miles, it was very dark, & he had to avoid the mud by stepping from sleeper to sleeper. On reaching the station, the station master asked how he had come, & he said on the line whereupon a village policeman who was by, arrested him (?) & suggested that they should go off together. "But how far is it?" "Fourteen miles." "Don't you think it would be rather inconvenient to go all that way now?" The policeman seemed to fall in with this idea on his own account, & the matter ended by the stationmaster's pointing out that Ford's nearest way to Rye was on along the line. He also had an adventure with a tramp. When he got to Rye he found another policeman who offered him his bed as he was on night duty, & gave him breakfast in the morning, as he didn't want any himself, then refused remuneration. "Do you know whose cottage you are in." "Yours." "Ah yes, but do you know Fletcher?" "The prize-fighter?" "No the poet." So he had been sleeping under Fletcher's roof as well. Altogether, during that spell of fine weather he seems to have had a good time.

We discussed society strata with contempt. Mathematical music (Prout) v. Poetical music (Wagner.) The coming reign of lawlessness. Mrs. Thorne.

We went into the dining-room, where we had a long & uninterrupted argument, just for the pleasure of thinking & talking, & exchanging impressions, with never the possibility of agreeing or convincing—But still delightful enough besides, a voyage of discovery into an intelligent being's mind, seasoned with laughter, is intoxicating always. I was however very much shocked when Ford admitted that as a relief from the gospel of perfect indifference to everything, he sought refuge in bigoted pietism in the Brompton Oratory, not that he thought that Catholicism was rational, outside its circle, but that it satisfied his sensual religious needs, he found poetry in it, etc.

In fact he started the paradox theory saying that in the mean lies torpor in extremes madness, he balanced the two parts of his nature one against the other. Atheistic indifference on the one hand, bigoted pietism on the other. To my well ordered & I think carefully trained little rational mind, such confession seemed to reveal an abyss at my feet. . . . His conscience does not reproach him for conceit or selfishness, nor would it for any crime; what is crime? But this way lies madness.

Thursday, June 9 [1892]
When the visitors had gone, we sat on the grass plot. He is going to Paris shortly for possibly 3 months.[6] He has been studying the Neo-platonists beginning a 3 volume novel, expects the Feather to be out shortly, has been playing tennis, writing till 4 in the morning & then going out for a walk in the streets of London. That was about all except that he gave me a splendid letter to read which he had sent to the Manchester Guardian re his grandfather's fresco. It is impossible to do justice to this in description, thoroughly Brown, Hueffer, & Ford, its combined daring & cleverness almost took my breath away & it seems to have shaken up the Manchester folk a bit since they replied saying that so far was it from being true that they did not care for babies, that they had actually founded several societies for prevention of cruelty to Children. But the

letter is simply delicious. . . . I must say that his lordly air is caviare to me, it delights me hugely, it is so absolutely unblushingly put on. I said that he might repent sitting up so late one day, that health was the most precious possession & so forth—the usual platitudes. "We were speaking of Goethe, I think" he said when I paused.

He caught a man trying to steal his watch. "I did not prosecute him—ah, too much trouble." I said that I had been depressed about my writing, it was not robust enough for the public. "Take some oatmeal everyday." He was going to dinner somewhere but lingered, Edward came out of the B. M. at last, bowed low with mock ceremony & then hit him in the chest after which they proceeded to business. The Hueffer imagination is most refreshing. It had never occurred to me that a torch light procession over the Museum roofs was an ordinary & agreeable amusement for the residents at night, or that flowers springing up in the grass plot as I walked along would be an easy and infallible method for getting a garden, & so easy of course. Oh dear I wonder if one would get very much bored if all ones friends were original people.

Ford's memorable walk of late March had taken him to Rye and thus surely to nearby Winchelsea and fifteen-year-old Elsie Martindale, his chum from the modern, coeducational Praetorius School in Folkestone. Olive's first reference to Ford's "conquest . . . the all absorbing topic" concludes: "what becomes of the young lady at Hampstead in whose beauty and virtues I so firmly believe?" (c. October 29, 1892).[7] Thus, although Ford and Elsie appear to have been childhood sweethearts at Folkestone, and although Ford's first novel, *The Shifting of the Fire*, reflects, as we shall see, his love for Elsie, already there were others. Ford's four-page letter to Olive the previous February about her unfinished allegory certainly indicates considerable fondness for *her*, as do his long conversations with her that spring.

Olive watched with great interest the progress of Ford's courtship. She was also aware from the first of Elsie's older sister Mary and early saw them together in Regent's Park: "there came walking towards me two ladies dressed in an art shade of bright green velvet in the aesthetic style, with capes to match their dresses & green hats. The youngest one looked very handsome, she was Elsie Martindale" (April 23, 1893). Olive, however, knew no more than the lovers the chief reason for the Martindales' adamant opposition to the marriage: the parents feared that their unstable older daughter would lose her mind if her sister rather than she got Ford.[8] Despite Ford's ignorance of Mary's passion at the time, he must have enjoyed her frequent presence, as he doubtless enjoyed Olive's. Ford seems always to have needed another admiring woman in addition to the beloved. By having a second female looking enviously upon his happy situation, he was perhaps unconsciously taking revenge on the time when he had first had to observe his beautiful mother loving not him but his pretty baby sister.

Olive realized only that Ford was getting a lovely, talented, devoted, and ultimately—despite a history of ill health—strong young woman. She noted, too, that Ford's responses to the excitement and terrors of his forbidden courtship were indeed mixed. At the beginning Olive emphasizes the delicate health of both lovers. (The first reason given for postponing the engagement was Elsie's physical condition.) Although Ford told his grandfather that he was engaged, and his grandfather told "everyone except one or two" (March 9, 1893), the Martindale parents, "while liking Ford very much & allowing them to see one another, will not allow that it is a formal engagement, till she is stronger" (March 15, 1893). Olive Rossetti gave Olive Garnett the medical details: "an iron kneecap & a hole in her breast. Diseased bones show consumption, her family is consumptive & so is she. At the same time her health improves" (March 24, 1893).[9] Ford's friends and relations were far more concerned about *his* condition: "his mother is anxious about him, about his heart, he is not at all well & taking his grandfather's advice has gone to Salisbury to walk about there. [This is but one of many occasions when Ford and his fictional heroes will seek relief in that part of the world.] Oliver has gone with him to look after him. This news makes me realize how very dear they are to me, those two" (March 9, 1893). Ford refused to see a doctor: "he says that he knows all about himself, his heart *is* weak" (March 15, 1893).

Olive loved Elsie the instant she saw her, and indeed they became lifelong friends.

> She is a charming girl, exceedingly pretty & not merely so, but she has a soul in her face. I recognised the gold thread in her brown hair, the oval sweep from ear to chin, and the light deep down in her hazel eyes, especially the light in her eyes. At times she smiled in their depths as at a secret happiness. She has too, charming manners & neither conceit nor shyness. Ford looked proud of her—as well he might. . . . She looked the more robust of the two. I hope that we shall become friends. I like best the "unconsciousness" in her, but perhaps that is because she is in love. (March 16, 1893)

By the following winter, Olive had such affection and sympathy for the thwarted pair that she wrote: "I wish I had a lapful of good things to shower on her and Ford" (February 21, 1894). They needed them. Within a few weeks Mr. Martindale had forbidden the lovers' meeting, and Ford had even proposed a suicide pact: "we can always cut our throats and have it over . . . at worst there's a garter—or a second storey window—or your hair—your soft hair, that too would be like kisses . . ."[10] The Martindales had other reasons than Mary's condition for opposing the marriage. To these conventional people, Oliver Hueffer's succession of fiancées, his hobnobbing with the rich, the kaleidoscopic changes in his career plans, and his persistent indebtedness were anathema. Ford himself, despite his characteristically persistent industry as a writer, had no money. This was not his fault, and Olive wisely recorded another Fordian paradox. On the one hand, she saw his "unreliability, inaccuracy &—genius" (March 26, 1892); on the other, she perceived that he was "ultra-respectable and steady going" (March 16, 1894). To the Martindales, Ford's anarchistic Rossetti cousins must have been another black mark against him. At precisely this time, early March, 1894, the Rossetti house was being watched by the police. Young Arthur Rossetti, an amateur chemist, was suspected of being involved in the February 15 bombing at Greenwich (the source of Conrad's *Secret Agent*). William Michael Rossetti threw out his son's chemicals and destroyed the *Torch* press in his house. Ford and Oliver blamed the Rossettis for the Martindales' hostility.

On March 16, 1894, Elsie gave Mary the slip at Ashford Station, where they were changing trains en route to Winchelsea. She returned to London and, apparently by previous arrangement with Olive's lawyer-brother Robert Singleton Garnett, fled across the country to Bath and to secret asylum in Clifton, near Gloucester, with Garnett cousins. From there she moved to Gloucester to stay with Mrs. Garnett's retired personal maid Chapple. When her father still refused to permit the engagement and began legal steps to get his daughter back, Elsie and Ford, in Olive's words, "went to a registry office in Gloucester on Thursday with a license, & said that they were of age . . . [they] have gone to Lynton for a short honeymoon" (Sunday, May 20, 1894).[11] Soon the newlyweds were back in London, staying at the Garnetts', and appearing in court to face the wrathful Mr. Martindale. During these tumultuous months, the Garnetts were much aware of Elsie's fortitude and charm, Ford's anxiety and excitement, the literary quality of the adventures, and the fun they were all having. After all, they were young: Robert 28, Edward 26, Olive 22, Ford 20, Elsie 17.

On learning, the day of Elsie's flight, of Mr. Martindale's intention to prosecute, Ford hastened by hansom in pursuit of Robert. He caught him on the top of an omnibus and said: "I am in great trouble." Olive gathered that Ford was "very much excited & seems to think that by this time the whole of London is talking about the affair." Olive thought that "Elsie seems to have acted in a most determined manner for her age" (March 16, 1894). Her opinion was confirmed by Robert when he and Ford returned from visiting Elsie several days later: "Elsie," Robert reported, "was well & safe & calm as a millpond" (March 19, 1894). When Robert on Easter (March 25) weekend moved Elsie from Clifton to Gloucester, he

> spent sunday walking about Robin Hood's Hill with Elsie, & getting to know her. He says she is most attractive. Sketches, sings beautifully when she has any voice, is full of fun, walks well & looks so lovely that the people in the street turn round to look at her. But he also thinks her hard, extravagant, very youthful, changeable, loving only Ford, & him to distraction. (March 26, 1894)

Olive's sober comment on the marriage suggests that Ford was less wholly committed than Elsie: "Notwithstanding the great responsibilities which—penniless as they are— they are taking upon themselves, I myself do not see what else was to be done, considering their position. Elsie will at any rate be happier" (May 20, 1894). At the trial, initially occasioned by Mr. Martindale's efforts to make Elsie a ward of the court and thus force her to be returned, Elsie continued to look strong and in control: "She was very much excited and flushed, though outwardly calm & lent well back that she might not be seen, every minute grasping my arm to ask questions as to who was in court & so on." Ford, on the other hand, was "pink & white &

limp—he had been obliged to take brandy beforehand"
(June 14, re June 6, 1894). When the judge refused "to sus-
pend the order restricting intercourse," Ford had to stay at
his mother's, Elsie at the Garnetts':

> I saw Elsie undressed with her hair down & she lay on
> the bed so & explained her system of underclothing.
> She is built much in the same way as Olive Rossetti. In
> some ways she is very young, her nature is quite sim-
> ple & direct. I like her very much. (June 14, re June 7,
> 1894)

Since the judge considered the case in private sessions,
Olive got her reports secondhand, from Ford, Elsie, and
Robert. On one occasion, when contempt of court was
mentioned, Ford "glared back so fiercely" that the judge
actually dropped his eyes. Yet Ford, characteristically as
we shall see, "hardly knew what was going on" (June 14,
re June 9).

That the groom agonized more than the child bride is interesting and, by hindsight of course, ominous. Still,
Olive's narrative mainly gives an impression of the excitement and fun the forbidden marriage engendered. All
these literary types saw the adventure in terms of fiction or
family history; "Robert said he felt as if he were acting in
one of Meredith's novels & as if Ford were his grandfather
come to life" (March 19). "Everything has happened as in a
sensational novel" (June 5). "We talked over the whole affair as if it were someone else's novel we had been reading,
& became quite gleeful with the aid of some thimblefuls of
sloe gin" (June 14, re June 6). The whole affair was, in a
sense, Ford's, and perhaps Elsie's, novel. Ford's newest
fairy tale, *The Queen Who Flew*, was announced ten days before Elsie's flight, and no one missed the appropriateness
of the title, least of all Ford. Indeed, getting a journalist
friend to write a newspaper story yoking the new book
with the private court proceedings caused Ford to pay
costs on contempt charges. (Ford often needed to have the
reality of his adventures confirmed by seeing them in

print.) Similarly, Elsie wore her hat with a feather for both the escape from Mary and her appearances in court, thus recalling Ford's previous fairy tale, *The Feather*. Olive gathered that Elsie spent her time in Gloucester "writing a novel" (April 9). The excitement of the adventure stimulated Ford and Olive to have the most enjoyable talk of her life:

> It seemed to be tacitly agreed upon that we were real friends, & meant to take and enjoy just for the moment what we found good in one another. Trouble behind, trouble ahead, & that lent a zest to the present, just this little oasis of time—a dinner—in which we might rest, & which we were wise to make the most of. . . . I had never found Ford so delightful, so good, the ideal so near and conversation so enthralling. I shall never forget that dinner. (March 20)

The drama of those days did not keep Ford from planning new literary projects. On June 9, Ford, Elsie, and Olive "spent a jubilant evening" together celebrating the judge's decision to quash the order "forbidding intercourse." "Ford played & Elsie sang . . . magnificently & afterwards Ford talked enthusiastically of literary plans. He has been asked to write a life of his grandfather & thinks of reissuing the remainder of Oliver Brown's Literary Remains in new covers." With the judge's decision June 23 to withhold judgment some weeks on the contempt charges, Ford and Elsie no longer needed constant support from Robert and Olive. Settled temporarily in Mrs. Hueffer's house, they invited their friends over for the next day. "Robert and I did not go to Brooke Green by mutual consent. We both felt that it would be good to rest a little from the Hueffers." This proved to be only one of many occasions when the Garnetts, or subsequent best friends, or lovers would need respite from poor Ford's recurrent imbroglios. It is amazing that even in this first youthful courtship, Ford should so unerringly have put himself into a tangle that prefigured future entanglements: an injured, attached—if only in her imagination—lady (Mary), her angry supporters, and legal complications. The outraged Mr. Martindale acted as if Ford were destroying a relationship rather than confirming one.

Closely observing Ford and Elsie, Olive recorded a mutually devoted couple. Yet two passages suggest in retrospect that young Elsie would have a rough road ahead. The first night of Olive's first visit, her brother was there as well: "Edward amused us incessantly, his mock reverence for Elsie's masculine powers & treating Ford like a well meaning baby. 'Are you awake?' Stroking his hair patting him on the back etc." (November 17, 1894). This gently comic episode would not be worth mentioning were Ford not later to appear so frequently as a baby in his own writings and in the comments of his friends. The second prefigurative passage has to do with a dream of Elsie's. The day of the dream the trio had traveled from Bonnington to Limpsfield by train—and on foot. At Ashford, Elsie had gone on an errand, lost Ford and Olive, and become alarmed. On finding them at the famous station, Elsie said she had "thought you two had gone off in the train & left me." Olive comments: "This brings back that other day here when she escaped from her sister Mary & began for Ford and herself their present life." That night, after supper with Edward and his wife Constance at Frog Hole, they all went in the starlight night to look at the unfinished Cearne, the stone, medieval-style cottage Edward and Connie were proudly building. Elsie and Olive slept together at a neighbor's and Elsie talked in her sleep: "The roof is coming down. I can't hold it up any longer" (November 18, 1895). Within the context, one can speculate that the roofless Cearne provided the manifest content for a number of latent meanings—including Elsie's weary sense of responsibility for the marriage, her recollection of its complicated history, and her anxiety as to its permanence.

As Dowell asserts in *The Good Soldier*, the Fordian man falls in love to find peace: " 'Du Bist die Ruh' " is one of

Ford's earliest poems to Elsie.[12] Ford seems initially to have found rest and happiness with Elsie. Paying them, some six months after the marriage, an extended visit at their primitive semidetached villa in isolated Bonnington, South Kent, Olive found the couple completely happy. After one particularly good day full of conversation and long walks, Olive lay "awake so contented & happy thinking how much I love the two sleeping below & that there are good people in the world after all" (November 20, 1894). Although Elsie would later recall with pain their poverty in those days, Olive's version suggests it was all mainly a lark: "They had only 1/- with which to pay the sweep if he came on Tuesday. They proposed to lie in bed & afterwards to write saying they 'had heard that he had come & would he come again' " (November 25, 1894). The arrangements were indeed primitive: "there is no system of drainage, & all the drinking water has to be fetched from a mile away" (July 17, 1894). Yet even this is turned into a joke: "method of cleaning boots to tie a cord round them & lower them into a well." Although Conrad in 1898 would find Ford in a potato patch playing the role of market gardener, Ford and Elsie at the beginning were playing bohemian Pre-Raphaelites. They "smoked shag in a cutty pipe . . . constantly on their walks, & were known as the Frenchies" (November 9, 1894). Elsie made herself a dress and cloak of spring green Liberty furniture serge, with "large loose sleeves gathered into a wristband . . . ornamented by feather stitching in yellow wool." The dress was "secured round the waist by a girdle of rope (like a monk's) & can be hitched up over this for walking." To Olive the costume "looks as if it had come from an old street scene at the Lyceum" (November 14, 1894). Ford complemented Elsie well on their walks together, "carrying his famous Rossettian coat" (November 18, 1895), which his sister remembered as black with a floating cape.[13] After a time in Bonnington, Ford and Elsie acquired some appropriate possessions; Olive "was soon admiring the Christina Rossetti furniture at each piece of which she 'wrote all her poems,' as Ford playfully put it" (November 16, 1895).

DR. HUEFFER, D. G. ROSSETTI, AND
THE SHIFTING OF THE FIRE

Ford began his first novel, *The Shifting of the Fire*, very soon after his father's death. Before finishing it, he was courting Elsie; and on receiving, in October 1892, the first printed copies, he asked for her hand. Not surprisingly, Ford's father, his grandfather, their friend Rossetti, Elsie, and her pharmaceutical-chemist father all seem to have figured in Ford's imagination as he wrote this youthful, strangely impressive novel.

Its subject was to dominate all Ford's most interesting fiction—passion in the modern world. The title suggests his attitude: passion changes; passion destroys. What on earth would the "ultra-respectable" sixteen-year-old son of a scholarly German journalist know about passion's flame? Dr. Hueffer's academic specialty was, it is true, the medieval, Provençal "troubadour," or court poet—a major source of our wretched Western tradition of hopeless, self-consuming, romantic love. So Ford would have known, from his father's interests, something of passion in a bookish way. He would have discovered from Francis Hueffer's chief work, *The Troubadours* (1878), that "the ever recurring burden of Provençal poetry" is a highborn "lady dissatisfied with her husband and openly calling for death to come and kill him soon in order that she may be united to her lover." Courting operated, to be sure, on a very high plane: "the noblest duty of the mediaeval knight was his service and devotion to the lady of his heart, a feeling akin to the religious veneration of that type of immaculate womanhood which the wisdom of the Roman Church has placed on a par almost with the Deity itself." Nevertheless, Dr. Hueffer's main theme remains this: "not all ladies were inexorable: not all troubadours contented with a purely ideal worship. Ardent wooings led to passionate attachments, and lovers' bliss was frequently followed by lovers' quarrels."[14]

But young Ford had a much nearer, much more vivid guide to passion than his father's dull prose about twelfth- and thirteenth-century poets. From his colorful, garrulous painter-grandfather, Ford would have known a great deal, more perhaps than he wanted to know, of the real-life loves of his glamorous, sinister "uncle," Dante Gabriel Rossetti. Madox Brown was present at all the more horrendous crises in his friend's "vexed and trampled"[15] life. Rossetti's impact on Ford's work is obvious. Ford wrote a book about him in 1902 and treated him extensively in other books about the Pre-Raphaelites as well as in various reminiscences. In *The Good Soldier* Florence paraphrases Rossetti, in *Parade's End* Christopher Tietjens hates him while Macmaster reveres him, and in *The Rash Act* Henry Martin remembers vividly Rossetti's *doppelgänger* painting.

In the early nineties, a decade after his death, Rossetti's romantic legend loomed large in England. And Ford, aware of Rossetti since earliest childhood, must have been permeated with it. Although Ford's cousin Helen Rossetti Angeli might say that Rossetti "idealized" the beauty of women "as the mainspring of all that is dearest and noblest in life and as the symbol of Divine Love," Arthur Symons puts it more succinctly, and persuasively: "his life was passion consumed by passion."[16] Rossetti's life of passion began at the age of twenty-two when, in the spring of 1850, he met the sixteen-year-old model Elizabeth Eleanor "Lizzie" Siddal. From their engagement in 1852, to their marriage in 1860, to her death in 1862 from an overdose of laudanum, probably deliberately self-administered, their life together was one of "sickness, seriousness, reproach, rancour, misunderstanding and lack of sympathy."[17] Throughout Rossetti's career he picked for models and mistresses other heavily maned "stunners" like Fanny Cornforth and, especially, Jane Burden Morris. Her husband, William Morris, ever the obliging friend, even went off to Iceland leaving Kelmscott Manor to Janey and

Rossetti. Like Lizzie in love, Janey soon became seriously ill while Rossetti suffered semiblindness and insomnia. Obsessed with the mystery of Lizzie's death, the fear of losing Janey, and the critical attacks on the immorality of his verse, he attempted suicide, also by an overdose of laudanum, and spent his remaining decade chiefly as a gloomy recluse. In his book on Rossetti, Ford claims "intimate" knowledge of his subject's "pagan" life of satisfying "his desires as they came" (153-54). We can only speculate as to precisely what Rossetti's poems and paintings meant to Ford at sixteen. Many of Rossetti's early works do idealize women, and those of his middle period often celebrate the joys of female beauty and earthly love. Still, a dark strain of fear and hostility runs through Rossetti's work from the very early ballad, "Sister Helen," whose subject damns her lover to hell by melting a waxen image of him, to the very late painting *Venus Astarte*, who is, in Symons' words, "a dark and unintelligible menace."[18]

Conspicuous in both the poetry and the painting is the recurring symbol, either blatant or implied, of the apple.[19] Rossetti used it quite early, in his 1857 fresco of Launcelot and Guinevere. He describes the scene:

> Sir Lancelot prevented by his sin from entering the chapel of the San Grail. He has fallen asleep before the shrine full of angels, and , between him and it, rises in his dream the image of Queen Guinevere, *the cause of all*. She stands gazing at him with her arms extended in the branches of an apple-tree.[20]

Rossetti neglects to mention that Guinevere's left hand holds an apple. Ford significantly praises in the fresco the sleeping figure of Launcelot: a study in "extreme muscular exhaustion" (82).

Implicitly part of this tradition of apple symbolism are the Lilith paintings and sonnet of the mid-sixties, inspired by the opulent charms of Fanny Cornforth. Ford tells us that "Lilith was the witch-wife of Adam; she stood for illicit love, for the women who bring sorrow to the Eves of this world and disaster to the hearth." In repainting *Lilith*, Rossetti, Ford goes on, forced the "note of corruption and what we now call *decadence*" (140-41). The sonnet "Body's Beauty" tells how Lilith deceived Adam before the snake did, how her spell goes through a youth, and leaves "his straight neck bent / And round his heart one strangling golden hair."[21] The ballad "Eden Bower" explains that evil came into the world not through the agency of a masculine serpent but through Adam's witch-wife. Lilith's passion has a lesbian aspect: she will seduce Eve. Lilith's passion is also narcissistic: she will return from her mission in the form of a snake to embrace her lover-snake, who will be arrayed in Lilith's own body.

"Troy Town" and "Cassandra" show Venus's apple to be the ultimate cause of Troy's burning, but it is "The Orchard-Pit," an unfinished five-stanza poem, that expresses most vividly the idea of female menace in terms of apples and breasts. The poet keeps dreaming the same terrifying dream of a pit in an apple orchard full of dead men. In a "soft dell, among the apple-trees" a siren "stands, / And . . . sings"; she gives the men "her magic hour of ease, / And those her apples." The poet continues: "her hair / Crosses my lips and draws my burning breath. . . . Life's eyes are gleaming from her forehead fair, / And from her breasts the ravishing eyes of Death."[22] The story obviously had considerable impact on Ford, for it is a chief source of *The Young Lovell*, the novel he wrote immediately before *The Good Soldier*.[23]

Ford discusses at some length Rossetti's pictures *Proserpine, Launcelot and Guinevere, Lilith,* and *Venus Verticordia*; he stresses, too, Rossetti's fascination with "the epic figure of Helen of Troy; or the epic tale portraying so vastly the dangers of the love of women" (106). When Ford Madox Brown designed for Rossetti's grave a headstone in the form of an Irish cross, he included in each of its four angles the figure of Lilith of Eden Bower. Below them is a marriage ceremony being conducted by a blindfolded priest. Madox Brown's Irish cross, which Ford and Elsie went to see during their courtship, adequately symbolizes what must have been the lesson for young Ford of Rossetti's life and works. Passion is delicious, evil, destructive; in the woman it includes lesbian and narcissistic aspects. Marriage is always a mistake which speedily brings illness, despair, suicide. Passion exists only outside marriage, usually with someone else's wife, perhaps with the wife of a dear friend.

A conversation between Olive Garnett and Ford on March 25, 1892, a month after he delivered the manuscript of *The Shifting of the Fire* to Edward Garnett and six months before he gave the book to Elsie, suggests how close Ford was then to Rossetti's view of things. Olive relates that she was "much surprised when Ford also declared that the only thing really interesting & unfathomable was love, not the higher kind, but the lower kind. 'Helen of Troy the everlasting symbol.' Men to become beasts etc." Ford's first novel, *The Shifting of the Fire* (1892), only too obviously reflects Rossetti's life and attitudes; and it is seriously flawed. Soon after its publication, Ford turned against it, as he was to turn against almost everything he wrote. On November 23, 1895, he said to Olive Garnett of *The Shifting of the Fire*:

> "I have been reading it over again, I wrote it when I was sixteen & I think it is one of the most vulgar books I have ever read. But it is a bit of life." . . . Ford attributed this [Olive comments] to his having been brought up among ultra refined people, & afterwards revelling in what he imagined to be nearer real life.[24]

Nevertheless, it is well to remember that Edward Garnett, perhaps the best talent scout of his generation, discovered Ford's literary gifts through this book and, to Olive's irritation, steadfastly held to his "exaggerated view" of it. Indeed, despite all its flaws, the energy of this first naive novel foreshadows Ford's masterpiece, *The Good Soldier*.[25] Edward Garnett, with his unerring eye for genuine distinction, must have sensed the promise.[26]

Four of the five chief characters of *The Shifting of the Fire*
clearly prefigure the Dowell-Ashburnham quartet of *The
Good Soldier*. Clem Hollebone, mild-mannered, studious,
immensely wealthy, is engaged to beautiful Edith Ryland.
Her roommate, Julia Tubbs, falls in love with a writer,
Jemmy Ryves, son of a very old, *nouveau-riche* merchant,
Mr. Kasker-Ryves. Clem has a passion for Edith but also
finds Julia a "jolly girl" whose company he enjoys. In fact,
when he has to talk in private to Julia about his problems
with Edith, their meeting has the look of an assignation.
Edith even accuses Julia of trying to steal away Clem. Just
as Ford partially reflects both Ashburnham and Dowell, so
he reflects both these young men, the blond writer Ryves
and the gentle, industrious, slightly foreign Clem, a descendant of Holbein. As Ashburnham has several love affairs, and even the timid Dowell finds himself attracted to
various women, so Jemmy Ryves feels remorse about having sowed some wild oats and Clem is attracted not only to
Julia but also to a young American cousin.

The Shifting of the Fire is ostensibly concerned with the
complications arising from the youthful, misapplied self-
sacrifices of Clem and Edith. Actually, if fitfully, this novel,
like *The Good Soldier*, dramatizes the destructiveness of
passion and shows human beings murderously preying
upon one another. It resounds with echoes of Rossetti's
career, vibrates with sexual anxiety, and casts its influence
upon Ford's later fictions and even upon the very actions
of his "real life." In writing a novel so early and dedicating
it to Ford Madox Brown, Ford was himself half-consciously
re-enacting for his grandfather the life of that beloved,
ever-lamented son Nolly. This was so in more senses than
one, for Rossetti had been deeply disturbed to find among
Nolly's writings a story that seemed to be about him.

Kasker-Ryves belongs because of his age to the generation of Rossetti and Madox Brown. He has "ruined" his
son's mother and driven her, like Lizzie Siddal Rossetti, to
suicide. Sometimes guilt-ridden, Kasker-Ryves generally
is given, like Rossetti, to "justifying those excesses on

philosophic grounds" (108). Clem, too, partakes of the tradition by writing Rossettian Lilith-poems to Edith:

> My love did send to me a single strand
> From her great golden Heav'n of hair, . . .
> Alas! the treacherous hair twines round my heart . . .
>   (225)

On her birthday, Clem presents to Edith, as a joke, the fruits of his chemical research: a bottle of a new kind of poison, more deadly than prussic acid. Edith at first is not amused: "it's just as if you wanted me to commit suicide" (8). But later, more cheerfully, she admits that the poison may come in handy: "It will do to kill my future husband if he ill-treats me" (18). Much later, after she has married old Kasker-Ryves, in order to become a wealthy widow for the impoverished Clem, Edith chooses for her bedtime reading Browning's *Fifine at the Fair*, the poem Rossetti believed was inspired by his mistreatment of Lizzie.

After Edith's marriage, Clem loathes her as if she were a "snake" and identifies with her husband, "poor fellow" (142). Still, Clem cannot put her out of his mind. "This love, this opiate emasculates me and paralyses the engines of my brain" (231). In a recurrent, highly charged, grotesque scene, depicting a powerful Kasker-Ryves, an inert Edith, and a terrorized, fascinated young man, Ford comes close to dramatizing successfully his sexual anxieties. Its most vivid version portrays Clem and Edith finding her husband dead, Clem believing Edith has poisoned him, and Edith falling to the ground with her arms about Kasker-Ryves's neck. Even in death, the old man remains a potent Rossetti. Clem stands "in paralyzed amazement surveying the grotesque figure of the corpse as it lay, stiff and unnatural like an artist's lay figure, across Edith" (289). What finally emerges is that all the characters are, figuratively speaking, killers, even Julia with her "rash apologia for murder" (304). Nevertheless, Ford, inspired presumably by the hope of perfect bliss with Elsie, managed to give a happy ending to his first seriously intended novel of modern love. He was unable to do this again until *A Man Could Stand Up*, thirty-four years later.

After Madox Brown's death, Ford, Elsie, and the Martindales proceeded to act out portions of Ford's first novel as if it were a scenario written especially for them. Edith's roommate Julia is attracted to Clem much as Elsie's sister Mary was attracted to Ford. Edith's parents actively disdain the arts and forbid their daughter to marry a penniless suitor; so did the Martindales. Whereas the old and wrathful Kasker-Ryves stamps to pieces Edith's Stradivarius, Mr. Martindale simply confiscated Elsie's violin. Just as Edith sings to Clem Tennyson's "Ring out the old, Ring in the new," so Elsie, still remembered for her lovely voice, sang it for Ford and Olive (June 9, 1894). Ford and Elsie went to live in Bonnington, Kent, a few miles from Dymchurch where Clem practices medicine, Kasker-Ryves dies, and Edith and Clem are reconciled. Like the fictional lovers, Ford and Elsie followed Rossetti's example in the way they dressed, and Ford threatened to hang himself with Elsie's hair.

Unhappily, the fictitious events of *The Shifting of the Fire* continued uncannily to recur in Ford's history. Although Edith only talks about administering or taking Clem's poison and old Kasker-Ryves only appears to take it, old Mr. Martindale, according to Olive's diary, in a fit of melancholia in 1902, actually took a lethal dose of prussic acid (February 7, 1902). Violet Hunt, Ford's mistress from 1909 to 1919, apparently came to believe as an old lady that she had lived with and loved not Ford Madox Hueffer but Dante Gabriel Rossetti. For, in her last book, *The Wife of Rossetti*, she identifies wholly with the barbarously treated Lizzie Siddal.

FORD MADOX BROWN AND THE THREE
FAIRY TALES

Although Rossetti can conveniently introduce Ford's obsessive concern with passion, he cannot, warmly generous though he was, adequately symbolize for us Ford's other persistent obsession, with passion's opposite—altruism. Edith's self-sacrificing marriage and Clem's self-denying impulses suggest Ford's longing to believe in the existence of genuine goodness to counteract the murderousness of passion. The overwhelming instance of such superhuman goodness in Ford's early life was, significantly, male—his grandfather, Ford Madox Brown. As long as Ford lived, he believed his grandfather to be the best person he had ever known. Madox Brown's influence, only implicit in *The Shifting of the Fire*, exerted a constant, powerful effect on what Ford wrote and how he lived. In trying to imagine what his grandfather meant to Ford in the nineties, we should remember that Ford's adoration of the old man was shared by all the young people who knew him, including the Garnett children. Practically the earliest entry in Olive Garnett's diary (June 11, 1890) records the good omen of Madox Brown's being among the first callers at the Garnetts' new home in the British Museum. Olive "took it as a very high compliment" that, during his call, Madox Brown told her he would use her face if he ever came to paint a portrait of Shelley.

Before he was twenty-one, Ford began writing his grandfather's official biography. Dull as it is, the book manages to convey Ford's sense of the selfless benefactor. Madox Brown sacrificed himself for Rossetti from their first meeting in 1848, when the older man agreed to teach Rossetti to paint, through countless domestic disasters and an endless battle against drug addiction, clear to Rossetti's death in 1882 and even beyond, to raising money for memorials and then executing them himself. But Madox Brown was generous to all his artist friends, constantly exerting himself to find buyers for their works, giving them practical suggestions to improve their artistry, and, after their deaths, taking care of their destitute widows and children. Rossetti was finally moved to write a letter begging him "to stop this kind of preoccupation rigorously" (283). Even his artist-enemies, whenever they had fallen from prosperity, benefited, according to Ford, from Madox Brown's generosity "by stealth" (401). He did not confine his charity to artists. During one particularly severe winter, he and his wife ran a "soup-kitchen in their own house" (172). Meanwhile, his own income was always modest, his pictures at no time brought prices like Rossetti's, and he was sometimes distinctly hard up.

Madox Brown's generosity expressed a fundamental quality in his temperament. Along with his "elaborate courteousness of a *grand seigneur*" went a profound sense of human equality (392). In fact, says Ford, his impulse was always to rate the opinion of a British hand laborer above that of a philosopher. The central figure of his masterpiece *Work*, a product itself of eleven years' labor, is a stalwart young construction worker in the act of thrusting forward a shovel. This egalitarian (Ford would come to call it "Tory") outlook especially endeared him to the young: "His reverence for youth was a most touching thing to see; the opinions of a young man, if uttered in his presence or to him, were canons that almost certainly ousted his own, formulated though they might have been from the bitterest of experiences" (393).

If Madox Brown selflessly devoted himself to his friends (most of whom were to some extent competitors), he also gave himself utterly to his art. He was from the beginning, as Ford says, an "indefatigable worker," in his sixties still painting from 10 a.m. to 8 p.m.; indeed, he worked a full day the day before the onset of his last, brief illness (17). First trained in his teens in Antwerp under Baron Wappers, Madox Brown early mastered every technique in the plastic arts. He was strictly a professional, with scorn for English amateurishness in artistic and critical matters. By his mid-twenties he was an "artistic revolutionist" (409), anticipating the "Plein Air" school in France and the Pre-Raphaelite movement in England. Like Conrad and Ford after him, he scorned coterie art and believed that the treatment of a subject should make itself clear to ordinary viewers (429). In his modesty Madox Brown never would do anything to further his reputation. He associated exclusively with artists and eschewed the "moneyed class, among which picture buyers are to be found" (109). He treated the Royal Academy with open contempt; he ignored John Ruskin, whose favor brought fame and fortune to Rossetti. Madox Brown, painter of big pictures celebrating great, and often physically powerful, men—Elijah, Jesus, Lear, Harold, Wickliffe, Chaucer, Cromwell—was naively delighted with the anonymous critic who spoke of him as a "great force . . . quietly and modestly doing solid and lasting work" (318).

The Ford Madox Brown known intimately to the young Garnetts, Hueffers, and Rossettis was simply a saint: "in the autumn of his life he was the most loveable, the sweetest, of all men" (399). Yet Ford knew, not only from family lore, but also from early photographs and self-portraits, that the late saintliness had been bought at a heavy price. Madox Brown's first wife died tragically young, and he had suffered, too, from that "morbidness which not infrequently casts a shadow on the mind of the ignored innovator" (51). In the eighteen-fifties his face looked to his friend Arthur Hughes "impressive and rather severe," with that "disappointed and half resentful" look (70) worn by the emigrant staring over the stern of the departing ship in Madox Brown's famous painting, *The Last of England* (1855). In 1853 he suffered some sort of nervous breakdown and, on doctor's orders, left his wife and children to live alone in various places in London. The experience made him sympathetic with the mental illnesses of Rossetti and other friends. Madox Brown came to believe that no one accomplishes anything significant without having, some time in his thirties, passed through a phase of nervous hysteria (315). Throughout his life, he showed neurotic tendencies. He suffered, his grandson says, from "exaggerated, almost incomprehensible, suspiciousness" (96); "the most courteous and genial of men," he "repeatedly damaged his prospects by resenting over-hastily and answering unguardedly slights that were frequently imagined" (175-76). Only in the late eighteen-sixties and early seventies did Madox Brown experience a period of relative prosperity, active social life, and personal happiness. But that ended in 1874 with Nolly's death. Beginning in the early eighties when Rossetti died, Madox Brown started losing his oldest and best friends without acquiring any new ones. Ford's reading of his grandfather's life here clearly reflects his own anxieties and self-doubts: "Madox Brown's proneness to feel new impressions made each successive loss seem a more and more predominant presage, not so much of his own end, as of a time when he might stand alone and unbefriended" (354).

If Ford could idealize Madox Brown's generosity and see his own anxious fears for the future confirmed by his grandfather's past suffering, he must nevertheless have felt a great gulf between his sense of his own quivering self and his grandfather's blatant manliness. Immediately after discussing the "strong influence" of Cromwell's "virile personality" upon the mind of Madox Brown (311), Ford describes the 1875 self-portrait. Almost every word suggests largeness and power.

> We see the artist—a man of great handsomeness of a masculine cast—Roman-nosed, broad of forehead, with rather long, almond-shaped eyes; the face rather oval and broad at the cheeks. The profuse grey hair, carefully parted in the middle, and falling mane-like on each side, and the sweeping grey beard, beginning to grow white, impart an almost patriarchal air to a face otherwise vigorous enough. (313-14)

No doubt young Ford not only loved and envied his old grandfather, but tried to be like him. While Madox Brown was still alive, his grandson was successfully imitating him as a raconteur. To the amusement of his friends, Ford often talked like someone even older than Madox Brown. Olive Garnett notes in her diary on March 23, 1893: "It is true that Ford speaks to everybody as if he were their great-grandfather." A few years later, Stephen Crane predicted

that Ford "will end up by patronizing God who will have
to get used to it and they will be friends."[27] Erik Erikson
says that such youthful, antique solemnity is common
among the most gifted, and notes that Luther at eighteen
acted so old and profound a part that his classmates called
him"*Philosophus*."[28] Ford's reason for wanting, *right away*,
to be his grandfather can easily be guessed.[29] His first
novel suggests that he already knew that suffering, especially sexual suffering, is the lot of man. Ford must have
envied that white-bearded, benign old fellow, who had
most of his painful losses and sexual anxieties behind him.
In a discussion with Olive on November 20, 1895, Ford
spoke of the "childlike old age of Madox Brown. . . . The
last state the perfect one in which man through failing
power renounces." At eighteen, Ford must have been
eager to fly away into the future whence he could look
back in safety upon those flames of passion he feared were
about to erupt.

Longing to be in every way like his grandfather, Ford
seems never to have wondered whether pernicious motives of egoism or overweening vanity could lie behind the
old man's persistent meddlesome generosity. Yet a quarrel
with Olive Garnett on November 22, 1895 suggests that
Ford had some strong, if unconscious, anxieties about the
psychological sources of altruism. Olive had been translating from the Russian a friend's memoirs. In reading from
them an account of the self-sacrifice of someone named
Fomin, Olive included a note of psychological explanation
by her famous Russian revolutionary and novelist friend
Stepniak:

> This set Ford off. He threw back his head & in his
> slowest & most tempered tones inveighed bitterly
> against Stepniak, myself & my family. "You are all
> alike the simplest, most sacred, indisputable altruism
> is twisted and turned by you to suit your own worldly
> convenience. Give up all & follow Christ. Could any-
> thing be plainer. Fomin does here in this story & here

Stepniak puts in his own wretched philistine, bourgeois note to *explain* forsooth, to explain it away, & you agree, you would publish it." Fomin was right, you are wrong, etc. etc. "I thought Stepniak was such a wonderful person," said Elsie, & Ford said some rude, damning things, if they were true "To die for the truth, what is finer, truer, higher? According to me erred only in one thing when giving himself up to the police prompted by physical pain; had he let himself starve he would have been perfect." Logical, I replied, not perfect, only perfectly logical, as it is not given to human nature, even to Fomin to be, Fomin who is while still a young man leading a useless existence, supported by the very authorities of whom he disapproves. We argued on, Ford lucidly, logically, I lamely, confusedly, yet clinging clinging to some idea I knew was implanted in me & in Stepniak. How can I describe my feelings, my wounds! Ford's brutality certainly had moved me, even to tears.

The quarrel shows the gulf between Fordian idealism and Garnettian common sense, and the intensity of Ford's feelings. Why would a psychological explanation of altruism so outrage Ford? Perhaps partly at least he wondered whether he himself could be faithful to Madox Brown's high ideals. Perhaps he unconsciously wondered whether his commitment to altruism masked an ultimately irresistible tendency toward self-indulgence.

Ford's earliest fictional efforts were fairy tales: *The Brown Owl* (1891) and *The Feather* (1892); after *The Shifting of the Fire*, he published still another fairy tale, *The Queen Who Flew* (1894). All three reflect his idealization of altruism and his longing to escape from himself. All reflect, in varying degrees, his devotion to his grandfather and the latter's affection for little girls. *The Brown Owl*, as its title suggests, can be read as a private family allegory. Ford wrote it with the sole purpose of amusing his little sister Juliet, who had been only eight when her father died.[30] The tale in fact

starts with the young Princess weeping over the death-
cold face of her father. Almost immediately an owl appears, perches on her shoulder, and covers her face with
his "soft brown feathers." "The touch of the Owl seemed
to have driven away her grief. . . . it seemed as if the Owl
had become a companion to her that would take the place
of her father" (19). By night, he sits at the head of the bed
to protect her. By day, he plays hide and seek with her,
exposes and ousts the evil minister Merrymineral, drives
away a dragon, and manages her romance with the Prince
of India. In a tournament staged for the Princess's hand,
the unknown Knight of London defeats the Prince of India, and the Princess cruelly rejects her lover for the new-
comer. Thereupon the Owl magically expands in size,
takes the Princess on his back, carries her to a secret castle,
and there reveals to her the infamy of the Knight of London and his defenselessness against weapons made of
paper. The Princess regrets her treatment of the Prince of
India, returns to him, revives his sunken spirits, and tells
him how to defeat the Knight of London in a rematch. The
Knight proves to be none other than evil old Merrymineral
in disguise, and the Owl proves to be the Princess's own
father, who was not dead after all. Nevertheless, he gives
his kingdom to his daughter and her lover, reassumes the
shape of the Brown Owl, and promises to return every
seven years. And so here, in his very first published work,
Ford dramatizes the faultless altruism and wisdom of an
ancient king/brown owl and the charm of a lovely young
girl with long hair. Together they easily defeat the ugly old
demons and witches. At the same time, the little girl/
princess reveals capriciousness and considerable determination: at one point she unfairly rejects her wounded, de-
feated young man; but then, after her flight, she mends
him physically and inspires him to victory, a rather literary
triumph as his secret weapon is paper.

Ford's two succeeding fairy tales, *The Feather* and *The
Queen Who Flew*, follow the formula of *The Brown Owl*. The
dedication of *The Queen Who Flew* to a "Princess of the Old

Time" who came "over the leas . . . on the sward of the cliffs that breast the sea" recalls Ford's and Elsie's school days together on the Folkestone Leas, high above the Straits of Dover. As Madox Brown encouraged those young lovers, a "dear good old bat" teaches young Queen Elrida to fly, by means of a coronet of windflowers, to meet her young man, a blind plowman. (Ford was no doubt thinking of how prettily Elsie sang "Twist me a crown of windflowers" to him and Olive, June 9, 1894.) Ultimately the Queen cures the young man's blindness by sacrificing her coronet to make a magical tea. Her plowman says hopefully, "I dare say you won't want it again, unless you get very tired of me" (82).

In writing his four fictions of the early nineties, Ford, it seems, was trying symbolically to replace first Juliet's deceased and then Elsie's estranged father. In recompense they were presumably to give him not only the love they once gave their fathers, but rest as well. But far from achieving peace and happiness by winning Elsie, Ford would shortly be suffering recurrent eye trouble (like Rossetti during his breakdowns) and would soon be creating a host of stumbling, staggering, half-blind, sick young heroes. As for Elsie, she would finally fly to a solitary cottage overlooking the English Channel and forever renounce life with Ford, although never her legal ties to him.

CHAPTER TWO

Women and Men, I
1894–1908

JOSEPH CONRAD TO THE RESCUE
(*THE INHERITORS* AND *ROMANCE*)

Despite Olive's charming pictures[1] of the young Hueffers, things from the beginning did not go well in the vital matters of producing either fiction or children. Olive reports in the course of 1894 reading one Ford novel in manuscript, "The Wooing of the Wind," and hearing of another, "The Sowing of the Oats." (Clearly, the author of *The Shifting of the Fire* was still in a participial phase.) Both manuscripts needed extensive "working up"; neither became a book. Although Ford did publish his biography of Madox Brown in 1896, he had had, while writing it, to endure Edward Garnett's harsh criticism: "German—cumbrous—slovenly—vague will generalise about things of which he knows nothing etc." (September 28, 1895). Meanwhile, the previous February Olive was reporting Elsie first as "enormous" and then as unwell, foretelling the miscarriage. During her subsequent pregnancy, Elsie had to take to her bed and call on Mary to come and help. Happily, Christina Margaret Madox Hueffer arrived safe and sound July 3, 1897. The other bright spot of those early years was reconciliation with the Martindales, duly reported by Olive:

A little while ago Mrs. Martindale sent Elsie a packet containing her childhood's treasures, clothes & violin. Elsie wrote a 'kind' letter, & now Mr. and Mrs. Martindale have each written to Ford and Elsie amiable letters inviting them to spend Xmas at Winchelsea. Ford is in a 'whirl.' So here ends the romance. (December 10, 1895)

Martindale support meant that they could, on October 15, 1896, move out of crowded, primitive Blomfield Villas and into the attractive, relatively comfortable Pent Farm. Yet even with this move and the birth of their daughter, they were still discontented. By March 1898 they had sublet the Pent and moved next door to Edward and Constance Garnett, in Limpsfield, Surrey. There that spring and summer Ford wrote a draft of an historical novel, "Seraphina," also clearly unpublishable. Twenty-six years later Ford remembered this as the "most depressing period" of his life (JC, 17).

Into it, probably in September 1898,[2] through Edward Garnett, came Joseph Conrad.[3] Conrad and Ford responded to each other immediately. In no time, they were planning to collaborate, the Conrads had taken over the Pent, and the Hueffers had left Limpsfield for Stock's Hall, Aldington, a few miles from the Conrads. Having Conrad in his house made Ford feel as if he were entertaining a king (JC, 38).

It was a remarkable relationship. Is there another instance in literary history of so early and intimate a friendship, including collaboration, between two novelists of such ultimate distinction? It is true, of course, that two years earlier, on his honeymoon with youthful, conventional, unliterary Jessie George, the middle-aged Conrad had begun his first masterpiece, *The Nigger of the "Narcissus"*. Moreover, before he met Ford, he had discovered his narrator Marlow while writing the very fine "Youth" in May 1898. Nevertheless, this complex, Polish disciple of Flaubert and James required, in addition to a comforting bosom, literary conversation of a high order. Immediately upon meeting Ford and moving to the Pent, Conrad wrote, in quick succession, all his other masterpieces (except, some would say, for *Under Western Eyes*, "The Secret Sharer," and *The Shadow-Line*).

The two writers were certainly ready for each other. By the summer of 1898, Conrad had lost, through a quarrel, his intimate friend of twenty years, Adolf P. Krieger, had acquired as competitor an infant son, had made pressing publishing commitments, and could not finish "The Rescuer."[4] Ford appeared with unpublished manuscripts, an apparently uncomfortable marriage, a competing infant, and probably the need for a great artist to worship as he had worshipped Madox Brown. Violet Hunt says that Ford "adored" Conrad and Conrad "loved" Ford.[5] Ford would later call the friendship a "very beautiful thing" best characterized by the word "intimacy."[6] Conrad's letters to Ford tend to support this view. Indeed, the letters of February 3, 1902 and July 29, 1904, on the occasions respectively of Mr. Martindale's shocking death and Ford's nervous breakdown, use the word "intimate" to describe the friendship.[7] And Conrad's last truly loving letter until 1916, that of late April 1909, calls upon "ten years of perfect confidence and intimacy" as witness to his commitment to Ford.[8] Still, the relationship moved through stages, paralleling Ford's phases, and from the beginning contained the seeds of its own destruction. The first five and a half years, from September 1898 to March 1904, were intimate in the senses of both love and constant communication. During the second five years, Conrad and Ford saw much less of each other, and the affection Conrad shows in his letters, though still warm, has a more formal quality. In the spring of 1909, the friends quarreled bitterly, were completely estranged for two years, and thereafter maintained only a wary, sporadic relationship.

All sorts of ties bound them together. There were the financial connections: landlord to tenant, creditor to debtor, editor to contributor. Their closest bond was, of course, literary collaboration which was almost continuous, in some form, throughout the decade. The intensity of the relationship comes out in Conrad's frequent, disparaging references to third parties, with the implication that only Conrad really understands Ford and can protect him against the world. That James, for example, saw Ford as merely "un jeune homme modeste" had for Conrad "an effect of farcical blindness."[9] Typically, Jessie belonged among the outsiders, whereas Elsie Hueffer was one of us—another bond. Conrad took seriously Elsie's translation of de Maupassant: "We must get into a closer heap together when she is ready to commence—if not sooner! I want you and have wanted you for some time."[10] Bernard C. Meyer has stressed the obsessive concern of the two close friends with each other's physical and mental states. Conrad's first surviving letter to Ford says the move to the Pent is necessary to "preserve . . . my sanity."[11] The second finds Conrad "concerned to hear your body is making itself so objectionable to you. . . . What is it about your eyes? It sounds so very serious."[12] Conrad's constant references to his own fatigue look forward to a host of weary Fordian heroes: "I am tired! I am tired of sitting on the knees of the unpropitious gods."[13] Probably the high point in Conrad's correspondence is his response upon receiving a copy of *The Fifth Queen*, dedicated to himself:

> What your modesty and tenderness prompt you to say of myself I reject utterly in its literal sense. It is a delusion of your affection—and as a delusion I accept it with a melancholy eagerness; for it is a delusion which, for me, is of infinite "douceur." And presently after reading it once more I shall burn your letter.[14]

Even here there appears, in the last sentence, a curious Conradian reservation, doubt of self, perhaps, and doubt of friend as well. We remember, sadly, that though Conrad dedicated books to Krieger, Garnett, Galsworthy, Cunninghame Graham, and Wells, he never got around to dedicating one to Ford.

Because they chose each other out of similar needs and weaknesses, the friendship, with all its intensity, had certain built-in problems. Especially it had to contain Ford's frequent bouts of depression, which began long before he met Conrad. Conrad had constantly to reassure Ford of his affection. Yet Ford had some basis for feeling exploited.

His career went nowhere those first five years, while Conrad was doing his best work. To his credit, Conrad's letters reflect remorse at using Ford and awareness that Ford longed to make a splash. Perhaps beyond this, Ford sensed something ultimately provisional in Conrad's love for him. Certainly, given his traumatized childhood, unsettled sailing years, and marriage with a limited, jealous spouse (Borys Conrad said his mother's opinion of Ford was "unprintable"),[15] Conrad at forty could hardly have committed himself wholly and eternally to the Hueffers. Yet his other, less intense, literary friendships did endure, and Conrad in 1905 still believed that Ford was a "lifelong habit."[16]

Besides Conrad's general wariness about human relations, his letters reflect specific uneasiness about Ford. Conrad recurrently wonders whether Ford has his facts straight, whether he fully understands some financial arrangement, whether he sees why a particular fictional scene is illogical. In a letter to Elsie about Ford's preface to her de Maupassant volume, Conrad simply blows up over what he sees as the inaccuracy, inappropriateness, and blindness to reality of a comment of Ford's. Twice Conrad asks what Ford *means*, as he will do years later in his angriest letter. Here, Conrad is asking Elsie:

> What does Ford mean in the preface about Maupassant being or even seeming a rhetorician in the *last sentences* of the chair mender? It is either perverseness or carelessness—or I don't know what rhetoric is, to me it's sheer narrative—sheer report—bare statement of facts about horses, dogs, the relations of doctor to chemist and the tears in the Marquesa's eyes. If it is only one of his little jokes I am sorry that he let himself become folâtre before the high altar. It's the sort of thing that hardly pays. C'est une triste passion.

And then Conrad allows himself to wonder if Ford has even got the right story! "Did he mean the last par. of Mlle. Perle—by chance?"[17]

Conrad's uneasiness about Ford emerges chiefly, and

understandably, in literary discussions. For Conrad, "actuality," "substance," "conception" take precedence over "technique." To improve, Ford must "sweat" and get "nearer to life, to reality." Where a section of *Romance* "must be given hard *reality*," where its treatment "is too much in the air," Conrad will "do the thing myself." Frederick R. Karl interestingly relates comments of this sort to Ford's and Conrad's esthetic theories, which look forward to Pound's and Olson's.[18] Our concern here, however, is merely the human relations between two remarkable friends. Conrad's insistence upon overall conception and hard reality reflects, it seems to me, his doubts about the ability of Ford the writer to find a significant subject and the capacity of Ford the man to think things through and stick to the real world. I think, in short, that Conrad had a lurking fear of Ford's mental instability and that this fear brought about a subtle change in the relationship in 1904, and a drastic one in 1909.

When Conrad proposed collaboration to Ford in the fall of 1898, he obviously had in mind their reworking Ford's "Seraphina," with its West Indian setting that recalled his earliest sailing days. Instead, Ford showed up the following October with the opening chapters of a fantasy on contemporary politics. Conrad helped a little with the writing and added his name, so that at last, in 1901, nine years after *The Shifting of the Fire*, Ford had, to his (partial) credit, another novel, *The Inheritors*.[19] Conrad's impact on the work is striking. The political subject, King Leopold's exploitation of the Congo, comes from "Heart of Darkness"; one major setting, a Legitimist salon in Paris, looks forward to Conrad's writings about the Carlist revolutionaries in France. But the hero's psychic state and his responses to passion and altruism are strictly Fordian.

In *The Shifting of the Fire* Ford had portrayed most of the character-types of his later fiction: the powerful, bad, old man (Kasker-Ryves); the idealistic, talented, infirm, young man (Clem); the idealistic, determined, maternal, young woman (Edith). To this gallery the fairy tales contributed three other types: the kind, faultless, old benefactor; the beautiful, innocent, defenseless, little girl; the wicked witch.[20] Several peculiarities of these characters seem worth mentioning. Kasker-Ryves, for example, is not *thoroughly* bad. Even though, like Mr. Martindale, he is strictly a *nouveau riche* in his country estate, he is "universally esteemed" there (89) by both the peasantry and the county aristocracy. Oddly enough, he looks a great deal like Ford Madox Brown: "a remarkably noble-looking, white-haired old gentleman, with a smile of overpowering sweetness" (51); like Madox Brown he has "all the airs of 'grand seigneur'" (36-37). When Kasker-Ryves marries Edith, Clem identifies with, rather than hates, him. That is to say, the type of the bad old man threatens to dissolve into the types of either the faultless old benefactor or the idealistic, infirm young hero. Again, the innocent, defenseless little girls in the fairy tales show amazing determination in crises, ultimately relate to their young lovers more as nursing mothers than as wives or daughters, and tend to turn into the type of the determined, maternal young heroine. Finally, Ford betrays significant flashes of fear and hostility toward these young heroines; to their vulnerable lovers, they could become not nurturing mothers but frightening witches. In short, despite the apparent variety of character-types in Ford's eighteen-nineties portrait gallery, one painting threatens to overshadow, absorb all the rest. It is Rossetti's picture of Guinevere "looking rather contemplatively and without emotion at her sleeping lover" (R, 82) and effectively, permanently, blocking Launcelot's way to the Holy Grail.

From the nineties to the Great War, Ford was to portray passion obsessively and with varying degrees of unsuccess. The hero of *The Inheritors*, Etchingham Granger, is another Clem—talented, infirm, drawn to women but afraid of them. The man Granger admires most, a politician named Churchill, with his sanity, his traditionalism, manliness, "probity," and "conscious rectitude," belongs among the old benefactors (285, 189, 312). But the heroine, a lady from the Fourth Dimension—"sinister," "cold," "sinuous," "inscrutable," "threatening," "overpowering"—belongs among the witches and her fellow Fourth Dimensionists among the evil old kings and demons of the fairy tales (7, 15, 174, 234, 160, 222). The heroine's purpose is "to sound the knell . . . of altruism." She accomplishes it by inspiring in the hero a passion for her: "if you had not loved me you would not have betrayed your—your very self." (321-22). She belongs, that is, with Lilith and Guinevere; and the hero belongs with Launcelot and "muscular exhaustion."

Although intended as a serious political novel, *The Inheritors* is a neurotic portrait of a neurotic hero; it partakes of the hero's own listlessness, dimness, sense of unreality, and reminds us of Elsie's, Olive's, and Conrad's concern at the time for Ford's health—his bad eyes, indigestion, insomnia—and low spirits. When Granger, "a convalescent" (7), says that he "never quite understood the bearings of that scene" (199), he could be speaking for the author. Throughout the novel, the hero sways on his legs and suffers fits of "giddiness" (9). He undergoes psychotic distortions of reality during which enormous buildings "topple forwards" (297) and the tower of Canterbury Cathedral reels "out of the perpendicular" (8). He simply cannot trust his senses: "A little behind them . . . there was a space. Perhaps I was mistaken; perhaps there was no space—I don't know" (159). He is perpetually baffled: "I was overcome . . . I did not know what to do" (144). "So tired, so dog-tired," he must tire himself still more if he is "to come through it sane" (237).

The hero's confusion is never greater than when he is with the heroine. He believes he loves her: "I want you, I want you, I want you." Her reply, "If you had wanted me I have [*sic*] been here" (234), is quite true. On their first secluded walk together, a "panic of prudence" keeps him from kissing her hand (18). When they were alone together in Paris, he "wanted to make love to her—oh, immensely, but I was never in the mood." "I was forever screwing my courage up and feeling it die away." "She overpowered me so that I actually dwindled" (205, 174). Granger, however, is partially protected from her by the possibility that she is his sister reincarnated, a hint, in the light of imminent developments, that Ford's sister-in-law Mary may have been a partial inspiration.

Churchill's role is important in Ford's canon. His political support comes from "county" aristocracy with which the hero, like Clem, has family connections. Ford, moreover, associates Churchill with Jenkins, a great disregarded old painter obviously based on Madox Brown. Finally, Churchill, like Conrad, seeks the hero's assistance in collaborating on a book. Although the hero insists upon his love for the heroine, the only dramatized affection is strictly masculine, between the hero and Churchill. Granger's account of his last moment with Churchill looks forward to Dowell's account of Ashburnham's last affectionate words and his own useless devotion.[21]

Yet, strangely, at the end the hero views the ruin of Churchill with appalling equanimity. Like a patient who has mastered the language of psychoanalysis without really being cured, Ford asserts, without being able to dramatize or criticize it, that his hero's enormous vanity scarcely conceals an anxious self-loathing. The heroine pronounces judgment upon the hero: " 'It is yourself that you bemoan. That is your tragedy, that you can never go again to Churchill with the old look in your eyes, that you can never go to anyone for fear of contempt' " (322-23).

Romance (1903), Ford's next novel and second collaboration with Conrad, is the much delayed reworking of "Seraphina." Although it does not elicit from either writer his very best prose, the escape in the fog and the death of Manuel-del-Popolo are Conradian triumphs worthy of *Nostromo*, and the trial of John Kemp is an effective, Fordian scene.[22] Moreover, Kemp's love for Seraphina yields useful insights into Ford's attitude toward passion and toward himself as an artist.

According to Ford, the story of Aaron Smith, the last

pirate to be tried at the Old Bailey, had interested him because Richard Garnett considered Smith the prey of gov-
ernmental mistreatment (RY, 174). Presumably Ford's obsessive guilt feelings coupled with his sense, like Lord
Jim's, of "innate blamelessness" made him an avid fan of
unjust trials.[23] (We have already seen how frightened, yet
fascinated, he was by the legal proceedings issuing out of
Elsie's flight.) John Kemp suffers not only at the hands of a
harsh and corrupt legal system but in other ways as well.
In generously refusing to kill his two worst enemies, he
endangers the lives of his two best friends and thus feels
"guilty of cruelty for the sake of my conscience" (217).
Whereas Conrad, in *The Nigger of the "Narcissus"*, is deeply
skeptical of the moral and practical value of pity and, in
Nostromo, finds destructive egoism lurking beneath the fair
robes of idealism, Conrad and Ford shield Kemp from all
real blame in *Romance*. Neither conscience nor honor is
subjected to persuasive skeptical questioning. Even when
Kemp asks himself, "Had I acted like an Englishman and a
gentleman, or only like a fool satisfying his sentiment at
other people's expense?" (217), the issue is not in doubt.
Kemp is a *good* man.

Yet Kemp suffers from other, less conscious and more
convincing, varieties of guilt. For example, as the "heretic
Inglez" in Roman Catholic Cuba, he seems to feel a strange
religious guilt in courting Seraphina. Since Ford joined the
Roman Catholic church immediately upon proposing to
the Protestant Elsie and then went on to marry her in a
registry office, he might well, by the time of *Romance*, have
been blaming his woes on disloyalty to the Faith. Conrad
playfully equated Elsie with Seraphina, habitually calling
her in his letters "the Señora." Ford made the important
contribution of senility to the character of Seraphina's
father and wrote the section, highly praised by Conrad,
about the old man's funeral only a week or so before the
death of Mr. Martindale.[24]

The Aaron Smith story must have attracted Ford not
only because of the trials of the hero but also because of the

heroine's situation. The story of a beautiful orphaned girl
rescued from a pirate stronghold would have reminded
Ford of his beloved *Lorna Doone*, that great Victorian
adventure-romance he read so often that he claimed he
knew it by heart (AL, 180).[25] Like it, *Romance* is told by an
old man looking back to the romantic time of his
youth. Ford's dedicatory poem to Elsie and Jessie expresses his characteristic longing to leap out of the present
so that he can look back at it:

If we could have remembrance now
And see, as in the days to come
We shall, what's venturous in these hours:
The swift, intangible romance of fields at home . . .[26]

Like Lorna Doone, Seraphina is young, beautiful, exotic,
highborn, orphaned, trapped among outlaws and intended for their leader. But unlike the simple yeoman John
Ridd and like his Fordian predecessors and successors,
John Kemp belongs to county aristocracy.

The men and women of *Romance* partake of both Ford's
fairy-tale characters and the more or less realistic figures
from *The Shifting of the Fire*. Seraphina, "frail," "innocent,"
"tender," "defenceless," looking "lost like a little child"
(197, 198), resembles "a fabulous apparition from a half-
forgotten tale" (119-20). The treatment of Seraphina happily never suffers from her creators' literary misogyny.
Like other Ford heroines, she acts as nurse, but always
charitably and without dominance. Chiefly she is an ever-
faithful Lorna Doone. Kemp, however, resembles Ford's
previous infirm young men: he has had a "rather bitter
childhood";[27] in the West Indies, he feels "very lonely"
and wants "to cry" (43); in the last part of the novel, written almost wholly by Ford, he seeks a mother's lap: "I had
suffered too much; I wanted rest, woman's love, slacken-
ing off" (402).[28] Ford's inability to imagine a successful
marriage and happy ending is underlined by the following:
it was Conrad and Jessie who insisted that the reunion between Seraphina and Kemp be made explicit, Conrad who

qualified the word "suffering" with "not despair," but Ford who made of that reunion "a sense of rest . . . like the fall of a beneficent and welcome death."[29]

Ford's most interesting contribution to *Romance* is John Kemp's long speech to the court at the end. In it Ford reveals many of the notions about narrative art that would inform all his subsequent fiction and criticism. Nothing has ever been more important to Kemp than that he tell his story well: "If there were to be any possibility of saving my life, I had to tell what I had been through—and to tell it vividly." Ford early learned his narrative skill from his grandfather, Kemp from his "old, pale" father: "I knew how to do it, I had it in the blood" (454). As Ford would dictate *The Good Soldier* to the one he loved, so Kemp fixes his eyes on the face of a pretty girl in the audience: "I was telling the story for that young girl" (453). And Kemp is successful in precisely Ford's and Conrad's impressionistic terms: "I had made them see things" (456).

Yet Kemp's speech has disturbing aspects which are also, alas, characteristic of Ford's artistic career. Kemp finds the presence of the older generation inhibiting: "the white face of my father . . . distracted me, threw me off my balance, my coolness was gone. It was as if something had snapped" (453). Although Kemp glows with pride at having made his audience "see things," his real appeal to them is for pity. Aged far beyond his years, utterly exhausted, ill-used, his wrists scarred by manacles, his hands "smashed . . . upon the spikes of the rail," one arm "impaled and the blood running down" (452), Kemp is a whining Christ: "Look at my hands, I say. Look at my wrists. . . ." (455). Like Granger, Kemp sometimes does not know where he is. "A cloud of the perfume of a West Indian bean" is so strong, Kemp thinks he is "back in Cuba again. The people in the court disappeared in the deepening shadows" (454). Sometimes the court moves "slowly up and down" in front of him "like the deck of a ship," and a roaring noise makes him think he is "on a beach by the sea" (459, 461). But Kemp's ultimate artistic goal proves to be neither to make his audience see his life, nor to make them pity him for it, but to enable himself to escape utterly from that life. To Ford's credit, Kemp remains clear-sighted enough to recognize the futility of his longing: "And suddenly it came into my head that even if I did save my life by talking about these things, it would be absolutely useless. I could never go back again; never be the boy again; never again hear the true voice of the Ever Faithful Island" (454).

MARY MARTINDALE (*THE BENEFACTOR* AND *THE FIFTH QUEEN* TRILOGY)

Even the excitement of Conrad's friendship and the ultimate, inestimable benefit of his example to Ford's artistry brought about no improvement in Ford's mental and physical health. On June 19, 1899, Olive recorded that "Ford looked very ill" and, on August 23, that he said: "I haven't got any friends but you and the Cowlishaws."[30] The birth of a second daughter, Katharine Mary Madox Hueffer, April 16, 1900, was apparently a mixed blessing. Jessie Conrad wrote to a friend concerning the parents' reaction: "I am afraid they are both awfully disappointed it is not a son." (In poems written for subsequent partners Violet Hunt and Stella Bowen, Ford's recurrent longings for a son suggest his continuing anxiety about his masculinity.)[31] The arrival of the second infant had a more immediate result: the inconveniences and isolation of Stock's Hall proved intolerable. By the following January Mr. Martindale had offered them a house near his in Winchelsea. Olive's entry for February 10 suggests that Ford thought that *this* change would surely be a good thing: "Ford has his cottage." Olive's subconscious doubts surface a week later: "Dreamed this morning that Ford was dead: an affection of the heart. I cried in my dream & went about telling everyone 'I have dreamed that Ford is dead.' " Although the dream was not literally prophetic, the move to Winchelsea, in April 1901, meant living near Mary, and was followed by horrendous changes in Ford's and Elsie's lives.

The first of these occurred early the next year. Olive's entries are as follows: February 2, 1902, "Robert & Ford dined & spent afternoon. Ford left after tea to go down to Winchelsea. Just before going, Robert whispered that Ford had just heard of the death of Mr. Martindale in sad circumstances"; February 5, "Mr. M. took prussic acid on Sunday morning. Melancholia." February 7, "Ford hopes to take Elsie to Paris directly. Mr. M. wrote 'thank Ford' at the end of his letter." We shall probably never know the intention of that cryptic remark. It could, of course, be bitterly sardonic; more likely, in the light of Ford's tenderness to sufferers and previous helpfulness to his father-in-law, the words are affectionate. The suicide must have been especially painful to Elsie with her never-to-be-forgotten knowledge that, in 1894, she had flagrantly disobeyed her father. In any case, from his death onward, Olive repeatedly refers to Elsie's ill health as well as to Ford's. Her visit to Winchelsea more than a year after the death revealed a depressing situation: "Elsie is rather thinner & less active than formerly, & bent on 'writing.' She wears conventional clothes, mourning" (March 30, 1903). "Ford said he must see his doctor at Hythe for indigestion & sleeplessness . . ." (March 31). "Elsie had a headache & her story was rejected. Ford was out of sorts, & attacked me at lunch à propos of 'Joseph' [Conrad] & his non-understanding of women; about Tourguenieff who did understand them. We kept our tempers . . ." (April 4). One interesting bright spot is also revealing: "We had tea at the Mermaid . . . & a grand discussion à propos of the psychology of Edward's celebrated article about the 'Wings of the Dove' " (April 5). The entry echoes an earlier one (February 11) about a discussion of the novel with Ford in London; it reminds us, too, that Ford and James corresponded and talked about that novel of sexual betrayal and that Ford saw himself as its unfortunate hero.[32] Olive con-

cludes her account of the visit: "Elsie lonely. Left Winchelsea at 1.50."

Olive gives no hint of when Ford's affair with Mary Martindale actually began; perhaps she never knew about it.
Mary had moved in with her parents at Glebe Cottage
about the time the Hueffers had also settled in Winchelsea.
Mizener says only that Ford and Mary "became lovers . . .
sometime after the Hueffers' arrival." Mrs. Katharine
Hueffer Lamb believed, but was not certain, that the beginning of the affair was in 1903.[33]

In any case, 1903 continued to be a bad year both financially and physically. The tepid reception of *Romance*, published in October, deeply disappointed Ford. In November, Elsie broke her arm badly. Determined to get out of
Winchelsea, the Hueffers first planned to spend the winter
in St. Jean de Luz with the Conrads, then considered S. S.
McClure's suggestion that they go to the United States for
the American publication of *Romance*; finally they rented
Ford's brother's house in Airlie Gardens, Campden Hill,
Kensington, and the Conrads took rooms nearby. Ford
later remembered the first quarter of 1904 as "the most terrible period" in his and Conrad's lives (JC, 212). Influenza
wracked both households. Jessie fell in the street and permanently injured her knees. Conrad so suffered from
writer's block that Ford had not only to extract from him by
dictation sections of *The Mirror of the Sea* but also even to
write for him a brief portion of *Nostromo*.[34] One day Christina's hair caught fire (RY, 297). Olive's entry for March 6
wholly confirms Ford's later vivid account and provides a
key to the nervous breakdown that would color the remainder of Ford's life and his most important writings.

Robert went to Airlie Gardens yesterday & found a
scene of desolation. Elsie in bed with something internal, a trained nurse with her. Christina's hair & chin
burned. Nurse burned. All talking of returning to the
country, & leaving Winchelsea, Mrs. Conrad already

returned homesick to the Pent. Ford & Elsie got into
such a state of depression & "nerves" that they attributed their misfortunes to the possession of the opal
ring Ford gave Elsie; Ford tried to lose it down drains,
& at last, meeting a Little Sister of the Poor gave it to
her, asking her to sell it for charity. Elsie now says it
should have been put under running water to break
the charm. Very sad! (March 6, 1904)

Although London and protracted intimacy with the Conrads had proven a disaster, Winchelsea still seemed impossible. More importantly, their fixing upon the ring that
Ford gave to Elsie surely suggests their own sense that,
however their ill luck had manifested itself, something was
radically wrong with their union.

Once again in his anxiety Ford headed inland, first to the
New Forest, then to the Salisbury Plain. On Saturday,
April 9, Olive noted that "Ford and the children had already gone to farmhouse lodgings near Brockenhurst, &
Elsie was going on Tuesday." By early June, they had
moved to Bridge House, Winterbourne Stoke, near Salisbury. On July 8, 1904, Olive received a letter which she
summarized in her diary: "Elsie who has burnt her face
with carbolic acid wishes me to go down to Salisbury at
once." Olive went on the eleventh, found Ford in an acute
state of mental depression, and stayed with them for ten
painful days. Nearly fifty years later, inspired by David
Garnett's *The Golden Echo*, Olive wrote, and left with her
diary, her recollections of Ford's illness. Of her visit, she
recounted:

Ford met me with trap & seemed pleased to see me. I
think I had never heard then of neurasthenia: & for a
few days all went well; but it was a hot July, & on leaving Lake House (to which a college friend had given
me a general invitation), to walk over the Plain to
Amesbury, Ford had an attack of agoraphobia, & said
if I didn't take his arm he would fall down. I held on in
all the blaze for miles, it seemed to me, but the town

reached, he walked off briskly to get tobacco & a
shave; and when I pointed this out to Elsie she said
"nerves." He can't cross wide open spaces. She said
he had already consulted a local doctor. We explored
further & went to Stonehenge, but he got worse. Elsie
was usually silent while I argued & philosophised on
our walks. But at last he burst out in a vitriolic attack
on "respectable" Garnetts & said "*I* would rather be
notorious & hanged," and was tearful: and next day
on the plain as we lay about in the heat, we all wept. It
seemed so hopeless. I was put up in a cottage across
the road, & next morning Elsie came over & woke me
& said I could catch the nine o'clock bus, with the
market-women to Salisbury. Ford was asleep &
wouldn't be up till mid-day. He had gone down stairs
at 2 a.m. & afraid that he might commit suicide, she
had crept after him, & found he was only putting the
kettle on. Evidently I could do no good by staying
longer & had better go.

Olive had based this belated account on the very brief,
very guarded diary entries she had made between July 11
and 19. But the entry for Monday, July 18, illuminates
Olive's desperate remark, above: "It all seemed so hopeless."

Ford's state acute. Very uncomfortable day: we three
went on to the plain in the evening & picked cam-
panulas & lay about. Tearful. "The bowl is broken . . .
the axe is laid to the root." (H. James's letters, *London*,
their prospects. Elsie's arm etc.) Ford rather relented,
but we parted stupidly.

The parenthetic note about Ford's unplaced book, *Soul of
London*, which James had generously assured him would
not compete with his own London book, projected for the
distant future, and about Elsie's and Ford's "prospects"
shows Olive's awareness of the very real, material causes
of their despair. But the broken bowl surely betokens

Olive's sense of either a shattered marriage or a shattered friendship. (There is no indication they were aware that James, at that very time, was finishing *The Golden Bowl*.)

The doctors seemed to blame the marriage. When Elsie suddenly brought Ford to the Robert Garnetts' in London on July 30, Dr. Tunnicliffe, a specialist recommended by Elsie's brother, told Ford to leave England without his wife. Olive's late reminiscence summarizes the events from their arrival to Ford's departure for Germany:

> It wasn't till the end of July that Elsie wired to expect them that evening, Ford had to see a specialist. The verdict was "nervous breakdown: recovery *might* be in two years: sea voyage & no work for 6 months." I went over to West Hill, & Ford walked over to sleep there, sitting down on every seat & putting a lozenge into his mouth against agoraphobia. We kept Elsie who went to see Conrad; Robert & Edward consulted & as there was no money for a long sea voyage, Edward had Ford at the Cearne & finally Robert saw him off from London docks for a voyage up the Rhine to his aunt at Bonn.

According to the diary, Ford seemed "decidedly better" (August 3) when he went to lunch with Edward and Galsworthy while Olive was dispatching Elsie to Waterloo Station for the return to Winterbourne Stoke. Olive's concluding remark recalls her final response to the court trial a decade earlier: "Peace." But when Robert and, presumably, Ford's mother saw him off about August 6, Ford's agoraphobia was, in Mizener's words, "so bad that he could not get up the ship's gangplank without support."[35]

As Ford's correspondence with Olive, her brief diary entries, and Mizener's narrative all make clear, Ford's trip to Germany was a disaster. On October 9, Ford wrote that he was taking a milk cure, staggering along the streets, and constantly losing his belongings. In a postcard from Stein Am Rhein on October 20 Ford wonders how he will be able to walk back to his hotel. Two days later, Olive noted in her diary: "Mrs. H. has gone out to him." In November, Ford was said to be looking worse. December 11, Olive noted: "Ford suddenly returned & is in London."

Conrad surely knew of his best friend's depressed mental state. Whether he also knew then that Ford was bearing the guilt of his secret affair with Mary Martindale is much less likely. Even in the light of Conrad's concerns over *Nostromo* and Jessie's injury, however, his surviving letters to Ford for the rest of 1904 are curiously infrequent, detached, and sparse of reference to Ford's illness. Conrad did not write to Ford until April 25, having mislaid the address. A letter of May 29 begins promisingly: "I am awfully grieved to hear of your state." It continues less so: "Mine though not identical is just as bad."[36] After Ford's agoraphobia in July and the doctor's dire prognosis, Elsie on August 1 went alone to the Pent to report Ford's imminent departure for Germany and to ask, fruitlessly, for some of the £100 Conrad owed Ford. Conrad apparently did not try to see his best friend then and wrote to him only three letters during Ford's four months in Germany. Ford returned, no better, in December; the Conrads departed for Capri in January.

I think that Conrad could not bear the notion of Ford's illness. While Ford was falling apart, Conrad was writing about the suicide of his own alter-ego, Decoud, and about Nostromo's bizarre, self-destructive passion for the sister of his betrothed. In 1904, as he would temporarily in 1909, Conrad staved off a mental breakdown with hard work. (He wrote Ford September 5 that his mind was running "on disconnected like the free wheel of a bicycle" and described himself on October 15 as "too shaky in mind and body" to write "anything inspiring to you.")[37] Despite *Nostromo*'s greatness, many readers find its second half inferior to the first. After finishing it, Conrad felt "left behind," fundamentally changed, his imagination "quieted-down."[38] And really, he was never again to write so beautifully as he had upon marrying Jessie or so profoundly as he had upon meeting Ford. The early months of

1904 must have reaffirmed for Conrad the lessons of his childhood and demonstrated the human vulnerability of his two most necessary props—the domestic Jessie and the literary Ford.

As if by tacit, self-preserving agreement, the two couples henceforth saw much less of each other. The Conrads went three successive winters to the Continent and then, in 1907, spent over a year away from Kent in Bedfordshire. Fewer than half as many Conrad letters to Ford survive from these second five years, and, warm as they are, they lack the earlier spontaneous exclamations of love and need.[39]

Although Olive had begun referring to Elsie's being unwell soon after Mr. Martindale's death, the bulk of her medical reports had been about Ford. Elsie was continuing to appear, as she had during the courtship, the more robust of the two. She wanted in August to take Ford to Germany; in October she wanted to join him. Then, seeing that London, the New Forest, the Salisbury Plain, and Germany had not worked, she began preparing a better life for Ford back in Winchelsea. Despite his own worries over money and his explicit wish that Elsie not mortgage her Hurst Cottage property in Aldington, she did just that in order to have a studio added to the Winchelsea bungalow. Olive wrote later: "Elsie had employed Harry [Cowlishaw] to build on a large room at the back of the small Winchelsea Cottage as a homecoming surprise, & William Rossetti who was going abroad offered 3 St. Edmund's Terrace for them all to live in." Olive's first sight of Ford on his return confirms the impression of a sturdy Elsie and recalls Olive's picture of the couple in the courtroom a decade earlier: "walked across Park to No. 3 & found Ford on the dining-room sofa. Chatted with him till Elsie & tea came in. Ford was smiling and limp. Elsie energetic and worried" (December 20, 1904). Olive had already heard from Robert (December 14) that Conrad had taken his physician, Dr. Tebb, to Ford. Elsie told Olive that "now F. would not even let her go down the road at St. E. Terr:

to post a letter." But on January 15, 1905, Olive reported a dramatic change in what proved to be her last picture of her friends as a happy couple: "Ford and Elsie, radiant to supper. Not only 'London' but 'George' is accepted through Pinker. . . . Ford looks very much better." Olive later said that Ford's cure "came suddenly" with the "boom of *The Soul of London*" (reported in her diary on May 2, 1905). Ford's own recollection, however, that he remained ill at least until his and Elsie's return from America in the autumn of 1906 is corroborated by considerable external evidence, including Olive's own references to Ford's dependence on Dr. Tebb.

Nevertheless, Olive's sympathy was henceforth to be focused on Elsie and the refrain "Poor Ford" (November 7, 1904) heard no more. Scarcely a week after Olive had seen Ford and Elsie "radiant," she noted: "Elsie ill at Broadhurst Gdns.," her mother's London residence (January 23, 1905). The illness proved to be the beginning of tuberculosis of the kidney, not properly diagnosed until May 1908. Perhaps this was the moment when Elsie discovered that Ford was having an affair with her sister Mary. If Elsie knew of it earlier, she must have tried initially to forgive Ford or she would not have been so eager to care for him in his illness. Whatever her conscious attitudes, her unconscious ones could well have rejected the marriage by January 1905 and contributed to the return of tuberculosis.[40]

While all these troubles were besetting the Hueffers, Ford was struggling with two highly significant fictional works. As early as November 12, 1901, Olive noted: "Ford read as much as he has written of George in the afternoon & . . . Katharine Howard aloud after supper." "George" was the original title of *The Benefactor*, the novel intended "as an 'extension' of the character of Ford's father-in-law" Mr. Martindale.[41] "Katharine Howard," probably a verse play, testifies to Ford's early interest in the fifth queen of Henry VIII, England's most famous practitioner of unsuccessful marriages.

When *The Benefactor* finally appeared, Ford at first hotly denied to Olive that it was autobiographical, but soon acknowledged: " 'The Benefactor' represented me up to three months ago" (November 2, 1905). Some of the connections between the hero and Ford are obvious and relatively innocent. George Moffat has written the official biography of his late father, a "great portrait painter" (8), who, like Ford Madox Brown, counseled him: "never lose a chance of helping any lame dog over a style" (9). Again, somewhat like Ford with Conrad, George has thrown away his inheritance helping other writers, all of whom eventually betray him.[42] George's wife recalls Elsie. A simple, direct woman, one of two sisters, she has become increasingly unable to bear her husband's self-sacrifices, especially for militant agnostics. She has left George in order to lead alone "a determined, forceful life . . . in the recesses of a northern moor, among her own people" (4). (The Martindales came from Carlisle.) Since George now loves "clean run" Clara Brede (*also* one of two sisters), *The Benefactor* becomes Ford's first novel to raise explicitly the question of adultery. Clara's life, presumably analogous to Mary's, has been wasted nursing first an invalid mother and then a mentally deranged father. Her "dazzling and solid" shoulders (94) and her voice of a "great hardness" (39) suggest that George has left one formidable nurse for another. Mr. Brede, a "ponderous," titanic old man, plays the same inhibiting role as does Kasker-Ryves of Ford's first novel; and George, somewhat like Clem, feels "a warm liking for the great, uncouth and passionate man" (24, 293). Although Ford tries to treat ironically George's altruistic meddlesomeness, he cannot remain critically detached. Clara's view, "You are such a good man," dominates the book (40).

Like Granger in *The Inheritors*, George believes himself passionately in love; Ford believes it, too: "He wanted Clara Brede. He wanted her love; he wanted her to be enthralled. . . ." (278). Interestingly, the fact of that love first reveals itself to George when he is far away from Clara, in a big bed in his father's house: "It stood straight up against him and filled him with an embarrassed and intense dislike for the frailty of his own nature" (247). The barrier to their union is not his marriage (Clara is willing to live with him unwed on the Continent), but George's sense of honor. He feels himself to be in a position of trust toward Clara, as Ford no doubt felt toward Mary. It is as if George were courting her under the pretext of trying to cure her mentally ill father.

Once again, Ford dramatizes his hero's fear of a powerful father and of his own impotence. When all the barriers are down, when he has money and Mr. Brede has been permanently institutionalized, George simply cannot take Clara. Ford tells us why. A powerful old man has said no: "The black and tremendous figure of her father had risen before George's eyes." He cannot do it (346). Clara, feeling "a cold anger, a cruel pride" against "this man who had thrown her away," walks out of his life (348).

The Fifth Queen trilogy (published as *The Fifth Queen*, 1906; *Privy Seal*, 1907; *The Fifth Queen Crowned*, 1908) appears to have originated in an idea similar to that of *Romance*—an innocent young person accused of capital crime. Practically everyone has agreed, for four centuries, that Katharine Howard as a very young girl was "unchaste" with one, two, or three men and that she concealed this from her husband Henry VIII. Moreover, just prior to her execution she was also "proven" to have been unfaithful to Henry after their marriage. Not all historians accept this second charge, but A. F. Pollard did so in his scholarly, influential biography of Henry, first published in 1902 when Ford was already meditating his trilogy. Ford must have wondered something like this: what if Katharine Howard had been "chaste as snow," after all? Even though, as a child, she had been exposed to all sorts of lewd conduct, what if she herself had remained pure? Even though, after her marriage, she received, late at night in her bedchamber, her former suitor Thomas Culpepper, what if Katharine had been merely nursing his madness and doing no sin? Even though she ultimately admitted to sexual misconduct, what if she had confessed falsely, out of despair at her hopeless position? Just what Ford "really" thought about Katharine Howard is hard to say. In 1904, he wrote a letter to old Richard Garnett saying he was going to whitewash his heroine.[43] No doubt his dismay at having betrayed Elsie, combined with his longings to be free, made the story of Katharine and Henry particularly vivid to him. Still, whatever commitment Ford feels in this trilogy seems invested in the notion of her doomed innocence in a corrupt world.

Wanting to write of goodness, Ford appropriately dedicated the first and last volumes to the two friends he most loved and idealized—Joseph Conrad and Arthur Marwood. He gave to the first volume a richness of detail reminiscent of *Romance* and set much of the last in Marwood's Yorkshire. But Ford's ethical attitude throughout the trilogy is characteristically, and almost fatally, confused.[44] On the one hand, he wants to see the world complexly, not in black and white but, in the words of Throckmorton, Thomas Cromwell's spy, "grey or piebald" (FQ, 218). "A man," says Throckmorton, "may act most evilly . . . and yet be the best man in the world" (FQ, 222). Nevertheless, Ford cannot bear to dramatize moral complexity or relativity. Instead he shows us an almost totally evil world, full of gossip, intrigue, spying, plotting.

A most ambitious portrait of a perfect idealist, Katharine scrupulously does not seek personal advantage (FQ, 266). Her sole purpose is to help Henry return his kingdom to God (FQC, 309). She recalls John Kemp in her refusal to fight unfairly in order to bring down even so deadly an enemy as Cromwell: "I will not stoop in evil ways" (PS, 210).

Ford molds Henry in the shape of earlier, aging benefactors, at the same time that he works toward the character of Ashburnham. Most frequently we see Henry as a weary old man; to Katharine he appears "heavy, unsuspicious and benevolent" (FQ, 256), incongruously Christlike, "a heavy man with bitter sorrows" (PS, 303). Time and again, Henry, like Ford, expresses his profound longings for peace. He loves to "let his eyes rest upon a great view . . . and to think nothing" (FQC, 16). Although history compelled Ford to make Henry, with all his congenial ways, a devious and cruel man, he tends to slide over the cruelty and have the deviousness serve good causes.

Whatever other roles Katharine's former lover Thomas Culpepper may play, his last is strictly that of the exhausted Launcelot. Mad for love of Katharine, he attempts suicide when she weds the King. Later, completely insane, his eyes "lacklustre" (FQC, 203), he invades her bedroom late at night to kill her. Katharine immediately controls him; in fact, she manages him much as Conrad's Lena was to handle Ricardo in *Victory*. That is, she takes his head in her lap and gently removes a dagger from his hand while he gazes upward at her face (FQC, 207). Passing his hand "over his eyes with a gesture of ineffable weariness," he recalls that he first wooed Katharine, as those deadly Rossetti women were wooed, "in an apple orchard" (FQC, 208).

Katharine tames Henry even more thoroughly. She will not allow him to spare her life, for he is "not such a man as I would live with willingly to preserve my life" (FQC, 312). Her final flick of the whip is to say that she will spend her last hours praying for the hated young rival Culpepper; Henry will never know for sure whether he did "feed after such a make of hound" (PS, 265). "Aye, there the shoe pinches!" says Katharine (FQC, 314).

Reading this trilogy, begun at the outset of Ford's first, terrible breakdown in 1904 and completed only a year before the separation from Elsie, one cannot resist making connections and wondering about the great fascination Henry and Katharine had for Ford. He liked to remember that his father looked like Henry and that he himself went to sleep every night in the mid-nineties by fantasizing about Henry. Katharine's very name, the same as his mother's and younger daughter's (he insisted on the identical spelling for the latter), surely had for Ford a special resonance. And attributing to Henry's fifth queen an idealistic devotion to the Church must have intrigued Ford, whose Elsie gave in to him by sending their daughters to a convent school during his 1904 illness and agreeing to their 1906 conversion to Catholicism.[45] Especially interesting in the light of Ford's imminent marital defection is his rage in the trilogy against all the evil efforts to separate Henry from Katharine. By ultimately damning Henry, Ford could punish himself for breaking his marriage vows. By whitewashing Katharine, he could deny the unthinkable fact that he and Mary had been unchaste. By pitying Katharine, he could pity Elsie for the suffering he had caused. Henceforth, however, Ford would devote himself to protecting the ego of the harried male.

ARTHUR MARWOOD TO THE RESCUE
(*THE NATURE OF A CRIME*)

Ford's origins, though perfectly respectable, were hardly aristocratic. Yet interestingly enough, his first four fictional heroes—Clem, Granger, Kemp, and George—all belong to "county" families. Joseph Conrad's distinguished heritage surely delighted Ford, but his blatant foreignness must have been to Ford an embarrassment as well as a bond. The "ultra-respectable" side of Ford no doubt longed to be more English than the English. Meeting Arthur Pierson Marwood provided him at last with intimate knowledge of the world of the English country gentleman.

Marwood's father, George Metcalfe Marwood of Busby Hall, Stokesley near Middlesbrough, Yorkshire, was an Oxford graduate (Christ Church, 1827), a landed proprietor, and a direct descendant of Edward III; his family had held the Busby estate as far back as the fifteenth century. He had first four sons, and then seven daughters. His oldest son died relatively young, the second became a distinguished civil servant in London, and the third was a battalion commander in India. Thus, Arthur, the youngest, might have run the estate if his health had permitted it. Born August 21, 1868, he attended Clifton College and matriculated at Trinity College, Cambridge, 1887, but did not finish.[46]

On February 3, 1903, in Leeds, he married his nurse, Caroline Cranswick, also thirty-four and a native of Yorkshire. For both, this was the first marriage.[47] Some time afterward they sought, for Marwood's tuberculosis, a milder climate, and chose Winchelsea because a sister of Marwood's lived there at the "Old Forge." Precisely when they arrived is not known, but a native of Winchelsea who worked for the Marwoods as a young girl puts the date early in 1905. Three of Marwood's sisters, who are remembered as "intellectual," had a large flat at 3rd The Mansions, near Earl's Court. Thus the Marwoods had a London base.[48]

Ford knew Marwood well enough to present him with an inscribed copy of *Rossetti* for Christmas, 1905. By February 1906, Ford's letters to Elsie, then on an extended visit to Ford's Rossetti cousins in Rome, were indicating that a close friendship had developed with the Marwoods. Ford and his mother took Caroline Marwood along when visiting Ford's daughters at their convent school in Rye. Another time, after tea with Henry James, Ford walked with Marwood to the sea. In April, Ford took Wells to lunch in Winchelsea, "where H. G. had a fine argument with the great Marwood."[49] By the end of June, the Conrads, recently returned from wintering in Montpellier, had been introduced to Marwood by Ford.[50] Among Ford's closest friends, only Olive Garnett seems not to have met Marwood.[51]

Coinciding with Ford's sudden intimacy with the Marwoods early in 1906 were the cooling of his friendship with Olive and the reaffirmation of his friendship with Conrad. Olive was clearly irritated with Ford's evident ability to do without Elsie. On January 23, 1906, she noted: "Ford to tea. . . . Elsie was not going to California, but might go to Rome next week. Would I go with her? I said I would if he would come too!" Olive was conscious at the time of mutual hostility. "We had a Free trade discourse; & a moment of hate? distrust? something peeped out." By mid-March, *The Fifth Queen* was out, to good reviews, and Olive was not particularly pleased: "Ford's happiness & success. His journalist admirers, speeches at clubs, portrait in *Bystander* reviews and pecuniary satisfactions" (March 21, 1906). Conrad, however, was delighted. Writing from Montpellier on March 29, he called the novel "A triumph: my dear boy, a triumph!" and asked Ford to convey to his mother and mother-in-law his "sincere congratulations on the vogue of the Vth Queen." Conrad's last words are particularly significant: "But before all to Mary in special terms and with very special regard."[52] Surely Ford would have read this as Conrad's acceptance of his love affair. Fortified by this support and by the new gratifying friendship with Marwood, Ford would presumably be better able to shake off the recurrent depression he had been suffering for the past two years.

After the Conrads returned to England in April, Ford spent two long weekends with them in Winchelsea, and it was probably then that he and Conrad began their last collaboration.[53] Although very short and very slight, *The Nature of a Crime* is important because it initiates Ford's custom of bringing into his fictions suggestions of both Conrad and Marwood.[54] Like the previous two collaborations and several of Conrad's greatest works, but unlike any of Ford's own novels before *The Good Soldier, The Nature of a Crime* has a personal narrator. Told in the form of a letter written by a weary skeptic in London to the woman he loves in Rome just prior to his intended but unconsummated suicide, this collaboration resembles Decoud's letter in *Nostromo*, written to his sister in Europe shortly before his actual, if unpremeditated, suicide.

In the preface he wrote for the 1924 edition, Conrad acknowledges that their narrator "was conceived for purposes of irony; but our conception of him, I fear, is too fantastic." Conrad remembers, too, his "panic" over "all

those people" they had created, and his gratitude at the
"neatness" with which Ford threw them "overboard" (6,
7). Perhaps Conrad had panicked partly, at least, at the
realization that Ford was dragging him into a fantasy on
their "real" lives. In effect, Ford was making him help
write a love letter to a married woman whose situation resembled Elsie's.

The Nature of a Crime opens thus: "You are, I suppose, by
now in Rome" (15). Elsie's 1906 visit to Rome had inspired
Ford to write, in language close to that of the novel,
"Views," perhaps the finest poetical expression of his impressionism.[55] The poet, speaking from London, addresses his beloved in Rome and wonders whether she will
be going "up to the Hill." He was there yesterday, in his
imagination, and she came to him. She has her Rome, and
he has "my You." In London, "this unreal town of real
things," his "You" stands beside him. If the novel's language and solipsistic attitude make the nameless narrator
Fordian, its chronology makes him Conradian. The narrator has known the heroine for seven years and three
months (26); it is now early March, presumably 1906.
Thus, he and the heroine met in late 1898, the time when
Conrad first knew Elsie. Like Conrad unalterably skeptical,
he does not believe in "Providence" (30).

Despite these Conradian suggestions, the narrator is
chiefly the Fordian neurotic and megalomaniac. Pretending to perfectly rational self-control just before his carefully
thought out "suicide," he is far from sane. The outside
world seems peculiar to him, totally without interest and
yet "fascinating, vivid." For some reason, he has no senses
left except those of sight and sound. "Vivid: that is the
word. . . . They were the clearest moments I have ever
spent upon the earth—those when I was dead" (96-97).
The narrator asserts that in these moments he is seeing the
world for the first time with "utterly unbiased eyes" (97),
but a dubious reader may instead find these to be characteristically Fordian hallucinated moments, typical of the
other collaborations. It is certainly an infirm Fordian voice

speaking these words near the end of this last Conrad-Ford effort:

> My dear, I am a very tired man. If you knew what it was to long for you as I have longed for you all these years, you would wonder that I did not, sitting in that chair, put the ring up to my teeth . . . and end it. I have an irresistible longing for rest—or perhaps it is only your support. (101)

The narrator is also interestingly Fordian in his Olympian attitude toward the chief figure in the subplot. He enjoys playing "the Godhead" to his ward, young Edward Burden, shocking him with cynical speeches and looking forward to his dismay when he discovers his guardian has stolen from him. Although Ford always writes with reverence of Arthur Marwood's vigorous brain, encyclopedic knowledge, and powerful grasp of world affairs, a letter from Conrad to Ford and some comments by Violet Hunt suggest that, at least in the early years of their friendship, Ford was quite capable of condescending to Marwood.[56] In creating the "good" Edward Burden, that conventional, aristocratic, open, trusting, wealthy, foolish young man, Ford seems to be expressing some of his less attractive feelings for his new friend. As the recently married Marwoods loomed large in Ford's letters to Elsie in Rome, so do the about-to-be married Burdens in Conrad and Ford's narrator's letter to his beloved in Rome. Never afterward was Marwood to depart from Ford's creative imagination.

FRIENDS AND LOVERS (AN ENGLISH GIRL, THE "HALF-MOON," AND MR. APOLLO)

During the five years after his 1904 breakdown, Ford, in addition to completing The Fifth Queen trilogy and collaborating briefly with Conrad, wrote three minor novels: a study of modern love, an historical novel, and a contemporary, satirical fantasy.[57] This mixture of fictional genres recalls Ford's unpublished manuscripts during his first five

years with Elsie; it also resembles what Ford, with Conrad's help, completed in the next five years. The mixture
further looks forward to his productions during the five
years after his liaison with Violet Hunt began in 1909. Indeed, Ford's productivity throughout his career fell into
five-year periods, coinciding with the remarkably regular
appearances of new loves in his life. (However, these
five-year segments were importantly and irregularly mod-
ified by Ford's relations with Conrad and Marwood and by
the cataclysm of the war.)[58]

The novels of 1907 to 1909 naturally reflect the external
events of Ford's and Elsie's life together, most notably
their trip to America in August and September 1906. Thus,
An English Girl tells how an idealistic young couple go on
an unsuccessful mission to New York, and *The "Half-
Moon"* tells how a newly married man from Rye becomes
the first European to die on the Hudson River. *Mr. Apollo*,
a London novel, reflects the Hueffers' leasing, in March
1907, a maisonette on Holland Park Avenue. More interestingly, these novels show that Ford, despite his success
with Mary (the affair persisted after Elsie's discovery of it)
and the admiration of Conrad and Marwood, continued to
deal obsessively with sick young men and their powerful,
frightening women.

Don Kelleg, the hero of *An English Girl*, only too obviously reflects the author, most of all in his unabashedly
Fordian psyche.[59] Though his manner suggests "stability"
(7), underneath that calm exterior Don is, in fact, "hysterical" (132). Like Ford, he *"can* talk" (16). Eleanor Greville
wishes "that her lover might at times dispense with his
tremendous flow of words" (82). Don is given to "inac-
curacies in his generalisations," "indifference to fact" (40,
42). Sometimes Don finds it difficult to tell a story because
while he is seeing everything in so many different ways,
he can't hope to accomplish anything (129). Don's dilemma haunted Ford throughout his life. Beneath Don's
impressive capacity for seeing so many aspects lies a terrified skepticism about his ability to understand reality at

all. He no sooner arrives in New York than he suffers "nervous prostration" (214). In New York, Don complains, you "don't know who's who, or what's what" (227). Don cannot bear America both because it is incomprehensible and because it is the adopted land of his father. The italics in Don's first words—"My father *is* dead" (1)—indicate that the truth of the death has been in doubt. But the truth of the novel is that old Kelleg never dies. He lives on in Don's mind as the dead Kasker-Ryves does in Clem's and the mad, imprisoned Mr. Brede in George's. Kelleg lives on to cripple Don's sexuality. For Don, Eleanor does not represent "passion," but "a feeling of . . . heavenly peace" (13). Ford underlines Don's sexual timidity by contrasting him with "Oggie" Greville, Eleanor's cousin and Don's lawyer, who calls Don "the tamest sort of cat" and tells Eleanor she "cannot make a man out of that—that sponge" (80).

Don puts the purpose of his trip to America in unconsciously sexual terms. Their expedition is just like "going down into the basement to borrow a hammer. . . . Only . . . I've *got* the hammer. My father's left it me" (33-34). Much as Dowell will cross the Atlantic to distribute his inheritance and try to prove his manhood, Don takes Eleanor, Mr. Greville, and Oggie to New York to break his father's trust and try to repay the people he cheated. Oggie telephones the results of Don's efforts from Boston to the New York suite where Don and Eleanor wait together. The scene is made for love, but Don's thoughts are far otherwise. The tapestries on the walls, the chairs, the candlelight all affect him

> with a sense of solitude, a sense of smallness, a sense of impotence that he hadn't felt since he had been a small child. And the repeated mention of his father's name had brought a tense sense of his father again before him. . . . He suddenly felt as if his father were once more saying: "Not this time, sonny." (279)

And then Oggie's malicious voice comes to him: "it amounts to this . . . that you're absolutely impotent . . .

absolutely . . . absolutely . . . impotent!" (280). Don and
Eleanor return to England without having "so much as got
the hammer" (286). Although there is nothing now to prevent their marriage, Don suddenly, and typically, flees
from his beloved, to return to America.

The character in *An English Girl* who most resembles
Conrad, Don's Italian step-brother, is of considerable biographical interest. In a letter to Eleanor, he defends Don's
vacillation and blames everything on her, the unaware
English woman with "the strong, placid, powerful gaze of
the bull" (304). Don, his step-brother asserts, is a "genius"
(306). Eleanor's "duty was to be good, to be kind, to be dear
to the noblest and best man you've ever seen" (305). The
letter concludes: "you have stabbed my brother. May God
forgive you. . . . Don was a child and you have injured
him!" (308). With its epistolary form, its Elsie-like addressee, and its passionate, non-English, aristocratic,
olive-skinned, aquiline-featured, black-mustached, auto-
mobile-enthusiast author, this epilogue to *An English Girl*
looks back a year to *The Nature of a Crime* and forward to a
whole series of Conradian figures, including even Dowell.
It suggests that Ford's private purpose in writing the novel
was to beg Elsie for understanding, especially by using
Conrad, their most distinguished mutual friend, as Ford's
advocate.

The "Half-Moon" takes a different tack. One of Ford's
most explicitly misogynistic novels, it takes its subject from
Rossetti's ballad "Sister Helen" and begins with Anne Jeal
singing an old ballad, "What maketh lads so cruel to be?"
Like Elsie, she has a lovely voice and is the daughter of the
mayor of a Sussex town; like Florence, she combines determination with fearful superstition. She loves to distraction the handsome shipowner Edward Colman and, despite her own French and Spanish blood, hates all the
foreigners in Rye, especially Colman's fiancée, the fair,
strong, gentle, enduring Magdalena. (*Mary* Magdalen?) To
prevent the marriage, Anne Jeal betrays Colman's smug-
gling activities. Her efforts, however, fail, and she must
witness the wedding. When she, like Elsie finding Ford's

telegram to Mary,[60] sees a letter from Colman to Magdalena, she at last realizes that the new love is permanent.
With "one only thought of revenge" (173), she acquires
two waxen church candles, makes them into the shape of a
cross, bares her left breast, which stood "out, white and
firm from her red coat, as if she were about to give suck,"
performs a parody of the mass, drives a bodkin into "the
point of her breast," models, with the blood and wax, a
doll in the shape of Colman, gazes at it with a face "full of
triumph and a fearful malice," and lies on the bed "with
the little image pressed to her breast" (176-78). She kills
Colman by melting and stabbing the waxen image. The
murder is an orgasm: "Anne Jeal fell back against the table,
panting, and her eyes wide open. Suddenly she screamed
out in triumph" (335).

The "Half-Moon" reminds us of the powerful, paradoxical influence on Ford of Roman Catholicism. Anne Jeal is
emphatically a Catholic witch, and the one and only way
Colman could have escaped her witchcraft would have
been to take "the communion of the Old Faith" (180).
Ashburnham and Tietjens, nominal Protestants emotionally drawn to Roman Catholicism, suffer at the hands of
their Catholic wives. Curiously, none of Ford's real-life
loves—Elsie Hueffer, Violet Hunt, Brigit Patmore—who,
as I see it, at various times inspire Catholic characters in
the novels, was herself a Catholic. This should serve as a
stern warning to biographical critics.

Like *An English Girl* but unlike *The "Half-Moon," Mr.
Apollo* gives us an Elsie-inspired character almost as sympathetic as the Fordian infirm young man. Alfred and
Frances Milne's tiny upstairs flat recalls Olive's description
of the Hueffers' maisonette. On March 23, 1907, Olive
found Elsie there, "lying down, & thin, said the doctor
said 'it was nerves.' " Frances Milne recalls Elsie in her
"ample limbs," her striking eyes, her "generally loose
gown," and her "powerful restfulness" (107). Frances's
long poem on her sheltered nook in a wood is very close in
spirit to essays Elsie soon published in the *English Review*.

Among Ford's idealistic, infirm young men, the youthful
elementary school teacher Alfred Milne appears something
of an anomaly: he is happily married. Nevertheless, Ford
successfully protects himself against imagining any sex life
for his sympathetic hero. Because of their poverty, Alfred
and Frances Milne "must avoid the chance of children"
(99). "Weary," "ill," "chilly," "very tired" (81, 167, 166,
164), Alfred Milne spends much of the novel stretched out
on the truckle bed. Resembling Ford's own neurotic periods and the lassitude of the hero of *The Inheritors*, Alfred's
illness is one of "morale" (167) as well as "physique" (99).
He wants something to restore "faith in himself." He
needs to be shown that he still has "the faculty to attract, to
soothe, to influence" (167-68).

More importantly, *Mr. Apollo* follows *An English Girl*
(and *The Nature of a Crime*) in presenting a Conradian
and/or Marwoodian figure who supports the infirm young
man and involves himself somehow with the robust young
woman. Olive's keen eyes had early noted Conrad's re-
sponsiveness to Elsie's beauty: "We sat by the fire in Conrad's room (old drawing-room), drank bovril, & tried to
keep warm. I looked at Japanese books & discussed the
legitimate in art. Conrad looked at Elsie. She wore her cape
& new gloves & veil" (November 15, 1901). Years later
Marwood would prove to be a good deal more obviously
drawn to Elsie.

In *Mr. Apollo*, both Marwoodian and Conradian characters help the infirm young man regain faith in himself. This
delightful novel tells what would happen if a "real" God
should descend into contemporary London. Mr. Apollo's
large blond handsomeness, splendid evening attire, and
power to assist the Fordian hero must owe much to Arthur
Marwood. Typical of the Marwoodian figure, Mr. Apollo
contains a great deal of Ford and, as we shall see later, acts
as beneficent double to the infirm young Alfred. The London Ford was at once the semi-indigent journalist in his
inadequate lodgings and the sparkling dandy strolling
through Kensington Gardens en route to a few hours of

writing at the Club. And so the following charming pictures of "Phoebus Apollo, the son of Maia" (32), are not wholly incompatible with Ford's view of himself in his more, let us say, exalted moods: "Mr. Apollo, standing, tall-hatted and erect, absolutely unmoved . . . the Top Toff of all" (151); Mr. Apollo in court, talking "like a book" (9) (as Ford would, during the war, to amuse the Tommies); Mr. Apollo at the pianola, playing "a little thing of my own" (63); Mr. Apollo saying, "Time has no existence for me!!" (31). The ladies love him because they can talk to him about anything and he will listen with interest. Sometimes he says "the oddest things—but it was the right sort of oddness. . . ." (241). Mr. Apollo's greatest gift reminds us of many eloquent Fordian heroes: he can "read the hearts of men" (88) and, "by one small speech," "change" them (136). That Ford can so easily imagine himself a god should not surprise us. After all, Olive Garnett acclaimed his "lordly air" when he was scarcely eighteen; Richard Aldington in 1914 portrayed him as on the most familiar terms with God.[61] Jean Rhys in 1928 had Ford's fictional counterpart, Hugh Heidler, say: "God's a pal of mine. . . . He probably looks rather like me, with cold eyes and fattish hands. I'm in His image or He's in mine. It's all one."[62]

Alfred Milne's best friend, the "elderly" Joseph Clarges, recalls his namesake Joseph Conrad in looks and actions.[63] A "diminutive, grey-bearded . . . man, with a coppery face, sharp features," an "alert and hawk-like" appearance (92-93), "this little wasp-like and vigorous man" moves in a "jerky manner" and has "swift and nervous fingers" (222-23). An "Individualist," Clarges is always throwing "back his head with little whistles and snorts of impatience," while the Milnes talk (94). Unintentionally the cause of the Milnes' poverty, Mr. Clarges so far has confined himself to giving them "moral support" (101). Still, when Alfred becomes terribly ill, Frances believes Clarges will give them money for a holiday somewhat the way Elsie tried (unsuccessfully) to get help from Conrad in 1904. Aggressively atheistic, also like Conrad, Mr. Clarges denies Mr. Apollo's divinity and calls him a "charlatan" and a pickpocket (182, 112).

Mr. Clarges is deeply devoted to Frances Milne, as Conrad was to Elsie, and furiously jealous of Mr. Apollo. Some consider Frances "a most dangerous woman." Not that she practices "coquetry," but that she has a way of so giving the whole of her attention "that it was as if indeed she gave very much more than she had any idea of giving. Thus some men—the worst sort—misunderstood her, and she seemed to lead them on" (179). But in Alfred's view, "if a man can't keep his wife's affections—or if a wife is not willing to defend herself from such advances—it's neither decent nor in any way useful for a man to interfere." The only way is to "take what comes . . . without much fuss." Alfred still insists that he is not "advocating promiscuity" and is "entirely contented" with Frances (202-204). Nevertheless, the distance between the trusting Alfred and chaste Frances on the one hand and the cuckolded Dowell and his predatory Florence on the other is not very great.

Alfred Milne and Mr. Apollo, the two characters most resembling Ford, figure in Ford's imagination as doubles. Ford, in fact, refers in the novel to the "double ganger" (267). Certainly the connections between Alfred and Mr. Apollo are extraordinarily close. When they quarrel, Alfred feels that he is "cast out from a charmed circle" (300) and suffers a total breakdown which can be cured only by "reconciliation" (302). At last, when Frances Milne calls directly upon God, Mr. Apollo appears. He reveals that he has in fact been with them throughout the three weeks and agrees to stay with them forever. We are left at the end presumably expected to believe that, through the constant presence of the potent Mr. Apollo, the Milnes' marriage will become healthy and happy.

Although the cheerful ending of Ford's fantasy proved in the long run cruelly unprophetic, it must have seemed at first uncannily true. He finished *Mr. Apollo* in April 1908; in May, thanks to Marwood's beneficence, Elsie had the operation that would finally bring her to health. By the time *Mr. Apollo* came out in late August, Ford, as editor of the forthcoming *English Review*, was already having an influence—thanks again to Marwood. But in a matter of months Ford was suffering far more than Alfred Milne ever does. Not only his benefactor but also his best friend and his wife hated him. However, into his life and works had walked a new nurse/mother—Violet Hunt.

CHAPTER THREE

Women and Men, II

1909–1913

VIOLET HUNT (*A CALL* AND *LADIES WHOSE BRIGHT EYES*)

As early as May 10, 1908, Olive had heard from Robert Garnett the "interesting news" of "Ford's proposed Review," and on September 9, from Edward, that the *English Review* would begin in November and would take at least one of her short stories. On February 10, 1909, she indicated misgivings: "To tea with Ford & stayed on till midnight listening to his new novel: & discussing all sorts of questions. . . . Am not now keen on appearing in the Review . . . (His secretaries & friends)." "Friends" no doubt included Violet Hunt, with whom Ford at the time was falling very seriously in love. Eleven years Ford's senior, the daughter of the late, Pre-Raphaelite water-colorist and Oxford don Alfred Hunt, she had inherited her literary interests from her novelist mother. Violet had several books and several former lovers to her credit when, on October 16, 1908, she came to the Hueffers' Kensington place to offer her stories to the *English Review*.

By the next spring, under the strain of the uncongenial task of trying to deal with the *Review*'s dire financial problems, its contributors' human vagaries, and his own complex temperament, Ford once again fell apart. He temporarily broke off relations with Marwood, permanently wounded Conrad, and quarreled with many old friends. Moreover, the unhappy marriage seeming at last intolerable, he asked Elsie for a divorce. Soon he was threatening suicide to Violet. On June 10, 1909, to save him and, with luck, to gain a husband, Violet became his mistress. On October 14, at Charing Cross Station, Elsie caught the two getting off the boat-train together after a clandestine vacation in France. Olive spent that Christmas with Elsie and "had a great deal of talk . . . about her affairs" (December 29, 1909). Over New Year's Olive "read a novel by Miss Violet Hunt as a specimen & don't wish to read another" (January 2, 1910). On January 11, the court gave Ford fourteen days to return to Elsie, her first move in winning custody of the children and, if she chose (which she ultimately did not), getting a divorce.[1] On January 23, 1910, Olive noted: "E[dward] says Ford says he is more at peace than he has been for 20 years," that is, since his father had died.

The manuscript Ford read to Olive the previous winter was *A Call*, his latest novel of modern love, written, like the earlier ones, to launch a new "phase" (to use his own, favorite term). He quickly followed *A Call* with the usual historical romance, the usual fantasy (also historical this time), a farcical novel, and three, less usual, satirical novels. All—in varying degrees—reflect the passions of his personal life and point toward the great artistic breakthrough of *The Good Soldier*.

Finished March 7, 1909, published serially that autumn and in book form the following February, *A Call* uncannily foretells Ford's and Violet's crazy marital maneuvers of 1911. It even proposes that the unmarried couple meet on the Continent and then return to London saying that they have just gotten married abroad (259). But the roots of *A Call* lie in Ford's previous fiction and in the deep past of his personal life. Like George in *The Benefactor*, Robert Grimshaw is a benevolent, middle-aged meddler; he sponsors the marriage of a protégé, Dudley Leicester, to a pretty young thing and himself pursues a woman of about thirty. But since Robert is a bachelor, the only bar to marriage is his fiancée's neurotic (and fictionally unconvincing) fear of the ceremony. Like George's Clara, Katya Lascarides explicitly offers herself as a mistress to her lover. A foreigner and the best friend of the wealthy, infirm young

Dudley, Robert recalls both Don's loyal brother and Milne's friend Joseph Clarges.

Behind this welter of fictional characters lies Ford's personal life, echoes of which resound throughout *A Call*. For the first time in his fiction Ford here tries to deal directly with a portion of the most important period of his life and the one that was to energize *The Good Soldier*: the 1904, London beginnings of his prolonged breakdown. And more explicitly than ever before he represents fictionally his most intimate friends. Robert Grimshaw resembles Joseph Conrad. He looks like a "Levantine pirate"; he has an "aquiline" nose and a "very black, short beard" which makes him appear to be fifty (19). A foreigner like Conrad, Robert feels alien and "lonely" in London; he is at his happiest speaking in Greek to an Orthodox priest in Kensington Gardens (214). Robert meddles frequently in the affairs of his young, naive friend Dudley, as Conrad, according to Violet, did in Ford's.

Despite his alleged stupidity, Dudley Leicester has striking connections with Arthur Marwood, who was in a few months to replace Ford in Conrad's affections. His old, emphatically "county" name, his public school and university education, his wealth, his careful attention to dress, his bewilderment at complex human relations, his lack of any profession, and even his fear of tuberculosis precisely recall Marwood. Interestingly, Dudley's wife is named Pauline, Marwood's Caroline.[2] Both are little; both prove to be expert nurses of their ill husbands. Katya represents, in Mizener's words, "Ford's conception of Elsie Martindale";[3] like Elsie, Katya has a sister.[4] Naturally though, looming over all these characters, and especially over the males, is the figure of Ford himself. Violet shrewdly equated him with Robert, and Mizener shows how Fordian is Robert's struggle between personal desire and public responsibility.[5] Robert resembles Ford, too, in being thirty-five, in marrying one of two sisters he had known since childhood, in insinuating himself into the lives of others solely to be helpful, and in sometimes experiencing panic

at moments of crisis and fearing he will go mad. Yet the
character Ford most blatantly resembles is Dudley, above
all in his nervous breakdown. It begins in March, in London, like Ford's, while his wife is in Brockenhurst, where
Ford and Elsie went in April. Dudley's chief symptoms—
physical collapse and inability, or unwillingness, to
speak—make him look like the Ford Olive saw supine in
Elsie's energetic presence. Finally, Dudley going "mad"
particularly resembles Ford. Katya's sister Ellida Langham says "that she had never before noticed he was
goggle-eyed. He stood, enormously tall, his legs very wide
apart, gazing at her with his mouth open . . . his hand
[raised] to his straw-coloured moustache" (93). The cause
of Dudley's crack-up—being discovered, by Robert's telephone call, in the house of his old flame Etta Stackpole—
reflects what must have been a major source of Ford's
crack-up, his affair with Mary.

It is Dudley, not Pauline or Katya, who inspires Robert's
deepest affection, despite the latter's superficial contempt
for him. Although Ford sometimes treats Dudley comically, Robert and Dudley are very devoted to each other.
They act in the novel virtually as doubles.[6] Robert's fiancée
Katya is not particularly jealous of Pauline; she is, rather,
terribly jealous of Robert's interest in Dudley:

> "No wonder you can't give in to me if you've got to be
> thinking of him all the time. Well, put it how you will,
> I have done with him, and I've done with you. Go
> your own idiotic ways together. . . . All my life you've
> tortured me . . . you had always someone like that,
> that you took an interest in; that you were always try-
> ing to get *me* to take an interest in." (253-54)

Katya's is a brilliant intuition and reads like Ford's version
of Elsie talking to him about Marwood.

What most fascinates Fordians about *A Call: A Tale of Two
Passions* is, of course, the way it foreshadows Ford's mas-
terly *Good Soldier: A Tale of Passion*. Despite the novel's
general failure to convince, *A Call* does occasionally convey

some of *The Good Soldier*'s sense of the pain that passion
can inflict. Katya is Robert's incomprehensibly unattainable mistress as Florence is Dowell's (253-54). Tiny Pauline
changes as dramatically for Dudley as does Nancy for Edward. Dudley watches Pauline "approach, wide-eyed and
panic-stricken, as if she held an animal trainer's whip"
(136). And yet Ford can, with utter sympathy and no sense
of incongruity, portray Robert's passion for Pauline thus:
"I want to watch Pauline Leicester. I want to; I want to; I
want to. . . . I should like to kneel down and put my face in
her lap and cry, and cry, and cry" (17-18). Clearly, Ford
here needs the perspective of a Dowell; but to achieve this
would take new knowledge, new courage, still four or five
years distant. As yet he could not, as Arnold Bennett noted
at the time in his journal, "get down to the real stuff."[7]

Of the three historical fictions Ford wrote during his Violet phase, the first, *The Portrait* (1910), though a very read-
able, amusing book, is the least relevant to our purposes.
Its chief interest lies in the detailed ways it foreshadows
Parade's End and thus dramatizes the impact Marwood had
already had upon Ford's creative imagination. Not surprisingly, *The Portrait*'s heroine Lady Eshetford is an attractive
projection of Violet, Ford's new love. Yet, at the end, when
all problems have been solved and Lady Eshetford has announced that, in half an hour, she and the Fordian hero
Squire Bettesworth are to marry, the latter, sitting alone
waiting for his beloved to bring in the parson, is so very
happy that he almost dies:

> he might as well have been carved out of wax. He felt
> singularly little of elation; but, upon the other hand,
> along with the sense of entire tranquillity he had that
> of presenting to the world an extremely fine figure. He
> seemed, in fact, to himself to be almost as perfect, to
> be almost as semi-divine as he had ever dreamed of
> being; at the same time it was as if his heart had for-
> gotten to beat and he had no desire to make any mo-
> tions of his limbs at all. (302)

Ladies Whose Bright Eyes, Ford's popular historical fantasy, is the last production of that brief period when Ford
still dreamed that he might succeed in freeing himself from
Elsie and legally marrying Violet. The novel has, for our
present purposes, two sources of interest: first, the characteristic ways in which Ford manipulates the fictional counters representing his intimate circle, expanded now to include not only Violet but her almost equally devoted niece
Rosamond; second, the increasingly violent, agonized
ways that sexual passion makes itself felt. Designed as a
corrective to *A Connecticut Yankee in King Arthur's Court*,
Ladies Whose Bright Eyes tells how a twentieth-century British publisher, Mr. (afterwards Sir) William Sorrell, is
knocked unconscious during a train wreck and plunged
into a protracted dream set in fourteenth-century Wiltshire
on the Salisbury Plain. There he becomes involved with
Lady Blanche de Coucy and Lady Dionissia de Egerton,
wives of the "Large" Knight of Coucy and the "Young"
Knight of Egerton. These five characters reflect, respectively, Marwood, Elsie, Rosamond/Violet, Ford, and
Conrad, and look forward, of course, to Ashburnham,
Florence, Nancy, Leonora, and Dowell. In terms of our
character types, Sorrell plays both benefactor and infirm
young man, Blanche witch, Dionissia doll/nurse, Coucy
benefactor, and Egerton infirm young man.[8]

The last two "boon companions" have very minor roles.
"A small man with brownish features" and a "foxy" expression (183), the Conradian Egerton speaks English "in-
differently" and is "subject to great changes of humour";
he has "a livid weal above his left breast" (193, 183, 204)
gotten in battle as Conrad (no doubt inaccurately) claimed
to have gotten his in a duel. Egerton's best friend and
next-door neighbor, the Knight of Coucy, represents a
self-idealization of Ford's situation in 1908 and 1909.[9]

Lady Blanche de Coucy must be the bitchiest heroine of
Ford's historical romances. Even the witch of *The "Half-
Moon"* cannot compete in unpleasantness with her. A
monster of jealousy, hostility, and aggressiveness toward
her husband, toward her cousin and closest friend, Lady

Dionissia, toward her servants and attendants, and ultimately even toward her new beloved, Sorrell, Blanche
lives in a perpetual rage over sex and money. We first see
her, characteristically without her husband, consumed by
frustration, groaning and twisting "her nails in aching solitude" (40). When she offers herself to Sorrell, he finds the
experience terrifying. Her eyes fill with "smouldering
fire"; she expands "her broad chest," erects a "fierce
head," and invites Sorrell, as "a very holy man," to kiss
her. "But I say," he asks, "is that a proper thing to do?
What about your husband?" Sorrell rightly considers her a
"savage tiger" (127). She intends not merely to slay her
rival but so to "cut and mangle" her face with a dagger that
"none shall ever call her fair again if they remember her"
(275). Such imagery looks forward to *The Good Soldier* and
to the attitudes of Florence, Leonora, and Nancy.

Ladies Whose Bright Eyes has chiefly to do with Mr. Sorrell, who looks and acts like Marwood. "Rising forty" (as
was Marwood when Ford was writing the novel), Sorrell is
"rather fair," with "pink, clear skin," "blue . . . slightly
threatening" eyes, and a "distinctly bulky" build (12, 14).
Like Marwood, he prefers "half-cooked" meats to fancy
dishes, carries a "large leather portmanteau" (143, 164),
disdains novels and "nonsense of that sort" (7), believes in
serious, factual works, and writes "to the papers" to correct wrongs (31). But in the following curious passage,
Ford seems, through Sorrell, to be foisting on Marwood
the role his grandfather played for him twenty years before:

> His eyes looked musingly at the young man. He was
> tall, slight, fair—very much what Sir William remem-
> bered himself to have been at that age, except for the
> boy's chin, which was no good. It was the chin that
> undoubtedly accounted for the scrape he had got into
> at Cambridge. . . . The young man wanted propping
> up; he wanted regular work, and Sir William was glad
> that he had promised . . . to give moral support to a
> boy with a weak chin. (340-41)

As with previous Marwoodian figures (notably Dudley Leicester), Sorrell contains a great deal of Ford. Especially, he exhibits those symptoms of his mental illness that Ford showed on the Salisbury Plain in July 1904 and that were to contribute to the creation of *The Good Soldier*. Ford, we recall, under the hot July sun, clung to Olive's arm so as not to fall from agoraphobia and said he would rather be hanged than be a Garnett. Sorrell, after the train wreck, finds himself walking "on, on, and on," his legs aching, his head "dizzy with the heat of the sun" (22), "practically a wandering lunatic." Longing for a sick-nurse and spying a nun in the distance, he wants desperately to meet her (35). This fact and Sorrell's anxiety to get rid of his golden cross recall how Ford, after much trouble, gave Elsie's opal ring to a Little Sister of the Poor.

Ford uses Sorrell's confusion about whether he is delirious, or simply caught up in a modern pageant, or "really" translated back to the Middle Ages to dramatize his own radical, skeptical impressionism, his profound doubts as to whether one person's reality is accessible to anyone else, whether, indeed, reality exists beyond the confines of one's own skull. At the end of the novel, Ford gives several new twists to the dream/reality paradox. On the one hand, Sorrell so persuades Nurse Morane of the reality of his medieval dream that she herself in 1909 can point to the stone on which he hit his head in the dream of 1326. On the other hand, he can assert that her constant bedside presence during his coma "made me dream" (359, 360). This last notion conforms to Ford's esthetic of fictional narration, which requires the presence of a silent, inspiring auditor, usually feminine, for the artist to create, whether he be John Kemp in the dock pleading for his life or John Dowell telling his saddest story to an imaginary listener.

Far more important than Sorrell's awakening to unreality is the motive that drives him there—again, and again, and again. Four times the terror of female sexuality and of his own response to it plunges Sorrell into madness and confronts him with an anguished vision of death. One such episode occurs at dinner when Dionissia turns her "deep and bewildered glance" upon him and Sorrell, aware for the first time of "the run of her limbs beneath her dress," suddenly becomes fatigued, mute (146). Almost immediately thereafter, he finds himself on a "terrible" white stallion, out defending Dionissia's castle. Without Sorrell doing anything, the horse attacks Dionissia's enemy, black-bearded Hugh FitzGreville, smashes "his head like a nut," tears his prostrate body "with its enormous teeth, until there remained only the pulp of the human being" and trots off, carrying his "powerless" rider clear into the stable where a mare awaits and where Sorrell, dismounted at last, becomes "violently ill" (154, 158). The final instance finds Dionissia and Sorrell at last united in their little castle, sitting by the fire, his head in her lap. Into this scene bursts the Knight of Egerton. He had ridden "furiously," his heart full of "black rage," inspired by lies he has heard about Sorrell and Dionissia from a "raging and cursing" Blanche, in bed with a broken leg (327-28). When Egerton knocks Sorrell unconscious against a stone wall, Dionissia, her eyes "enormously large . . . like two blue stones," drives her "long dagger" into Egerton "with such force that it stuck in the bones of his throat behind" (331). Dionissia thus becomes as murderous as Blanche of the "great sword" and "hard, green eyes" (71, 271).

These scenes invite a biographical gloss. First, despite Dionissia's superficial resemblances to the young Rosamond, her situation obviously reflects Violet's. Owing to certain legal barriers to their marriage, Sorrell must expend much gold to gain the Church's blessing. This, as well as Sorrell's sense of the great changes in his life that his new love entails and even the very language he addresses to Dionissia, resembles Violet's account of Ford's attempt to get a divorce in Germany and of their flurried romantic years together.[10] Second, *Ladies Whose Bright Eyes*, having been finished in 1910, belongs not only to the happy, hopeful time with Violet, but also to the period of complete estrangement from Conrad. Ford believed later, and probably at the time as well, that the chief reason for Conrad's wrath was "my relationships with women."[11] He also knew that during the first months of 1910 Conrad had had a complete nervous collapse. These scenes, then, appear to dramatize the sexual excitement, wonder, and terror engendered by Ford's new, forbidden liaison with Violet. The sudden death of black-bearded Hugh FitzGreville, savaged by Dionissia's stallion, suggests (probably unconsciously) either Conrad's suffering from Ford's affair or Ford's desire for revenge. The last scene surely fantasizes Elsie complaining about Ford and Violet to Conrad, who confronts the happy couple and dies at the hands of Violet's triumphant sexuality while Ford lies unconscious in the corner.[12]

The Panel, published in 1912 and comically intended, sadly reflects its author's new agonies. By the winter of 1912-1913, Elsie's lawyers were after Ford, his finances were a shambles, and a new, three-year siege of neurasthenia was beginning. Hence, *The Panel* usually wallows in pity for the hero while blackening beyond all credibility his hateful, Elsie-like fiancée.

However, one genuinely amusing scene sheds some light on how Ford might make a masterpiece out of unpromising and regressive materials. One night, in a manor house, Major Edward Brent Foster (the Fordian/Marwoodian hero) is trying to get little Flossie Delamare, clad in her foamy pink peignoir, out of his room through the same secret panel she had inadvertently entered by. Although the major, with Flossie's candle, hunts first for the hidden spring, it is she who finds it: "It's this knobby thistle thing that does the trick." He implores her to "do the trick and get back to your room . . . and let's have a night's rest." After "wiggling the button thing" for all she's worth, Flossie gives up (120). Thereupon the major "with a face full of a sort of awe" begins "clicking the thistle-like knob"—to no effect (121). Sweating now, the major tries his pen knife; next he tries "pressing," then "pulling"; finally he tries "fumbling in his kit-bag for a little oil-can he

always carried" (122). Meanwhile, Flossie sits in his arm-
chair, extends her stockinged feet to the fire, and mocks
the major as Etta mocked Dudley's "fumbling" with the
telephone: "Oh, go on wiggling, I can wait." At last,
though, Flossie takes pity and agrees to depart another
way, first offering him a kiss: "I don't *really* think I want to,
Flossie. . . . I don't—I don't believe I *can* be very well"
(124).

This scene is important as well as funny. Promisingly it
shows Ford able to laugh at his hero's ineptitude. Indeed,
in this novel Ford defines that aspect of the comic which
gives *The Good Soldier* its distinctive flavor: "I daresay it is
grotesque—a mixture of the sorrowful and the funny" (95).
Also, the scene, like that of the supine Don hearing in Oggie's voice over the telephone his father's words, "Not this
time, sonny," underlines the hero's impotence when in
the threatening presence of father figures. The major's
unmanageable panel consists of a painting featuring "three
fierce men," all "Ancestors" (64).

EXIT CONRAD (*THE SIMPLE LIFE LIMITED*)

At precisely the same time as Ford was gaining Violet's
love, he was losing the greatest friendship of his life—that
with Joseph Conrad. Appropriately, the chief external
cause involved Marwood. In the early spring of 1909, Elsie
told Ford that Marwood was making improper advances to
her; Ford apparently wrote crushing letters to Marwood on
this and other subjects; Elsie told the Conrads of Marwood's supposed villainy and asked them to invite Ford
down from London to their place in Aldington; Marwood
insisted upon his innocence.

In response to this storm, Conrad at the end of April
wrote to Ford a long, complicated, affectionate, and extremely important letter.[13] In it he tries to show Ford how
irrational he has become of late and to warn him that such
behavior may cost him Conrad's friendship. Conrad's language interestingly recalls the terms he used when talking

about Ford's prose. Ford's activity reveals "the reckless wasting of your substance." Ford's quarrel with *Spectator* magazine is "vapouring." Fawning on S. S. McClure is "not worthy of you." As to Ford's plan to "crush" Marwood and prove himself reconciled to Elsie by visiting, not her, but the Conrads: "What purpose can be served by re-creating an equivocal situation? By much juggling with the realities of life an atmosphere of plots and accusations and suspicions is created. I can't breathe in situations that are not clear." Here Conrad's underlying misgivings about Ford's relations with the real world come to light. Twice Conrad equates Ford with the gods, mentioning his "Olympian severity" and saying obscurely: "God only knows. You too perhaps." Conrad suggests his doubts of his friend's stability by speaking of his McClure "phase" and his *Spectator* "phase," and hoping that both phases "are over." Ford's wrangle with *The Spectator* is "For nothing at all. Nothing! Less than nothing." Yet at the same time Ford threatens the reality of their friendship, "ten years of perfect confidence and intimacy." The letter has, too, its pathos and irony. Conrad's saying he is unable to breathe calls to mind those striking images of claustrophobia in his greatest fiction. At the height of his powers in *Lord Jim*, he could revel imaginatively in an "equivocal situation"; now, in real life, he cannot bear "situations that are not clear."

Toward the end of the letter, Conrad uses the familiar image of himself and Ford against the world: "Unless words are wind, facts are mist, the confidence you've given me a mere caprice of fancy, and unless an absolute loyalty of thought and act on my part contra mundum gives no privilege I have the right to warn you that you will find yourself at forty with only the wrecks of friendships at your feet." Conrad's prediction came true. Ford at forty wrote *The Good Soldier* out of the wreckage of his relations with Conrad, Marwood, Elsie, and Violet.

As Conrad feared in his letter, Ford dismissed his advice, and Conrad broke with him. The next two letters, the last for nearly two years, are simply furious. (The one of May 20 re Willa Cather begins: "What means your letter?" and later says: "The question is—What do you mean? What the devil do you mean?") More explicit are Conrad's letters to mutual friends about Ford's "mania." To their literary agent Pinker, he describes Ford as a "megalomaniac who imagines that he is managing the Universe and that everybody treats him with the blackest ingratitude. . . . there are cases, not quite as bad, under medical treatment."[14]

Insanity must be about the worst of human terrors. For the literary impressionist, who relies upon the reality of his own sensations, the possibility of the brain's going awry must be particularly horrifying. As Meyer has shown, Conrad himself greatly feared mental illness.[15] In 1909, he held on only long enough to write "The Secret Sharer" and finish *Under Western Eyes* before taking to his bed for three months, holding "converse" with his fictional characters, and accusing Jessie of "trying to put him into an asylum."[16] He recovered but emerged even more fundamentally changed than after the 1904 nightmare with *Nostromo*, Jessie's injury, and his friend's breakdown.

Despite continued productivity after 1909, Ford fared little better. Like Elsie in 1904, Violet in 1909 feared Ford would commit suicide. Linking himself to Violet that summer brought temporary respite, but from 1912 to 1915 he was chronically neurasthenic.[17] Starting in March 1911, however, he and Conrad did correspond sporadically, and Conrad once even wrote: "to me my dear Ford [those old days] are a very precious possession. In fact I have nothing else that I can call my own."[18] But those days were indeed gone forever.

The friendship between Conrad and Ford seems to me one of the saddest stories. But I do not see how, given their personalities, they could have acted differently. Probably Conrad, seeing in Ford his own weaknesses writ large, was a little ashamed of him. They related as father to son, and fathers are sometimes like that. Or they related as Marlow to Jim; Conrad called Ford "dear boy," but no doubt considered him unsound even as he leaned on him. Ford said *Lord Jim* had "entered into me like the blood in my veins."[19] To Edward Garnett Ford wrote long afterwards: "My affection for Conrad was so great and remains so unchanged that I have never been able really to believe in his death, and at this moment it is as if he were sitting behind me waiting to read what I have tapped out."[20] Ford must be remembering here Conrad's loveliest expression of a man's affection for a friend, inspired perhaps by Ford's presence but uttered, alas, behind the protective veil of Marlow:

> "at times it seems as though he must come in presently and tell the story in his own words, in his careless yet feeling voice, with his offhand manner, a little puzzled, a little bothered, a little hurt. . . . It's difficult to believe he will never come. I shall never hear his voice again, nor shall I see his smooth tan-and-pink face with a white line on the forehead, and the youthful eyes darkened by excitement to a profound, unfathomable blue."[21]

Whether Marlow, at the end, felt obscurely betrayed by Jim I do not know. But I think that Conrad felt so about Ford in the spring of 1909. It is a pity that Conrad could not have viewed their relationship in the generous spirit of a statement from his newly composed reminiscences (inspired by Ford and dictated in part to him): "It would take too long to explain the intimate alliance of contradictions in human nature which makes love itself wear at times the desperate shape of betrayal."[22] At least Conrad admitted in a letter to Blackwood, December 31, 1909, "after eleven years of intimacy one feels the breach."[23]

What Conrad got from Ford during the early wonderful years of 1898 to 1904 was probably just immense moral support. Meyer's phrase for the relationship, "the secret sharers," is perfectly apt.[24] Ford was serving Conrad as Fliess, at almost the same time, served Freud, as much earlier Louis Bouilhet had served their mutual hero Flaubert, and as a generation later Phil Stone would serve Faulkner. Clearly empathy, patience, generosity, and some knowledge are needed for the subservient sharer's role—but not remarkable intelligence or talent, let alone genius. In truth, Conrad probably got much more intellectual stimulation in 1898 from Cunninghame Graham than from Ford. Whether Conrad ever did recognize Ford's ultimate distinction—even after reading *The Good Soldier* and *Some Do Not*—is doubtful.

Ford, buoyed up at first by Violet's approval, completed, as we have seen, his customary novels of modern love, historical romance, and fantasy. He was also able to write, somewhat in the vein of *The Inheritors* and *Mr. Apollo*, but much superior to them, a satire on contemporary times, *The Simple Life Limited*. For this hilarious *roman à clef* he chose a pseudonym, Daniel Chaucer. Olive Garnett was not amused. On April 10, 1911, she noted in her diary: "Julius West asked me if I had written the 'Simple Life' "; at the top of the page, in a much later, shaky, outraged hand, she scrawled: "i.e. Ford Hueffer—a pot boiler and scandalous." On July 8 she wrote, presumably in reference to the pseudonym: "The cat now completely out of the bag. It is a relief." To anyone who knew anything of the Conrads, Hueffers, or Garnetts, the identity of the main characters would have been obvious. The book even refers explicitly to Ford Madox Hueffer as an "esteemed" author and to the *English Review* as a source of "literature of an idealistic nature or of a hygienic materialism" (55, 94). The only reason Ford's authorship might have been in doubt is that Horatio Gubb, the character modeled chiefly on Ford, is one of the least sympathetic figures in the novel.

Besides wanting to make money, Ford (perhaps with Violet's help)[25] must have written the book to celebrate Marwood, who had re-established his intimacy with Ford, and to avenge himself on Conrad, who had rejected him. And yet, in order to bring himself to denigrate the dearest friend of his life, Ford apparently had not only to make himself out to be far worse than Conrad but even, at the end of the novel, to let Conrad become the hero. *The Simple Life Limited* thus fulfills a need beyond revenge, Ford's need to express his profound self-loathing, the inevitable counterpart of his boundless vanity. D. H. Lawrence at about this time wrote of Ford, to Violet: "He is really such a lot better fellow than he thinks he ought to be, . . . but he daubs his dove-grey kindliness with a villainous selfish tar, and hops forth a very rook among rooks."[26] Yet maybe even this was a self-protective tactic. If Ford made himself out to be worse than he was, possibly his erstwhile friends would pity, forgive, and once more love him.

The Simple Life Limited is, in short, an immensely interesting key to Ford's state of mind four years before writing *The Good Soldier*. Moreover, despite padding and sloppiness, the novel has many rewarding moments, usually when making cruelest fun of Ford's alter ego Gubb. Ostensibly set at the time of the South African war, *The Simple Life Limited* conflates events of the nineties and those of the *English Review* days. Its locale, established by explicit reference to Frog Hole on the border between Kent and Surrey (48, 49), is clearly that of Limpsfield, where Edward and Constance Garnett built their pseudomedieval stone house, the Cearne, in 1895. For part of that year the Russian revolutionary and novelist Sergius Stepniak and his wife Fanny had a cottage at Crockham Hill, a village near Frog Hole and Limpsfield. After Stepniak's sudden death in December 1895, Fanny settled there permanently. In September 1898, another Russian revolutionary, David Soskice, arrived; subsequently he divorced his wife and married Ford's sister Juliet. The colony was at its most literary in 1898. That spring and summer Ford and Elsie were living next to the Cearne in Gracie's Cottage; Stephen Crane was staying in nearby Oxted. At this time, too, the Conrads visited the Edward Garnetts and met the Hueffers. The area also sported such important English Fabians as the Peases and the Hobsons, and Henry Salt, whom David Garnett calls "the leading humanitarian and vege-

tarian in England."[27] Into his marvelous material for utopian satire Ford injected for contrast the wise, common-
sensical Arthur Marwood, who really belonged to the next
decade and the other end of Kent. But Ford imagines
Marwood occupying the ancestral home, "Coombe Luscombe," on what is clearly Limpsfield Common, and acting for a while as patron to the Colony of Simple Lifers,
much as Marwood did for the *English Review*.

Gerald Luscombe, the most thoroughly and consistently
admirable character in the novel, exhibits many Marwoodian features. He is six feet tall, blond, heavy, broad-
shouldered, full-chested, with a mustache, sagacious eyes,
and white level teeth. Graduate of a fine public school and
Cambridge, he is a Tory who fears God, honors the
Queen, and dislikes advanced opinions. His wife is
Evangeline (Marwood's Caroline). As a model landlord,
beloved of his servants and popular with his tenants, some
of whose families have been with his family for centuries,
Luscombe plays the role Marwood, save for his health,
would presumably have played at Busby Hall.

To almost the same degree that he elevates Marwood,
Ford brings down Conrad and makes of England's greatest
living novelist a ridiculous (and very funny) comic butt.
Moreover, the portrait is often too close to reality to have
seemed very amusing to its helpless model. Although Ford
first describes Bransdon as enormously fat with a very long
beard, he ultimately makes him look like the Conrad of
1910 lying supine after the betrayal by his long-time disciple Gubb, now become Don Juan. With "black and white
hair combed back from the great forehead," "tufted eye-
brows," "eyes glancing doggedly" at his feet, "sharp"
nose, "peaked beard, pointing upwards with a sinister
cock," Bransdon resembles "a recumbent effigy of the
Commendatore in Don Giovanni" (241).

Bransdon's history is that of Jozef Teodor Konrad Kor-
zeniowski. Born Simeon Brandetski, he anglicizes his
name to Simon Bransdon at the suggestion of Parmont (a
condescending portrait of Edward Garnett). Bransdon is

"possibly Polish, possibly Lithuanian, possibly Little Russian Jew" (69), this last recalling Violet's assertion that Ford when "riding one of his high horses" would deliberately miscall Conrad a Jew.[28] First an adventurer in the Congo, walloping "nigger" railway crews, Bransdon becomes a writer after ruining his health there. Conrad must especially have resented Ford's emphasis upon Bransdon's lack of productivity, his poverty, and his irregular sex life. The fictional rendering of all three comes too close to the truth for comfort. Ford calls Bransdon "one of the laziest men" alive, hating any exertion, "even standing still." He wants "to be in a hammock for ever and ever"; he thinks he leads "a dog's life" (73). Here Ford comically exposes Conrad's characteristic psychological trait—a neurotic attraction to total inertia; the last phrase reminds us that Conrad spoke of the life of a writer as *"le vrai métier du chien."* Bransdon's literary productivity suffers not only from his laziness (67) but also—and this again is too much like Conrad—from recurrent mental illness. The "turning point in his life" occurs when he flies into a rage and beats to death his clumsy but affectionate bulldog. Unable to forget the animal's eyes, Bransdon has a nervous breakdown, ceases to converse, and walks "up and down his rooms, holding his untidy head in both his hands" (77). (Since the bulldog beating recurs in *Parade's End*, with Sylvia Tietjens as the sadist, it presumably figures in Ford's imagination as a metaphor for his own mistreatment first by Conrad, later by Violet.) Much as Conrad, when delirious, would call out in Polish to his terrified, uncomprehending Jessie, so Bransdon cannot understand English and speaks only Russian "which he had completely forgotten" (77). His brain having "so entirely succumbed to shock" (82), Bransdon can write no fiction but only dictate poetic prose to Gubb. All this corresponds roughly to Conrad's dictating memoirs to Ford during unproductive periods in 1904 and 1908. Literary productivity was, incidentally, the one way in which Ford indisputably surpassed Conrad. Between the book publications of *Nostromo* in 1904 and *Under Western Eyes* in 1911, Conrad published one novel, Ford eleven.

Discovering that the great Bransdon is "grotesquely poor" and hopelessly indebted, as Conrad was with the unfinished "Rescuer" in 1898, to publishers for advances on novels he cannot finish (80), Gubb takes over his affairs. He pays Bransdon's bills and installs him in the cottage next door as Ford sublet the Pent to Conrad, moved nearby, and lent Conrad £100. Though not especially interested in women, Bransdon has sometimes taken a woman companion to a Brighton hotel for a week. On Parmont's recommendation, Bransdon engages a secretary. "His habit of writing late into the night and lying on his back conducing to it, she became in course of time his mistress" and, at Parmont's scandalized insistence, his wife (75-76). Installed by Gubb in a country cottage, the city-bred Mrs. Bransdon longs for their "dark and untidy Bloomsbury lodgings," "the smell of cabbage water," and most of all the sales, "the chance . . . to buy a soiled blouse" (83-84). Jessie Conrad, typist daughter of a poor Londoner, must have been apoplectic.[29]

If Ford ridicules mercilessly "the great Mr. Bransdon," he simply demolishes "his chief disciple Mr. Gubb" (17). Although unquestionably a self-portrait, Horatio Gubb is, naturally, partially disguised. His initials, his resemblance to a "Sunfish in outline" (53), his illegitimate child, his lack of a classical education, and his persistent if hypocritical socialist politics recall Wells, who had played a conspicuous, exasperating role in the founding of the *English Review* and was to figure prominently in Ford's other "Daniel Chaucer" novel. Nevertheless, Gubb is very Fordian, funny, and unattractive. "Pink and white," with "golden" hair, Gubb, like Ford, talks all the time, uttering in "peculiarly honied" and "yet didactic tones," his "gentle flow of good doctrine" (53, 59, 57, 58). Ford, with amazing self-awareness, exposes Gubb's vanity, a vanity so great that he looks upon the truth as something to be manipulated, and people as objects to be exploited. When Bransdon protests against faking a dictation scene with Gubb in order to impress a possible benefactress, Gubb gives a familiar Fordian rationalization for fibbing. Admitting that the dictation is something of a "display," Gubb insists it isn't really "meretricious or deceptive" since it is the "usual sort" of thing they do. "It was the sort of thing to give a new visitor a true idea" of them (145).

Much of the last third of the novel is devoted to a series of humiliations for Gubb. In answer to Gubb's request for more money, Luscombe quietly points out that Gubb has been personally making three or four hundred pounds a year out of the Colony, asks him to "move the whole show" elsewhere, and admits he does not like Gubb's methods (276). Bransdon, too, exposes Gubb, going so far as to advise Miss Egmont against marrying him. "If that man doesn't work you one way, he'll work you another, and he'll turn you into a pitiful sort of slave at the end of it" (250). Only Everard, the theater impresario, has praise for Gubb—as a trickster:

> "That chap Gubb is working just as hard as a juggler keeping sixteen balls in the air at a time. . . . Everything's crumbling round him. . . . And there he stands up there on that platform, calm and smiling." (347)

Perhaps the most interesting aspect of *The Simple Life Limited* is Ford's insight into the change in his relationship with Conrad. Fairly early in the novel, Bransdon is casting looks of "savage dislike" at Gubb and sneering at his pretense of devotion (143). In a delightful episode that probably reflects Ford's attempts, in May 1909, to send Willa Cather to call on an outraged Conrad, Bransdon betrays the familiar Conradian characteristics. He is irritated because Gubb bursts in unannounced; his eyes under shaggy brows are at once piercing and lazy. Accustomed as Gubb is to Bransdon's querulousness, he does not expect the new imperiousness. Bransdon rejects both Gubb's suggestion that they stage a dictation scene and Gubb's affectionate address: "Oh, don't 'dear friend' me," Bransdon acidly remarks. "There's nobody to hear you" (141-42).

Somewhat later in the novel, Gubb at last senses the profound shift in their relationship and sees Mr. Bransdon cut loose from him and able to survive on his own (239). Yet by a characteristically Fordian paradox, Gubb also believes the opposite, that Bransdon can never really be cured: "Men whose brains have once been touched never escape again" (240). The scene is remarkably perceptive and prescient. On the one hand, Bransdon is only pretending illness to escape Gubb, as Ford probably suspected Conrad of doing when, in the spring of 1909, he begged off writing any more reminiscences for the *English Review*. On the other hand, Ford would have known of Conrad's total mental collapse in January 1910. Between the quarrel and the collapse, Conrad had written his famous "double" story, "The Secret Sharer," which Meyer reads as a partial allegory upon Conrad's separation from Ford and his acceptance of a new, independent commanding role.[30] The confident ending of "The Secret Sharer" is curiously echoed in *The Simple Life Limited* when Bransdon regains the strength and simplicity he had lost during his years of close association with Gubb. It is Bransdon and, significantly, his new Marwoodian friend Luscombe, not Gubb, who risk their lives at the last by charging the hideout of an armed arsonist. Rejecting forever the "slackness" of life with Gubb, Bransdon resolves to see him just one last time, "so as to face the matter out . . ." (249). In that last conversation, Bransdon tells him the simple truth: since Gubb has spent his whole life doing nothing but "wrestling with respectable shadows it's hard to have to come out into the open and face things" (370). Nevertheless, Bransdon wants them to part friends, to let bygones be bygones. Instead Gubb, like Ford in his less good moments, accuses Bransdon and all the other Colonists of "ingratitude." And amazingly, with what mixture of feelings it is hard to imagine, Ford has Gubb tell Bransdon, while pointing at the arsonist's corpse, that he would like to see Bransdon "lying dead" at his feet, "Like that!" (369). For all his laziness and apathy, for all his hairiness, his clammy hands, and his drooping eyelids that give him "the appearance of oriental and semi-blind imbecility" (53), Bransdon ultimately appears sympathetic, heroic, and healthy. Yet we recall Gubb's hunch that Bransdon would never *really* get better. The truth is that after Conrad, in 1911, simplified his view of things, rejected slackness, and wrote affirmatively, the quality of his fiction declined markedly and his health did not particularly improve.[31]

One fact dramatizes the closeness of the secret sharers: while Ford was penning his satiric portrait of Conrad, Conrad was doing the same to Ford. In his March 1911 letter resuming relations with Ford, Conrad mentions that he is "trying to make a fresh start with a thing called *Chance*."[32] Ford would have remembered that when he saw the beginning of *Chance* in October 1905 he described it to Olive as "something magnificent" (November 2, 1905). A letter from Conrad to Galsworthy at the end of March 1912 reports the completion of *Chance* and a visit by "the great F.M.H."[33] Conrad, having spent the past year writing about "the Great de Barral," could hardly have avoided applying the epithet to his former dearest friend. Ford must have been much on Conrad's mind while creating that cold, vain, self-deluded charlatan. De Barral looks, talks, and acts like Ford; and his situation at the time of his greatness surely owes something to Ford's in his *English Review* days. Although de Barral aboard the *Ferndale* reflects little of Ford's life after the *English Review*, the *donnée* recalls Ford's fiction, especially *An English Girl*. Both it and *Chance* feature a sea voyage involving a father, his daughter, and her lover, with the last so diffident and undemonstrative that the girl feels neglected.[34] But the situation in *Chance* is far more compelling than that in Ford's 1907 novel. Not until *The Good Soldier* would Ford portray that situation with an overwhelming intensity.

EXIT MARWOOD (*THE NEW HUMPTY-DUMPTY*
AND *MR. FLEIGHT*)

Predictably, the course of true love did not, after a few years, run smooth for Ford. This was due not only to the inevitable failure of the ideal to become reality, but also to Ford's inability to fulfill his pledge to divorce Elsie and marry Violet legally. Olive's diary gives a vivid sense of how often in those prewar years Ford had to face Elsie in court. Olive gloried in Elsie's legal victories. Indeed, her language describing the conflict prepares suitably for World War I. Between 1910 and 1914, Olive recorded at least five triumphs for Elsie. For one court appearance, on May 16, 1910, Elsie was appropriately clad "in royal purple." On July 13, 1910: "I never saw her look so pale before. She met Ford face to face in court this morning & obtained an order against him. Byles supported him & his counsel said Mr. Hueffer did not come there to plead poverty." (It was presumably on this ocassion that Ford was put in Brixton Gaol for ten days for refusing to pay the allowance awarded in April.)

No sooner had Elsie gained custody of her children, in the summer of 1911, than she had to defend against newspapers and magazines her exclusive right to her married name. Ford had rashly told a newspaper reporter that he had in Germany divorced Elsie and married Violet. To Elsie and Olive this was "the bolt from the blue in the *Daily Mirror*" (October 23, 1911). Three days later Elsie appeared at Olive's: "Her solicitor says she must deny the D. Mirr. statement as it is a libel, for which she can claim damages. . . . Elsie seemed very well. Says there is a lot of fiction in F.M.H.'s statement." Ford seems to have been still undaunted, and undiplomatic. Elsie wrote on November 8 that Ford had written "her solicitor regretting the publishing given his re-marriage by the press, as he had wished to spare his client 'mortification.' " Although Elsie soon reported that "the Mirror climbs down," she remained "very indignant with 'Daily Mirror' and H——s" (December 7 and 11, 1911). Olive spent the holidays with Elsie: "A grand Xmas Dinner. . . . It was a fine day." Even better was January 8, 1912: "A great day. The 'Mirror' inserted 'apology & withdrawal' and pays Elsie £350 damages."

Although Ford weathered the *Daily Mirror*, he was sunk when the *Throne*, a magazine run by his friend René Byles, incautiously on April 3, 1912, described Violet Hunt as "(now Mrs. Ford Madox Hueffer)." Olive's account on April 29 is a masterpiece of economy: "Letter from Elsie. (The throne and Byles . . . F.'s nervous breakdown.)" On June 18, Elsie told her, "Ford seems to be a wreck & V. H. is managing everything." Elsie came to Olive in London on September 24, and the next day delivered her "ultimatum re Throne action & income." If Olive felt any pity at all for Ford, she neglected to mention it in her diary. November 23: "tea with Edw. and Con. . . . F.M.H. morally done for." At the end of January, Elsie, in London, "looked very charming. F & V. H. said to be in Germany" (January 26, 1913). Although Ford was too ill to attend the trial, Violet did, and so, to be sure, did Olive. "Mr. Holman Gregory's opening of Elsie's case. Mr. Justice Avory very 'sympathetic.' " "All day in [King's Bench] No. 8. Verdict for the plaintiff & £300 damages. . . . Mr. Justice Avory's smile. Triumph" (February 6 and 7). Poor Ford had still more to endure. On March 28, there was a "summons proceedings" about his failure to pay the support money: "F. sent excuse from [Dr.] Tebb. V.H. present." But on July 22, Ford had to face his nemesis: "Elsie attended before the registrars' [in Bankruptcy Court] & her counsel got further adjournment to examine F's accounts. F & V.H. appeared."

No doubt what made these events most painful for Ford was the apparent hardheartedness of Conrad and Marwood. Although Conrad did write a courteous letter to Violet regretting his inability to attend their grandly defiant garden party of July 1, 1913, he seems not to have written to Ford at all between March 1913 and the spring of 1915.[35] Conrad's reason could simply have been distaste for the *Throne* case publicity, but, more likely, he was backing up Marwood, who had broken totally with Ford that winter. Before speculating upon the reasons for Marwood's wrath, we should recall earlier evidences of tension in the Conrad-Ford-Marwood relationship. Jessie says that as soon as Ford introduced Conrad to Marwood, the latter *"usurped* a place completely in my husband's regard."[36] Moreover, Violet calls an epistolary reference of Conrad's to " 'the good Marwood' . . . a little dig at the eternal rival."[37] Many years later, Ford himself would tell how his "place as general cook and bottle washer in Conrad's literary establishment" was taken over by Marwood (RY, 198). Unconsciously, Ford must have wanted it this way. It would be a token of his love for Conrad that he should wish to give Marwood to his closest friend. Similarly, in collaborating with Conrad on *The Nature of a Crime*, Ford was symbolically giving Elsie to Conrad. Conrad's gallantry toward Elsie suggests that he was willing, a little, to play that game.

A major cause of Conrad's anger at Ford in 1909 was a similar, if more overt, game, involving Elsie, Marwood, and Ford. Elsie (as we have seen) believed and said that Marwood had attacked her honor; Marwood denied it; Ford was equivocal, and Conrad was furious. The truth is, as usual, unclear. Marwood may have been attracted to Elsie from the first. At least, her younger daughter Katharine recalled her mother telling how Marwood had behaved improperly toward her even while Katharine was sitting in her lap. Robert Garnett excused Marwood's 1909 overtures to Elsie on the grounds of Marwood's sympathy for her neglected state, being himself "a highly impressionable and *unhappy* person."[38] (Marwood's unhappiness was the result, no doubt, of his chronic ill health and, perhaps, the fact that his wife did treat him as an invalid.)[39] Although Conrad described Elsie and Ford as "guillotin[ing]" Marwood, Ford's letter to Elsie about Marwood's attack on "yr virtue and my honour" is rather mild, its diction unconsciously amusing: "It is a horrible and very ticklish matter for me. On the one hand I do not like you to be misjudged: on the other certain very ticklish negotiations are just being consummated, involving Marwood, Soskice, Robert and myself."

My belief is that the really intense triangle involved not Elsie, Marwood, and Ford, but three men: Conrad, Marwood, and Ford. If Conrad broke with Ford out of a furious, desperate sense of the other's "fierce and exasperating vanity" and recurrent instability, Ford must have been angry with Conrad partly out of jealousy over Marwood. Conrad's letters of the *English Review* period show him favoring Marwood at Ford's expense. On March 9, 1909, Conrad relayed with approval Marwood's damning account of *The Fifth Queen* dramatization: "M'wood imparted to me horrid news of '*The Vth Queen*' . . . but may be he exaggerated his account of utter disorganisation of the production." Whether Ford blew this up into a belief that Marwood was also attacking his management of the *Review*, or gossip to that effect had reached Ford, he told Elsie that he had written to Marwood "that it was possible" that "misrepresentations had taken place," that he was "getting all the discredit of the Review's failures . . . whilst *all* the credit was claimed by various other persons, that I was not in a state to be very companionable and that, in consequence, I thought I had better not see him till I felt more composed."[40] Conrad's long, important letter to Ford in late April, while recognizing that Marwood may have committed "faults of tact, or even grave failures of discretion," nevertheless comes out wholly on the side of Marwood against Ford. Moreover, in stressing Marwood's excessive devotion to Ford, Conrad reveals his own feelings of jealousy:

> This evening the people in question [Marwoods] have called. The man when we were alone said he felt bound to inform me that he had just dispatched a letter to you breaking-off your intimate relations. He told me he was very unhappy and in truth he looked ill. As

he is of good birth and upbringing and has always
seemed to me a gallant-homme I can't give him up for
a ruffian as long as he remains in this neighbourhood
which I imagine won't be for long. He was your friend
not mine and I have never sought his acquaintance.
His devotion to you was notorious—a matter of public
knowledge. What advantage he sought, what ends he
had in view when he trotted about after you like a
faithful dog, God only knows. You too perhaps. In
this case if it is any satisfaction to you you have done
some crushing.[41]

It took female observers to perceive that the storm really
rose out of jealousy among three English gentlemen. Violet
Hunt, referring to Ford's "suddenly unprovoked quarrel
with Marwood," goes on shrewdly, if with deliberate
obscurity:

Poor Marwood was a nervous man, full of feeling, but
not endowed by nature with the means of letting off
steam possessed by the two doyens of the pen. . . .
Perhaps he was too clever to look for, too simple to
realise, the capacity for petty jealousies implicit in the
psychology of these great *névroses*, the incidence of
that earnest regard . . . which men of the same *métier*,
which is their unique preoccupation, come to have for
one another. . . . Marwood, in his noble simplicity,
was caught between two deeply sophisticated personalities, and went about looking ill and unhappy.[42]

Jessie Conrad puts it more succinctly: "F.M.H. had a cottage quite close to us in Aldington. . . . The intimacy was
not now so great, and there was, I feel sure, some little
jealousy on account of Joseph Conrad's great affection for
that other neighbour, Arthur Marwood."[43]

Nevertheless, Ford managed, in contrast to the definitive rupture with Conrad, to patch things up rather quickly
with Marwood.[44] They remained good friends until 1912 or
early 1913, when Marwood broke far more completely with

Ford than Conrad had done or would do. Meanwhile, Conrad had come to rely much upon Marwood, and the two men exchanged, without fail, weekly visits between Capel House and Water Farm until Marwood's fatal illness.[45] Dame Rebecca West said that at this time Ford's relations with Conrad were "very strained," and she remembered hearing Violet say that Marwood was so painful a subject one did not dare mention his name in Ford's presence.[46] Violet gives, in her usual opaque fashion, several reasons for Marwood's wrath: Marwood believed he had found himself in a Ford novel and did not like it; Marwood believed Ford had "left his children to starve"; and, more generally, about "other things, Marwood had believed what was not, and could not have been."[47] (Whether Marwood really believed that Ford had neglected his children is hard to say. Violet's vehement denial has a ring of sincere conviction about it, but so do Elsie's daughter's recollections of their poverty in those days.) The novel in question is surely *The New Humpty-Dumpty*, Ford's other Daniel Chaucer *roman à clef*. In it he yokes to the founding of the *English Review* a Conradian political situation, that of a counterrevolutionary movement to restore the Bourbon pretender to a Spanish provincial throne.[48] But though he is using the same autobiographical material as in *The Simple Life Limited*, the tone is very different. The earlier work is comic; the later, originally titled "The Dark Forest," is intended to be tragic. Certainly the events immediately preceding its July 1912 publication showed Ford tottering on his wall: *Mirror* damages, beginnings of the *Throne* case, a new attack of neurasthenia. Whereas in *The Simple Life Limited* Ford had taken Gubb's marital difficulties lightly, he takes Count Macdonald's passionate involvements very solemnly indeed. *The New Humpty-Dumpty* presents, wholly without distancing, the sorrows of Ford Madox Hueffer and is thus at once fascinating and awful fiction. It tries to prove that Ford is perfect and Violet virtually so, and that insofar as Conrad and Marwood partake of Ford, they are too; it makes murder-

ers of Wells, Robert Garnett, and above all Elsie; insofar as
Conrad and Marwood are opposed to Ford, they are mur-
derers as well. If the satiric *Simple Life Limited* showed
Ford's potential for achieving perspective on himself, the
self-pitying *New Humpty-Dumpty* shows his potential for
seeing at last that passion means suffering.

The epigraph dramatizes at once the hopelessness of
that particular fictional enterprise and the possibility of
creating *The Good Soldier*. The first line—"There be summer
queens and dukes of a day"—prepares for the grandeur of
the fantasy: Lady Aldington has her regal moment, and
Count Macdonald does become a duke—though really for
less than a day. The second line—"But the heart of another
is a dark forest"—proposes, plausibly, that others are unknowable but implies, unpromisingly, that evil resides
only in others. These points Ford insists on throughout the
novel with his emphasis, as in *The Good Soldier*, upon
hearts. Although the "dark forest" line comes from
Turgenev,[49] it figures in Ford's imagination as Conradian.
"Tambov," the reputed author of the epigraph, is the
home of the quixotic little Russian in "Heart of Darkness."
Conrad's great tale, like Ford's great novel, anticipates
Freud's equally dark *Civilization and Its Discontents*.[50]

The chief characters resolve themselves into the familiar
pattern that would finally achieve its perfect form in
The Good Soldier. However, probably because *The New
Humpty-Dumpty* is so nakedly, if fantastically, drawn from
"real life," so artistically unimagined, its correspondences
to Ford's most fully imagined fiction are extremely unstable. Insofar as Sergius Mihailovitch Macdonald is foreign,
neurotic, sexually chaste, and married to a flirtatious wife,
he prefigures Dowell; but as the tall, blond, active aristocratic hero who dies on the last page, he prefigures
Ashburnham. Similarly, to the extent that the Duke of Kintyre is the tall English aristocrat of "fine traditions" (74),
"member of the ruling classes" (73), graduate of a fine old
public school yet of no great intellect, who "philanders"
with (but does not seduce) the wife of his "best friend"

(356, 224), *he* prefigures Ashburnham. Nevertheless, in his total devotion to that best friend and in his skeptical impressionism—" 'Any man,' he said slowly, 'is any sort of man, some time or other, you know.' " (211-12)— Kintyre looks forward to Dowell. Countess Macdonald, in her vulgarity, flirtatiousness, and awe of titles, presages Florence, but her dominant impulse to torture, disfigure, and murder her husband most closely resembles the imagery Dowell associates with Leonora toward the end of the novel. Lady Aldington, however, prefigures only the good, early Leonora. First seen in the novel in a German opera house, accompanied by her unfaithful husband whom she initially idealized and whose finances she now controls, Lady Aldington is certainly in the situation of Leonora at the beginning of *The Good Soldier*. And she has Leonora's vehicle: aged thirty-one, in excellent health, with blonde hair and fair skin, and a tall, thin figure, she rides every morning (3, 1, 12).

To tell how the Count and Countess Macdonald and Emily Aldington resemble Ford, Elsie, and Violet would be virtually to retell the novel. Moreover, Mizener has effectively established how closely the Countess's treatment of the Count conforms to Ford's vision of Elsie, how closely the Count's wooing of Lady Aldington conforms to Violet's version of their courtship. Violet, indeed, says, "to have stood for Lady Aldington, any woman in England might be proud"; whereas "Countess Macdonald is, so I hear, not best pleased."[51] Whatever caused the Hueffers' marriage to fail, the Macdonalds' fails because of the wife's inability to keep up intellectually with the husband's dramatic progress. Ford emphasizes the Countess's stagnation by fixing her in Elsie's aesthetic garb of the nineties, even to the gown made from Madox Brown's curtains: "She still dressed in clothes of sage green, her sleeves still swept the floor; round her neck was a rope of amber beads" (44). After litigation begins, the Countess acquires a brilliant ruby dress to prove to her husband "how desirable" she is (204, 205), thus recalling Olive's tributes to Elsie's handsome costumes for court appearances.

The Countess's worst marital tirade has an appalling air of historical veracity about it. In the railway carriage, her voice drones over her husband, groaning and huddling in his seat, too weak to "raise a hand":

> "you are hankering after another woman. . . . Do you suppose that I have not any eyes in my head? Do you suppose that if it had not been for her you would ever have had the courage to tell me that you wanted to separate? . . . I dare say you will tell me that you never so much as wanted to kiss the doll of a creature that it is. And I dare say it is true enough. This is the sort of effeminate creature that you are, and you will call it chivalry or honour." (92-94)

The Countess institutes divorce proceedings just "to beggar" (215) her husband and with no intention of completing them. She spreads the lies that ultimately cause his death: he took money of his best friend "as the price of his own dishonour" and "money of his mistress to give to his creature!" (351). The Countess is last seen lying in wait for the Count, revolver and vitriol in hand.

Despite Ford's efforts to make Count Macdonald a political mastermind and superb organizer, he most convincingly portrays him as a hopeless neurotic. When plans go awry, he responds hysterically. His view of reality and the past is remote, to put it mildly. Looking back, he remembers only "spots of things here and there." When he recalls what he has been through, "it just seems like a dark forest." He sees plainly neither people nor scenes: "It's just a darkness" (257).

Nevertheless, the real world constantly undoes him, particularly when money and/or sex is involved. The curious result is that, when his two worst enemies try to blackmail him, the wholly innocent Count Macdonald feels immense guilt: "so horrible is the approach of any kind of blackmailer—that Sergius Mihailovitch for the time being really felt that he was the type of man" he had been accused of being. He begins to think that if everyone believes that he is a *"souteneur,"* that he has accepted Kintyre's and Lady Aldington's money, that he has "left his wife to starve," then "these things . . . must be true" (367). Despite its weaknesses, *The New Humpty-Dumpty* takes one giant step toward the triumphant truth of *The Good Soldier*: it is Ford's first novel of modern love in which the hero really dies. Granted, Macdonald does not die by his own hand, and his death reveals no enlightenment in the character and little in the creator. Nonetheless, the death suggests some dim sense that human passion and violence do have effects, can really hurt. Ford, as usual, cannot imagine a sexual role for himself without a disaster immediately ensuing to prevent consummation. Thus, Macdonald must die quickly of an injury to the spine on his wedding day, prefiguring both Ashburnham's death by cutting his throat and the total paralysis of Mark Tietjens on the occasion of his brother's long-delayed conquest of Valentine. This meaning is implicit, however, in almost every novel: the Fordian lover usually looks weak in the joints, unstrung.

Macdonald utters his last words, "The dear dark Forest," just after turning "his head into Lady Aldington's lap" (432). He is, of course, quite right. Sexual passion is the major source of the dark forest. Still, Ford asserts that Macdonald's "depressions" come "from that essential dark forest which is the heart of another," and that "his fellow-beings" are "wolves" (303). What Ford could not bear to see all his life—except once—was that in his own heart, too, lay a dark forest and in that forest lurked a beast. But once, like Kurtz, Ford looked into that dark heart, discovered he had something to say, and said it.

Why would *The New Humpty-Dumpty* have been so infuriating to Marwood? The Duke of Kintyre, the character customarily equated with Marwood, is a wholly attractive figure.[52] However, Ford's portrait of Lady Aldington's

ex-husband might well have hurt Marwood. Lord Aldington's name belongs to the Kentish village where the
Conrads, Marwoods, and Hueffers so disastrously congre-
gated in early 1909. Lord Aldington comes originally from
Yorkshire, where his family acquired wealth through the
iron ore found on their property; he now has a place in the
South of England and one in London. Aldington has
graduated from a good public school, but has dropped out
of university. Finally, he is six feet tall, forty inches around
the chest, with a heavy, fair face, "expressionless" blue
eyes, a "shapeless" figure, and a "heavy slouch" (6, 7, 268,
80, 9). All this is true of Marwood. Although the Ald-
ingtons' way of life does not at all resemble the Marwoods', it certainly looks forward to the Ashburnhams'.
Lord Aldington, formerly a Guards officer, is a persistently
unfaithful husband. This "extremely model" (11) couple
do not share a bed and rarely speak in private; their
finances are wholly in Lady Aldington's hands. They lead
a carefully scheduled life among their various houses and
including always three summer weeks taking the baths at a
German spa. Still, Lord Aldington is basically an English
brute; Ashburnham, after all, is not. The former was sent
down from Oxford for ill-treating a cat; all the maidser-
vants hate him; his sexual conquests are exclusively among
vulgar women of the barmaid sort; he has been careless
enough to father three bastards. Yet for all that, when his
wife finally, understandably, acts to get rid of him, Ford
evinces enough sympathy for him as a wiferidden male to
have Lord Aldington, surprisingly, act like a gentleman
and make easy his wife's divorce plans. The portrait of
Lord Aldington thus includes sympathetic identification as
well as hostility.

Ford's creative intentions toward the brutal Lord Aldington are unclear. Perhaps he merely wanted to provide
sympathy for Lady Aldington and to "justify" her wealth
and her availability to Count Macdonald. Nevertheless,
Ford had, to Conrad's mind, badly mistreated Marwood in
1909, suggesting that Ford's devotion to his best Tory

friend included hostility. According to Violet, a fictional portrait in 1912 (undoubtedly in *The New Humpty-Dumpty*) was one cause of Marwood's anger; and thus Ford lost, in Violet's words, "the best, most loving friend an editor ever had—and wasted."[53] Whereas professional writers like Conrad and Wells seem not to have let Ford's fictional portraits of themselves affect their personal relations with Ford, but merely responded in kind in *Chance* and *The Bulpington of Blup*, Marwood took the matter seriously.[54] The widow of a nephew of his remembered this, quite unprompted and long, long after Marwood's death:

> the thing about the [Tietjens] books which all the Marwoods . . . detested Ford for, was that to make a story he mixed up "Tietjens" & "Mark" with all his *own* rather horrid love affairs. All the Marwood men were . . . *completely* proper in their dealings with women . . .[55]

Marwood signaled his break with Ford by demanding immediate payment of the 400 guineas he had lent him in 1908 for Elsie's surgery. The outcome remains in dispute: the Marwoods say it was never paid; Violet says it was— "on the nail."[56] In any case, Marwood's demand for money would have reminded the bankrupt Ford one more time of how far from reality was his fantasy of himself as grand seigneur distributing largesse to a grateful peasantry. Further, the debt would have revived memories of the mistreated Elsie of 1909, who had become in 1913 his nemesis. Especially, that debt would have revived Ford's nightmares about sexual complications. The fact that Marwood had lent the money for the beautiful ailing Elsie had been powerful support for her belief in 1909 that he was in love with her. (Ford would both wish for this and be unable to bear it.) The money would then have been in Ford's fantasies a bribe for the injured husband. Marwood's demanding the money back in 1913 would have seemed punishment for the years Ford and Violet had been living, less and less happily, in sin. At the same time, Marwood's rejection must have been oddly satisfying. For the other Ford, the ideal, ever-loving, loyal, generous, self-sacrificing Ford, would need to have been grossly misjudged and misused by his remaining best friend.

Not only Violet, in her dramatic account of the 1913 breakup, but also Conrad, in his role as unsuccessful (and perhaps grimly amused) mediator, lays heavy emphasis on the money question. Conrad, in his March 27, 1913 letter to Ford (the last for two years) about the debts, stresses Marwood's ill health and makes no allusion to any personal hostility on anyone's part. Marwood had said, Conrad writes: "['] I'll give Ford 6 months to pay the £40 [sic]. I'll give him more if he likes only the matter must be settled.['] I suppose you know he nearly died this winter and wants to get his affairs in order in case of another illness." The letter goes on to make clear that Ford has been up to his old tricks with the male triangle of shifting identities, replacing one loved friend with another or, to use Conrad's 1909 phrase, "juggling with the realities of life." Conrad opines that Marwood would not "think much" of Ford's idea that Marwood, in lieu of repayment, should take over *Conrad's* debt to Ford of £40 interest on the £100 Conrad borrowed a dozen years before. Then Conrad throws himself into the game and begins to speak for their mutual friend. Marwood "would say," Conrad is certain, " 'I know how Conrad stands. He's always hard up. And if he were to die I couldn't press his widow.' "[57] Thus Conrad not only refuses to substitute himself for Ford but equates himself with Marwood: both would die soon. In Conrad's short story of that time "The Planter of Malata," the Conradian hero's assistant and then the hero die, leaving to the Fordian "Editor" only a grave and a deserted beach. What nonsense. The first one to die would be—Ford Madox Hueffer.

But first, Ford would try, in the only way he knew, through his fiction, to win back Marwood's affection. Like *Ladies Whose Bright Eyes* and the Daniel Chaucer novels, *Mr. Fleight* (1913) deeply involves Marwood and draws on

the *English Review* days. Indeed, the titular Conrad / Ford
hero and his Marwood / Ford benefactor Mr. Blood found
the highbrow *New Review* with a staff that includes as
poetry editor an obsessively talkative, emerald shirted, bad
tennis-playing young man (Pound), and as chief editor an
intrepid, tough, beautiful, sexy but chaperoned woman,
Augusta McPhail (Violet) (30, 267). Still, the real interest
lies in the intensity of Aaron Rothweil Fleight's devotion to
Mr. Blood.

A big man, a wealthy landowner, a club man who is un-
involved in the world (1), the "greatest intellect of the day"
(6), "an anachronism" (8), a "great reader" of books about
"solid, real things or solid, real people" (9), with a pair of
horses' hoofs "set in silver" and an enormous silver cigar-
box (10), Blood bears most of the marks of Marwood and
many of Ashburnham and Tietjens.[58] In his cynical comments about modern marriage, Blood not only looks forward a decade to Tietjens, but also reflects some of Ford's
remarks in *Women & Men* and of Marlow's in *Chance*, both
essentially contemporaneous with *Mr. Fleight*: "In this
country the business of marriage is to join two loving
hearts in a union that it's better not to talk about, compounded of sympathy and bearing up and not letting the
servants know that you quarrel" (291). Blood's chief topic,
however, is "modern life . . . the disgusting thing that it
has become" (193-94). Although Blood exhibits almost no
sexual desires, he is, like Marwood, a passionate man. Indeed, he once strangled a groom with his bare hands for
accepting an American millionaire's bribe to drug Blood's
show horses. For Blood, as for Ashburnham, horses represent the old virtues. *Mr. Fleight* thus begins with Blood at
his club window on Derby Day ritualistically making a
statistical comparison between horses and motor vehicles.

Although Fleight has long admired Blood and desires to
become "what Blood ought to have been" (7), it is years
before he has the courage even to speak to him. Fleight
does not presume to ask for friendship; all he wants is to be
Blood's "instrument," his "flail" (4) with which to punish

society. As Fleight says to a friend: "it is my intention to be absolutely and entirely loyal to Mr. Blood. . . . the point is that he *is* the director of my career" (166-67).

Fleight has only two solaces—talking to Blood and imagining total escape. During his longest conversation with his benefactor, Fleight remains seated because it is "more respectful." This day "is almost the greatest" of Fleight's life. His chief ambition has always been to be invited to Blood's country place and have him "talking by the hour" only to him (235). Fleight's other way of coping with his misery is to dream of "strong, cheap tea at the end of the day, and cheap, strong cheese. And a rabbit that's been poached. And father will give you a taste of his beer if he's in a good temper . . ." (173). But at the end of his long talk with Blood, Fleight makes his desires even more modest: "I want to sit quiet in the corner" (254).

Mr. Fleight can be read, then, as Ford's pledge of allegiance to Marwood, as his longing, even, to *be* Marwood. Speaking of himself as Marwood's flail is not all that far-fetched. By 1911 Ford was invoking his very best Tory friends in his journalism, and by 1913 he was referring explicitly to Blood and implicitly to Marwood in his *Outlook* columns. The novel can be read also as Ford's plea to Marwood for forgiveness and renewed friendship. That Ford was still hoping for the best is suggested by the "kindly" (303) look Ford has Blood give to Fleight at the end, prefiguring Ashburnham's last moment with Dowell. *Mr. Fleight*, moreover, concludes happily with the infirm young man, accompanied by his benefactor, walking toward his wedding. Conversely, the next two novels of the Violet phase end with their heroes in very, very quiet corners—or dead.

BRIGIT PATMORE AND *THE YOUNG LOVELL*

One of the more surprising turns in Ford's perpetually surprising career is just how very little *The Young Lovell* foreshadows its immediate, peerless successor *The Good*

Soldier. Indeed, if one had been asked to prophesy what would happen next to *The Young Lovell*'s author, one might well have predicted that he would write no more or even that he would destroy himself. The book is appalling in its pervasive lethargy and its final extreme quietness.[59] Instead of Blood's cynical rage against things as they are, *The Young Lovell* offers only indifference. Published in October 1913, it was written at the nadir of Ford's fortunes. "Well, it was Joseph Leopold's funeral," says Violet cheerfully of the celebrated *Throne* trial of February 7, 1913.[60] Immediately afterward she brought to Ford in Boulogne the news that Elsie had won £300 damages and that every London tabloid had had a field day with the tale of the two Mrs. Hueffers. So unstrung he was unable to speak, Ford refused to hear any details. On the advice of a French doctor, Violet took him south to Montpellier ("a wash out"), to Carcassonne ("where rabies was raging"), to Les Baux ("depressed us immeasurably"), to St. Rémy (where the mistral cut with "its knife-blade of cold").[61] During this grotesque rest cure, Ford wrote most of *The Young Lovell* and received a letter from Elsie demanding more money and one from Conrad confirming Marwood's implacable enmity.

Except for the hero, the characters of this sadly begotten fiction are so dim that to shove them into categories would be a meaningless exercise. But the Young Lovell vacillates distinctly between the roles of perfect benefactor and infirm young man. Probably no Fordian character before Henry Martin of *The Rash Act* is more explicitly a double man than he: on the one hand, the perfect hero, the "fairest knight of Christendom" (241); on the other hand, a desperate neurotic, utterly weary of his mortal beloved and longing to escape completely from this world into the arms of his "White Lady" (222). Ford dramatizes the split by having wayward thoughts of the lady conflict with responsible thoughts of masculine action. He knows he must be moving on, but the memory of her girdle-crossed breasts keeps "him languishing there in the hot sun as if his limbs had lost their young strength" (79). Once again the Fordian hero barely staggers along, recalling Pound's characterization of Ford as "paralysed" by his distinct vision of "the Venus immortal crossing the tram tracks."[62]

The Young Lovell begins in a nightmare inspired by Venus come to prevent his betrothal to Margaret. It ends in his fantasy of being with Venus on her island. But instead of eliciting scenes of terror and violence, potentially sexual situations in *The Young Lovell* translate the hero into visionary scenes of complete quietude. Although sometimes rather beautiful, the portraits of Venus are strangely static and significantly inconsistent; the personality of each character who looks at her determines the vision and suggests that the lady exists in everyone. Despite her kindliness and occasional suggestions of Christian attributes, she probably means to Ford what the Bishop avers: "All those women were one woman! . . . This apparition . . . appeareth with many faces and bodies, being the spirit that most snareth men to carnal desires. So doth she show herself to each man in the image that should snare him to sin . . ." (234, 238). The Bishop's word "image" appropriately defines the apparition's other important aspect, its resemblance to art rather than life. For Lovell, she duplicates the Botticelli Venus. For Margaret, she takes a pose leaning against a tree "with her arm over her head in an attitude of great leisure" (154), recalling Rossetti's study of Guinevere that so enchanted Ford. All this tends to support Violet's shrewd analysis of Fordian love:

> Love without breadth, depth, or thickness, without dimension. Subjective, purely. For the object—set up like an ikon to be worshipped, perfunctorily, with genuflections and lip-service, a queen in the game of knights and castles—any sort of fetish, glittering, shining, compelling, will do.[63]

By the same token, the vision of this love object in a stroke obliterates the real world or renders it meaningless: "ever since you saw that lady's face this world has seemed as a mirror and an unreality to you" (133).

The Young Lovell has a doubly quiet ending, appropriate

to its divided hero. His "mortal body" (310) lies immured until death in a stinking Northumberland hermitage. His spirit, translated by Venus to her magic island, first does fierce but loving battle with Paris. Then the two heroes, their limbs anointed by women so that their wounds are healed, lie down with the ladies on beds of herbs to discuss what would have been the outcome of the combat if it had "been fought upon the wearisome fields known to mortal man" (308-309).

Despite the completeness of its impulse to escape human existence, *The Young Lovell*, like its predecessors, proves to have some connections with Ford's real life, and one link, after all, with his masterpiece. The legal barriers to Lovell's marriage to Margaret, his weariness at the thought of her, and his remorseful sense of her continuing loyalty to him surely reflect Ford's relations with Violet in 1913. Perhaps Lovell's harmless, happy battle with Paris is a wish-fulfillment fantasy upon Ford's ruined relations with Marwood.

The fairy lady must reflect Ford's newest love, the beautiful young Irish woman Brigit Patmore. Born in Dublin January 25, 1882, Ethel Elizabeth Morrison-Scott, who always wished to be called Brigit, married, in 1907, a Londoner, John Deighton Patmore, grandson of the popular Victorian poet Coventry Patmore. Violet, knowing the Patmore family through her Pre-Raphaelite father, called upon the couple in Putney. When the Patmores moved to Kensington some five years later, Violet and Brigit became fast friends. Soon they were seeing each other weekly, often at Ford and Violet's South Lodge. Sometime in 1913, or early 1914, Ford fell in love with her. Although Brigit said much later that "he never attracted me," Violet Hunt, in her diary, quotes Brigit as admitting to her once that she had succumbed to Ford.[64]

The prevailing unreality of *The Young Lovell* suggests that Ford's spirits were so low in Provence that he could scarcely think of anyone to long for, or remember who Elsie was, or blame Violet for his not loving her. The over-

whelming feeling is one of pathos; the novelist just wants
to escape. *The Young Lovell* points, in short, to the quiet despair at the end of *The Good Soldier*. Like Ashburnham
clinging to the crucifix in a futile effort to drive Nancy from
his mind, Lovell senses the hopelessness of seeking religious help to ward off the lady. Unable to take up again the
responsibility of being a great lord or to assume his role as
Margaret's husband, Lovell, during a driving rainstorm,
has himself confined in "that little hermit's kennel" (305),
where the stench of the previous tenant's "rotten corpse"
still lingers (304). The feeling here must be close to that of
Ashburnham in his stable taking out his "little neat pen-
knife" and telling Dowell he "must have a bit of rest"
(294). And Dowell, whose name so resembles Lovell's and
whose ultimate silent solitude is so like a hermit's, echoes
the language and the locale of the last pages of *The Young
Lovell*: "Is there then any terrestrial paradise where, amidst
the whispering of the olive-leaves, people can be with
whom they like and have what they like and take their ease
in shadows and in coolness?" (273).[65]

With his personal life in disarray and his twenty-one
years of professional commitment still unrewarded, Ford
in July 1913 shared Lovell's solitary despair. Yet almost
immediately he sprang forth to begin what is clearly his
masterpiece and one of the great novels of the century. For
half those years he had been practicing his craft under England's greatest master. For the entire period, he had been
dealing with, or pretending to deal with, essentially the
same subject-matter—enticing, menacing, unfulfilled sexual passion—and with a virtually unchanged pattern of
characters. Moreover, the idea of *The Good Soldier* itself
went back at least to his writing of *The Spirit of the People* in
the spring of 1906, and possibly to 1903, perhaps even to
1901.[66] Why, then, should Ford, at last and only this one
time, have triumphed so completely? Graham Greene, a
lifelong admirer of Ford, provides a wise guess. Greene's
strongest impression of the novel is a "sense of Ford's involvement." The source of that deeper involvement must

be biographical: "A novelist is not a vegetable absorbing nourishment mechanically from soil and air: material is not easily or painlessly gained, and one cannot help wondering what agonies of frustration and error lay behind *The Saddest Story*."[67]

For Ford the courage to start every new, serious novel about modern love had to come from a new woman. In the case of *The Good Soldier*, it was Brigit Patmore. The time, just five years after he fell in love with Violet, reminds us once more of the appalling regularity with which his phases coincided with the decades and half-decades of his life. In January 1889, at the age of fifteen, Ford suffered the twin shocks of losing his father and finding his family more or less penniless. However, at the age of twenty, in May 1894, after an agonized courtship that included thoughts of suicide, he found happiness in the arms of Elsie Martindale. By September 1898, three months before his twenty-fifth birthday, he was in utter despair. Conrad's arrival at the Pent that fall provided a temporary respite. Nevertheless, despite Conrad's friendship and, at some point, the favors of Mary Martindale, Ford found himself, in the summer of 1904 at the age of thirty, agoraphobic and suicidal. Although he was enjoying his new friendship with Arthur Marwood in 1906 and founding a great review in 1908, by 1909, when Ford was thirty-five, he was again so desperate as to be threatening suicide and again in love, with Violet Hunt. After finding happiness for a while with Violet, he was, the spring after his fortieth year, in love with Brigit Patmore and expecting to die soon. He was also writing his greatest novel. Then, after years of increasing estrangement from Violet and a long stretch of military service including mental and physical breakdowns in France, Ford, at the age of forty-five, in the spring of 1919, was happy once again, this time with Stella Bowen. After publishing the first section of his second-best novel and founding a new review, he was (in 1924, at the age of fifty) having an affair with Jean Rhys and alienating Stella. By August 1928, a few months before his fifty-fifth birthday, Ford had not only lost Stella, but was losing her intended replacement and was once again talking about suicide.[68] In May 1930, Janice Biala appeared, all the more welcome for being a year late, and Ford was soon at work on one of his most interesting novels. The spring and summer of 1936 found him writing one of his finest love poems, but this time in celebration of continuing devotion to Janice. Ford's last phase ended on June 26, 1939, cheated by Death of its tenth year.

With four wives and at least three extramarital attachments to work with, what psychobiographer could not invent a five-year plan? And with those 79 books, 57 contributions to books, 416 articles, and many unpublished manuscripts, with all those works of fiction, poetry, biography, history, criticism, sociology, and reminiscence, with all that, who could not devise any number of patterns?

On the other hand, a five-year plan for Ford may only reflect the normal emotional fluctuations of poor, suffering humankind. A distinguished American psychologist once observed, à propos of Erik Erikson's work on identity crises and the eight stages of man, that people have identity crises about every five years, that his own octogenerian father was undergoing one at the time.[69] Dame Rebecca West takes a more particularized view: "You say as a total outsider that 'usually Ford could stay in love five years, and stay attached only ten.' This seems to me characteristic of many of your sex and cannot, I think, be counted as an idiosyncrasy of Ford."[70]

Lovely and inspiring a muse as Brigit was (to Pound at the same time and to Richard Aldington later), she was nevertheless playing a very familiar Fordian role. But *The Good Soldier* is a unique achievement. No, the "agonies of frustration and error" that Greene "cannot help wondering about" must have come chiefly out of drastically altered relations with the people he had loved longest and most, the people whose shades were coming more and more to dominate his fiction. Not, in short, the women in his life, but Joseph Conrad and Arthur Marwood. By the summer of 1913, Ford must have realized that neither his artist-friend, who was like a father to him, nor his country gentleman-friend, who embodied his grandfather's generous traditions—that neither of these former boon companions really, really loved him anymore.

The experience was killing to Ford. If 1898 was the "most depressing period" and 1904 "the most terrible period" of his life, if he threatened suicide in 1904 and 1909, still the year of *The Good Soldier* seems even more oriented toward a final ending. In 1934, Ford was to say that "F.M.F. . . . went down the drain Anno MCMXIV & since that date abandoned all hope of a glorious resurrection."[71] In 1927 he said that he considered himself in 1914 "as the Great Auk" that, having reached its allotted time and laid its "one egg . . . might as well die."[72] More to the point, in his 1914 journalism he spoke of himself as one of those "relatively speaking, about to die" and announced his determination "to drop creative writing for good and all."[73] More to the point still is Olive's laconic reference to a letter from Ford to his older daughter in May 1914: "Ford wrote to Xtina that he was dying." Paradoxically, then, Ford drew the courage to write *The Good Soldier* from the comforting presences of a real Brigit Patmore and an imagined imminent death. But to accomplish *The Good Soldier* required not only courage, but perspective—the latter supplied, according to my speculation, by the losses of Conrad and Marwood.

The saddest story is that love dies, dies because man is mad. (Sane he would perhaps not love at all.) I do not mean, however, that a simple desire of Ford's to avenge himself on Conrad and Marwood resulted in the magnificent achievement of *The Good Soldier*. After all, Dowell genuinely loves Ashburnham, Ashburnham may love Dowell, and Ford loves them both. Rather, *Chance*, with its reminder that Conrad no longer loved Ford as he once had,[74] and Marwood's irrevocable silence pressed the real world upon Ford's consciousness with an importunity it may not have exhibited since Francis Hueffer died in 1889. Almost surely, it was merely Ford's words—in preposterous Olympian letters to his friends, in fantastic statements to the press, in childish legal maneuverings, in foolish fictions like *The New Humpty-Dumpty*—it was surely just in his words and not through any vicious acts that he at last irretrievably disgusted, dismayed, and disillusioned Marwood. Conrad had warned Ford in 1909 that words were *not* "wind," but Ford could not see it. Perhaps their reconciliation in 1911 deluded Ford into thinking that he could say anything and all might yet be well. But Conrad's new silence and *Chance*'s publication dramatized Conrad's true estimate of Ford. Equally important, Marwood's absolute refusal to take up relations again, despite Ford's self-abasement to him in *Mr. Fleight*, would have shown Ford that words really do things in a world that is in some sense real. Especially, words can kill love, which, once dead, can never come back again. Love, of course, is awfully demanding, hard to bear. Maybe seeing those two loves stripped away was partly a relief to Ford, who had probably feared all his life that he was unlovable.

CHAPTER FOUR

Impressionism, Agoraphobia, and *The Good Soldier*

1913–1914

FROM REALITY TO MIRAGE

Ford may, or may not, have been reading Conrad's *Chance*—that last, most intricate instance of Marlovian impressionism—as he began *The Good Soldier*. But we know that he was reading James, since the book he wrote just before *The Good Soldier* was his *Henry James*, begun immediately after the completion of *The Young Lovell* on July 7, in proof by September 2, though not published until January 1, 1914.[1]

The very last words in Ford's book on James are "*The Golden Bowl*." That novel echoes in *The Good Soldier* so strikingly as to have inspired an ingenious if perverse interpretation of Ford's masterpiece as a conscious parody of James's own four-square coterie.[2] To an impressive list of parallels between the two little, naive, cuckolded American millionaires, Adam Verver and John Dowell, can be added such precise details as their blue ties and their habit of carefully counting their steps. Both the wife-dominated Prince and Ashburnham not only are successful with other women but are termed, with complex irony, "stupid."[3] More seriously, both novels are about the difficulty of human communications, the impossibility of really knowing, the Anglo-American resistance to looking into things. Indeed, both novels use obsessively variations on the key words "know" and "impression." The last half of *The Golden Bowl*, told from Maggie's point of view, is a great early instance in modern fiction of conjectural narration, thus making it a distinguished progenitor of *Absalom, Absalom!* as well as of *Chance* and *The Good Soldier*. And finally, both classics, *The Golden Bowl* and *The Good Soldier*, make very dark reports on the human condition. As the Prince says to Maggie: "Everything's terrible, *cara*—in the heart of man."[4]

Henry James reminds us that Ford was a profound student of the art of the novel, that his masterpiece owes much to James's, and that its existence is partly the result of a technical breakthrough.[5] The James book reminds us, too, that the year of *The Good Soldier* was also the year of Ford's best literary criticism, in his two, two-part essays on impressionism, and in his wonderful, weekly "Literary Portraits" in *The Outlook*. Only *Joseph Conrad*, written in a rush under the painful inspiration of his best friend's death, August 5, 1924, approaches in quality the criticism of 1913-1914. The James book reminds us finally that besides nineteen pre-*Good Soldier* novels, Ford wrote eleven volumes of nonfictional prose. Four of these, the trilogy of impressionistic journalism, *The Soul of London, The Heart of the Country*, and *The Spirit of the People*, written during the 1904-1906 nervous breakdown, and *Ancient Lights*, written just after Ford's defection to Violet, have perhaps more vitality and human interest than any of his fiction of the period. Moreover, they are immensely useful guides to Ford's characteristic state of mind during the first half of his literary career. And his state of mind, in turn, helps us a good deal in understanding his version of literary impressionism.

The history of literary impressionism remains to be written. It will have to take into account eighteenth-century British empiricism, romantic theory, positivism, French realism, French impressionist painting, pragmatism, and phenomenology—at least. It will need to make precise distinctions among the various impressionisms of Dickens, James, Crane, Conrad, and Ford. It will need especially to remain lucid about the intimate connections and contradictions between literary realism and literary impressionism. It will probably never be written.[6] The aim of the French impressionist painters was, in the words of Ian Watt, "to give a pictorial equivalent of the visual sensations of a particular individual at a particular time and place."[7] Thus, to a greater extent than earlier traditions, literary impressionism's chief source has as a central interest epistemology. The classic, impressionist model of the mind is of course Walter Pater's beautiful definition of experience in his Conclusion to *The Renaissance*. He makes only too clear that the logical extreme of the impressionist view of reality is a terrifying solipsism:

> Experience, already reduced to a swarm of impressions, is ringed round for each one of us by that thick wall of personality through which no real voice has ever pierced on its way to us, or from us to that which we can only conjecture to be without. Every one of those impressions is the impression of the individual in his isolation, each mind keeping as a solitary prisoner its own dream of a world.[8]

Now the James of "The Art of Fiction," taking as his observer "one on whom nothing is lost," believes that one can learn from experience and make reasonable connections between areas of experience. He sees the novelist as an historian, and Conrad later movingly celebrated James as the "historian of fine consciences."[9] Though Marlow's encounter with Kurtz seems to shed a kind of light, Conrad is obviously much less sure how much can be learned and whether what is learned can ever be successfully communicated to another. Nevertheless, he has no doubt about the existence of a material world.[10] "For Conrad," to quote Watt again, "the world of the senses is not a picture but a presence, a presence . . . intense, unconditional, and unanswerable."[11] Ford's impressionist position, like his life, is shot through with contradictions. More explicitly, more blatantly, more insistently than James and Conrad, he celebrates the novelist as the exact scientist and the his-

torian of his own times. And yet, in the end, for Ford, external reality is almost literally a mirage.[12]

Much as those definitive breaks with his dearest male
friends merely climax a recurrent pattern of personal relationships that Ford had been compulsively arranging since
childhood, so the critical ideas of 1913-1914 represent only
a ripening of what he early acquired from his grandfather
and the Pre-Raphaelite milieu. Ford is surely poeticizing
only a little when he says in July 1914 that he has been advocating the same literary doctrines since he was fifteen.[13]
He is probably not poeticizing at all when he says in the
Conrad book that Conrad's 1897 message ("My task which
I am trying to achieve is, by the power of the written word
. . . to make you *see*") is a belief that Ford had previously
held.[14] Ford was from the first committed to "realism" and
to all the good old words that go with it: truth, honesty,
sincerity, exactitude, nature. If he admires a particular artist, the highest praise he can bestow has to do with the
realism of the portrayal. Thus in 1896 Ford is celebrating
his grandfather's "strenuous efforts to be absolutely realistic" (FMB, 412). De Maupassant's "rendering" is "true,"[15]
Holbein's "sincere" (H, 172), Trollope's "exact." Hudson
is a "scientist,"[16] Henry James, "the only unbiassed, vo-
luminous and truthful historian of our day" (HJ, 66). Some
of Ford's most striking and most loving pictures of Conrad
portray him carefully observing his physical surroundings.
Ford says that Conrad, on entering a room, would move
"his head once semi-circularly" in order "to master that
room . . . his chief passion being the realisation of aspects
to himself." Conrad's mind formed and held ideas only
"after he had contemplated a sufficient number of facts or
documents" (JC, 11, 56). If the writer is to render life
exactly, he must write from his own personal experience
(Ford here being far more prescriptive than James): "a
writer can only really write with assurance of the life which
he himself has lived" (CA, 92). Moreover, if the writer is to
have universal appeal, he ought first to have been a "man
of action," ought to have led a "normal" life (AL, 242).

Examples of Ford's commitment to traditional realism could be multiplied indefinitely. Yet many of them contain qualifying phrases suggesting uneasiness about the possibility of writing realistically. In praising James for limiting himself "to what he knows intimately," Ford feels compelled to add "and within himself" (HJ, 123). Indeed, more often than not in talking about realism Ford's emphasis is not upon the reality observed but upon the mentality of the observer. In *The Spirit of the People*, Ford limits "himself to attempting to produce an image of the world he has lived in, *reflected in his own personality*" (xiv, my italics). Although Conrad "presents us with facts not theories,"[17] Ford feels facts do not matter: "It is all one whether the artist be right or wrong as to his facts; his business is to render rightly the appearance of things" (SP, xv). Moreover, those appearances of modern life in Ford's brain are singularly difficult to render. Life these days, he says, is "much more bewildered" than at any time since the Dark Ages; it is merely a series of "meaningless episodes beneath the shadow of doom" (CA, 28; HJ, 155). In his essays of *The Good Soldier* year, reality seems particularly hopeless of depiction: any careful "rendering of any material object has power to . . . point the moral of the impermanence of matter." The "roots of poetry draw their nourishment from seeing and from beliefs. Here I see nothing."[18]

Although Ford kept on saying that, besides giving pleasure, the other chief purpose of art is to render life, provide knowledge, present truth, and so on, the ultimate effect of his statements about art is to underline how hard, how really impossible it is to know much of anything, let alone convey it to another human being.[19] Indeed, by 1914 the voice of Ford the journalistic critic is virtually indistinguishable from that of Dowell the fictional narrator: the theme of both is "I don't know." Sometimes Ford thinks that a truth is relative to an era, that the great artist's truth is ahead of his times: "For Art . . . whose truths become apparent only to future generations, can make very little appeal to the everyday mind of its time" (CA, 109). Or, truth is relative to one's culture, Conrad's truth relative to the Polish aristocratic idea of honor, Ford's to the morals of Campden Hill.[20] Sometimes Ford goes so far as to say essentially that it is impossible to tell the truth or that truth is irrelevant to the conduct of life. The typical Englishman's weakness is that he believes that truth will prevail; whereas "with his eyes closed—he might see a thousand instances in which truth has not prevailed." Ford, indeed, can conceive of a society based upon a lie. Truth is really just "a convenience, a simplification of relationships" (SP, 162).

If truth for Ford is relative, irrelevant, and ever-changing, present-day external reality is vague, and its effects upon the subject indefinite. A writer, to render reality properly, must get its indefiniteness into his works. The impressionist method is especially effective in conveying "a sense of the complexity, the tantalisation, the shimmering, the haze, that life is" (JC, 191). In their novels he and Conrad wanted to suggest, in dialogue, "the sort of indefiniteness that is characteristic of all human conversations" (JC, 135).

Presumably this last is so because no real human communication is possible. Sometimes Ford seems to think that the gulf between persons is strictly a modern phenomenon. In his grandfather's time, "intimacies between man and man, and woman and woman, were comparatively frequent. . . . We are all men and women nowadays, and we have not got any friends" (AL, 273-74). Ford admits poignantly that it "will never now be known" whether Conrad had any affection for him. "You may live with another for years and years in a condition of the closest daily intimacy and never know what, at the bottom of the heart, goes on in your companion" (JC, 123). Ford's account of how he and Conrad handled fictional conversations suggests not only their mutual awareness of the difficulties inherent in human communication, but also a crucial difference in their attitudes. They agreed that a character's speech should never answer that of another character because "in real life . . . few people listen." Thus, when conversing with Mr. Slack, "you hardly notice" what he tells you "because you are dying to tell him" something; you "miss Mr. Slack's next two speeches" because you are thinking about your daughter Millicent. Nevertheless, there comes a moment at "which the characters do directly answer each other." Significantly, and this is the point, "in this department," Conrad was "matchless," Ford "very deficient" (JC, 188-89, 191).

Ford's puzzlement about the hearts of others is not confined to real and fictional characters of modern life. Having spent many years doing historical research on Henry VIII, Ford concludes that he really knows "nothing whatever" about him: "all that I *know* about this king could be reported in the words of Maupassant . . . that he was a gentleman with red whiskers who always went first through a door" (CW, 38). Ford's illustration shows that the closest he can come to knowledge is a momentary visual observation and that he feels perfectly free to draw his concrete instance from a different, and fictional, context. The discussion of Henry VIII follows Ford's charming commentary on Hogarth's four-line drawing of a watchman carrying a pike on his shoulder with his dog beside him "going in at a door" (36). Ford's point is the familiar Jamesian one: let the observer fill in his own details and thus intensify his belief. More importantly, these juxtaposed images of men disappearing through doors underline Ford's sense of the elusiveness of reality and his longing to escape from it.

This reality that it is his bounden duty, as his grandfather's disciple, to render seems to him much of the time simply unknowable. Throughout his pre-*Good Soldier* prose, Ford sounds with surely more than usual frequency Dowell's refrain. In 1911, "I don't know; and I don't know that it all affects my argument" (WM, 20). By 1914, the idea has become obsessive: "I do not know why I should have been especially asked to write about Impressionism. . . . A few years ago, I should languidly have denied that . . . I knew anything about the school . . . I don't know; I just write books . . ." "But with verse I just do not know: I do not know anything at all" (CW, 34, 140). Ford's bafflement reaches its climax when war breaks out: "We writers go out. . . . What then is the good of it all? I don't know." "But the present period, for the moment, is too much for me. I cannot get the hang of it. . . . I do not know whether I am a hero or just a tired person."[21]

A propos of reviewing a book by Conal O'Riordan in April 1914, Ford tells an anecdote about five Irish politicians each telling his own version of the same story. The experience symbolizes for Ford the incomprehensibility of reality and possibly its conscious intention to harm. He despairs of conveying the suspicious, mysterious, gloating atmosphere enveloping "those five extraordinarily different narrations." All five seem to think that Ford understands the farce they are conducting. But indeed, he does not at all know the one basic truth he is supposed to know: "it was rather like being taken for a Freemason and having mystic but incomprehensible signs made to one . . . indeed whenever I see the Irishry . . . I seem to see a crowd of unreal people playing an unreal game with unknown laws."[22] No doubt, besides being interested in the literary and political ferment in Ireland, Ford was particularly obsessed with the Irish because of Brigit Patmore. But he includes in his bafflement a great many non-Irish writers. We can sympathize with his reading James's *The American Scene* "with a sense of deep, of complete, and finally of utter, non-comprehension," with his finding James's Prefaces mystifying and bewildering (HJ, 21, 135). But what of all these? Of Gissing, "one knows nothing." "I don't just figure out what [Wyndham Lewis] means." A book on poetic theory "just bewilders me." "Now, here is Mr. Titterton's book. I do not know much what to make of that . . . I may have misread him." And of a book by R. H. Benson: "perhaps I am wrong and missing the point. . . . Perhaps it is I who am tired."[23]

Such comments take one away, rather forcibly, from the reality observed and back to the self observing. The fault is in ourselves, and this is precisely what for Ford the impressionistic method can teach: "a profoundly significant lesson as to the self-engrossment of humanity" (JC, 190). "Impressionism," Ford says, "is a frank expression of personality." And although you need to make every fictional motive "convincing to your reader," you first "will try to make it convincing also to yourself, since you yourself in this solitary world of ours will be the only reader that you really and truly know" (CW, 36, 46). Still, just how well the artist can know even himself is a dubious matter. Ford remarks cheerfully of James: "as to what may go on within the cavernous recesses of his artist's mind, we have simply no means of knowing, and very likely he has simply no means of knowing himself" (HJ, 28). Ford admits that his own "emotions move so quickly that I never have time to catch hold of them."[24] His sense impressions are equally mysterious: "I simply don't know. One's glass . . . is so small, and one is compelled to drink solely in that glass, that one might come the most frightful howlers if one trusted to one's own observation. And whom is one to trust?"[25]

Although Ford says his task is to make us see, he cannot see himself. He cannot see because, when he looks, his purpose is not observation but tranquillity. He cannot see also because his mind is usually not on its surroundings. Although Ford shares his grandfather's devotion to Holbein's realistic renderings, he says that Holbein's great gift to humanity was "tranquillity" (H, 110). A field naturalist does not observe the rabbit, stoat, or chaffinch in order to understand external reality: "He is building up his little house of observations; he is filling in the chinks of the wattle-wall that shuts out for him the monotony of his life." The sound of wind, the lines of trees, the smell of grass, these operate to "soothe his mind" (HC, 102).

In his heart of hearts, Ford hardly believes that direct observation is possible, or even natural, to humanity. He delights in such directions as these: "You go down the lane till you come to the place where Farmer Banks's old barn used to stand when he kept six cows in it" (HC, 213). In the Conrad book, Ford says that anyone who has been in combat knows how little a part the actual fighting plays in one's mind: "You would be lying on your stomach, in a beast of a funk. . . . But . . . your thoughts were concentrated . . . on your daughter Millicent's hair, on the fall of the Asquith Ministry. . . . You were there, but great shafts of thought from the outside, distant and unattainable world . . . occupied your mind" (JC, 192).

Ford would go so far as to believe sometimes that he was not really there and indeed that, as with Gertrude Stein's Oakland, there was really no there there. The world, Ford says, "is an extraordinarily unreal mirage." He notes three sharp stones in his driveway, a broken bucket in his orchard, the rain beating against his window, the furniture in need of painting, the baker at his gate. But all these demanding realities are actually "mirage; there is nothing real about the stones, or the discarded bucket, or the rain, or the baker coming in at the gate. Myself, my own self, is miles away—thirty miles away, thinking of things how different—how utterly different!"[26]

For Ford then, the impressionistic method serves not to render the external world but to dramatize a mind in a state of dislocation. The method, says Ford, can appropriately convey "a sense of two, of three, of as many as you will, places, persons, emotions, all going on simultaneously in the emotions of the writer." A writer, he goes on, can quite plausibly "have the sense, when he is in one room, that he is in another, or when he is speaking to one person he may be so intensely haunted by the memory or desire for another person that he may be absent-minded or distraught." And then he illustrates his idea with one of those images that tell us so much about his own psyche and thus about *The Good Soldier*. "Indeed," he says, "I suppose that Impressionism exists to render those queer effects of real life that are like so many views seen through bright glass—through glass so bright that whilst you perceive through it a landscape or a backyard, you are aware that, on its surface, it reflects a face of a person behind you." Here is Ford, haunted by the desire for, probably, a woman. His simile puts her reflection between the observer and the scene and puts her "really" behind the observer, a potential comfort—or threat. Moreover, the simile puts Ford characteristically by a window through which he can escape. "For the whole of life is really like that; we are almost always in one place with our minds somewhere quite other" (CW, 40-41).

If Ford's thoughts are not somewhere else, they are—in his most profound experiences with art—blissfully nonexistent, the self obliterated. He says he has visited the National Gallery innumerable times to look at Holbein's *Christina: Duchess of Milan*, "simply to think nothing. It is not for me a picture; it is not even a personage with whom I am in love. But simply a mood—a mood of profound lack of thought, of profound self-forgetfulness . . ." (H, 150-52). In a review of Dostoevsky's *The Idiot*, Ford describes his ideal book and in so doing gives his most moving account of the value of art as escape:

> what is to be aimed at in a style is something so unobtrusive and so quiet—and so beautiful if possible—that the reader shall not know that he is reading, and be conscious only that he is living in the life of the book. . . . a book so quiet in tone, so clearly and so unobtrusively worded, that it should give the effect of a long monologue spoken by a lover at a little distance from his mistress's ear—a book about the invisible relationships between man and man; about the values of life; about the nature of God—the sort of book that nowadays one could read in as one used to do when one was a child, pressed against a tall window-pane for hours and hours, utterly oblivious of oneself, in the twilight.[27]

The subject matter is irrelevant, the need for oblivion overwhelming.[28] Once again the image translates Ford out of the present time and place and puts him back in the past and up against a window, where dreams of escape are so much easier.

Ford's notions of art as escape are hardly original. He could have gotten them, for instance, from his father's hero Schopenhauer.[29] Those ideas were, moreover, coming to the fore among modern poets. They achieve particularly beautiful expression in Wallace Stevens' "The House Was Quiet and the World Was Calm," its statement, "The reader became the book," recalling Ford's "living the life of the book."[30] But surely one cause above all moved Ford to see reality as a mirage and to desire oblivion: his early experiences—painful and funny—of mental distress.

FORD'S MENTAL ILLNESS

To try to get at the roots of Ford's mental illness, let us start with two hypotheses. Let us assume that by 1913 Ford had come to know a good deal about his difficulties. Violet Hunt and Stella Bowen agree that he was a superb psychologist. Let us further assume that Ford's relations with his father were the chief source of his distress: "What I remember of him most was that he called me 'the patient but extremely stupid donkey' " (AL, ix). That judgment would have had particular force for the son; he thought of his father as a "ferocious critic," as "a man of great rectitude," "of great erudition and force of character," "of an encyclopedic knowledge" (AL, 83, ix, 10, 41). The judgment would have been reinforced by Ford's awareness that his younger brother was always considered "very much the sharper of the two" sons (AL, 102). Moreover, Francis Hueffer's early death meant that no matter what the boy did he could never prove himself. The loss must have been catastrophic. It inspired his first known poem and his first book.

Ancient Lights begins with two reproductions; they are, as illustrations should try to be, very illustrative. The first, facing the title page, is a photograph of Madox Brown's doorway on Fitzroy Square; there is a quotation: "with a funeral urn in the centre of the entry." We shall return to it shortly as the proper entry into Ford's agoraphobia. The second illustration, facing Ford's prefatory dedication to his daughters, is Madox Brown's painting of little Fordie as *Tell's Son*. It, too, carries a quotation: "I seem to be looking at myself from outside." The little boy is holding the split halves of the apple and looking out with very strange eyes. Those eyes do not seem to say: "See the fine thing my father has done." Still, they are not stupid. Perhaps they say: "Well, here it is, the thing you grownups were all excited about. I don't understand, and I am worried." The inscription certainly suggests that Ford wants no longer to be inside that blond head.

That inscription comes from Ford's account, in the "Dedication," of his earliest memory. He can see himself as a very small child at an enormous window where his grandmother keeps a breeding-box containing ring-doves. By standing on tiptoe he can just manage to look inside the box, where he can just make out "greyish and almost shapeless objects with, upon them, little speckles, like the very short spines of hedgehogs, and I stand with the first surprise of my life and with the first wonder of my life. I ask myself: can these be doves?—these unrecognizable, panting morsels of flesh." His grandmother discovers him and angrily tells him "that if the mother dove is disturbed, she will eat her young." Though Ford now believes this is incorrect, "I know quite well that for many days afterwards I thought I had destroyed life and that I was exceedingly sinful. . . . my first conscious conviction was one of great sin, of a deep criminality" (AL, viii-ix). The passage is a Freudian's delight. This recollection of an illicit peek into a box of "greyish and almost shapeless objects with . . . little speckles, like the very short spines of hedgehogs," of "unrecognizable, panting morsels of flesh" associated with a mother dove and a human grandmother, this recollection surely stands for the male child's earliest enlightenment as to the mysterious, terrifyingly *not* phallic nature of the female sex organ. To little boys, such

knowledge is utterly forbidden, the punishment annihila-
tion. The "very tiny child" who has disturbed the "angry"
mother-figure is going to be devoured like the "young" of
the "disturbed" mother dove. Worse still, this scene is
connected directly by its inscription to the painting of the
tiny Ford-child holding up his apple neatly split by
Father's arrow. Moreover, this passage ends with Dr.
Hueffer calling his son a "stupid donkey." In short, father
will castrate him and mother will devour him. "Stupid"
suggests that the apple means not only human sexuality
but knowledge in general. The father considers his son
stupid because the father understands things the son cannot possibly understand: in these instances of the breeding
doves and the apple, where babies (impossible siblings?)
come from, the primal act, and thus all our woe. What the
terrified Ford-child chiefly experiences is the incomprehensible explosion of murderous feelings in gigantic
persons. Much later Ford was to remember that as a child
he believed that except for himself the world was popu-
lated wholly by devils (RY, 72).

   This picture of himself caught, by an adult, in some
frightening situation and found sinful or stupid recurs at
least a dozen times in *Ancient Lights* as well as in many
other places in Ford's journalism. It works as Ford's sign of
his own relation to the world. Although most of these
scenes naturally have to do with artistic, rather than sexual, encounters, they often feature the disturbing noises so
characteristic of, to use the psychoanalytic jargon, "primal
scene content." In some, Ford is not necessarily to blame.
Indeed, in the first three instances in *Ancient Lights*, a
father-figure has left him to his doom. In several cases,
adults have clothed him in some grotesque costume that
adds to his misery. These scenes serve together to illustrate
Ford's abiding memory of having to "stand nervous and
trembling . . . before some enormous creature" and feeling
in his "heart a terrible fear of precipitating a torrent of
moral indignation" (CA, 174). And yet these scenes also
inspire some of Ford's most enjoyable, most memorable

writing. Thus Ford, "a small child in a blue pinafore," finds himself alone in his grandfather's studio with Turgenev and his translator Ralston, both six-foot giants, and exclaims, "in a high treble: 'Won't you take a chair?' " (AL, 187). Or, clad for a concert in a "suit of greenish-yellow corduroy velveteen with gold buttons, and two stockings of which the one was red and the other green . . . the curse of my young existence," Ford finds himself abandoned by his father's assistant in the front row. Franz Liszt, for a joke, and in the presence of King Edward, lifts Ford out of his seat, sits in it and leaves Ford "standing, the very small lonely child with the long golden curls, underneath all those eyes and stupefied by the immense sounds of applause" (AL, 70, 71). Ford, delivered "to the full educational fury" of Aunt Lucy, appears in a Greek play, "a lanky boy of twelve . . . draped in robes of the most flimsy butter muslin . . . imbecilely flapping my naked arms" before an audience of the Pre-Raphaelite great, hearing from time to time "the rather high voice of my father . . . 'Speak up, Fordie!' " (AL, 101-103).

So impressed was Ford with such experiences of exposed childhood that, in reviewing Mme. Pawlowska's autobiography, he quotes from a similar scene and says that the passage contains "the whole tragedy of childhood" and, further, that "all of us adults are feeling . . . these agonies . . . every moment of our lives, which are lives of misunderstanding between man and man."[31] Ford indeed pictures himself no better off as a young adult. The poet Mathilde Blind reduces him to a "miserable muteness" and herself becomes his father, calling "Fordie . . . as stupid as a donkey" (AL, 51-52). His contemporaries "brow-beat" him in an effort to make him see that all of James's novels contain a "Profound Moral Purpose" (HJ, 45).

Such episodes become for Ford almost a convention, his way of telling how he relates to such heroes and friends as Hudson, Marwood, and Conrad. Naturally the tone is comic and the point of the story not wholly Ford's discomfiture. Yet each anecdote dramatizes the same muddled, suffering Ford. The middle-aged man is astonished at how little he seems to have changed since he was a very small boy. He feels as though he has never grown up; he still expects to be " 'spoken to' or spanked by a mysterious *They*" (AL, 253-54). At his first meeting with Hudson, Ford is not sinful, merely stupid because he thinks Hudson is someone come to buy Conrad's mare (JC, 155-56). Later, when Ford offers a literary comment in praise of Hudson's style, he becomes sinful as well: "He turned upon me with an extraordinary aquiline fury and exclaimed: 'Stylist! Me a stylist! Stevenson was a stylist, Pater was a stylist, I have no time for that twiddling nonsense' " (AL, 111). Marwood, "part proprietor of the *E——h Re——w*," simply addresses the editor "in tones of despair . . . 'It's a perfectly rotten number!' "[32] Conrad's groaning response to Ford's reading aloud "Seraphina" elicits from Ford the counterresponse "dumb obstinacy"—that stupid donkey again! (JC, 23).

Francis Hueffer, then, has pronounced judgment upon his sinful, muddled son. As Ford sees it, everyone agrees. Moreover, sin must be punished—by death or by mental suffering. That punishment will come from the air above (though on one memorable occasion from poison taken inadvertently). Ford frequently dramatizes his terror through images that suggest the chief symptom of his illness—agoraphobia.

Our *locus classicus* is the frontispiece to *Ancient Lights*, the photograph of Madox Brown's doorway. It was there, in his grandfather's house, that Ford's "eyes first opened" to an unforgettable visual impression. He still remembers himself "as a very small boy, shuddering . . . upon the door-step at the thought that the great stone urn" sitting above the door on a stone shelf "the size and shape of a folio book, might fall upon me and crush me entirely out of existence" (AL, 2). Little Fordie, inadequately protected by a book-shaped stone, shrinks from going out into the London streets. The first recorded instance of Ford's agoraphobia was in Kensington, in March 1904, when he was physically unable to walk to the Thames to throw away Elsie's opal. This was also when he was writing *The Soul of London*, in which the typical Londoner sees himself as a child: "there will remain to him always an odd sensation of being very little, of peering round the corners of gray and gigantic buildings upon grayer vistas of buildings more gigantic" (4). The just-arrived provincial looks even more like little Ford: "He will stand perhaps . . . at his own doorstep, for a moment at a loss what to do. . . . He will not ever have been so alone" (7). Ford memorably pictures his Londoner "glancing aside in his moments of terror, of perplexity, of passion, of grief. . . . The square fronts of houses peep down on you as you run beneath; constant footbridges overhead . . . shudder and quiver. We, who are not made for strong impressions, are ourselves inclined to shudder . . . all the limitless stretches of roofs . . . the miles and miles of buildings, the myriads of plane-trees, of almonds, of elms—all these appalling regions of London . . . fuse in our minds into one cloud" (27, 58, 160).

It is in *The Heart of the Country* that Ford most movingly describes his agoraphobia, his depression, and his terror of judgment from above. He pretends he is talking about someone named Waring who inhabits a room of a laborer's cottage in a little village. The details obviously refer to Ford: a writer is trying unsuccessfully to work on his historical novel; he is overwhelmed by guilt and self-pity; he considers suicide, all this on a hot summer's night, in sheep country, far inland:

> He remembers it always as it was at night, with all the doors and windows open in a breathless June, and two candles burning motionlessly above white paper. The peculiar whimper of sheep bells comes always down the hill. . . . It was like . . . being hidden in a little lighted chamber of an immense cavern—a place deep down in the eternal blackness of the earth's centre.
> And, according to his view, no man in the world

was ever more terribly burdened with griefs of a hundred kinds. . . . at given moments the whole circle of his life may seem to crumble away and leave him naked beneath the pitiless stars. . . . At times the razor that lay on the shelf behind his back had the fascination of a lodestone, and on a hot, blazing moonlight night he would rush out from his room and wander, appalled and shaken, to the middle of the white silent village, with the thatches on the wall-tops silver, and the shadows vertical beneath the moon. (14-15)

For anyone who cares for Ford, the phrase that has to be heartbreaking is "naked beneath the pitiless stars." It reveals its full meaning later in the book in a passage more specifically agoraphobic. Ford is explaining how "no landscape is restful" to him "unless the horizon is somewhere broken into by the line of the sea." He then recurs to the earlier episode: "Far inland I seem to be beneath an impalpable weight, and on an absolutely naked down I am conscious of glancing round, in search of at least a clump of trees in which I might take refuge from the great gaze of the sky" (98-99).

These passages explain a good deal. They explain how a man with a passion for views can fear open and public places. To be outside, either in London or in the heart of the country, is for Ford to be trapped and alone. But to be able to see the pink cliffs of Boulogne is to have an escape hatch and a comforting, if distant, companion. To be outside and alone is to be vulnerable; it is to be exposed to the judgment of the "pitiless stars" and the "great gaze of the sky." Freud, who himself at a most creative period suffered from agoraphobia and required the traveling companionship of his sister-in-law, equates the sun with the father in his great study of Dr. Schreber. In Freud's case history of little Hans, the latter's fear of going out relates directly to fear of the father. Agoraphobia rarely, however, begins in childhood. Although its onset may be preceded by years of uneasiness about going out alone, the peak ages for first experiencing it are twenty and thirty (Ford was thirty). Interestingly, the large majority of agoraphobics are women. Yet we recall that, coincidentally with its onset, Ford was beginning his whitewash of Katharine Howard, his most sustained effort to enter a woman's point of view. Finally, according to some psychiatric studies, a majority of agoraphobics have suffered from childhood fears and night terrors.[33]

Ford memorably records such an episode and further describes his ailment in a Literary Portrait of 1914. Let this be our last symptom of poor Ford's mental distress. The incident occurred when he was nine, and he is convinced that it was the "most important" and "agonising event" of his life. "A muddle-headed, absent-minded child," he was "given to long reveries" during which he was unaware of what his hands were doing. One night in pitch darkness he found himself "sucking the end of a burnt match." Remembering that phosphorous was poisonous, he screamed

> for ages and ages, in a blackness that was palpable and stifling. . . . And I can say with absolute assurance, so as to form a document for educationists or psycho-therapeutists, that every fear of my life from that day has been that fear—and every mental agony that agony and no other. If I have committed unworthy actions, if I do now commit unworthy actions, it is, I am subconsciously but quite clearly aware, because I am afraid of that fear—that same fear—that day by day recurs to me.[34]

We can readily imagine why Ford at nine would have experienced a terrible dread of dying of poison. He would surely by then have picked up some notion of Lizzie Siddal's death and Rossetti's attempted suicide. At once blighting and fascinating would have been his grandfather's ceaseless mourning for his only son, dead of blood poisoning the year after Ford's birth: "so frail a thing is genius and so tenuous its hold upon existence" says the inscription for Oliver Madox Brown's photograph in *Ancient Lights*.

Before turning to Ford's efforts to cope with his fears, let us consider again the possible causes of his 1904 to 1906 breakdown. We have already speculated, on the basis of Olive's account of the period and of Mizener's discovery of the affair with Mary, that Ford's guilt at the failure of his marriage was a major cause. Although he would of course never say so explicitly, his poem to Elsie, "From Inland," written in Germany in 1904 about a tired, aged couple who will never again experience their early, happy love, certainly suggests a similar diagnosis. And his list of Waring's "griefs"—"hopeless passion . . . the disclosure of hidden baseness in himself, the consciousness of personal failure"—suggests that Ford thought at the time that sexual misconduct was part of the cause of his illness.

It was surely not the whole cause. The Garnetts and Conrad obviously thought the main source was Pinker's difficulty in placing Ford's manuscripts. Conrad alludes to Pinker in his letters to the ill Ford with the greatest delicacy. When *The Benefactor* is finally placed in January 1905, Olive reports Elsie "radiant"; when Ford's publishers engineer a "boom" in the spring, Edward, Olive, and Galsworthy are ecstatic. And Conrad writes from Montpellier (May 9, 1905): "Hurrah for *The Soul of London!*"[35]

But since we are taking seriously Ford's own views, let us consider his self-diagnosis in the Conrad book. There he says that "during the writing of *Nostromo* the continual weight of Conrad's depression broke the writer [Ford] down" (211-13). One evening, Conrad had made an impassioned statement to Ford about the writer's craft being a dog's life. You write and write, Conrad said, and no one understands, either what you're trying to say or how much blood and sweat you have put into the work. It's as if you had rowed about all your life in a huge river in dense fog. You row endlessly without ever seeing a signal light on the invisible banks to indicate whether you're going upstream or drifting with the current. You experience every kind of deprivation. And never in your life do you find one soul to tell you if you're the greatest genius in the world or if you're the most miserable hack (255-56).[36] A statement like that, coming from Conrad, *could* have broken Ford. The fears Conrad expresses, that no one will understand your most sincere, agonized literary efforts and that you will never know whether your work is really any good, are fears that, as Stella Bowen testifies, obsessed Ford his whole life.

But what has this to do with Francis Hueffer and the "extremely stupid donkey"? Everything. The muddled child moves about among giants who know how to make babies and other works of art. When the child tries to find out anything, he gets yelled at. (Ford would say something "in all innocence, but no doubt with stupidity. And then the floodgates of heaven would open.")[37] These giants dress him up and move him about for purposes totally incomprehensible to him. Events explode in his face; he does not know why. Sitting in the train compartment with Conrad and seeing they have arrived at Charing Cross, Ford touches Conrad's shoulder: " 'We're there!' Conrad's face was most extraordinary—suffused and madly vicious. He sprang to his feet and straight at the writer's throat . . ." (JC, 157). Ford is sitting in a music hall when "suddenly the large, respectable house appeared to go mad, and I asked my neighbour why he was excited. He said that the song was called 'Following the Something or Other,' but I could not catch what it was."[38] His father, in short, condemns him to life imprisonment within his skull; subsequent experience keeps confirming the sentence; and then the greatest living writer and Ford's dearest friend says in despair that you write and write and no one in the world understands.

Nevertheless, although "horror, despair and incessant striving are the lot" of man, each endures "them as a rule with commonsense and cheerfulness" (CW, 49). So Ford struggled with his solitude. He tried the two obvious solutions: first, to break out of his skull and achieve genuine communication with another human being; second, to escape—into his own imagination, or into oblivion, or into another's consciousness. Father said, "Speak up, Fordie," and he wanted to try. He seems particularly to have felt during the terrible years of 1904 to 1906 that suppression of self was the cause of his unhappiness and that it was a national disease. Suppression is indeed the central theme of *The Spirit of the People*, completed in the spring of 1906. Although England's greatness lies in its "rule of thumb system" whereby men can "live together in large masses," she has accomplished this only by means of a "ferocious lack of . . . that imagination which is insight." Because Englishmen feel very deeply, they take refuge in an "official optimism"; the whole nation appears "extraordinarily tongue-tied" (26, 28, 27, 144, 147). Ford's classic illustration is of course the germ for *The Good Soldier*, the story of the married couple—"good people"—and their young ward. The husband falls in love with her, the wife senses it, and the girl is sent off on a world cruise. Ford accompanies the ward and husband in the dogcart to the station, where, of course, nothing is said: "Miss W—— died at Brindisi on the voyage out, and P—— spent the next three years at various places on the Continent where nerve cures are attempted. . . . it seems to me," Ford comments, "that at that moment of separation a word or two might have saved the girl's life and the man's misery" (148, 150). Two questions suggest themselves. How? How would a few words have done anything to ameliorate hopeless passion? And, who? We shall probably never know. Elsie being in Rome, Ford was seeing a lot of the Marwoods while writing *The Spirit of the People*. Yet it is unlikely that he would use his new friends so blatantly and then give them a copy of the book. P——'s breakdown and cure to some extent recall Ford's. Still, since Ford is "so apt to identify myself with anyone's sufferings," we need only say that he feels very much in poor silent P——'s shoes.[39] Surely the longing for communication must have been one of the chief motives in his recurrent romances. "Every man or

every woman of the modern world has a certain number
. . . of passionate experiences. During those moments of
passion the man or the woman will be alive to the member
of the opposite sex who for the time being attracts him"
(WM, 36). The hitch here is "for the time being."

The other, more enduring route to communication
through social contacts lay for Ford in the founding of
literary schools. In one of the few optimistic passages in
Ancient Lights, he idealizes the relations among the Pre-
Raphaelites and lovingly describes old Madox Brown and
"Topsy" Morris coming together affectionately one last
time. Insofar as *Ancient Lights* is Ford's apology to Conrad
for botching the *English Review* and their friendship, the
book strongly implies Ford's noble purpose in founding
the magazine. Elsewhere he says explicitly its aim was to
encourage the formation of "a society of men eagerly discussing their Art, sinking personal jealousies . . . in the divine curiosity to discover how things are done" (CA, 48).
For Ford, "the pleasure of eternal technical discussion with
Conrad" was reason enough for continuing their collaboration (JC, 49).

But the most important way of communicating, and the
way that filled the two friends with despair, was of course
writing books. And though they despaired, they never
quit. Ford always said that to be a proper man you must
write a book. Writing books answered Father, too.
Whereas Madox Brown was eager for Ford to be an artist,
his dying father exhorted him never to write a book (AL,
156). Also, Ford's fantastic fecundity, in many genres, including his father's literary journalism, would be an answer to his father's "encyclopaedic mind." Ford was obviously delighted when Conrad, in his preface to *The Secret
Agent*, called Ford "omniscient" (JC, 229). Yet he could
have it both ways, be omniscient and still "have for facts a
most profound contempt" (AL, xv). Writing books, novels
especially, meant more than answering Father: it was the
most profound, the most personal form of communication.
Ford's whole effort was to devise a style that would have

the effect of being spoken into someone's ear. Every word he wrote after meeting Conrad was set down with the idea of reading it aloud to Conrad (JC, 203).

And yet for Ford neither the spoken nor the written forms of communication worked; neither love nor literature would break through the wall of solitary suffering. Mainly, he just tried to escape, chiefly into the world of his imagination. His favorite imaginative themes are familiar to us, and hardly exclusive to himself: nature, religion, romantic love, literary creation. Before the "threatening gleam" of young Fabian eyes, Ford "fled—into the country" (AL, 241). There he finds that "almost sublime forgetfulness of self that the Anglo-Saxon will feel when looking at animals, at flower-filled woods" (SP, 14). Alone in despair in Germany in 1904, he is "obsessed always with an intense longing to see once more the sails of ships above the sea wall, the wide stretch of land, the church spire of Lydd breaking the distant horizon" (SP, 172). We know from Olive that Ford "found poetry in" Roman Catholicism. Ford's most marvelous account of what religion does for him occurs in an important Literary Portrait of 1914 which has to do with, presumably, Marwood's mother's austere Anglicanism. As a contrast to her, and in order to express "pretty exactly what religion means for me," Ford quotes from a "friend, like myself, a German Papist, resident for many years in England." The language is Fordian; the "friend" was no doubt Ford. For him, religion is not at all austere; it is "a matter of little friendly quaintnesses and communications." Taking Holy Water is an "intimate satisfaction." The candles and the religious medals are "so 'freundlich'," the whole "business" is "so intimately childish and homelike. Yes, it is like going home." For Ford's Catholic friend, the world of religion is more real than his daily life. Packing his things for a journey, his mind is on going to the Cathedral chapel: "upon my soul, I was not in my dressing-room at that moment; I was in the rather dark chapel, with the candles burning and some people kneeling about, and I was standing and looking on . . ."[40]

Another avenue of imaginative escape was through romantic love. Although Ford sometimes sees love as communication, a moment of passion when one is particularly aware of someone of the opposite sex, the overriding purpose of each new romance is peace. And although Ford makes fun of the Pre-Raphaelite view of medieval love as "a great but rather sloppy passion" whose hell is "pleasant enough," still that view no doubt attracts him (AL, 62-63). Ford's wooing of Elsie was, as we have seen, very Pre-Raphaelite indeed. So, too, was " 'Du Bist die Ruh,' " his most devoted poem to her, published first in 1900 in *Poems for Pictures*, reprinted in 1907, but, significantly, never thereafter.

Finally, and most obviously Ford's imagination sought rest in the writing of books. If the novel was his instrument for showing where we stand, expressing his real self, or communicating with the beloved or Joseph Conrad, preeminently the novel was a means of escape. Until 1915, Ford was *always* writing novels, even if not publishing them. In his worst periods he was turning out stuff as good as *The Fifth Queen* and as thin as *The Young Lovell*. Besides being potboilers, the minor novels represent his necessary, regular, daily escapes behind protective fantasies—which is probably why they are no better than they are. Much as a landscape provides "a back cloth . . . an aching pageantry . . . to those whose thoughts centre upon themselves," so in despair Waring the writer would try to populate his room with imagined characters, "a whole galantry-show of kings and queens in mediaeval garnitures passing dimly from door to door" (HC, 104, 15). So, too, Ford must have put in many hours groping for *"le mot juste."* He pictures himself so engrossed in such activity that the news of his best friend's death can scarcely break through the wall. Ford was driving in an area of France reminiscent of Kent and asking himself how he would "render" the wheatfield he was passing through. Just so, many times in the past, he and Conrad would discuss the precise phrasing necessary to catch the wind blowing over wheat-fields, a most restful occupation. Ford continues thinking of wheat while buying train tickets, while buying the *Daily Mail*, and even while reading the words: "Sudden Death of Joseph Conrad." "Je m'occupais de la recherche des mots justes qui rendraient ces champs chuchotants et dorés. . . . Et j'entendis ma voix qui criait: à ma compagne: 'Look . . . Look . . . Regardez!' " (JC, 31-33, 254).

This episode dramatizes vividly the depth of Ford's reveries, but the escape is not total. The ultimate solution is to cease to be Ford. We have already seen how, from time to time, he came close enough to suicide to frighten the women who loved him. But sometimes oblivion seems to have come to Ford involuntarily, unbidden. Ford views cheerfully these strange psychic experiences; yet they seem terrifying, almost pathological. "The course of a life," he says, "becomes visible" only "in the marking time." And you realize this best when you are just standing and not thinking, looking down at the ceaseless traffic passing beneath your club window:

> You live only with your eyes, and they lull you. So Time becomes manifest like a slow pulse, the world stands still; a four-wheeler takes as it were two years to crawl from one lamp-post to another. . . . That is your deep and blessed leisure: the pause in the beat of the clock . . . (SL, 122-23)[41]

Ford relates a striking instance of this state of "suspension of the intellectual faculties" (SL, 123) to the time of his mental illness. The vividness of the image he paints recalls not only Pre-Raphaelite colors, but also those reported by people in psychotic, hypnotic, or hallucinogenic states. But again, the episode, by a window, was ultimately satisfying to Ford. "[P]assing through a period of extreme mental distress . . . for which there was no remedy," he had one day glimpsed through a window "a shape of an extremely vivid—but an incredibly vivid!—green." Its color transcended "any thinkable color . . . any green flame, any possible painted surface, and it was extremely clear and sharp in outline." It proved to be the underside of a parrot climbing a trellis. At the sight of it "an extraordinary calmness descended" on Ford's depression. It was, he says "like the end of the Church service when the clergyman says 'The peace of God which passes all understanding.' "[42]

A final way by which Ford achieved oblivion, escaped being Ford, was, almost literally, to become someone else and look at the world with someone else's eyes. The episode of this sort that seemed most important to him occurred in New York City in 1906, when he was still ill. It is important to us because of the light it sheds on both *The Good Soldier* and what Ford became subsequently. In *New York is Not America*, he tells of taking a walk from East Fourteenth Street down Fifth Avenue. In the course of that walk, he suddenly conceived a "half-philosophical, half-literary idea" that has since become the basis for his technique as a writer and the "mainspring" of his actions. One morning he was looking across the street at the deeply shadowed Flatiron Building and feeling intensely lonely. But then he "suddenly conjured up . . . the figure" of a friend who had been walking with him there a day or so before: "And it occurred to me suddenly to think how the imagination of that figure made the Flatiron live for me . . ." (85-86).[43] This experience is close to that of the hero of Dostoevsky's *The Double*. Mr. Golyadkin, walking the November night streets of St. Petersburg in despair, suddenly splits psychically, involuntarily creates a double to give himself company. Ford's New York experience resembles one he had in London, though on that occasion the helpful viewer was really there and did not have to be "conjured up." Ford is standing outside a bank, gazing down Pall Mall and "thinking nothing at all," when he is accosted by "an old, shrunken, wizened man. . . . in one tortured eye a round piece of dirty window-glass." Ford, of course, takes him for "an atrocious old usurer," and, of course, it is Conrad.

But, within three minutes, as he stood and talked, . . . the monocle sparkled like cut crystal, the eyes glowed. And, almost more wonderfully, Pall Mall became alive as we went towards the Bodega: it became alive as towns of the true belief awaken in the presence of the Prince of True Believers, come to saunter through his slave market. (JC, 238-39)

In *The Spirit of the People*, the last of the 1904-1906 trilogy, Ford suggests what must have been his response to getting caught with Mary Martindale: "if you catch an Englishman, or if . . . he catches himself, in an act of meanness. . . . He will protest, and it will be true: 'This is not the real I' " (158-59).[44] Perhaps this, too, contributed to his impulse to exist in another person. The point is that poor Ford the impressionist, constrained by the sense of his own unworthiness, could not see. Without seeing, how could he render? Until Conrad appeared, he could not see Pall Mall. Until he conjured up the figure of a friend, he could scarcely see across Fifth Avenue. Using this method, he split into Dowell, a fictive person who he could really be, and thus wrote a great novel. Shortly thereafter he split into Marwood, a real, if dead, person, who he could never be. Since the strategy probably saved Ford's life, who can blame him? Yet becoming Marwood meant for Ford writing no other *Good Soldier*.

IMPRESSIONISTIC TECHNIQUES

Before turning to *The Good Soldier*, let us remind ourselves of some of the techniques Conrad and Ford devised or emphasized. As early as 1903, in his preface to Elsie's translations of de Maupassant, Ford calls "interest . . . the supreme, . . . the indispensable, quality of all art."[45] In the Conrad book, Ford says further that the one quality which gives "interest to Art" is "surprise" (JC, 189).[46] "Surprise" almost sums up Ford's view of experience. Seeing few connections between phenomena, and being perpetually absorbed in reverie, he finds every stimulus from the external world surprising. He yokes the notions of interest and surprise to most of the impressionist techniques particularly relevant to *The Good Soldier*.[47] The writer awakens interest through surprise chiefly by means of contrast: "actual contrasts vividly presented. This is what gives interest . . ." (SL, xv). And contrast is best achieved through that "unchronological" structuring Conrad devised for *Lord Jim* (JC, 99). Beyond the fact that, for Ford, disordered chronology is true to the way the mind works, the method has two other advantages. It involves "the reader amongst the personages of the story," makes the reader believe "that he is present at an affair in real life"; and it permits exciting and meaningful juxtapositions, what Ford calls "superimposed emotions" (CW, 43, 41).

But sometimes it is "concrete pictures" that inspire interest and surprise. In the de Maupassant preface Ford says that "The only thing of value is the concrete fact," and that only because it gives form to what is going on in the mind. But the sad truth is that Ford is seldom strikingly concrete. In talking about *Romance*, in 1911, he shows, with touching modesty and accuracy, "Conrad's desire for actualities, for hard and characteristic phrases set against his collaborator's more vague personality."[48] Only in *The Good Soldier* and sporadically in *Parade's End* does Ford's fictional presentation of concrete instances truly succeed.

One aspect of literary technique Ford absolves from the requirement of surprise: style, or language. For Ford, the ideal style is unnoticeable, as he likes himself "to pass unnoticed in the crowd."[49] His ideal book, we recall, is one the reader is not aware of reading, an impossibility if the style calls attention to itself. He and Conrad were after the "right" word. "Not the precious word; not even the startlingly real word. . . . *Too* startling words . . . are apt in the long run to be . . . fatiguing" (JC, 105, 193). The best style, the least obtrusive language, is that which is spoken. Thus Ford and Conrad wrote in "the language that we employed in talking the one to the other" (JC, 196). But in fact, Conrad, one of the great stylists in English, uses language far more heightened than Ford's dictum would permit, though less recherché than that of Conrad's greatest disciple, Faulkner.[50] Ford seems to sense this, pays tribute to Conrad's burning phrases, and permits the words "serene" and "azure" (albeit "a shade *chargés*") to remain in a glorious passage in "Youth" (JC, 99, 160-63).

By and large Ford succeeds in achieving a style free of characteristic quirks and oddities. I notice only two, both intimately related to his view of reality. If life is one blessed (or damned) thing after another, then one is overwhelmed, like Henry Adams, by multiplicity. Ford's style, far more than James's even, is studded with successions of odd plurals (e.g., "finenesses," "meannesses," "wrong-headednesses," "smoothnesses," "knowledges," "oddnesses," "charlatanries" [SP, 45; HJ, 33, 36, 126, 137]). The other striking oddity is the locution that makes him a passive object rather than an active agent, always acted upon, the battered recipient of impressions he does not want.

But Ford is not merely passive, and Ford strikes back, using the impressionist's ultimate weapon—exaggeration. By 1909, he has come to see this device, as much as contrast and concreteness, as a chief means of creating interest: "The first business of the author is to interest; his instrument wherewith he interests us is his exaggeration" (CA, 38).[51] Elsewhere, Ford makes clearer that by exaggeration he means the expression of the artist's personality: "The province of the imaginative writer is by exaggeration due to his particular character—by characteristic exaggeration, in fact—precisely to awaken thought" (CA, 32). In short, "exaggeration" takes us back one more time to his consistently subjective critical stance. As everyone knows who has read much Ford, exaggeration is endemic, and it is a problem. His journalism abounds in notable firsts, striking superlatives, absolutes both positive and negative—many of them quite unconvincing. When Ford owns up to conscious exaggeration, one does not know

whether to be grateful for his candor or to wonder how
many conscious exaggerations he has not owned up to, to
wonder how often he has been deliberately fooling us.

We have seen recurring in Ford's fiction the notion of the
artist as trickster. This is particularly the impression that
Gubb, in *The Simple Life Limited*, gives, up there juggling
before a hostile crowd. The idea recurs in Ford's criticism,
too. In the book on the Pre-Raphaelites, Ford equates "skill
in rendering" with "that subtle trickery of the beholder
into an oblivion of himself that is art" (31). Reviewing
some plays by Lord Dunsany, Ford pays tribute to "the
greatness of his particular conjuring trick." Ford uses the
same key word, but in a different figure when he compares
"laying out a novel" to planning the strategy of a bridge
hand after the dummy's cards are on the table: "every
word in a novel should help the story forward towards the
taking of that last trick which is your final effect."[52]

Finally, the "trick" brings us to still another metaphor
for technique, and the ultimate problem in Ford. The task
of Art, he says, is to bring persons into contact with one
another. The artist, then, is the "eternal mental prostitute"
who cries out in the marketplace: "Come into contact with
my thought, with my visions, with the sweet sounds that I
cause to arise—with my personality" (CA, 64). Is Ford pursuing this last metaphor when he later calls the art of in-
troducing a fictional character "the seductive occupation"?
He goes on to say that "what the artist needs is the man
with the quite virgin mind."

> To him, then, you will address your picture, your
> poem, your prose story, or your argument. You will
> seek to capture his interest; you will seek to hold his
> interest. You will do this by methods of surprise, of
> fatigue, by passages of sweetness in your language, by
> passages suggesting the sudden and brutal shock of
> suicide. You will give him passages of dulness, so that
> your bright effects may seem more bright; you will al-
> ternate, you will dwell for a long time upon an inti-

mate point; you will seek to exasperate so that you may the better enchant. You will, in short, employ all the devices of the prostitute. (CW, 39, 53, 54)[53]

This charming passage, vintage Ford, dramatizes beautifully the seductiveness of impressionistic fiction at its greatest. Yet, is it stuffy to regret the last word? Wouldn't "lover" be better? For by definition the virgin reader is a virgin only once. And if the seduction does not include a genuine longing for love, what is left after the deflowering? "Prostitute" does not adequately describe the best Ford, although maybe "seducer" does.

The impressionist wishes to foster his "reader's illusion that he is present at an affair in real life" (CW, 43). By "affair," Ford means "a parcel of life" involving "several human beings," as opposed to the huge casts of *Bleak House* or *Middlemarch* (CA, 89).[54] In this sense, "affair" applies to Conrad's fictions. For James, as for Flaubert and Ford, the affair is also usually the subject, a love affair. For Ford, the metaphor has a third meaning. He intends always to re-woo Conrad, and often to woo some woman: Elsie, Mary, Violet, Brigit, others. But it is while writing *The Good Soldier* that he bids "adieu" to creative writing not only because writing up to his "own standards is such an intolerable labour," but also because it is "such a thankless job, since it can't give me the one thing in the world that I desire" (CW, 46).

For the artist who would seduce his reader, "the whole of Art consists in selection" (JC, 182). But does the artist simply select any fact to make his effect, or must that fact be consistent with his fictive world? For Ford, "Truth is relative." But "relative" is different from "selective." Ford, when "on his high horse," ready to call Conrad a Jew or to say that a book of his has sold 12,000 (instead of 1,200) copies, is untrue to his passion for truth.[55]

In 1914 Ford writes that "none but a man with the seeds of lunacy in him can write" and that "no one who was not a little mad would seek to write an individual book."[56] He was a little mad—in his fiction, in the way he remembered things, in the acts of everyday life. To a young friend Edward Shanks, as to Pound, Ford "*was* a problem, and one which he was the last person to solve. How could he, indeed? He did not know from minute to minute who he was. . . ." Fond as Shanks was of Ford, he found his behavior sometimes "frightening." Once they were walking through a Sussex field discussing poetry when suddenly, à propos of nothing, Ford struck from Shanks's hand a wild mushroom he was about to eat. Shanks might—Ford said—have caught . . . "anthrax." "When we had gone a little further he spoke again, solemnly: 'There is only one thing I am more afraid of than anthrax and that is being savaged by a stallion.' This completely dumbfounded me and we walked on in silence . . ."[57] Stallions, of course, rage through Ford's prose, most notably in *Ladies Whose Bright Eyes*; and the anthrax recalls little Fordie sucking on the burnt match, Uncle Nolly's death by blood poisoning, Lizzie's laudanum. But what of the suddenly striking hand? Was this a Fordian "surprise," to "interest" Shanks? Or was Ford "really" afraid Shanks would catch anthrax? Probably Ford himself did not know, just "found" his hand swinging. The real question is this: could an agoraphobic, neurasthenic, impressionistic solipsist—with, surely, a schizoid personality—write a great novel? It seems unlikely—except that Ford did it.

THE GOOD SOLDIER AS IMPRESSIONISM

Ford initially entitled *The Good Soldier* "The Saddest Story"; he could almost have called it "The Strangest Story" because it is not only one of the grimmest but also one of the most mysterious of modern novels. Its strangeness comes both from the melodramatic story and from the odd way the odd narrator tells it. Yet for all that strangeness, *The Good Soldier* is an eminently accessible work; it deals with that most human of endeavors—trying to *know*—and with those most human of emotions—passion and friendship.

The Good Soldier certainly is "The Saddest Story." Five of its six characters are destroyed, and under rather un-glamorous circumstances. Little Maisie Maidan's heart simply stops when she learns that Edward Ashburnham now loves Florence Dowell. Precisely nine years later, Florence takes poison in her hotel room, because Edward now loves Nancy Rufford. When Edward realizes he can never have Nancy, he cuts his throat in his stable. Then when Nancy, en route to India, hears of Edward's death, she goes quietly, permanently, mad. Henceforth, she never speaks except to say "Shuttlecocks!" and to aver, in Latin, that she believes in one Omnipotent Deity. Her lover-caretaker is John Dowell, once Florence's deceived husband. He never slept with Florence because she pre-tended to a heart too fragile for sexual activity. Only Ed-ward's widow Leonora Ashburnham thrives, being in the end happily remarried and pregnant.

Thus, *The Good Soldier* is a strange as well as a sad tale. The reader is asked to believe that the narrator, John Dow-ell, an American millionaire, could accept for a dozen years his wife's alleged illness and an unconsummated union; could fail to notice her passionate affair with his best friend, Edward, although Edward's wife sees through it immediately; could continue to love the memory of Ed-ward even after learning that Edward has cuckolded him and that he has driven Florence to suicide and their be-loved Nancy to madness. As strange as the events Dowell relates is the tone of voice in which he tells them. That tone is an almost indescribable combination of irony, sentimen-tality, cynicism, and bafflement. So peculiar is *The Good Soldier* that many readers have seen the whole thing as some sort of put-on, with Ford laughing at his bumbling narrator and wanting us to do the same. The exact nature of Ford's conscious intentions is probably irrecoverable. My own belief is that he deeply sympathized with Dowell.

To stress too heavily the book's undoubtedly comic element is to miss its greatness.[58]

To anyone steeped in the early writings of Ford Madox Ford, *The Good Soldier* is overpoweringly Fordian. This is as Ford wants it: "The Impressionist author['s] . . . whole book, his whole poem, is merely an expression of his personality" (CW, 43). Take the famous first sentence: "This is the saddest story I have ever heard." The sadness is Fordian; the superlative is Fordian; a heard story is the proper subject for a novel. And finally, although the "I" of that first sentence proves to have been very much a participant in the events, his sense of the gulf between himself and external reality is so profound that his own life is as remote from himself as is a heard story.

Dowell's is incomparably the best narrative voice Ford ever found, and it is so, partly at least, because it is so Conradian. Although Ford admitted to writing some Jamesian pastiches, and although *The Good Soldier*'s quartet recalls that of *The Golden Bowl*, Ford was able, at last, to put everything he had learned about writing from Conrad into *The Good Soldier*. Dowell is as close to Marlow as Ford could ever get; he partakes of all four versions of Marlow. Dowell's years with his wife and the Ashburnhams prove ultimately as devastatingly enlightening to him as Marlow's trip to the Congo to him. Before Marlow embarked on his voyage of discovery, he was like "a silly little bird."[59] Dowell says that he himself was simply a fool. However, the contrast between the narrator's pre- and post-enlightenment phases is endemic to *The Good Soldier* as it is not to "Heart of Darkness." In the recurrent juxtaposition of an older, wiser Dowell with a young, naive one, we can see a trace of the relationship between old and young Marlow in "Youth." Old Marlow recounts in amazement how his younger self foolishly leapt into a smoking hold, promptly fainted, and was fished out with a boat hook. Dowell's tone is similar as he recalls how, on the night he eloped with Florence, he went up and down the ladder to her bedroom window "like a tranquil jumping jack" (98).

Dowell's choice of a hero is Marlovian as well. Like Jim, Edward is a big, blond, handsome, likeable, inarticulate Englishman with considerable skill in the service-profession he espouses, and with a subtle unsoundness not at all apparent to strangers. But whereas Jim's plague spot relates, tragically, to his professional performance, Edward's does not. On the other hand, Edward's overwhelming need to comfort a mournful female recalls Marlow's last subject, Captain Anthony of *Chance* and his Flora.

It surely goes without saying that Dowell especially resembles Marlow as a master (for the first time in Ford's career) of what Ford considered Conrad's greatest literary forte, the "architectonics" of the impressionistic novel (JC, 169). And so Dowell, in true Conradian style, gets in his strong first impression of Edward in the hotel dining room, especially as to the significant expression in the eyes, and then works backward and forward in time. Both narrators handle the reader's feelings with such consummate skill that the main, titular character, who has acted in some respects like a villain, proves ultimately sympathetic, even heroic, if ambiguously, suicidally so. Dowell, again like Marlow, handles masterfully the meaningful, illustrative digression. His apparently mindless tale of La Louve and her troubadour prepares us for himself as complacent husband, Florence as witch, and Ashburnham as victim with his flesh ultimately hanging from him like rags. Similarly, the digressive account of Nancy's wretched childhood, when her father accidentally knocked her unconscious, looks forward to her final senseless state.

Dowell is also Conradian in his beautifully flexible management of the chapter unit.[60] The first chapter of *The Good Soldier*'s third part looks to be wholly about the fact and circumstances of Florence's suicide. Indeed, the first eight pages (123-31) do stick to that. But Dowell must try to imagine what Florence heard Edward say to Nancy that made Florence run back to the hotel and take poison. Thus, from pages 131 to 137, Dowell talks about Edward's feelings for Nancy at that moment, Nancy's for Edward, and Dowell's own ideas about what makes a man fall in love. For those seven pages Florence is out of it, and Dowell returns to her with reluctance. He talks so desultorily about her and himself for four pages that one readily accepts his extraordinary insistence (141, 142) that Florence ceased to exist for him, that he never thought again of her. The last two pages of the chapter change the subject again, to Dowell's feeling for Nancy, with which the chapter began.

In more modest ways Dowell reflects Conrad's structuring skill. One of the great moments in *The Nigger of the "Narcissus"* is the philosophical paragraph opening Chapter Four (beginning "On men reprieved by its disdainful mercy, the immortal sea . . ."). As Albert J. Guerard has brilliantly shown, not only is the paragraph rich in meaning, but it carries the reader through the difficult transition from Singleton's heroic steering during the storm to the otherwise inevitably anticlimactic account of cleaning up the ship.[61] Similarly, Dowell opens the fourth chapter of Part III with an important digressive paragraph on why he calls his the saddest story rather than a tragedy. Not only does this passage point up Dowell's central notion of his characters drifting volitionlessly, it also manages the transition from Edward's almost farcical encounter with La Dolciquita to the more serious business of Leonora's takeover of his estate and his touching love affair with Mrs. Basil. That Ford was thinking of Conrad's *"Narcissus"* paragraph while writing *The Good Soldier* is suggested later by Dowell's phrase "dreary succession of days" (226) echoing Conrad's "weary succession of nights and days."

Finally, Dowell recalls Marlow in his propensity to talk about how difficult it is to fulfill their common purpose to make the reader see, and about how hard the impressionistic method really is. "I am, at any rate, trying to get you to see what sort of life it was I led with Florence," he says early in the novel (19). He admits elsewhere that he doesn't know the best way to put the story down (17). Like Marlow in *Chance*, he acknowledges that his rambling method may make it difficult for someone to find his way "through what may be a sort of maze" (213). Nevertheless, Dowell, like Marlow, insists upon the unquestionable, literal truth of his tale: "I console myself with thinking that this is a real story and that, after all, real stories are probably told best in the way a person telling a story would tell them" (213). When he unintentionally gives a misleading impression, he endeavors to correct it (103). He is scrupulous when he is not sure: "I said to her something like—" (80). And he refuses to go beyond the strict confines of his own evidence: Leonora "probably said a good deal more to Edward than I have been able to report; but that is all that she has told me and I am not going to make up speeches" (245).

One fundamental, technical difference between Dowell's tale and the tales told by Marlow forcibly reminds us how Fordian a narrator Dowell is. Although Dowell tells the reader to pretend that they are spending a fortnight together in a cottage by the sea and that he is talking, in a low voice, to his sympathetic auditor, all this is emphatically pretense. Dowell is not talking: he is "really" writing down this sad story, and over a period of two years. The closest Marlow comes to written narration is the account of Jim's last days that he mails to his privileged listener. The difference is crucial because it allows Ford to give full rein to his solipsistic beliefs (Dowell is really writing only to himself) and to his devastating tendency to change his mind. Although Marlow's attitude always includes bewilderment, although "Heart of Darkness" and *Chance* are unique narratives inspired by special circumstances rather than frequently told yarns, and although Marlow's narratives are characteristically "inconclusive," one never has the sense that Marlow would change events or his attitude. But as Dowell writes, he comes to dislike Leonora, for whom he earlier would have given his life. Again, as Dowell writes, he suddenly sees events very differently from his earlier recollection of them. His impression at one time is that during their married years Florence was never out of his sight. The method is congenial to Ford and provides excuses for apparent errors and inconsistencies. On the other hand, it is a common experience suddenly to remember correctly something one has misremembered; it is not unknown to change one's attitude toward a friend and to harden one's heart even more against an enemy.

Marlow's auditors in "Heart of Darkness" exist as real presences who may, if they wish, talk back; Dowell's auditor is imaginary and therefore mute: "listener . . . you are so silent" (19). Interestingly enough, whereas Marlow can recount long, complicated conversations, Dowell sticks to Ford's dictum that since one cannot, in reality, precisely remember long speeches, one should never quote more than a couple of lines (JC, 186). Most significantly, Dowell gives us virtually nothing from his all-night-long conversation with Edward. Yet, since Dowell supposedly loves Edward more than anyone in the world, that night must have been a great event in his life.

Dowell differs from Marlow in one last, important way. Ford said that it was all right for a novelist to "create himself" if, in so doing, he would present himself as imperfect, "as benevolent but meddlesome, fine yet malicious, generous but naturally unsound" (CA, 34). Clearly Ford has in mind a character very different from Marlow, who is not only Conrad (albeit Anglicized) but also, despite his many claims to self-doubt, as perfect, in Conrad's terms, as anyone could hope to be. Dowell would seem to fit Ford's prescription of the author's self with many imperfections. In choosing Dowell to be his eyes and voice, Ford chose a man who would try to tell what he saw but who, like Ford, saw badly; who admired passionate creatures as Ford admired Conrad's passion (JC, 20) and yet himself feared intense feeling; who nevertheless was human and thus inevitably involved in suffering. To the extent that he can, Dowell suffers, his mind circling "in a weary, baffled space of pain" (267). Blind as he has been and perhaps still is, he has seen agony great enough to drive people he loves to madness and suicide. Dowell's conviction of the meaninglessness of existence is even more desperate than Marlow's. For the latter, Jim's dilemma has fascinating ethical and metaphysical implications for all men that make his story worth telling again and again. But characteristically of Ford, Dowell is unsure whether other people's lives are at all like the lives of those good people the Ashburnhams and the Dowells. His ostensible purpose in telling the tale is not to understand it but to get it out of his head.

Such a notion has more to do, of course, with Ford the human being than with Ford the craftsman. Let us then turn from Dowell in his strictly technical function to Dowell as a profoundly human character in the novel. As the sole source of knowledge, Dowell is only too Fordian in his carelessness and inconsistency; as a painter of scenes, he is predominantly Pre-Raphaelite, with more than a touch of nocturnal terror and agonized agoraphobia. Embracing, overriding all aspects, remains Dowell the Fordian impressionist, desperate solipsist, hopeless epistemologist.

In talking of Dowell as an effective, humanly moving Fordian figure, we might as well grant at the outset that he contains (how could he escape it?) a measure of "the bad Ford." By this I mean the Ford with a godlike power over dates, a megalomanic disregard for facts, a self-destructive contempt for his own works of art. Dowell's most notorious carelessness is with the most important date in the novel (and maybe in Ford's life), August 4, 1904. This date obviously gave Ford trouble during the writing. In the manuscript he used instead July 1906.[62] Both dates were the occasions for Ford of traumatic trips to Germany: in 1904, he was shipped off in a state of despair and near-madness to seek mental health in German spas; in 1906, after some five months of separation from Elsie, when his "domestic affairs" in Jessie's words "were not exactly to his liking,"[63] he took their daughters to Elsie in Germany for their reception into the Roman Church, after which he and Elsie went to America. But also, that later date, the one Ford first lit on for his saddest story, is the time, as we

know, of Ford's first recorded connection with the Marwoods, the time also of his collaboration with Conrad on
that strange prefiguration of *The Good Soldier*, *The Nature of
a Crime*, and the time finally, according to Jessie, when he
introduced Marwood to the Conrads. Clearly, his two
dearest male friends and his terrible breakdown were in
the forefront of his mind as he wrote *The Good Soldier*. In
the novel, August 4, 1904 is the date both of the two
couples' trip to M—— and of Maisie Maidan's death (78,
91). It is also, and impossibly, the day when the Ashburnhams arrive in Nauheim with Maisie and first meet
the Dowells—impossible because the couples meet at the
evening meal whereas the trip to M—— occurs in the afternoon (50) and Florence planned it "some days before"
(49). Indeed, the Dowells knew the Ashburnhams and
Maisie for a month before their trip and her death (217-19).
Similar chronological confusion attends Edward's death.
The fatal night when Leonora comes into Nancy's bedroom is that of November 12 (256); the following morning
Edward cables Dowell to come to them from America
(266). A fortnight passes between his arrival and Nancy's
departure for India (280). Sufficient time passes after that
for Edward to get the gardener's daughter off for murder-
ing her baby, to hunt twice, and to give two political addresses (289). Then Nancy's fatal telegram arrives from
Brindisi and precipitates Edward's suicide. Ten days later,
that is, mid-December at the earliest, Dowell begins to
learn the truth from Leonora "of a windy November evening" (124). And yet, earlier in the novel, Ford has Dowell
be present the night that Leonora goes into Nancy's bedroom (233).

Other inconsistencies are also associated with the idea of
death. After Dowell sees Florence run by and hears from
Bagshawe of her affair with Jimmie, how long does he sit
in the hotel lounge chair before going up to find her dead?
Sometimes, he thinks he went up "immediately afterwards" (127) and thus "do[es]n't know how Florence had
time to write to her aunt" (229). Yet, in his first account, he

went up "a long time afterwards" (119). If he had "run up sooner," he "might have prevented her" (142). Dowell's references to Nancy are almost as mysterious. In Part I, his vision of judgment shows Edward and Nancy in a close embrace, with Florence dangling alone (82-83). The clear implication is that all three are dead. Not until the second chapter of Part IV do we realize that Nancy would be much better off "if she were dead" (238). The precise circumstances of Edward's last minutes are mysterious too. On page 282, Dowell implies that he and Edward discussed Nancy's awful telegram. Yet eleven pages later, Dowell reports that Edward merely "whispered something that [characteristically] I did not catch," took out the penknife, told Dowell to take the wire to Leonora, and said he needed "a bit of a rest" (293-94).

What sort of artist, what sort of fanatic for *le mot juste*, would permit these distracting contradictions? Perhaps, for biographical reasons, these deaths caused Ford extreme anxiety. Perhaps, in his megalomania, he thought that his reader, the man of good will with the perpetually virginal mind, would swallow anything. Perhaps, in his self-doubts and despite the many verbal changes in the manuscript, he could not bear to recheck with meticulous care the facts of this affair. A remark in his early *Pre-Raphaelite Brotherhood* on the artist's difficulty in evolving and sticking to the rules of his art may help to explain Ford's characteristic revulsion from thinking about a completed novel:

> It is as if one should with infinite care in the placing of each card build up a tall card-house, and then cry out that the only way to build a house of cards is to shake the table and begin in quite another way—because one is sick and tired of the house once it is built. (31)

Still another reason suggests itself, especially in the instance of Edward's death. Since Ford has earlier had Dowell mention Edward's comments about Nancy's wire, perhaps Ford assumes the reader will recall these comments even though Dowell omits them on the last page.

"Sometimes," Ford says in the Conrad book, "to render anything at all in a given space will take up too much room—even to render the effect and delivery of a speech" (JC, 184). The problem with justification, Ford says, is that the writer must handle it so carefully that it does not delay the action of a story (JC, 207). Sensible as is Ford's conviction that any rule can be overthrown in order either to achieve a necessary effect or to get on with the tale, it has, I suspect, a deeply personal aspect. Central to Ford's creativity is the need to get rid of or to suppress an emotion. Sometimes, in his anxiety, he probably needs to fill in as quickly as possible those chinks in the wattle-wall of his imagination so as to block out for a while the perpetual assaults of a threatening reality.

We would do well, however, not to pounce too greedily upon Ford's carelessness. Mizener has shown that Dowell's apparent inconsistency in discussing Edward's pigskin cases dramatizes the important differences between Dowell's original sense of Edward and his sense of him after his death, which deepens even as Dowell writes.[64] Another, far more disconcerting instance of apparent inconsistency appears in Dowell's two presentations of Nancy offering herself to Edward, at night, by his bed. The first implies that Nancy's motive is sympathy: "You have to imagine her . . . suddenly offering herself to him—to save his reason!" (233-34). Presumably at the time of writing this, Dowell has known, for six months, from Edward and Leonora, that Nancy "desired to see Edward suffer" (274). Yet Dowell does not explicitly say this for over forty pages. Four pages after that he offers his second version:

> I have told you that the girl came one night to his room. And that was the real hell for him. . . . she looked at him with her straight eyes of an unflinching cruelty and she said: "I am ready to belong to you—to save your life." (278)

Ford's purpose is, of course, *progression d'effet*, a climax of horrors ending with Edward's quite small penknife. Yet our inconsistency has genuine meaning. Eighteen months have passed. Dowell now sees Nancy totally mad, and Leonora estranged from her past with Edward and from Nancy and Dowell. The appalling intensity of the two women's feelings is now fully evident to Dowell, as it was not quite at the time of the first telling.

If Dowell is, for better as well as for worse, a Fordian teller of tales, he is also very much a Fordian viewer of scenes and maker of images. Dowell contains a large measure of the Pre-Raphaelite: he longs for the unattainable; he sees things in bright, intense colors; his vision includes the grotesque, at once comic and terrifying. These qualities derive, no doubt, both from Ford's artistic heritage and from his tortured psyche. Dowell's hopeless Pre-Raphaelite longing for the ideal, for the "terrestrial paradise," hardly needs documentation (273). His most extended and serene description, the famous view from the train window on the trip to M——, is explicitly Pre-Raphaelite. The moment is propitious for such a vision because he is "off duty" and "out for enjoyment" (51). The scene recalls Ford's memory in the Conrad book of their early years together "as a time of great tranquillity" like "the surface of an old bright painting" (JC, 52).[65] It recalls Ford's summary of the Pre-Raphaelites as succeeding "very miraculously in rendering a very charming, a very tranquil, and a very secure England" (PRB, 164). The German countryside, with its greens and reds and emeralds and purples, and with its peasant women in native dress, specifically recalls what Ford is seeing from a German train in *Ancient Lights* when he learns of the death of Holman Hunt: "It was—and the words came to my lips at the very moment—too brave, too Pre-Raphaelite!" (209-10). Of course, Dowell's "little mounds of hay that will be grey-green on the sunny side and purple in the shadows" (50) go much farther back, to the note Madox Brown wrote about painting *The Hayfield* (FMB, 102).

But at the same time, Dowell's Pre-Raphaelite eye records the comic aspects of things. He bursts out laughing when he sees from the window "a brown cow hitch its horns under the stomach of a black and white animal" and throw it neatly into a small stream (50). The episode has its appropriateness. An apparent digression, it prepares for the next scene in which the Florence-cow lays her finger on Edward's wrist and thus metaphorically tosses the Leonora-cow right down the stairs. That battle of the cows as seen from a train window is characteristically Fordian. The beginnings of both *Ladies Whose Bright Eyes* and *Some Do Not* feature tranquil heroes traveling unconsciously toward scenes of sexual suffering. But the episode is Pre-Raphaelite too. In his solemn youth, Ford did not know what to do with his grandfather's use of occasional exaggeration and comic grotesquerie. By the time he wrote of these in *Rossetti*, he was becoming more tolerant. By *The Good Soldier*, he was doing it superbly himself.

In praising Rossetti's *Wedding of St. George*, Ford does not point to the wealth of the bride's thick hair falling forward to ensnare St. George, but he rightly contrasts her reality "with a quite idealised Italian-mediaeval golden Knight; . . . and with a deliberately humorous dragon's head sticking out of a box" (92-93). The dragon's charming toothy grin, lolling tongue, and devilish eye suggest that St. George has fallen into a woman trap. This of course is what happens to Edward and to such an innocent bystander as Maisie Maidan: "She had died so grotesquely that her little body had fallen forward into the trunk . . . like the jaws of a gigantic alligator" (88). If Dowell gives Maisie a grotesquely comic death, he nevertheless provides her with a lovely Pre-Raphaelite farewell, as pretty as Millais' *Ophelia*, picturing Lizzie Siddal lying in the bright water, the flowers in her hand reaching her shoulder and flowers hanging over her as well (PRB, 107, 122).

> I saw her, with the long lashes on the cheeks, with the smile about the lips, with the flowers all about her. The stem of a white lily rested in her hand so that the spike of flowers was upon her shoulder. She looked

like a bride in the sunlight of the mortuary candles . . .
(88)

Moreover, Dowell's equation of the nuns' coifs to swans is
appropriate in a general way to Ophelia's watery grave.[66]
But who operates those alligator jaws that deal so cruelly
with little Maisie Maidan? Florence, of course, even
though Leonora insists on sharing the blame. With her
complacent foolish husband, with a lover she will soon be
treating hellishly, Florence is clearly La Louve who gets
her poor troubadour "torn with fangs" (21). Leonora
proves to be a different kind of killer. Although equated
with a cat (to Edward's pigeon, 153), and a "hungry dog"
(to Edward's lamb, 263), Leonora is most memorably depicted as a whipper. In a rage she boxes Maisie's ears (62).
She would have liked, Dowell tells us, "to bring her
riding-whip down on Nancy's young face . . . cut deep into
the flesh and . . . leave a lasting wheal" (242). Simultaneously, Leonora is "lashing, like a cold fiend, into the unfortunate Edward" (243). She trains Nancy to the same
trade, and "those two women" flay "the skin off him as if
they had done it with whips" (274-75).

And what images does Dowell provide for the men?
Male sexuality is here, as elsewhere in Ford (to say nothing
of D. H. Lawrence), associated with horses. Edward is
surely the "proper man . . . a raging stallion forever neigh-
ing after his neighbour's womenkind" (16). The reason for
Edward's "heart" is "approximately, polo" (8). The image
is contextually appropriate. The first time Edward sees
Florence, his eyes have the "challenging look" Dowell will
notice again at a polo match when Edward gets the ball
away from Count Lelöffel as neatly as he gets Florence
away from Dowell (36). Yet, Edward proves not to be a
stallion after all, and the novel's only truly successful sexual man turns out to be Rodney Bayham, "rather like a
rabbit" (274).

Besides observing brilliant set pieces reminiscent of
Holman Hunt, Madox Brown, Rossetti, and Millais, Dow-

ell's Pre-Raphaelite eye shows in small ways. He likes in general to render vivid colors: Edward's hair, "golden and perfectly brushed"; his eyes, "blue as the sides of a certain type of box of matches"; his complexion, "brick dust red"; the eyes thus looking "like a mosaic of blue porcelain set in pink china" (35, 293). Dowell's most vivid recollection of the night of Forence's death is the "pinkish effulgence from the electric-lamps in the hotel lounge" (127). His account of Florence's first lover calls to notice Jimmie's six gold teeth (105-106).

In his attention to minutiae, Dowell is also Pre-Raphaelite. Leonora's lines conduct his gaze to her wrist and "a gold circlet with a little chain supporting a very small golden key to a dispatch box. Perhaps it was that in which she locked up her heart and her feelings" (39-40). Dowell's propensity to fix upon tiny concrete instances prevents any suspicion of Florence's suicide; seeing the flask of nitrate of amyl clutched in her hand, he seizes at once on the notion of heart failure: "In such circumstances of clamour, of outcry . . . it is some little material object, always, that catches the eye and that appeals to the imagination" (126-27). Remembering that Leonora's key, caught in Maisie's hair, attracted Florence's attention and caused all the trouble, and that Florence's bottle freed both men fatally to love Nancy, a Freudian would probably call both killers phallic women.[67] Or, at least, the similarity of the details and their explicit relation to the two women's hearts suggest their impenetrability to Dowell's understanding: "Ah, [Florence] was a riddle; but then, all other women are riddles" (29). But chiefly, much as Dowell's brain likes to count steps to fend off chaos, so his eyes, especially at moments of crisis, positively leap to distractions.

If, then, some of the most vivid visual images in *The Good Soldier* remind us forcibly that Ford is indeed the last Pre-Raphaelite, others even more forcibly recall poor Ford, the victim of agoraphobia and nocturnal terrors. In characterizing the impressionist's task, Ford catches perfectly the visual impact of his masterpiece: "drawing dreary pictures

of the hell that this world is."[68] Dowell the agoraphobic is
the perfect artist for the job. The first time he portrays himself he calls to mind Ford's pictures of himself as little and
lonely in London: being in Nauheim gives Dowell the feeling "almost of nakedness—the nakedness that one feels on
the sea-shore or in any great open space" (27). Looking out
at a sunlit world, from the steps of his hotel, he feels
"rather small" (29-30). His most terrible picture of hell is
his vision of Florence, Nancy, and Edward hanging above
a plain, recalling poor Ford on the Salisbury Plain under
the great gaze of the July 1904 sky:

> It is almost too terrible, the picture of that judgment
> . . . upon an immense plain, suspended in mid-air, I
> seem to see three figures, two of them clasped close in
> an intense embrace, and one intolerably solitary. . . .
> And the immense plain is the hand of God, stretching
> out for miles and miles, with great spaces above it and
> below it. And they are in the sight of God, and it is
> Florence that is alone . . . (82)

Trying to imagine his own posthumous role, Dowell
speculates that he will be given an elevator to run (83). This
pathetic, comic image has its appropriateness too. It belongs with such modern gadgets as the electrical device
supposedly attached to Florence and designed to sound an
alarm when pressed (104); the electric light hanging from
the ceiling at which the dead Florence looks (141); Edward's telephone, over which he talks in his gentle voice
(265). That elevator connects too with Dowell's other
grotesque implement, the rope ladder to Florence's window. The elevator's repetitious travels point to: Nancy as
shuttlecock "tossed backwards and forwards" between the
"violent" Ashburnhams; Leonora, "picked up and thrown
down" by Edward and Nancy; Edward, being sent "backwards and forwards like a blooming parcel" with insuffi-
cient postage (290-91).
  Dowell's other memorable pictures of hell reflect the
nocturnal terrors of Ford's mental illness, the despair of

"Waring" at the open windows and doors of the inland cottage. In a 1914 review, Ford refers to a "post-impression of swept, cold, and windy emptiness in the black and silent depths of a sleeping house" as giving him a "chill."[69] Dowell does the same thing in recounting Leonora's horror in Branshaw Teleragh: "Their rooms all gave on to the gallery. . . . The sight of those three open doors, side by side, gaping to receive whom the chances of the black night might bring, made Leonora shudder all over her body." She has just left Edward, cleaning his gun by the light of a green-shaded lamp, and is headed for her room, as unstrung as an agoraphobic, stumbling over rugs, scarcely able to "drag one limb after the other" (246). Leonora's next human encounter is equally frightening and oddly resembles Conrad's most vivid picture of Lena in the precisely contemporary *Victory*. Leonora finds Nancy "sitting perfectly still" in her room. Her hair falls, "black and like a pall," over her shoulders. Her fire burns brightly. She wears a white silk kimono. Inspiring in Leonora "horror" and "grief," Nancy gives her "a queer, far-away smile—as if she were a thousand years old, as if Leonora were a tiny child" (247-49). Nancy in white has an even more devastating effect on Florence, and the picture Dowell conjectures recalls not only hell but madhouses: "It was a very black night and the girl was dressed in cream-coloured muslin, that must have glimmered under the tall trees of the dark park like a phosphorescent fish in a cupboard" (129). To Dowell the image is not comic: "I tell you I see that thing as clearly as if it were a dream that never left me" (130). That phosphorescent fish has sinister echoes: the "phosphorescent gleam" of Annette's dress as she comes "tottering, pallid" out of the terrifying Riesenberg woods toward the German madhouse; the "phosphorescent light," flickering on Leggatt's apparently "headless corpse" in Conrad's story of "mental stress" (Ford's phrase), "The Secret Sharer."[70]

Although most of Dowell's pictures of hell are in black and white, the most appalling has a touch of color, recalling Leggatt's "greenish cadaverous glow"; it also has that horror Ford conveys in finding himself, as a child, sucking a match, and shrieking. Dowell begs the reader to imagine Nancy, a sudden apparition in the half-light at the foot of Edward's bed: "that was the real hell for him. That was the picture that never left his imagination. . . . He said that it seemed to have a greenish sort of effect as if there were a greenish tinge in the shadows of the tall bedposts that framed her body" (232-33, 278).

Although Dowell looks at everything through Pre-Raphaelite eyes, these pictures of the innocent Nancy putting everyone into hell are in intention surely anti-Pre-Raphaelite. Ford says in *Ancient Lights* that according to the Pre-Raphaelites, love "excused all sins." Those who were in hell because of love found there only "snow-flakes of fire" and still held their lovers in their arms. Rossetti's Paolo and Francesca did not suffer; whereas authentic medieval love was much like ours and usually exacted painful, grotesque retribution. "Dante's lovers in hell felt bitter cold, stinging flame, shame, horror, despair . . ." (62-64). Thus although Dowell at the beginning of his narration can imagine Edward and Nancy eternally clasped together, at the end he imagines only "poor Edward, naked and reclining amidst darkness, upon cold rocks, like one of the ancient Greek damned" (290). Pre-Raphaelism means a belief in the possibility of eternal joy which neither Dowell nor Ford can quite accept. Even Ford's image of the good old days with Conrad as a bright painting has its surface "cracked . . . with the agonies of Conrad's poverty, unsuccess, negotiations and misgivings" (JC, 52).

If Dowell looks out with anxious, Fordian eyes, he also philosophizes and psychologizes in Fordian ideas expressed in Fordian locutions. He is, in short, the pessimist and solipsist. And in this century of black books, *The Good Soldier* must be one of the blackest. Ford, let it be said, does not see Dowell's vision as unique. Henry James's "final note is despair" (HJ, 144). The conversations of James's characters, like those of the inmates of Branshaw Teleragh, "will convey to your mind that the quiet talkers are living in an atmosphere of horror, of bankruptcy, of passion hopeless as the Dies Irae!" (HJ, 153). This was Ford's view of Conrad, too: "the gloomy aristocrat . . . who mused unceasingly upon the treacheries, the muddles, the lack of imagination, the imbecilities which make up the conduct of human affairs" (JC, 237). Ford's statements in his own person, particularly in the year of *The Good Soldier*, convey the same attitude. Life is "always a sad affair."[71]

That Dowell participates in all these grim views needs no documentation. Pain, agony, and suffering, these are the recurrent words and the recurrent states of most of the characters he depicts, except, ironically, Florence, the one who first destroys herself. "The record of humanity," says Dowell, "is a record of sorrows" (238). Inherent in life's pain is its incomprehensibility and irremediability. Questions are Dowell's most characteristic form of address to the reader. Into them he manages to cram much of the grief and puzzlement of his narrative: "are all men's lives like the lives of us good people . . . broken, tumultuous, agonised and unromantic lives, periods punctuated by screams, by imbecilities, by deaths, by agonies? Who the devil knows?" (273). Whereas prior to *The Good Soldier*, Ford wanted to blame his woes on others—"the heart of another is a dark forest "—Dowell is reassuringly willing to include himself in the mystery: "Who in this world knows anything of any other heart—or of his own?" (182).[72]

Truth remains for Dowell utterly relative to the imperfect state of one's own perceptions. At the beginning of the novel he asks if, for him, they were just four people of similar tastes, "isn't that the truth?" (11). At the end, in the hell of Branshaw Teleragh, he is still maintaining that, for him who knew them so well, they were "just good people!" (233). Human actions are inexplicable and mainly volitionless in Dowell's view: "Why does one do things? I just drifted in and wanted Florence" (20). He doubts that the Ashburnhams even much wanted to go on that definitive trip to M—— (47). Edward and Leonora "were two noble natures, drifting down life, like fireships afloat on a lagoon and causing miseries, heartaches, agony . . ." Even Major Basil, a potential villain, is only a "slack, loose, shiftless sort of fellow" (192).

Many of Dowell's locutions underline the total lack of will. Practically nobody thinks anything, recognizes anything, believes anything. Instead, Florence arrives at a frame of mind; Leonora suddenly seems to begin to perceive; Edward seems to see a net closing round him (116, 166, 170). Ultimately, Dowell "cannot conceal" from himself either the fact that he dislikes Leonora or the fact that he loved Edward (290, 291). People do not notice things; rather, things force themselves upon their attention. Characters speak without realizing it. Dowell, thinking "nothing," says something "extraordinary" (123). Edward suddenly hears himself say something (202). Characters frequently begin actions quite unconsciously. Nancy, for example, finds herself playing the piano, without knowing how she happened to do it, and soon finds herself weeping (257-58).

Small wonder, then, that Dowell considers it impossible to predict how anyone will act. He sees no consistency or continuity in human characters: "no man really knows what he would have done in any given case" (106). Himself the most timid and restrained of men, he explodes at an old family retainer for dropping a leather grip. As an instance of human unpredictability, he cites the case of Florence's utterly reliable maid who "suddenly" steals a ring. He and Florence could never have believed she could do it, nor could the maid herself: "It was nothing in her character" (179, 182). That Fordian "suddenly" turns up everywhere, clear to the end: "It suddenly occurs to me that I have forgotten to say how Edward met his death" (292-93). Because human characters are so unstable and discontinuous, they are constantly having unique, extreme experiences. "Never, in all the years of her life" did Florence so smile at Dowell as once outside the baths (29). On the occasion of their first meeting, Leonora exhibits more gaiety than Dowell ever again observes in her (37).

Such locutions can be dismissed as Ford's desperate efforts to create suspense and surprise the reader. But I think they come as much from his genuine conviction that people do live in extremes. If "odd" and "queer" are two of the most frequently used words, "extraordinary" is another. When Ford has Dowell make the following remark, he intends it, I am sure, to be taken as a serious instance of Edward's innocence. "It will give you some idea of the extraordinary naïveté of Edward Ashburnham that, at the time of his marriage and for perhaps a couple of years after, he did not really know how children are produced. Neither did Leonora" (171). Although we may wonder what those country people thought stallions and mares were up to, we had better accept the literal truth of the statement if we are to appreciate Ford's grostesque world (a world surely not one-tenth so grotesque as, say, the real world of European politics in the summer of 1914). So, too, we must accept Dowell's extreme statement of his own naiveté: "the fourth of August, 1913, the last day of my absolute ignorance—and, I assure you, of my perfect happiness" (117). More commonly, however, the characters fluctuate among extremes rather than move from one fixed position to another. Leonora keeps changing her point of view, ready to yield to her passion for Edward at one moment, ready to denounce Mrs. Basil at another. Nancy's past, her looks, her temperament are also composed of extreme contradiction. Her father knocks her unconscious for three days; she remembers "rough kindnesses from him" (148). Her convent school is a "mixture of saturnalia and discipline" (148). Her looks reflect the same mixtures: "she had a tortured mouth, agonised eyes, and a quite extraordinary sense of fun . . . at times she was exceedingly grotesque and at times extraordinarily beautiful" (146). No wonder Dowell calls her a "queer girl . . . very difficult to describe" (145).

Dowell says at the beginning that the two couples were not dancing the minuet, they were "a prison full of screaming hysterics" (11). Under the force of passion, all the chief characters at some point go mad, reminding us again that August 1904 was the time Ford went to Germany to try to cure his mental illness, the time when he genuinely feared he might go insane. When Florence runs into the hotel, she sticks "her hands over her face as if she wished to push her eyes out" (118). When La Dolciquita refuses Edward her favors, he goes "mad," his world stands "on its head," the palm trees dance "grotesque dances" (188). When Leonora tells Nancy about divorce, her blue eyes fill with horror and the external world disintegrates: andirons appear "unreal"; burning logs become merely burning logs instead of the "comfortable symbols of an indestructible mode of life" they formerly were (254). When Dowell tells us at last of Nancy's permanent insanity, he does so by repeating "mad" five times (270-71). Even Leonora, "the perfectly normal woman," cannot act normally in an abnormal situation; the whole world is "mad around her," and so she, in her agony, takes "on the complexion of a madwoman" (275-76).

How can Dowell respond to these horrors that are revealed to him after his last day of perfect happiness? He tends to take one of two possible, and extreme, attitudes: complete cynicism or pitying sentimentality. Both attitudes preclude judgment. Maybe all men are like Edward even though they would all be "offended if you suggested they weren't the sort of person you could trust your wife alone with." To which Dowell adds: "that is if you can trust anybody alone with anybody" (15). Blaming Florence for Maisie's death, Dowell still realizes that Edward would have left Maisie for some other woman. Leonora's priests probably gave her bad advice: "But then, who would not have been mistaken with Edward?" (167). Leonora blames their troubles on her childlessness; Dowell disagrees (171). Edward blames the Kilsyte case for putting into his head the idea of adultery; Dowell doesn't believe it (184). The closest Dowell comes to implying that rationality is possible in human affairs is a solitary reference to Colonel Whelen's wife, apparently the "only sensible person" the Ashburnhams ever knew (189). At one point Dowell's despair is so extreme he seems to doubt the value of even trying to portray these people: "It is very difficult to give an all-round impression. . . . It is even very difficult to see how such things matter" (177).

Often Dowell's hopelessness is wrapped up in pity for these helpless ceatures. Although he feels that Leonora acted "wrongly," he refuses "to condemn her" (215). Despite his usual hostility to Florence, he on one occasion explicitly says that he does not blame her (12). *Ancient Lights* concludes with the same weary acceptance: "No one is to blame; it can't be cured; it can't be helped" (AL, 295). Overwhelmed by the sense of the helplessness of them all, Dowell cannot see what else they all should have done (268). He especially exempts Edward from judgment. Admitting that speaking love to Nancy is "the most monstrously wicked thing" Edward "ever did," Dowell still says his "permanent view" of Edward is as "straight, upright and honourable" (133-34). The other chief recipient of Dowell's pity is Nancy, the second of the "Beati Immaculati" of the novel's epigraph. His tribute to her is an almost hysterical version of Marlow's tribute to Jim: "And there was a little colour in her cheeks and light in her deep blue eyes. And to think that that vivid white thing, that saintly and swanlike being—to think that. . . . Why, she will never do anything again" (150). Dowell at least recognizes that he is "as much of a sentimentalist as" Edward (291). Ford, too, can see himself as sometimes "abominably sentimental."[73]

Dowell himself as a character in the drama epitomizes the hell that is the world of *The Good Soldier*. In his own way poor Dowell is as solitary as Gregor Samsa. Moreover, not only must he endure an impassable gulf between himself and the external world but also a gulf within, between at least two selves. Dowell's rootlessness is obvious: carrying around his title-deeds as if they were all that attached him to any place on the earth, describing himself as a "wanderer" among public resorts (9, 27). At the beginning he implies things were better once (11-12). Yet his previous nine years of perfect happiness reveal a singular lack of communicativeness on the part of the Ashburnhams and response from the Dowells that similarly has left out "the personal note" (42). Early in the relationship, Dowell, sounding like Ford telling Olive he has no friends, says to Leonora that he does not believe anyone has ever been as fond of him as he believes her to be (79). He has, alas, few grounds for the latter belief. The first time Leonora pays him "any attention," he finds the experience "mortifying"; she looks at him the way a kind woman might look at a man in a wheelchair (40). Ultimately, of course, Dowell recognizes his estrangement from Leonora and knows she does not like him. Nancy, being mad, ignores him. Edward, though he talks all night to him about Nancy, probably considers Dowell "like a woman or a solicitor" (272, 287). At least, Dowell can remember that, just before his death, Edward looks at him with eyes "soft and almost affectionate" (294). On the other hand, Dowell insists that he "loves" Leonora, Nancy, Edward. But the point is that he cannot communicate that love. He goes looking for Nancy one night, to tell her, but does not find her. He wants to tell Edward, at the end, "God bless you," but decides it "would not be quite English good form." All he can do is try to be "serviceable," at which he has never been any good—that stupid donkey again (294, 270).

Dowell is no good at it, because he is, with good reason, too afraid of human relations. He remains the muddled Ford-child, terrified by the incomprehensible passions that explode in his face. Leonora and Florence both stupefy him. On his wedding night, he receives Florence's "advances with a certain amount of absence of mind" and hustles down the ladder (97). When Florence lays her finger on Edward's wrist, Dowell expects they will all four "run and cry out . . . averting our heads" (53-54). In response to

Leonora's "don't you see what's going on?" poor Dowell mutters and stutters: "No! What's the matter?" (54).[74] He successfully suppresses his first correct notion, that Leonora must be "madly jealous," even though her face is precisely "that of a person looking into the pit of hell" (55). Exactly nine years later, Florence, running, repeats Leonora's clawing gesture, shows the same sort of face, to induce in Dowell the same panic, which this time lasts ten days. At first, he cannot move at all, and he does not know what he must have looked like to Bagshawe (118-19). Although Dowell evades the meaning of Florence's death and even turns his mind to Nancy, he is nevertheless in a "cataleptic" state. When he is led to the grave, he stands beside it. If he had, he says, been taken to a river bank, he would have drowned: "I was the walking dead" (129). Trying later to understand how he could have said to Leonora only two hours after Florence's death, "Now I can marry the girl," Dowell decides he must have a "dual personality" (123). Clearly, Dowell believes here that the statement coming out of his unconscious is the real truth. His "inner soul" had long ago understood that Florence had "a personality of paper" (142).[75]

In a final instance of the muddled Ford-child, confused rather than panic-stricken, Dowell again resorts to his other self. Over three months after Florence's death and some ten days after Edward's, Dowell gets "the news—full in the face," from Leonora, of Florence's affair with Edward and her suicide: "I didn't say anything and I don't suppose I felt anything" (124). Earlier, he makes a similar remark: "You ask how it feels to be a deceived husband. . . . It feels just nothing at all" (81, 82). Dowell, that is, in the face of catastrophic revelations, finds himself cut off from himself. He experiences something like Ford's characteristic sense of time infinitely slowed down, an "extraordinary sense of leisure. . . . It wasn't as if we were waiting for a train . . . it was just that there was nothing to wait for" (125). In the course of mulling over that revelatory scene with Leonora, Dowell has recourse to his notion of a dual personality. He feels only with "that mysterious and unconscious self that underlies most people" and imagines that "unconscious or walking in my sleep I may go and spit upon poor Edward's grave" (124). Elsewhere in the novel, the unconscious stands for the truth. But against the evidence here of Dowell's unconscious hatred of Edward must be set the later, powerful insistence on his love for Edward. Probably the biographical sources for Edward have something to do with Dowell's unresolved feelings.

One thing, however, is certain. If there were not somewhere in Dowell a self capable of viewing Edward and the others ironically, Dowell would be a far less effective narrator. Often his irony appears in the curious form of an apparently mindless repetition of words, phrases, even sentences. In this and other ways, he achieves an impressive range of ironic effects. We have already noticed his ironic treatment of his earlier, unenlightened self, recalling Conrad's "Youth." Sometimes his irony recalls Hardy's, that of people working hopelessly at cross-purposes. Dowell terms it "part of the peculiar irony of things" that only because Edward bought a third-class railway ticket to please Leonora did he kiss the nursemaid and thus initiate all their troubles (174). But Bagshawe's presence in the lobby when Florence runs in is sheer chance, "a grin on the face of Fate" (141).

At one point Dowell says pathetically: "Forgive my writing of these monstrous things in this frivolous manner. If I did not I should break down and cry" (71). Presumably, it is in this spirit that he says: "It would have done [Edward] a great deal of good to get killed" (199).[76] Yet many of Dowell's ironic comments act not as a defense against pain but to express a healthy scorn for the sentimentality of "that poor imbecile of an Edward" and for the self-indulgence of Florence. Dowell says that Florence justified marrying him in order to rejoin Jimmie on the grounds of an "overmastering passion. Well, I always say that an overmastering passion is a good excuse for feelings. You cannot help them" (99). Twice he says condescendingly of

Edward: "He was such a serious person" (186, 220). When La Dolciquita kicks Edward out, Dowell says "his sentimentalism required of him an attitude of Byronic gloom—as if his court had gone into half-mourning" (191). Even in the more sympathetic case of Mrs. Basil, Dowell is capable of a nice irony. Leonora gave Edward a horse to go prancing about India on while she was on religious retreat, which "was very good for her health. . . . It was probably also very good for Edward's health, because he pranced about mostly with Mrs. Basil, who was . . . very, very kind to him" (196). More surprising, Dowell with an apt adverb can treat ironically Edward's love of Nancy: Edward "believed maunderingly" that the girl kept on loving him because of some basic attractiveness he possessed (282). Dowell can even heap scorn on the reader: "there is always Leonora to cheer you up; I don't want to sadden you" (292). Sometimes the tone is very mysterious, very painful as in the "little neat pen-knife—quite a small pen-knife" (294).[77] He makes two especially odd repetitions concerning Nancy. "She called first upon her sweet Saviour—and she thought of Our Lord as her sweet Saviour!" Dowell must be not only commenting on the mystery of faith in suffering but also preparing for Nancy's late obsessive "Credo in unum Deum Omnipotentum" (269). Dowell says later that he would marry Nancy "if her reason were ever sufficiently restored to let her appreciate the meaning of the Anglican marriage service. But it is probable that her reason will never be sufficiently restored to let her appreciate the meaning of the Anglican marriage service" (272). Why this daft repetition? Perhaps Dowell is trying, rather successfully, to convey the hellish ennui of life at Branshaw Teleragh: "It is," as he says, "all very humdrum, as far as I am concerned" (271).

If Dowell is the overwhelming source of our sense that *The Good Soldier* is the most personal of Ford's novels, other characters, Edward especially, also make their Fordian contributions. Edward has Ford's Pre-Raphaelite and Tory attitudes. He feels the same way about love as Ford and has a similar psychological make-up. Moreover, Edward acts consistently as the double of Ford's alter ego Dowell,[78] and, despite his handsomeness, resembles Ford physically. Indeed, when Brigit Patmore describes Ford in her memoir, she may be remembering the novel rather than the man.[79] If Edward's voice is not fluffy and swallowed like Ford's, he still talks, as Ford did, like a book (34). Like Ford, Edward is an altruist, with all those virtues Madox Brown practiced: "I don't know how many ill-used people he did not pick up and provide with careers" (69). It is for his innumerable kindly acts that Dowell so likes him (109). Politically, Edward belongs of course to the Tory party (72), which is, for Ford, in a 1911 article, "the stupid party because we are the sentimental party."[80] Thus those early references in the novel to Edward as "stupid" (13, 35) perhaps intend less contempt than appears. Indeed, Ford's uses of "stupid" elsewhere almost suggest affection. In his journalism, Ford frequently calls himself a Papist, as well as sentimental, stupid, and a Tory. "In a mild way I should call myself a sentimental Tory and a Roman Catholic" (AL, 292). He makes clear, though, that the religion he means is not the English but the Continental variety, the religion of "friendly quaintnesses," as we have noted. When Ford thinks of the Anglicanism of the mother of his friend (surely Marwood), he is thinking of something very different. He seems

> to see, at the end of an immense, serenely dark Jacobean room, an immensely tall square mirror. . . . The mirror reflects nothing but the black serene emptiness of the room, and behind it is an immensely tall window, with square panes giving on to a perfectly black night. . . . Indeed, I am a little afraid; I recognise a goodness that, to me, is almost a wickedness and almost certainly a cruelty. It is so apparently austere, restrained, non-communicative. It is so nearly exactly what I don't want religion to be; though it is also so near Papistry. . . . It is no doubt English to regard

rather the austerities than the friendlinesses of religion—no doubt the spirit of the High Church martyrs
and . . . the English martyrs [was] . . . beautiful, austere, and flamelike—the spirit of the English College
at Rome, that sad, sad place . . .[81]

Thus Ford yokes Anglicans with English Catholics. The
familiar nocturnal, agoraphobic imagery suggests the inte-
rior of Branshaw Teleragh; his friend's mother's austerity
and cruelty recall the effects of Leonora's religion. But Edward, for a period, is "quite ready to become an emotional
Catholic" (167)—like Ford. Edward's suppressed love for
Nancy also places him in the camp of what Dowell calls the
"Continental Papists" (71). Leonora watches him sobbing
over a "tawdry . . . Prussian blue" image of the virgin that
Nancy had given to him (156-57). Dowell associates Edward's name with Roman Catholicism, commenting that
an Ashburnham had accompanied Charles I to the scaffold
(8). Ford had written of that Ashburnham in his youthful
Cinque Ports. For Ford, sentimental, Tory Papists are a van-
ished breed. Dowell does not think Edward "was wanted
in the world" (294). Of himself and Conrad, Ford writes:
"The world certainly did not want us" (JC, 38).

    If Edward is chiefly a stupid, sentimental, anachronistic
Tory, emotionally attracted to Catholicism, he also has
touches of Ford's Pre-Raphaelite heritage. Swinburne's
mother was an Ashburnham, and he and Ford's father
were much on Ford's mind at the time of *The Good Soldier*.
Edward sentimentally recites two lines from "Hymn to
Proserpine" (289). Edward's amorous gurgles (38, 74) not
only echo in Brigit's recollection of Ford, but recall Rossetti's "Guggum," his repeated pet name for Lizzie Siddall
(FMB, 113).[82] More seriously, Edward shares Dowell's and
Ford's Pre-Raphaelite longing for the ideal, in its most
characteristic form: "the mad passion to find an ultimately
satisfying woman" (60). Such a longing is not far from Edward's other Fordian need: "a bit of rest, you know" (294).

    Edward's attitude toward sex is thoroughly Fordian, as

others have noted.[83] Although he takes several mistresses, he never consciously intends sexual conquest (185). In fact, he feels revulsion from the mere idea of sex. Like Ford's version of himself and Conrad, Edward hates smoking-room stories (15-16; JC, 73-74). Having sex with Mrs. Basil is, to Edward's mind, "falling" (197). Not having it with Nancy is keeping himself "unspotted" (235). As Ford needed a loved one in order to be able to see, so Edward, according to Dowell, desires of his beloved "to see with the same eyes . . . to hear with the same ears, to lose his identity, to be enveloped, to be supported" (135). Leonora must also believe that the "sex-instinct" does not count "for very much in a really great passion" (135). For she does not determine to make Nancy hate Edward until Edward trips up and reveals that all he desires is that the girl continue loving him from a distance of five thousand miles (276-77).

Edward, as lover, reveals the same divided psyche as Ford and Dowell. He does not find the servant girl desirable until long afterward when, in the witness box, he thinks of her. He kisses La Dolciquita passionately because he remembers "suddenly" the servant girl (186). It is Edward's words that produce his love for Nancy: "as if the very words that he spoke, without knowing that he spoke them, created the passion as they went along" (137). Like the muddled Ford and the muddled Dowell, Edward stands either "thinking about nothing at all" (175) or with "a slightly reflective air . . . just opening one kind of case and just closing another" (33). Ford and Edward both have a dread of scenes in public places. Edward shares one of Ford's most touching traits, an unwillingness or inability to defend himself: "he remained dumb; he stretched out no finger to help himself" (277). Edward and Dowell have more in common than Fordian character traits. They are psychological doubles: "I loved Edward Ashburnham . . . because he was just myself" (291).[84] Certain key words unite them. Both are "fools" (65, 108). Both are good at "remorse" (71, 101). Both men have sexually uncooperative wives who have their moments of wishing their husbands would make sexual overtures. Edward trots about the ship carrying things for Maisie; Dowell trots off to Leonora with Nancy's wire. The two men find themselves in love with Nancy the same evening and express their love in the same unconscious, volitionless way.

As the other of the "Beati Immaculati" besides Edward, Nancy comes next closest to being like Ford (and Dowell). She, too, is dependent on others to provide a home. As with Ford, merely the sound of her father's voice can "unman her." "It brings back," she says, "those dreadful dreams" so that "the poor thing" is "always allowed a light at night" (151-52). Like Ford's, Dowell's, and Edward's, her love can operate "from a great distance" and remain "unspoken" (263). Still, Nancy has "a sense of rectitude . . . a thing like a knife that looked out of her eyes" (147). This, plus "the swift cruelty of youth" and "the swift solidarity that attaches woman to woman," unites Nancy with the cruel and rigidly principled Leonora (277). Yet even Leonora, despite her irreconcilable temperamental differences from Edward and despite the fact that she and Dowell come to dislike each other, belongs a little to the Fordian fraternity. She relates to the external world with that strange, characteristic combination of sentiment and absence of mind: "Leonora . . . gave the impression of being intensely sympathetic. When she listened to you she appeared also to be listening to some sound that was going on in the distance" (237-38). And, when faced with those open doors, Leonora has her moment of nocturnal terror and agoraphobic paralysis. Only Florence remains free of the familiar Fordian weaknesses and virtues. In Dowell's memorable vision, Florence hangs quite alone. Dowell expresses explicit hostility to her relatively early in the novel. And she expresses her "hard," damnable, "triumphant air" (100) as early as her wedding day and the trip to M———. The completeness of Dowell's judgment against Florence makes her a good deal less interesting and human than the others, although the hostility results in a memorable, sometimes hilarious caricature. But many readers consider her an artistic blemish and suspect Dowell of protesting too much.

FINAL BIOGRAPHICAL SPECULATIONS

Perhaps Ford's special attitude toward Florence arises out of her biographical sources. And perhaps a bit more needs to be said about the biographical sources of all the chief characters (except Dowell, whose Fordian and Conradian aspects we have surely considered sufficiently) and about the personal dramas that may have been going on even while Ford was writing *The Good Soldier*. Mizener, certain that "Florence is based on Violet," offers as usual solid textual evidence to support his view. Ford and Violet were in Nauheim together in 1910; they visited the Schloss at Marburg. Violet's account of herself in Germany in *The Desirable Alien* has verbal resemblances to Ford's account of Florence. Significantly, Ford cut one of the more obvious allusions to Violet from his manuscript. Also, Mizener finds the influence on Leonora of Elsie Martindale "less obvious but equally pervasive."[85]

Certainly something of Violet must have gone into little, chattery, stylish, modern Florence. Moreover, if there is any justice, Florence *should* reflect Violet. After all, Florence is the one who puts the finishing touch on a long, if not very happy, marriage between an unfaithful husband and an austere, determined wife. But justice has little to do with feelings in failed marriages or with the sources of imaginative creativity, especially Ford's sources. Surely Florence chiefly reflects the woman who once loved Ford to distraction, who triumphed so thoroughly over him in 1913, who must have been the woman he hated most in the year of *The Good Soldier*, Elsie Martindale Hueffer. Everyone agrees that Elsie is, so unjustly, the model for the Countess Macdonald in *The New Humpty-Dumpty*; and that vulgar character comes closer to Florence than any of Ford's previous heroines. Like Florence, Elsie belonged (in

Ford's mind) to that pseudo-intellectual, Fabian milieu of the nineties that he castigates in *Ancient Lights*. That is the period of the Browning Society (HJ, 44), where Dowell and Florence meet, the period when Ford was "anxious to make the world a little lighter,"[86] as Florence wants to leave "the world a little brighter" (48). If Ford went with Violet to Marburg and Provence, he had long before been to those places with Elsie. If Violet became ill and sexually unavailable, so had Elsie.[87] Moreover, Ford seems to have believed, incorrectly, that there was no physiological basis for Elsie's illness as there definitely was none for Florence's.[88] As Elsie loved playing Pre-Raphaelite damsel in amber beads and curtain serge, so Florence makes the quintessential Pre-Raphaelite remark: "And so the whole round table is begun" (41). Much as Florence's family attempts, for reasons incomprehensible to Dowell, to prevent their marriage, so had Elsie's family. Both couples ran off to get married. Most important of all is the fatal date, August 4, 1904, the time of Ford's mental breakdown, so intimately involved with Elsie and so long before Violet. Perhaps Florence's death by prussic acid is a cruel reminder of Mr. Martindale's.

Violet herself says, "I have to support the character of Leonora," which is hardly an enviable burden.[89] Can she really have inspired the creation of that "clean run" member of a county family? Well, surely, a little. By virtue of her artistic, academic, and social connections, Violet, as even Ford would grant, had a touch of class. The one time Ford alludes to Violet in the Conrad book, he calls her not only "cheerfully heartless" but also a "fine-lady" (JC, 20). I suspect that retrospectively Ford liked to think he had lowered himself by marrying into a pharmaceutical family, in trade, like Florence's wealthy Uncle Hurlbird. I suspect, too, that despite his disposition to tease Violet as a superficial novelist, he would nonetheless grant her far more genuine literary and historical culture than Elsie with her relatively few, if undeniably impressive, literary efforts. That is, I suspect that in matters cultural Ford would compare Elsie to Violet, as Dowell compares Florence to Leonora, a retriever trying to catch a greyhound (49). Again, in that awful picture of the judgment of God, Dowell predicts that "Leonora will burn, clear and serene, a northern light" (83). Violet always emphasized her own northern, Yorkshire roots, and was pleased that Rebecca West's review of *The Good Soldier* called Leonora that "Northern Light."[90] Finally, the way Leonora manages Edward's finances, takes over his family's heirlooms, and puts him on an allowance, recalls how Violet had to manage all Ford's affairs.

Yet Leonora as caretaker, northern light, and one of many daughters of an impecunious farming family, points to another source: Caroline Cranswick Marwood. Like Leonora with Dowell, she treated her husband as if he were an invalid. As Leonora takes over the management of Branshaw Teleragh, so Caroline had the sole responsibility of running Water Farm. As Leonora rides about Hampshire in a dogcart, so is Caroline remembered, in a dogcart, in Kent. As Leonora, a couple of years after Edward's death, marries her old admirer, the neighboring farmer Rodney Bayham, so Caroline, two years after Marwood's death and three years after *The Good Soldier*, was to marry their old farmer-friend and neighbor, Walter Pilcher—another of Ford's uncanny prophecies? Even more uncannily, Leonora Ashburnham Bayham becomes pregnant, and Caroline Marwood Pilcher adopted a child.

If the connections between Leonora and Caroline seem sketchy, there can be no doubt that the Ashburnhams as a model Tory couple owe a great deal to the Marwoods. In a group of articles, Ford mentions his "Yorkshire Tory friend," tells how the Tories love the Irish "with a deep, stupid, sentimental love" and how the best Tory he knows wept over Home Rule, and precisely prefigures Dowell on the eating habits of the Ashburnhams: "My best friends—my very best Tory friends—are an intolerable nuisance whenever they dine with me. They must always have the good, simple underdone English beef . . . a dismal thing that resembles tepid, moist, pink india-rubber."[91]

More seriously relevant to the background of *The Good Soldier*, and to the feelings Ford brought to the creation of Edward, Florence, Leonora, and Nancy, are the autobiographical asides in the journalism of 1913-1914. They hint especially at the intensity of Ford's hostility to these characters and at the source of his courage to handle his materials so well. Ford seems to realize his friendship with Marwood is really finished. "I *had* an Anglican friend for whose intellect I *had* a great admiration and for whose character I *had* a very real respect—and that is rare, for one really respects so few people; perhaps three or four in a lifetime!" (Madox Brown, Conrad, Marwood, James?) When this friend had told Ford that his "mother was a saint," Ford "accepted" it, thinking he meant that his "long dead" mother "did the pretty, kindly, or humorous things that, automatically, one expects of a saint of God." But Ford learns that his friend's mother was not like that: "and always, as I questioned him, he became more baffling in his attitude." Ford becomes conscious for the first time of "a great gulf fixed" between them. He is reminded of hearing two distinguished historians converse, one Lutheran and one Catholic: "it was as if they were talking in different languages of the affairs of another planet. They did not in the least quarrel; they never, as it were, got near enough to each other for that. . . . So with my friend and myself." Just as the mother's religion "is so nearly exactly what I don't want religion to be," so his friend's (and, subsequently, Christopher Tietjens') favorite poets—Herbert, Crashaw, Vaughan—and his friend's favorite poem, "Sweet day, so cool, so calm, so bright," are utterly alien to Ford: "I think I rather hate those poets and that poem, as indeed I think I hate all sad things." The article ends with Ford's current judgment against the Marwoods and the Ashburnhams: "But I am tired of the English county-family atmosphere."[92]

If Ford hints in the public press at the gulf between him-

self and Marwood, he alludes also to his concurrent relations with women. In the James book, he is obviously
thinking of Elsie: "In the afternoon, whilst the Courts or
the Stock Exchange or some woman up in town are sending you to the devil, you play a foursome . . . you know,
and they all know you know, that by the second of next
month not a soul there will talk to you" (HJ, 154-55). The
scene foreshadows, of course, the opening of *Some Do Not*,
but also surely reflects Ford's sense of Marwood and Conrad dropping him after the *Throne* trial and Elsie's
triumph.[93]

The journalism also hints at Ford's passion for the Irish
Brigit Patmore. In one article, of early January 1914, he
twice uses as a symbol for the wiles of woman a "bare-foot
girl of Kilronan fair . . . (These troublesome Irish)."[94] In the
first part of an article on impressionism published in June
1914, Ford tells how an impressionist would render a conversation at his club: "You will . . . remember that the man
at the same table with you was talking about morals, and
that your boots were too tight, whilst you were trying, in
your under mind, to arrange a meeting with some lady . . .
you would give a sense that your feet were burning, and
that the lady you wanted to meet had very clear and can-
did eyes. You would give a little description of her hair
. . ." (CW, 42). By December, in the second part of the essay, Ford is saying, as we have seen, that he cannot have
the one thing he desires. His impressionist subject, Mr.
Jones, is "developing a passion for a frivolous girl." One's
reader might be a "man mad as a hatter for love of a worth-
less creature" (CW, 44, 51).

Although Brigit Patmore later denied having an affair
with Ford, Violet suspected it at the time. Brigit took dictation from Ford for *The Good Soldier*, and she stayed with
Violet and Ford while recuperating from an operation in
January, February, and March, 1914.[95] Nevertheless, she
may have been idealizing only a little when she said that
Ford did not attract her. There is evidence, beyond his
1914 journalism, that Brigit rather quickly rejected Ford.

Violet's diary entry for March 22, 1917 says that Ford told her that Brigit treated him badly back in 1914. Moreover, the first novel Ford tried to write after *The Good Soldier* tells how the Fordian hero is thrown over by his glamorous, married mistress; he had hoped to have a son by her.[96]

Violet says that Brigit inspired the creation of Nancy Rufford in *The Good Soldier*.[97] Despite obvious differences in age, religion, and sexual experience, the resemblances are striking. Like Nancy, Brigit was Irish, "well educated," as Derek Patmore tells us, but "fundamentally simple"; she had studied music and played the piano "with a rare sensibility." She was lovely looking, with striking hair and eyes. She combined "a quiet sense of humor" with a melancholy temperament. Brigit attributes her own "love of sorrow" to her mother, who was "not very happy in her marriage," which is certainly true of the Ruffords.[98] As soon as Brigit settled in London, she was taken up by the Patmores' old family friend Violet Hunt, to whom she related much as Nancy relates to Leonora. Despite her husband's initial immense success in the insurance business and his interesting social connections, Brigit's early married life was not happy. Her husband was unfaithful, and her health was poor. Probably in December 1913, she had a major operation. In short, Brigit must have provided sufficient mournful material to inspire in a sentimentalist the wish to comfort—as Nancy does for Edward.

About the time that war broke out, Ford must have seen that Brigit's romantic interest in him was over. On August 15, 1914, he announced his "desire to be dead by . . . 1922, or even earlier"; and he appended two little poems ("Gothicisms") that are probably about Brigit and Violet. On September 12 he published another poem, the preamble to which suggests Brigit. In the first poem, "The White Raven," Ford bitterly terms the addressee a "white crow" and a "surgical scalpel"; he sarcastically calls her "kindest among women." "You have taken my manhood," he says. She has "had out" his eyes. The language reminds us that Nancy's "sense of rectitude" is "like a knife that looked out of her eyes" and that "it would have been better" if the inmates of Branshaw Teleragh "had all attempted to gouge out each other's eyes with carving knives" (147, 286). In the second poem, "The Mouldering Corpse" is speaking directly to "two whispering hyaenas." Nightly, they brush their claws in the sand above him. They grip his armbones. He hopes the marrow may "be very tasty to you two, . . . and green and putrescent!" If this poem does not describe Violet and Brigit handling Ford, it certainly shows Leonora and Nancy handling Edward; they are, Dowell says, "like ghouls with an immobile corpse in a tomb beside them" (275).[99]

A month later, Ford wrote that he had, surely because of Brigit, been thinking a good deal about Ovid's *Tristia* poems. They are about one who loves "some lady above him in station, so they carted him off to the confines of the empire. . . . And that depressed him a good deal." Nowadays, Ford says, "almost any lady is above a poet . . . the wives of stockbrokers, bill discounters, publishers, barristers." "When such a lady," he goes on, "to-day stoops the poor old poet would . . . bolt to distant suburbs. . . . And he would have a bad time." So Ford, imagining Ovid in such a modern quandary, "has produced quite a number of poems all addressed to the lady who brought about his downfall by breaking with him." And he appends an instance, called "That exploit of yours . . ." The poet is "here . . . in the vaulted and vaporous caverns of hell" as are Dowell and Edward by the end of *The Good Soldier*. The poet sometimes meets two soldiers there. One, "stuck by a pitchfork" while he was scaling a wall "to steal apples," recalls Dowell figuratively watching Edward "robbing the orchards" (291). The other, wearing a silver helmet and having been killed "from the fall of his horse on some tramlines," recalls Edward himself.[100]

Mizener gives good evidence for accepting Ford's recollection that he finished *The Good Soldier* in July 1914. A letter from Ford to his publisher, dated between August 10 and 19, refers to the manuscript as having been previously

delivered. The date (October 3, 1914) on the last page of
the printer's copy is consistent with a July completion.
Nevertheless, Richard Aldington's recollection that Ford
dictated to him a portion of *The Good Soldier* after the outbreak of war may still be correct. The last two chapters of
the manuscript are almost certainly in Aldington's
hand.[101] Moreover, Ford said on September 5: "Since this
war began I have written twenty poems and two chapters
of a novel!" The last two chapters Dowell writes eighteen
months after the completion of the previous chapter (268-
69). They are the only chapters that show Nancy giving
Edward "unimaginable hell" and that show her permanently insane. It is here, too, that Dowell says: "Well, it is
all over. Not one of us has got what he really wanted." "I
know nothing. I am very tired." "So life peters out" (274,
272, 282, 292). In that September 5 article, Ford says that he
has been trying to write a poem to a lady that will end:
"Well, that's all done!" He does not know whether he is "a
hero or just a tired person." He imagines himself to be "intellectually petering out. . . ."[102] Surely the outbreak of a
war involving his two homelands and his favorite country,
on the terrain he frequented with Violet, this war plus the
presumed loss of Brigit, must have made one month of
August seem to Ford as long as Dowell's eighteen. The
outbreak of war would also have kindled Ford's patriotism
and tended to mitigate his recently expressed hostility to
the "county-family atmosphere." In any case, Dowell's
most affectionate statements about Ashburnham occur in
those last two chapters of the novel.

The point of all this discussion is to underline how
Ford's immediate personal problems may have been ener-
gizing and shaping *The Good Soldier*. Yet explaining the
greatness of the novel is another matter. After all, his
agonizing troubles with Elsie and his winning of Violet lie
behind the vastly inferior *A Call*. How, this once, did Ford
dare attempt it, to undertake the first great work that follows Conrad's impressionistic manner and destroys or
dismisses Ford's most intimate friends? His journalism of

this period makes clear that he enjoys the role of ferocious critic. He acknowledges that "it is an exhilarating thing to do" to chuck his "cap into the faces of quite estimable people . . . we need the saeva indignatio . . . one wants to be reckless nowadays. . . . One wants it desperately . . . I should respect myself more if I could . . . just for once, say what I really think of a few people. But I have not the courage."[103] Except that he did have the courage—in the guise of fiction—to admit his dislike for Violet, give Elsie prussic acid, cut Marwood's throat and consider spitting on his grave. He had the courage to defy Conrad (and maybe James), to write his own masterpiece of impressionistic fiction. Ford had the courage because he had decided he was going to die soon. We can only speculate why that should be. Perhaps the *crise de la quarantaine* was upon him. He was also getting toward the age at which his father had died; Ford's children were likewise approaching his own and his brother's ages at the time of their father's death. Half-persuaded of his imminent demise, he so tender of skin could safely express his savage indignation.

And yet, *The Good Soldier* is great not so much for its bitter tone as for the almost filial love that Dowell feels for Edward (analogous presumably to Ford's deepest feelings for Marwood). If Edward's flaws of stupidity, self-indulgence, and sentimentality lie exposed, they are simply aspects of the great, living human being Ford was determined once in his life to create. Even if we do not believe that Edward, by virtue of his passion, quite belongs with Nancy among the "Beati Immaculati," he is appallingly human in his suffering.[104] A decade before *The Good Soldier*, in his little book on Holbein, Ford says that a "great portrait . . . makes its subject always a great man." "*Every* man," Ford goes on, "is great if viewed from the sympathetic point of view—great" not because of his actions, but because of his power to awaken interest. "Great art," Ford concludes, "is above all things generous, like the strong and merciful light of the sun that will render lovable the meanest fields, the barest walls" (124, 125).

Love of the father who had called him a stupid donkey and guilt for having enjoyed his death perhaps won out after all and helped make *The Good Soldier* the great novel that it is. We do not need merely to infer—from Ford's age, his death-thoughts, the misunderstandings with those two father-figures Conrad and Marwood—that Ford would at this time be thinking about his father. We know it from the journalism. The image of his father and Swinburne talking together becomes for him, in September 1914, when he has just completed *The Good Soldier*, the symbol of the good life lost. "A dim recollection" suddenly comes to Ford of his father and Swinburne, over a quarter of a century before, ardently discussing the identity of the *Satyricon's* author. Ford remembers "my father's high excited tones and Mr. Swinburne's mellow, exhortative, and beautiful organ." He likes thinking of his father and Swinburne "discussing with heat the identity of Petronius Arbiter, or whoever he was." It is a "picture of manners" he would "very willingly see revived . . ."[105]

Thus, at the very time Ford has apparently outraged Marwood and again dismayed Conrad, he is thinking of how as a child he just loved listening to his father talk. Ford's purpose in founding, with Marwood, the *English Review* was to promote discussion. And it was with Conrad—according to Violet—that "At Someries and The Pent they sat up all night helping each other to 'find the word.' "[106]

As a paean to both Conrad and Marwood, *The Good Soldier* succeeded in placating only the artist friend. Although Marwood apparently never again communicated with Ford, Conrad wrote a warm letter (undated but presumably of March 1915, or shortly thereafter) in praise of *The Good Soldier*.

The women are extraordinary—in the laudatory sense—and the whole vision of the subject perfectly amazing. And talking of cadences, one hears all through them a tone of fretful melancholy, extremely effective. Something new, this, in your work, my dear Ford—c'est très, très curieux. Et c'est très bien, très juste.[107]

Perhaps Conrad realized, too, that Ford was throwing himself into the war effort by writing propaganda, would soon enlist (making Conrad his literary executor), and would suffer sorely while trying to be a good soldier. Presumably Marwood's irrevocable rejection of him in 1913 instructed Ford that one's words and actions do have effects in the real world, a good lesson for a novelist who wishes to tell a true story. But the lesson seems to have held only for *The Good Soldier*. Like Dowell with Ashburnham, Ford came to the dangerous conclusion that Marwood was himself. In the twenties, by creating Christopher Tietjens for *Parade's End*, he turned from a true story to fantasy and produced very good work, but not the triumph of *The Good Soldier*.

---⋯⟨∽⟩⋯---

CHAPTER FIVE

Toward *Parade's End*

1914–1923

HOOFING OUT HUEFFER[1] (*WHEN BLOOD IS THEIR ARGUMENT* AND *BETWEEN ST. DENNIS AND ST. GEORGE*)

According to our theory, then, Marwood's determined rejection of Ford and Conrad's apparent withdrawal from him in 1913 so violated Ford's innate sense of blamelessness and so exacerbated his self-loathing that only one choice remained: to expunge Joseph Leopold Ford Hermann Madox Hueffer. By 1913 he had experienced much of the history of the typical, gifted, middle-aged, middle-class male suicide: early evidence of instability and disregard for the truth; rejection by father; early death of father; multiple marriages; heavy drinking; fluctuations in income; physical disability, especially involving shortness of breath; talk of self-destruction; a competitive or self-absorbed spouse.[2] But by writing *The Good Soldier* Ford had conquered the worst symptom of all: disappointment in the use of one's potential.

During his Violet period, the Fordian self had been predominantly Huefferian, Germanic, foreign. Nothing could more inspire loathing for that self than to see Germany attack Belgium, hence France, hence England, at the very spot where he proclaimed his marriage to Violet. Naturally, it took Ford a few days to absorb what had happened. An article of August 8 admits liking "so much" the South Germans and Austrians as well as the French, and blames the war on French politicians. But within three weeks Ford expects to be murdered by an English mob "for

my German sympathies"; very soon afterwards he begins
to extirpate his Huefferian self.[3] Of course political prudence played a large part. But Ford's motives must have
been deeply personal too. That German attack on the tenth
anniversary of his breakdown must have seemed to him,
like the anniversary appearance of Bagshawe to Florence,
"a grin on the face of Fate." Hounded by Elsie, chilled by
Violet, disappointed by Brigit, avoided by Conrad, rejected
by Marwood, Ford no longer wanted to be in Provence
with whom he pleased. He wanted to be a child again hearing his father and Swinburne talk about literature. Nevertheless, that past must be changed: father and son must
not be Germanic Hueffers. By the time Ford went into the
Army in August 1915, he had gotten rid of Joseph,
Leopold, and Hermann.[4] But even before that he had
taken steps to improve his past and to become Marwood
while writing his two books of war propaganda.

About one-third of *When Blood is Their Argument: An
Analysis of Prussian Culture* appeared serially in the *Outlook*
between September 1914 and February 1915. The revisions
of the serialized portions and the new material in the book
served to establish more firmly Ford's impressive knowledge of Germany while making more remote his personal
connections with it.[5] Significantly, Ford, while retaining
the lovely anecdote about Swinburne and his father as cul-
tivated, erudite Englishmen, omitted another equally long
account of his father. In it, he revealed that his father was
born in South Germany of Westphalian parents, could not
bear Prussianized professorial life there and "became the
most preposterously English person I have ever met."[6]

Besides minimizing his German connections in *When
Blood is Their Argument*, Ford transferred to Germany his
vision of the hell of Branshaw Teleragh in *The Good Soldier*
and the hell of the English literary and social scene of *The
Outlook* literary portraits. He described life in Germany as
"a frightfully worrying affair," with its people "leading
anxious lives . . . in an atmosphere of back-biting," the
whole country suffering such "strain," "tension," and

"agony" that it is "a hell to itself and a danger to the rest of the inhabited world" (191-92). Only three years earlier Ford had been calling Germany "my own amiable country" and referring to his readers as "you in England."[7] Clearly the revolution wringing his soul was even more extreme than his rejection, in *Ancient Lights*, of the Fabian past he had shared with Elsie. If Ford was seeing Britain as a "sack full of cats all at each others' throats" in his 1913-1914 journalism,[8] he now "cannot sufficiently emphasize to what an extent bitterness is the note of modern German life" (205). Although only a few months earlier he was weary of English country life, he prepares now for his transformation into Marwood and his union with a Stella Bowen he has not yet met. He tells how seriously he takes the traditions of English public-school life, "the traditions of responsibilities, duties, privileges, and no rights." It is ingrained in him that he "must give unceasingly" and in return, if he is lucky, some day "some one will spoil me a little . . ." (301).

Ford's propaganda book about the French, *Between St. Dennis and St. George*, is much less interesting than the really fine one on Germany. Nevertheless, it carries him along still further in altering his Germanic past and in making himself as preposterously English as Marwood. Although he once "had, for the German peoples, if not for the Prussian State, a considerable affection and some esteem," he is now "very tired of Germany." He feels as if Germany "had played upon me, personally, the shabbiest form of confidence-trick." He hopes Germany "will not exist much longer" (66). Only once, and very obliquely, does Ford refer to his own Germanic heritage: "descended, as I was, from . . . Roman Catholics in two . . . countries—Russia [sic!] and conquered Prussian territory" (49). Just how he persuaded himself of the Russian ancestry is hard to imagine. Frieda Lawrence later remembered that Violet said Ford was of "Russian descent." David Garnett presumably has *Between St. Dennis and St. George*

in mind when he says that Ford "wrote a book to prove he
was a Russian."[9] In any case, Ford also avoids referring to
his other heritage as South German and elsewhere makes
it more or less French. No barrier of race or creed divides,
he says, "the peoples of the South of Germany and the
peoples of France. Racially and historically these people
are Franks" (180).

If Ford Madox Hueffer, in *Between St. Dennis and St.
George*, disowns Germany and makes his ancestry Russian
and French, his main effort is to make himself as English as
Marwood and Ashburnham were, as Ford Madox Ford
and Christopher Tietjens will be: "I am about to give very
exactly phrased first-hand evidence, not of the Englishman
as he is or was, not of the Englishman as I have found him
to be, but of that individual as I have found myself to be"
(29). Ford epitomizes Englishness in a phrase, "correctness
of attitude," which he uses at least eight times (184, 186,
188, 189, 190, 191). The phrase recalls *The Good Soldier*—
and a far more complex view of things. At the end, "Edward's actions were perfectly—were monstrously, were
cruelly—correct." To Leonora, Edward is "abominably
selfish," however "perfectly correct" his actions. Dowell
"can't make out which of them" is right, and leaves it up to
the reader (283). War, however, encourages oversimplifi-
cations, and Ford embraces them in *Between St. Dennis and
St. George* for personal reasons, as he embraces his version
of Marwood.

What Ford really wants is peace. Yearning to be a child
again indicates this, as does "Félicité," the epilogue to *Between St. Dennis and St. George*. In France, there are no epistemological problems: "French men and women keep
themselves singularly in contact with the realities of life.
They know, extraordinarily . . . which things are real and
which are delusions." Yet those realities prove to look
Pre-Raphaelite and to smell of the grave. The views of
Boulogne and the Château d'Amour are in "painfully vivid
blue" and "painfully vivid pink." We need to get back to

Mme. Aubain and her servant Félicité, whose quiet rooms "smell a little of mould because the floor is a little lower than the garden" (195-96, 209, 204).

As it would probably have done Edward a great deal of good to have been killed in Transvaal, so it probably would have done Ford good, in France. Happily he not only survived but had twenty more years of incredible productivity. He served his king three-and-a-half years and suffered enough to satisfy his worst enemies. In the summer of 1916 he had two, brief, horrendous experiences close to the front; not surprisingly in view of his age and his medical history, he broke down physically and mentally. A second tour of duty in France a few months later resulted in another breakdown and his permanent return to England to serve the Army chiefly in educational functions.

THE GREEN NOOK (NO ENEMY)

Violet introduced Ford to Stella Bowen, a young Australian painter, in the autumn of 1917. By December 1918, he was promising her "quite a *little* cottage" in the country. Still, the first publishable prose he wrote after mustering out emphasizes his longing far more for peace than for companionship. This prose is the series of "English Country" essays, published in August and September 1919, excerpts from a work in progress that was finished in October, but not published until 1929, as No Enemy.[10] Despite stretches of triviality, No Enemy is a desperate, frequently moving account of Ford's deliberate decision to create for himself a "sanctuary." The book dramatizes his passion to find a "green nook" and to escape forever the pain of human relations by hiding out in a tiny piece of country (63, 221). The particular episodes from the war years that Ford recalls certainly show his helplessness before his overwhelming need to escape or, as he says, "to dig in." Most of them have, to my mind, a psychopathic aspect which Ford seems to recognize but also ultimately to desire. Although the episodes look to him like instances of "reality" breaking through to his consciousness, to the dispassionate reader they seem rather like those Fordian moments that Pound calls *halluciné*. Their dramatized meaning suggests not so much a way to deal with life in the future as a longing to escape human contacts, block from consciousness life's vicissitudes, and experience virtually a living death. *No Enemy* thus recalls the situations of total enclosure in which Lovell and Dowell ultimately find themselves.

Ford's alter ego in *No Enemy* is a middle-aged poet, called Gringoire (no doubt after the poet in *Notre-Dame de Paris*). In Flanders, Gringoire, like Dowell, feels "very isolated" as if he "were suspended . . . on a carpet in the infinitudes of space" (138). Like Ashburnham, as well as Dowell, he is without will; in France one is picked up and moved about like a parcel (259). Like Ford, Gringoire has rejected his past; the war has changed him utterly. Bad as the war was, it was less dreadful to him than his past. From his earliest childhood, he had been accustomed to the Fordian dreads "of bankruptcy, of incredible shyness, of insults, . . . of succumbing to blackmailers, forgers, brain-troubles, punishments, undeserved ingratitudes, betrayals" (64). Ford's odd emphasis throughout *No Enemy* upon the "shame" that the Germans would bring to "all the green champaign lands of the world" (21-22) seems to have a personal aspect. Part of him must have seen those gray legions bringing "contamination" and "humiliation" upon France and England as punishment for disloyalty to all his fathers (168, 28).

The heart of *No Enemy* is Gringoire's vision of four landscapes.[11] Before August 1914, he has lived chiefly through his eyes. But after that, the world becomes for him wholly gray (21). Only four times does he catch glimpses of reality, like "rifts in a mist" (24). Yet what Gringoire describes is a progressive withdrawal into fantasy. The first three glimpses do begin in the real world. The first reveals to him Kensington Gardens. But Gringoire's thinking that "old, stiff marionettes, rather homely courtiers and royal-

ties, might step out of the tall windows" of the Palace
suggests how private is the vista (25). The next two glimpses, though they also are inspired by the actual world,
begin in a strange psychic state and revert quickly to very
personal recollections. Gringoire, like Ford at his club
window, is thinking "nothing—a change in the beat of the
clock. . . . The whole world . . . noiseless; and immobile. . . .
And so the veil lifted for a second. The flat lands of Essex
were there, stretching out" (34). Gringoire's mind leaps,
almost immediately, to planting potatoes in Kent at the
end of the century, the time, place, occasion of Ford's
meeting Conrad (37). Convinced the war is lost, Gringoire
wants only to plant a garden. The third landscape, "an
immense sea . . . of swallows" in which Gringoire moves
as Lovell did and as Christopher Tietjens will, like "a
Greek God" (43, 44)—this experience, too, rises out of a
strange state: "rather like a dream . . . a numbness . . . like
being in the hands of doctors, on the way to an operation"
(51).

The last, the most memorable, of those landscapes that
become a "part of his immediate self" is literally a miracle
(48). Like the others, it appears at "a moment of the com-
pletest idleness" Gringoire has "known for many, many
months" (70). And what inspires the view is a piece of
French landscape, over the next shoulder, that the Camp
Commandant forbids him even to look at. Suddenly,
Gringoire begins to see in his mind "a nook . . . the closed
up end of a valley . . . a sanctuary" (62). This wholly imagined nook belongs to the world of dreams; its shape is
abstract, geometrical; its color is intensely bright; its image
lies between the senses and the external world; it recalls
works of art:

> There was a rhomboid of deeper, brighter green, of a
> green that was really alive, beyond the gray-green of
> the field they were in . It existed in front of the purple
> of scabrous flowers on the great shoulder that masked
> the battlefield. It wavered, precisely as you will see the

colored image cast on a sheet by a magic lantern, then
slowly, it hardened and brightened, took shape as a
recumbent oval, like eighteenth century vignettes.
(66-67)

To describe this nook and its effect, Gringoire reverts to
notions from childhood. The nook would have a fairy-tale
cottage (precisely the old cottage Gringoire now inhabits in
Sussex, 63, 9). His "subconscious mind" wants to believe
that after the war he will find a sanctuary where he can
cross his fingers in destiny's face and shout "Feignits" as
he did as a child playing at Prisoners' Base (67). He feels a
great longing "not for any humanity—but just for the
green country, the mists, the secure nook" (86). Although
to Gringoire the experience evokes images of childhood, to
me it recalls Ford's saving, if hallucinated, vision through
the window, in the depths of his mental breakdown, of
that greener than green parrot. In any case, precisely like
Ford's sight of the parrot's underside, Gringoire's glimpse
of the imaginary green nook brings to his mind "the peace
of God which passes all understanding" (68).

A month later, in a French village, a real visual image
persuades Gringoire that his illusory vision of the green
nook will enable him to survive in this world. Through a
dark window, his eyes make out a "white . . . triangular
patch," which proves to be the luminous forehead of a
Belgian war widow (244, 250). As she comes into her warm
kitchen with freshly dug potatoes, he "suddenly" sees
"again that vision in green—of the sanctuary!" (258). He
then remembers "extraordinarily" that familiar Fordian
experience of "digging potatoes at night" and finding "the
earth quite warm," exactly like thrusting "one's hand into
the breast of a woman" (259). And "suddenly," Gringoire
takes out a pad of paper and is able to write. Yet he con-
fesses that the frequently reappearing "recumbent oval of
green" has been frightening; he has wondered whether he
was about to have a seizure or succumb to some terrible
nervous disease (268). Now convinced that his vision of

the green oval is "not a visitation, but a sign," he believes that the Almighty will provide him with a place to dig himself in (269).

Ford being inspired to write by an instance of astonishing surprise, with sexual overtones, in the presence of a woman he has just met, is hardly a revelation. Still, *this* change of heart, beginning soon after *The Good Soldier* and receiving its most explicit discussion in *No Enemy*, represents a genuinely fresh departure. Although Gringoire calls his new state "aloofness of mind," he admits that he is weary of human beings and now prefers the society of vegetables and goats (120, 207). Thus, that aloofness he so admires seems not to mean artistic detachment, but a despairing withdrawal from human intimacy. And although his various visions mean that the war is over for him, the war in *No Enemy* is a metaphor for all the vicissitudes of life (267). Gringoire "must have a dugout, as proof as possible against the shells launched against me by blind and august destiny" (266). He identifies with the old, wrecked houses he has seen in Flanders and envies the total dissolution of one by fire, sinking "to the earth . . . luxuriously, as men stretch themselves down for a long rest" (199). And Ford's green nook becomes an image one might see, not when falling asleep, but when dying: "I hope . . . that, as the eyelids of those who fell closed on their glory, they had long, long visions, like that green vision that came to me . . ." (277).

BRINGING IN MARWOOD (*THUS TO REVISIT*)

Marwood had died of cancer May 13, 1916, some two months before Ford found himself at the Battle of the Somme. Almost as soon as Ford began publishing after the war, he wrote about Marwood at length and, for the first time, by name. He devoted most of an article of November 6, 1919, to Marwood. Gone is Ford's conviction of a profound gulf between himself and his friend. Their differences are now an occasion for amusement and affection:

"The novel . . . did not exist for this friend of mine. I don't mean that he despised novel-writing as an art; he simply did not know it was there . . . did not consider that novel-writing was a serious pursuit, any more than stamp collecting . . ." Except for that, Marwood is clearly Ford's ideal: "My friend the late Arthur Marwood . . . possessed, upon the whole, the widest and the most serene intelligence of any human being that I have yet met." (Serenity Ford never achieved, however phlegmatic his exterior! Significantly, he usually reserves that quality for people now dead, like Gaudier-Brzeska and Lieutenant Morgan, both of *No Enemy*.) Marwood's "tenacious . . . encyclopaedic" memory recalls, of course, Francis Hueffer's. Marwood's "singular wisdom . . . the ability to take various points of view that comes from a very wide knowledge and understanding of other given cases" is the sort of wisdom Ford five years later would attribute to Conrad. Marwood's "generalising habit" comes closest to Ford himself: "It was a sweeping statement to which my friend thus committed himself . . . For myself I love sweeping dicta; . . . the more obviously sweeping they are, the less they need to be taken *au pied de la lettre* . . ." And, of course, Marwood's politics are Ford's: "in essence, he was the last of the Tories."[12]

Marwood also appears several times in Ford's first published book after the war, *Thus to Revisit*, written in 1920 and published in 1921. A delightful, irreverent reminiscence, *Thus to Revisit* is devoted wholly to writing and writers, with the significant addition of Marwood. Ford's rich references to Marwood there serve to particularize the man and to strengthen the bonds between them. Ford describes him as "large, fair, clumsy, and gentle" (59). He provides a little history, mainly accurate: "He had no personal ambitions, being a Yorkshire Tory Squire, a distinguished mathematician and the Fellow of some Cambridge College—Trinity, I think" (59). He has the college right this time (later it would be Christ's) and the school, Clifton (RY, 398). Although he does not yet move Marwood's death back to before the war, he does poeticize Marwood's mathematical prowess a bit by making him a Senior Wrangler, an impossibility as Marwood was at Cambridge only two years (218). Ford repeats his paean to Marwood's mind in unverifiable but delightful particulars, telling how Marwood could hold forth accurately on rigging fruit schooners, rotating crops, "the home life of Ammianus Marcellinus, the vocabulary of Walter Pater . . . the rapture of Higher Mathematics, Napoleonic strategy, consubstantiation, or the Theory of Waves. . . ." (59).

Thus to Revisit discusses explicitly for the first time that bond between Marwood and himself that Ford had used so often in his fiction, the founding of the *English Review*: "In the lightness of our hearts and the inexperience of early middle age, Arthur Pearson [*sic*] Marwood—alas, that I must write: the late!—and myself set out to afford a nucleus for some sort of Movement that should combine some of the already Eminent with some of the Young . . ." (58). The *English Review* united its founders in pain and joy. A "familiar literary friend of Marwood and myself" (Conrad?) in a "full-dress letter of remonstrance" said they were "ruining [their] careers." Ford's language describing Marwood's anguish with the enterprise echoes what he always said of his own. Merciless and vengeful Destiny, he says, must have driven Marwood into the *Review* "to punish him for some sin unknown to the rest of the world. And if the enterprise did not ruin him as our friend had so forcibly predicted, it certainly inconvenienced him and caused him to endure a great deal of mental uneasiness and semi-public odium" (59-60). However, when *Les Jeunes*, Ezra Pound and all, appeared on the scene, the partners and a few friends shared the joy of being involved in a real literary revival (136).

Since Ford, characteristically in *Thus to Revisit*, damns the "erudition of fact . . . that kills alike true Learning and the love of it," he would seem to have a problem with Marwood, "the most factually-gifted soul that I have met" (167, 217-18). Not at all. "Temperamentally," Marwood

"was a poet" (218). Indeed, perhaps the closest bond between Marwood and Ford is their similar sufferings at the
hands of fact-stuffed schoolmasters. Ford learns this when
Marwood tells him one evening that "the characters of
Shakespeare and of Our Redeemer . . . bored him." Both
"had for him the aspects of Modern Educators." He saw
"them as if with the features of the 'English' master of Clifton . . . or . . . of Strauss who wrote the *Leben Jesu*." Ford
finds it tragic "that the beautiful spirit of Arthur Marwood
should have the beautiful features of Shakespeare and of
Our Lord ruined for him" (218-19). Ford makes the bond
explicit: "just as Shakespeare and Jesus were murdered for
my friend Marwood by one set of pedants, so was Shelley
murdered for me by . . ." (192. The ellipsis is Ford's and no
doubt stands for William Michael Rossetti). Incidentally,
Marwood's being damaged by a "cramming school" is a
specific tie with Edward Ashburnham (220).

Not surprisingly, Ford's immediately postwar prose also
contains allusions to his other best friend, Conrad. What is
surprising is that the earliest reference is an attack, the
only one I know, and that the subsequent references in
Thus to Revisit have a new emphasis. A week after the first
tribute to Marwood appeared came this curious discussion
of Conrad (the period of collaboration has been cut in half):
"Years and years ago I used to spend ages and ages . . . in
collaborating with Mr. Conrad. . . . It lasted for perhaps
half a decade. . . . I notice that Mr. Conrad is now engaged
in doing what is called *dénier des dieux de sa jeunesse*, and in
giving me the lie—which is all in the journey of a long
day."[13] Possible sources of Ford's wrath would be the reissuing of the collaborations without his name on the binding, which rightly outraged him, and the likelihood that he
was explicitly unwelcome at Conrad's handsome country
house "Oswalds" where the Conrads entertained frequently a new circle of friends. The separation is sadden-
ing because the war had brought the two friends back together. Ford made Conrad his literary executor before
going to France. That Ford associated his military adven-

ture with his hero's maritime youth is touchingly suggested by his request to borrow Conrad's old watch glasses. Conrad had regretfully to report they had long since disintegrated. From France, Ford wrote several agonized letters during his breakdowns, and Conrad responded, nobly, lovingly. Ford on several occasions visited Conrad's son Borys, a youthful artillery lieutenant.[14]

Ford's November 1919 attack on Conrad proved happily, and characteristically of Ford, only a temporary, human aberration. In *Thus to Revisit*, Conrad is "our Greatest Writer in the World," *Under Western Eyes* the "finest novel in the English language" (79, 91). Their collaboration lasted not for half a decade but "for many years" (39). Ford grants, what is perfectly true, that Conrad's later work may be getting "tired." *The Rescue* strikes him as "thinner and more pale" than *Chance* (80). Charitably, he does not even mention Conrad's two love stories, the only full-length novels of the war years. Perhaps this is because Ford recognizes Conrad's lack of interest in rendering the "relations of the sexes" (98). He imagines that Conrad would disapprove of de Maupassant's great expression of unbearably painful love, *Fort Comme la Mort*, a model for *The Good Soldier* (97).[15] Despite his appropriate praise for the political novels, Ford emphasizes in *Thus to Revisit* Conrad's Englishness. He titles the chapter, "Mr. Joseph Conrad and Anglo-Saxondom" (79). The reason for the success of *Chance* is that there Conrad gives "to Anglo-Saxondom the most attractive, the most pleasant, the most desirable of all views of . . . itself" (87). And he gives to Conrad that most English of virtues: Conrad's sailors always try to maintain "a certain standard of rectitude" (101). Conrad also appears importantly in *No Enemy*, coloring the character of Gringoire. His last words, spoken, of course, in "his heavy tired voice," must have been added after 1923: "Rest, . . . after toil, port after stormy seas. . . . Do greatly please!" (292). A quotation from *The Faerie Queene*, this serves as the epigraph to Conrad's last completed novel, *The Rover* (1923), and the epitaph on his tombstone. In *Thus to Revisit* Ford does not yet consign Conrad to the county aristocracy and lets him remain, for a few more years, "Elizabethan." Ford does, however, describe Henry James as a "country squire" (100, 116).

THE MARSDEN CASE

Although he legally substituted Ford for Hueffer in June 1919, Ford did not use his new name on a title page until he published *The Marsden Case*, his first novel after *The Good Soldier*: "By F. M. Ford (Ford Madox Hueffer)." Only one memorable paragraph and one brilliantly conceived, marvelously grotesque scene recall the Ford of *The Good Soldier* and make *The Marsden Case* a plausible preparation for *Parade's End*. Rather, the novel's chief interest is biographical and psychological.[16] A collage of bits of Ford's real and fictive pasts, it dramatizes how much of the old Hueffer the new Ford had to drag along with him. Much of the newness of the novel lies unfortunately in the indifference with which Ford treats formerly excruciating materials.

Although Ford said that *The Marsden Case* was based on an old story about Ralston, Turgenev's first English translator, the novel is transparently autobiographical.[17] The plot takes us instantly to the Ford (Hueffer) of the title page: George, the hero, goes by his mother's surname, Heimann, until he is nearly thirty (and looks forty), but his "real" name, that is, his patronymic, is the fine old English name of Marsden; indeed, he is the third Earl Marsden. Though their enemies call the Heimanns German Jews, George's mother's name is "really" Franco-Flemish. In terms of Ford's fantasy, not Hueffer but the purely English Ford is his "real name." And Hueffer is not German anyway but Russian and Frankish / French. The subject of *The Marsden Case* obviously reflects Violet's efforts, with Ford's uneasy cooperation, to call herself Mrs. Hueffer. George Heimann's sister Marie Elizabeth is determined to prove that she is a Marsden, even Lady Elizabeth Marsden.

George is reluctant because his father had rejected that name after being wrongfully removed from Gladstone's government. Going, in anger and sorrow, into early retirement on the Continent, he had pretended to be the maternal uncle, not the father, of his children. After his father's death, George remains reluctant to pursue the title out of affection for a paternal aunt whose cruel husband will make trouble for her if George and his sister prove their case.

Marie Elizabeth (Violet), backed up by her women friends and dressed in the newest fashions, constantly pushes poor George (Ford) into painful public scenes. When George proposes to enlist, his sister considers it "wicked" and tries to "get that stopped" (254). As usual, however, beneath the obvious surface of recent events lie earlier ones: the marriage to Elsie, her friendship with Olive, her 1909 response to Ford's defection. Marie Elizabeth combines the names of the Martindale sisters; her birthday, May 17, 1894, is Elsie's (and Ford's) wedding day. If her small compact body and scarlet make-up recall Violet, her memorable eyes and "beautiful chest" recall Countess Macdonald and Elsie. If her campaign to be called Marsden is very like Violet's, her legal efforts and longing to triumph resemble Elsie's. She is on a "crusade" to "bring to book a guilty man" (184). And Marie Elizabeth, unlike Violet and very like Elsie, does win. She is aided and abetted by her best friend, Miss Jeaffreson, and her solicitor brother, who have innumerable connections with Olive and Robert Garnett. Rather touchingly, if the novel castigates Miss Jeaffreson for her prurient meddlesomeness, it also praises her for coming to George's aid, holding him firmly by the arm, when he is suffering the onset of a nervous breakdown.

The book's crucial names, Heimann and Marsden, unite indissolubly Hueffer and Marwood. The character of George's father, Mr. Heimann (really the second Earl Marsden), fits Marwood. A "large, stooping" man with a "bulky body," "a man of great probity," he reads only "solid" books, "of the memoir type" and speaks "with calmness, precision, and balance" (48, 55, 113, 52, 53). Like the passionate Marwood, though, he occasionally makes violent statements. These are inspired not only by rage but by obscure physical pain, reminding us of Marwood's lifelong physical suffering. Heimann's unjust treatment by Gladstone (a "reverse" in "early life") has the same effect on him as Marwood's illness had on him: Heimann lives in shackles and dies unfulfilled at the beginning of the war (156, 59). Though of Whig, rather than Tory, ancestry, the Marsdens, like the Marwoods, are all, "high-falutin, sentimental, unpractical, and too clever by half" (173).

Two fine moments in *The Marsden Case* merit mentioning for themselves and for the light they shed on Ford's remarkable if uneven achievement in *Parade's End*. One moment has to do with Marwood, the other with the war. Speaking of the war, the narrator says:

> What is dreadful is that the world goes on and people go on being stupidly cruel—in the old ways and all the time. I used to think that, once out there, we should be surrounded by a magic and invisible tent that would keep from us all temporal cares. But we are not so surrounded, and it is not like that. . . . what is desolating, what is beyond everything hateful, is that, round your transparent tent, the old evils, the old heartbreaks and the old cruelties are unceasingly at work. (304-305)

This lovely passage (it provided the title for a good book on Ford's war novels) recalls, of course, the "sanctuary" of *No Enemy*.[18] It inaccurately suggests that the heroes (and Ford) did not find their green nook after all. But the neurasthenic Ford / Dowell narrator, Ernest Jessop, survives to tell the tale, and the handsome Ford / Ashburnham hero, George Heimann, wins the pretty young thing, Clarice Honeywill, and positively thrives.[19] The way that George does it is the key, in my opinion, to the way Ford was able to write *Parade's End*.

The lowest point in George's fortunes is his attempted suicide in September 1916 (the very time when Ford was having a breakdown on the western front). George intends to kill himself in part because of the death of his father. When the latter learns on August 4, 1914 that the Germans have crossed the Belgian border and hence that his Fordian dream of eternal Anglo-Teutonic friendship is a hollow mockery, he "hanged himself that afternoon from one of the immense beeches of an avenue outside the town. . . . pigs must have gone rooting beneath his father where he hung in the twilight; at any rate, the body was found by the City Swineherd, a State official" (208). George is so obsessed with mimicking the details of his father's suicide that he loses valuable time and flubs it anyway.

> He had wanted to reproduce to exactitude the tragedy of his father! The limb of the beech had to be twenty-seven feet above the ground. He would have liked swine to rout in the beechmast beneath his feet. He was an epicure in sensation. . . . In order to suit his connoisseur's taste George had hung himself from a very old beech tree that grew out of the bank, so that he had swung out sideways instead of taking a drop. (319)

Thus, he does not snap his neck; and he gives Clarice time to drive up in her car with the big police constable at her side, scoot under George's swinging body, catch him (as in "The Perils of Pauline"), and restore him to health and wealth and happiness.

Allegorically, the scene signifies Ford's half-conscious awareness that, though the war did not provide an invisible tent, the death of Marwood, his beloved father-figure, in May 1916 ("before the war"), may have saved his life. Marwood, in dying, would save Ford's life by making possible Ford's mad and detailed imitation of the man. But the best thing about the scene is George as "connoisseur." Ford is viewing his own rescue, his reincarnation as Marwood, with irony—comically even. Ford does not fool Ford

all of the time! The new Ford of *The Marsden Case* has not
escaped the past. His flight to a green nook is an escape to
a level below that of *The Good Soldier*. Nevertheless, there is
still life in him—if he will only play Marwood "to exactitude."

The first volume of the tetralogy, *Some Do Not*, takes its
odd title from Ford's next book, the delightful comic drama
in poetry, *Mister Bosphorus and the Muses*. The play tells
how a great but neglected English poet is abused by his
copper-haired, black-clad, hag-like Northern Muse (Violet?). The lovely, youthful Southern Muse, Clarissa, adores
the poet and determines to rescue him from her rival. Her
exclusive capacity to inspire to verse the weary Bosphorus
points obviously to Australian Stella Bowen. The translation of the poet and his youthful muse to the South prefigures Ford's and Stella's escape from English mud to the
Côte d'Azur immediately on finishing *Mister Bosphorus*.

Although Bosphorus does not, even symbolically, attempt suicide, he is, like George Heimann, a "connoisseur" (61). Moreover, he consciously and frequently plays
roles as when, in order to escape his enemies, he accedes
to his Southern Muse's injunction to "continue to appear
mad" (87). To achieve at last his perfect happiness of writing forever on a tablet pressed against the bosom of his beloved, on southern shores, Bosphorus first must, like Ford
in 1914, die and be reborn. Only then can he shake "off all
Northern shards" (110). But also the lovers must entertain
their enemies and the public with "buffoonery," "for these
are children here." "The Public," his Southern Muse in-
structs him, "Expect it of us . . ." Bosphorus begs her to
teach him "to come off well." She promises to bring him
"fitly off" and exhorts him to play his "part" as creditably
as he has the "art" for the sake of the fitness of things.
Ford never played his part better than in *Parade's End*. He
had the inspiration of having escaped from England into
Elysium. "The Gods," he says in *Mister Bosphorus*, give to
each person "a differing lot." Some, like Ford and Mr.
Bosphorus, "rest on snowy bosoms! Some do not!" (107-
108, 57).

CHAPTER SIX

Parade's End as
Christmas Pantomime
1924–1928

SOURCES AND PROBLEMS

The *Parade's End* tetralogy intends to show how Christopher Tietjens, the last of the Tories, learns to accept himself and live in the modern world. This self-awareness comes about through a series of painful experiences in love and war. In *Some Do Not*, Christopher, the saintly mealsack, not only agrees to take back his unfaithful bitch of a wife Sylvia, but also manages it so that no one except his best friend Vincent Macmaster even knows she ran off with another man. Simultaneously, Christopher and young, forthright Valentine Wannop fall in love; since, however, "some (that is, the best) do not," they heroically keep their love platonic. Ironically, little Macmaster has at the same time embarked on an adulterous affair with the elegant Edith Ethel Duchemin. Sylvia and others, including Christopher's godfather General Campion and his brother Mark Tietjens, sporadically believe that Christopher has had an illegitimate child by Valentine, stolen money to support them, had an affair with Mrs. Duchemin, and driven his father to suicide. *No More Parades* tells how Sylvia trails Christopher to wartime France, meddles with his Army career, and sets General Campion against him. As a result, Christopher loses his satisfying post in the Transportation Corps and, despite ill health, has to join an infantry battalion at the front. In *A Man Could Stand Up*, Christopher first proves valorous in battle and then suc-

cessful in love. On Armistice Day, he signalizes his rejection of the corrupt old world by leaving Sylvia, embracing
poverty, and making Valentine his mistress. *Last Post*,
viewed chiefly through the eyes of the bedfast, mute Mark
Tietjens, shows Valentine pregnant, her Christopher re-
storing antiques for a living, and Sylvia ultimately accepting their happiness and her loss.

As realism, even Fordian realism, these four wonderful,
if uneven, fictions betray one fundamental weakness: the
incredible perfection of the hero. This difference between
Christopher Tietjens, on the one hand, and John Dowell
and Edward Ashburnham, on the other, makes *Parade's
End*, despite its many admirable qualities, inferior to *The
Good Soldier*, and further illuminates Ford's basic psychological and artistic problems. The strengths of *Parade's End*
are almost wholly new to Ford.

That memorable first picture of the two young men of
the English public official class riding in the immaculate
new railway carriage bears unmistakably the signature of a
master. Unlike *The Good Soldier* which, in my view,
emerged from a single, if exceedingly complex, biographical situation, *Parade's End* must owe its happy genesis to a
great variety of inspirations. Partly Ford succeeded by
abandoning conditions and techniques that had worked
for *The Good Soldier* but not for *The Marsden Case*. Specifically, he gave up England. Although his assumption of
Marwood's identity reflected a determination to be more
English than the English, Ford needed the virgin territory
of France, and especially the dazzling skies of the Midi, to
light him on his way. Again, although Dowell had proven
a brilliant invention, Ernest Jessop as narrator of *The
Marsden Case* had not worked well, and Ford gave up the
method. Abandoning Marlovian first-person narration, he
no longer needed to worry about Conradian "justification." Indeed, although Ford subtitles each of the first
three volumes of *Parade's End* "A Novel," he is at his best,
probably against his conscious intentions, when writing
not in the mode of realism but in that of fairy tale, or of

Victorian pantomime. This change is the direct result of his retreat into a green nook and his more or less conscious, protective assumption of a new identity. Probably his personal, marital situation also contributed. Whereas writing *The Good Soldier* chiefly in agonized response to the loss of two male friendships results in a glimpse of reality, writing *Parade's End* under the beneficent female protection of Stella Bowen provides escape and rest. Nevertheless, one of the most powerful sources of Ford's triumph is his plunge again into the matter of *The Good Soldier*. Although *Parade's End* is explicitly about the war, it is also explicitly about Marwood. Moreover, although the alleged intent of the tetralogy is to project Marwood into a posthumous wartime existence, it in fact relies heavily upon Ford's own imaginative responses not only to his early relations with Marwood but also to those with Conrad and Elsie.

That opening scene in *Some Do Not* must owe its greatness to memories of three highly charged train rides, all uniting passion and literature. Christopher Tietjens and Vincent Macmaster, headed both for golf at Rye and a visit to a Rossetti-collecting clergyman, think and talk about passion. Christopher is virtually unstrung by the knowledge that he must take back the wife who has betrayed him. Macmaster, excitedly reading proof on his first book, about Rossetti, argues against Tietjens on the side of Pre-Raphaelite love. Unbeknownst to them and to the reader, both men are headed for their lives' passions. That very day Macmaster will meet Edith Ethel Duchemin, and Christopher, Valentine Wannop. By the next day's end, Macmaster will have committed adultery with Mrs. Duchemin and Christopher will be strongly attracted to Valentine.

The episode recalls, first of all, Ford's identical train ride to Rye in 1892, bearing his first novel to Elsie in order to launch his successful courtship. Although Elsie was young and unmarried, her father proved to be almost as difficult and mentally unstable as Mr. Duchemin. As Ford and Elsie played in appropriate costume at Pre-Raphaelite love, so would Macmaster and Mrs. Duchemin. The other two train rides admittedly lack explicit sexual content. They do, however, involve two men of "passion," literary work in preparation, and railway carriages on a South Kent line. The men are, of course, the chief catalysts of Ford's creativity. In *Joseph Conrad* he describes amusingly how he sat while Conrad read proof for their *Romance* on the train up to London. In *Return to Yesterday* Ford tells how Marwood and he would work on *English Review* materials while traveling together by train down to Aldington.

Thus, with such highly charged memories out of a past going back fifteen, twenty, more than thirty years, *Parade's End* begins. But just *when* does Ford imagine that episode as occurring in *Some Do Not*? When, indeed, does anything take place in the tetralogy? The question is immensely difficult, really impossible, to answer. But it is worth mentioning, if only to show how strongly certain events were pressing upon Ford, acting at once to distort the fabric, and to energize the content, of his fiction. A close look at the shifting ages of the characters and the timing of fictional events in *Some Do Not* reveals almost total confusion. Part One, consisting of Sylvia's adulterous escapade and Christopher's introduction to Valentine, probably occurs in June, 1912; but it could happen in June, 1906. Part Two, dealing with Sylvia's "exposure" of Christopher's supposed misdeeds and Christopher's recognition of his love for Valentine, takes place in August, 1917—or August, 1916.[1] Similar inconsistencies appear in the other three volumes.[2] Now what do these discrepancies show except that the small academic mind is more obsessed with consistency than is the great artistic one? Certainly, these "mistakes" in chronology do not tarnish what is truly brilliant about *Parade's End*. At their best, its characters are ageless grotesques out of Dickens,[3] the pantomime, and the puppet theater. The show that those fabulous creatures put on is essentially timeless. What the chronological discrepancies do suggest, I think, are the personal sources of Ford's creativity in *Parade's End*. It is best to think of two chronologies: one, official and conscious, the other personal, half-conscious. The official schedule places *Some Do Not* in 1912 and 1917; *No More Parades*, January 1918; *A Man Could Stand Up*, spring 1918 and Armistice Day; *Last Post*, well into the twenties. But a personal, more dynamic chronology would put *Some Do Not* at about 1906 and 1916; *No More Parades*, late 1916 or early 1917; *A Man Could Stand Up*, early 1917 and Armistice Day; *Last Post*, 1919. When in doubt about the timing, the reader should probably choose the earlier date. He should respond, that is, to Valentine's feeling that ten years have passed between their first meeting and Christopher's proposal, her feeling that two years more pass between proposal and Armistice Day consummation. One should accept Christopher's impression that he and Valentine met a long time ago; Sylvia's that she has been absolutely continent for many years; the shared impression that Mrs. Wannop has aged greatly and that Christopher's son, born seven months after the marriage, is eighteen and appears first in *Parade's End* in 1919.[4]

The summer-solstice opening of *Some Do Not*, with Christopher's wife having been abroad for four months and his best friend and protégé giving him moral support in the vicinity of Rye, recalls a specific, important moment in Ford's real and fantasy life. By early summer 1906, we remember, Elsie had been abroad for four months, Ford's domestic arrangements were not to his liking, he had been collaborating with Conrad in Winchelsea, he had seen a lot of the Marwoods, and he had probably introduced them to the Conrads.[5] There is, of course, no evidence that then, or at any other time, Elsie was attracted to, let alone involved with, another man. Nor is there any reason to think that Ford fell newly in love while Elsie was away.[6] Still, the chief characters of *Parade's End* in many ways reflect the central figures in Ford's real-life drama. Of course, Edith Ethel Duchemin recalls, chiefly, Elsie Martirdale Hueffer. (But the given names may be revenge on Ethel Elizabeth "Brigit" Patmore.) Vincent Macmaster recalls Conrad (and thus Ford). Sylvia Tietjens recalls, chiefly, Violet Hunt;

Christopher, Arthur Marwood (and thus Ford). Valentine Wannop clearly plays Stella Bowen's part, with other real or potential rescuers, even Violet, probably implicit.[7] Although it was over thirty years since Ford had fallen romantically in love with Elsie, twenty since their marriage had come to mean mainly illness and sorrow, fifteen since he had left her, and probably a decade since their last bitter meetings in the law courts, still Ford could not write fiction well without including her. She appears as Mrs. Duchemin, beautiful, dark and carmine complexioned, with straight nose, pointed chin, and "necklace of yellow polished amber" (70, 72).[8]

If Macmaster a little reflects Ford, he mainly recalls Conrad—not the great man of Ford's loving reminiscence but the bad Conrad Ford would revile to Violet and ridicule in *The Simple Life Limited*. Yet Ford, even in his unhappiness about Conrad's late works, would never have portrayed him as he does Macmaster, author of twenty-three critical monographs in the Eminent Bores series (MCS, 10). Into Macmaster must also have gone Ford's contempt for his own early self and his lifelong detestation of the typical academic critic of the Edmund (afterward Sir Edmund) Gosse variety.[9]

The presence of Conrad's and Elsie's shades suggests why Ford would keep pushing the opening events of *Parade's End* back toward 1906. But why the other impulse, to push the wartime portions toward 1916 and early 1917, despite compelling structural and historical reasons to set them in 1917 and early 1918? Since Ford's unhappy experiences in war-torn France occurred between mid-July 1916 and early March 1917, he would obviously be drawn to that time for the two novels set in France. But probably there was another reason, especially for placing Christopher's home service between March and August 1916. This was the time of Ford's own pre-France service; more important, it was the time, May 13, 1916, of Marwood's death. Conrad, we recall, had written to Ford in March 1913 that Marwood thought he was dying. In *The Good Sol-*

dier Ford had, with not remarkable foresight, portrayed Edward's death and, rather more remarkably, Leonora's remarriage to a neighboring farmer. In *The Marsden Case* he had again depicted the death of a Marwoodian character. In *Some Do Not*, although Christopher unabashedly reflects Marwood, the handling of old Mr. Tietjens' death probably reflects Ford's pained feelings about Marwood dying unreconciled with him. Mr. Tietjens, we recall, believes the lies Ruggles purveys about Christopher, that he takes money from his wife's lovers in order to pay for his own love affair with Valentine. Presumably this is Ford's fantasy upon what Marwood may have believed of Ford when he ceased communication in early 1913. Marwood's death without a friendly word to him must have hurt Ford very much. Why else would Ford have begun, by the preface of *Last Post*, to push that death back to the time before the war when they were still dear friends? Why else would Ford, contrary to historical fact and to Marwood's personality, have Marwoodian characters commit suicide?[10] Ford must have felt, however irrationally, that so cruel a departure had to have been deliberate. Christopher never forgives his father for killing himself and never forgets how, in the club writing room, the night before his death, his father had seen him, uniformed and sad, and would not acknowledge him (SDN, 261).

The beautiful Sylvia Tietjens—her reddish hair; her perfect figure; her wicked, witty tongue; her fashionable clothes, doting males, London social world, indifference to the war; her longing sometimes to whip, sometimes to cherish, her husband; her remorseless pursuit of her husband and his mistress after the war; and yet that persistent touch of class that keeps her from ever being really vulgar and extorts even from Christopher and Valentine a grudging respect—Sylvia as Violet needs no documentation.[11]

Valentine, by virtue of her role as the latest Only Possible She, is an anthology of Ford's female friends. First and foremost, of course, with her youthful, pug-nosed face and her rescue of the shattered soldier, she recalls the lovely Stella Bowen (NMP, 75). Other details connect her with other loves.[12]

Christopher himself is not only a portrait of Marwood, but a more accurate one than Ford would later provide in the reminiscences.[13] But since Ford had Marwood's height and coloring, apparently identified with him right away, and obviously idealized him, it is impossible to separate Christopher's Marwoodian from his Fordian traits. Both men probably shared Christopher's qualities of generosity with money and hospitality. However, all the wartime experiences, specifically the service first in a government office, the hospitalization in Rouen, the loss of memory, the terror of being taken prisoner, all these are exclusively Fordian (SDN, 282; NMP, 181, 204, 75; SDN, 210; MCS, 265). Then Christopher's sexual involvements are only too Fordian (MCS, 25). Indeed, a supreme irony informs any account of Ford's identification with Christopher. Long since an embarrassment to his friends for the frequent inaccuracy of his statements and for his inconvenient propensity to fall in love, Ford chose for his fictional hero a character who possesses a staggering store of facts, a brilliant statistical expertise, and an amazingly selfless honesty—a character who not only believes in monogamy and chastity but long practices them in the most trying situations.[14]

But of greater interest than similarities and differences between Christopher and Ford is the insight *Parade's End* provides into the workings of the Fordian mind. Certain remarks in the original prefaces make clear how conscious Ford was then of at least incorporating Marwood's point of view, if not of actually adopting his identity. The preface to *No More Parades* tells that it happened in September 1916, in the area known as the Salient: "I said to myself: How would all this look in the eyes of X . . . already dead, along with all English Tories?" (NMP, 7). The time and place are surely those of Ford's vision in *No Enemy* of the green nook to which he could escape. This, in turn, reminds us of his characteristic need to look with someone else's eyes.

Ford's preface to *Last Post* reveals how palpable the dead Marwood has become for him. "I have only to say to my mind, as the child on the knees of an adult says to its senior: 'Tell us a fairy tale!'—I have only to say: 'Tell us what he would here have done!' And at once he is there" (LP, vii). For Ford, the prototype for Christopher is even now "in Avignon," where Ford has been and to which he will return, "seated in front of the Taverne Riche under the planes . . . finding his Harris tweeds oppressive . . . mopping the whitish brow under his silver-streaked hair." He will keep going until "I myself cease" (LP, viii). However, although the dead Marwood is now alive in Provence, Ford pushes the living Marwood of 1913 into the conditional: "before the War even," he was in the habit of asking himself what Marwood "would have said . . . how he would have acted" (LP, vii). It is a further key to Ford's mind and to *Parade's End* that this preface should equate the mind inspiring the novels with an adult telling a fairy tale. He has already told us, with the voice of Gringoire in *No Enemy*, that he could, if he wished, write effectively about the war in the manner of a fairy tale (63).

Some of Christopher's comments suggest how Ford half-consciously adopted a new identity and employed it not just to view reality but to manipulate it. In *Some Do Not* Ford gives the formula for making oneself into a Marwood:

> In electing to be peculiarly English in habits and in as much of his temperament as he could control—for, though no man can choose the land of his birth or his ancestry, he can, if he have industry and determination, so watch over himself as materially to modify his automatic habits—Tietjens had quite advisedly and of set purpose adopted a habit of behaviour that he considered to be the best in the world for the normal life. (222)

Christopher believes it possible to modify not only one's own behavior but also past external events. When Valentine wonders whether they "*could* wash out this afternoon," Christopher says: "Yes, you *can*. . . . Cut it out; and join time up. . . . It *can* be done" (SDN, 348). So Ford had cut out the years of Marwood's anger. More typical of Ford, however, than the elimination of recalcitrant elements is their rearrangement. In fiction and probably in life, such changes sometimes serve to reactivate previously quieted anxieties. Having once upon a time decided that Christopher could not, after all, ever have been Edith Ethel Duchemin's lover, Valentine then experiences, after a couple of quiet years, a reversal of feelings: "But now after her farewell scene with Edith Ethel *a simple re-arrangement of the pattern* had brought many of the old doubts at least temporarily back" (SDN, 328, my italics). Recurrent allusions to patterns in the tetralogy remind us that Christopher and Ford share another habit, playing patience (solitaire) (SDN, 58). Christopher plays it while arranging his thoughts about how to respond to Sylvia's maneuvers; Ford characteristically played patience while planning an ensuing stage of a novel.[15]

Parade's End represents then, and owes its strengths partly to, a fantastic rearrangement of Ford's intimate, early history. Since this is also true of *The Good Soldier*, it is not surprising to find the earlier novel itself inextricably involved with the biographical sources of *Parade's End*. Indeed, *Parade's End*, especially for the first three volumes, is a kind of *Good Soldier* with a happy ending. The rough correspondences are fairly obvious. Both works feature two couples and an innocent young girl. However, although the Tietjens and the Macmaster couples, plus Valentine, roughly parallel the Ashburnhams and the Dowells, plus Nancy, the differences are striking, important, and necessary to the relatively happy ending of the later work. Christopher Tietjens of course resembles Edward Ashburnham in many ways: in his blond, blue-eyed, high-colored looks; his taciturnity as to his emotions; his total lack, in time present, of sexual relations with his wife; and his almost total lack of verbal communication with her (SDN, 23, 13, 53).[16] Although Christopher's attitude to-

ward love differs somewhat from Ashburnham's, both feel
that the real purpose of love is conversation and that sex is
merely the by-product (MCS, 203, 239). Still, as the chaste
husband of a formerly, if not currently, unfaithful wife,
Christopher plays a sexual part more analogous to Dowell's than to Ashburnham's. And so, when Christopher
finds that Sylvia has betrayed him with Perowne, he falls
into the same stupor Dowell does on learning of Florence's
long infidelity. Though not only not virginal but even the
father of a son, Christopher, like Dowell, wonders
whether he might be temperamentally a eunuch (NMP,
38). Again like Dowell (and Ford) but unlike Ashburnham,
Christopher detests Pre-Raphaelite sentimental, romantic
gurgling and considers it proper that Dante put Paolo and
Francesca in hell (SDN, 25, 27). Christopher shares both
Dowell's passion for caviar and his distaste for underdone
beef (SDN, 117, 133).

Similarly, although Macmaster mainly plays Dowell to
Christopher's Ashburnham, the occasional variations in
his hero induce reciprocal ones in himself. Smallish, neatly
attired, with a special kind of blue tie, Macmaster looks a
good bit like Dowell. While he begins *Parade's End* with a
sexual conquest, he is never subsequently portrayed as the
manly lover or husband. Rather he remains the "little . . .
drooping, deprecatory fellow," "the sort of person to
whom any Lady Macmaster would want—would have—to
be unfaithful" (MCS, 10). He seems, thinks Valentine, "to
ask for it" (SDN, 325). After Macmaster's death, Mark Tietjens takes over his role in the sense of being Christopher's
observant admirer and his sympathetic advocate against
the women who mistreat him. With none of Dowell's
flaws, he still recalls him in being connected by some sort
of alarm system to his wife,[17] and in his sense, not so terrified as Dowell's, of an enormous sky and an enormous,
eternal night (LP, 47, 278).

Like the men, Sylvia deviates on occasion from her
predecessor in *The Good Soldier*; but mainly she plays
Leonora to Christopher's Ashburnham. Both women are

Roman Catholics married to Anglicans. Though attractive to men, Sylvia remains throughout time present of *Parade's End* rigidly continent and longs to win her husband's love. She goes as far as Leonora in actively, if unsuccessfully, promoting an affair between her husband and Valentine in the hope that, once satisfied with the young girl, he will return to his wife (NMP, 94). Nevertheless, Sylvia differs widely from Leonora in having been unchaste before her marriage and unfaithful afterwards. That is, Sylvia plays Florence too, just as occasionally Christopher plays Dowell. Specifically, she invents chronic heart trouble to account for the anguished sound she must emit when her first lover comes to mind (SDN, 187). And much as Florence is observed by Bagshawe during her affair with Jimmie and then later exposed, Sylvia is seen by Thurston while in Brittany with Perowne (NMP, 263).

Still, Edith Ethel Duchemin chiefly fills the role of Florence. "A paulo-post pre-Raphaelite prostitute," in Christopher's memorable phrase, Edith Ethel succumbs as quickly to Macmaster as Florence to Ashburnham (SDN, 135, 284). Circumspect, continent, suave, apparently one of the bright beings of the earth, Edith Ethel proves ultimately disgustingly vulgar (SDN, 324). Despite the fine education and upbringing the Reverend Duchemin provided, Edith Ethel remains irretrievably lower middle class; her culture reveals itself as merely quotations memorized for use on the right occasions (MCS, 8).

Young, sexually inexperienced, idealistic, vibrating between devotion and detestation for her beloved, the considerably older Christopher, Valentine obviously resembles Nancy in a general way. Valentine, however, is of so much tougher stock that only one parallel is worth pursuing. Like Nancy on that fatal November ride to the train with Edward and Dowell in the dogcart, Valentine, improbably for a summer night, wears an otter-skin toque on her fatal ride in the dogcart with Christopher (SDN, 156). We shall return to the sexual content of the scene. Let us now simply remember how Ford's private chronology seemed to push this scene toward 1906, the original key date for *The Good Soldier*. Let us also remember that the source for that scene in *The Good Soldier* is *The Spirit of the People*, written in the spring of 1906. However, for Valentine and Christopher, the ride sets the seal on their mutual love and means a happy ending, whereas the ride with Nancy means the extinction of two beautiful souls and a tragic conclusion. That Ford, after a decade, should still be so in touch with his masterpiece indicates unwaning vitality. That he can so flexibly rearrange and reverse the biographical and fictional counters at his disposal suggests the continuing command of a master. But his tendency to take Christopher's improbable triumph as seriously as he took the painfully convincing destruction of Ashburnham brings us back to the fundamental weakness of *Parade's End*.

The tetralogy cannot wholly succeed because it attempts to paper over the radical division between Ford and Hueffer. Ford could say to himself that he had become Marwood, but no one can really become somebody else. Moreover, forty-five years of dragging along Hueffer were not to be denied. The theme of *Parade's End* is that Christopher Tietjens, last of the Tories, throws off his old ways and learns to live in the modern world. The visible symbol of his victory is Christopher's acceptance of Valentine's and his mutual if illicit love. The trouble is that in his heart Ford has never believed in happy endings in the real world and cannot do so even now, in the liberated twenties and with the protection of Marwood's persona. Ford remains a third generation Pre-Raphaelite, a child of the nineties, who knows only that love brings death. Ford's inability to accept his own sexuality and his resultant guilt and unhappiness are, of course, what make Ashburnham's story so sad and *The Good Soldier* so great.

PASSION

Ford's fundamental doubt about the validity of his theme expresses itself most vividly in a recurrent scene[18] that essentially denies any hope that union with Valentine will mean peace and happiness for Christopher. Of the previous, innumerable, Fordian scenes of interrupted passion, perhaps the most germane comes from *Ladies Whose Bright Eyes*. When Mr. Sorrell exchanges his first warm, long look with the Lady Dionissia, he immediately finds himself hurtling off to battle on the back of a raging stallion. The ride terrifies him and results in the fatal savaging of an enemy, whose death wins his pained sympathy. Scenes of this sort recur at the rate of two per volume throughout *Parade's End*. They usually take place just when Christopher is about to act upon his passionate longings. They commonly involve horses in some way; blood is often spilt; grotesque noises frequently accompany the action: the primal scene, in short, with father and son both taking a beating.

The *locus classicus* for such scenes of interrupted passion is, of course, also the first one in *Parade's End*, the memorable dogcart accident at dawn, in the Kentish, midsummer mist. The occasion is rife with Christopher's sexual longings and fears. When Valentine, like Lady Dionissia, takes "a long look at him . . . with immense eyes," he feels as if somehow "destiny" has looked at him (SDN, 171-72). Just when she tells him that he is actually not terribly ugly and lays her hand in his, General Campion's car, looking like "a black-laquered tea-tray," appears. The horse rears up out of the mist (173). There is "a crash and scraping: like twenty tea-trays" (174). The horse is pouring blood "like a red, varnished stocking." Tietjens staunches it with wadding made from Valentine's petticoat and then angrily confronts his godfather, who looks like "an enraged, scarlet scarecrow" (175). While the couple sit together afterwards on the road bank awaiting the horse-ambulance and Christopher tells Valentine about Groby and Valentine tells Christopher he will never take her there, Ford indicates the meaning of the accident. Christopher, shaken by sobs, thinks that, perhaps, he is not the father of his child, that, perhaps, he could not even beget a child, and that he is responsible for the horse's dreadful injury (178). In short, successful sexual communion has never been and can never be Christopher's; even to long for it means the spilling of blood. Moreover, that censorious, "scarlet" father figure may himself be as much a victim as a judge.

The scene is but the first of some half dozen memorable occasions of frustrated passion. But it also looks back to the great if underplayed scene in *The Good Soldier* when Edward and Nancy say "So long" forever. No blood is spilt at the time; the parting means merely that Edward will cut his throat. Perhaps that is what Dowell's image refers to: "The signal for the train's departure was a very bright red; that is about as passionate a statement as I can get into that scene" (288).

The other memorable scene of interrupted passion in *Some Do Not*, like that of the separation of Edward and Nancy, emphasizes neither horses nor violence. The obstacle to consummation is Valentine's drunken young brother, who insists on sitting beside the cab driver and grabbing at the reins as the trio returns late at night to the Wannop house. The scene is bloodless, but the boy has to be carried into the house, where his snoring provides plenty of distracting noise: "enormous, grotesque sounds, like the laughter of unknown races." Although Christopher has learned between the two episodes that he is indeed the father of his child and that Valentine wishes to be his mistress, still he and she decide that they are "the sort that . . . *do not!*" (345-47). (Had they decided otherwise, where would have been Ford's tetralogy?)

The two scenes of interrupted passion that take place under fire in France necessarily operate on the level of fantasy. Christopher, after all, can only dream about the absent Valentine. In the first instance in *No More Parades*, the spilt blood produces the image of the desirable girl rather than the other way around. Moreover, the familiar Fordian horse appears only by way of explicit reference to the dog-cart scene (35-36). On the other hand, the enormous, crashing sound of the air raid is described with the same figure as Campion's car, "an immense tea-tray, august, its voice filling the black circle of the horizon" (11). The blood belongs to O Nine Morgan, victimized by his woman's sexuality as General Campion and Christopher are by Sylvia's. "In the bright light," it looks "as if a whole pail of scarlet paint" had been poured over Morgan's face and body. Christopher feels "as he did when you patch up a horse that has been badly hurt." He remembers the horse from "whose chest the blood had streamed down . . . like a stocking" and, for the first time in the novel, the girl who had provided her petticoat (35). He can clearly see her face (36). Despite Valentine's promise at the end of the previous volume to be his when he comes back, Christopher now believes that he will never see her and that he is indeed a eunuch (37, 38). In much the way that he irrationally feels responsible for the horse's injury, he considers himself, quite unjustifiably and unconvincingly, to blame for O Nine Morgan's death.[19]

The parallel scene in *A Man Could Stand Up* unequivocally issues out of thoughts of Valentine Wannop. First, the "clean, blond, small" looks of Lance-Corporal Duckett and his "slightly peaked nose" remind Christopher of Valentine (160-62). She begins to "obsess" him, and he comes to his memorable conclusion that "you seduced a young woman in order to be able to finish your talks with her. . . . That in effect was love" (203). He decides that after the war he will live with Valentine (205). Christopher even admits to his little second-lieutenant, Aranjuez (like Campion, Morgan, and Christopher, a henpecked hero), that he has someone he loves and that he will "probably get her" (214). These are essentially his last words before a shell explodes with a terrible noise (215). He and Duckett and Aranjuez are blown up into the air and then partially buried. Although Christopher manages to dig them all out, Aranjuez is hit in the eye while being carried to safety: "The boy kicked, screamed, tore himself. . . . The scream was like a horse's in a stable on fire" (220). *A Man Could*

Stand Up seemingly ends without a second scene of interrupted passion. Valentine finds herself in Christopher's
arms, setting out on a "dear, meal-sack elephant" (275).

But, of course, in *Last Post* that elephant ride proves to
have been one long scene of unfulfilled passion resulting
in a whole roster of medical cases. Although Christopher
and Valentine do manage to embrace on the top step of St.
Martin's Church, they have had first to put the "raving
mad" McKechnie into a hospital for shell-shocked soldiers,
and to cope with the colonel's dying of cancer in their very
cab (187-88). When the happy couple returns to Christopher's flat for the purpose of, at long last, making love,
they find Sylvia waiting to block the way. Falsely claiming
that she too has cancer, Sylvia fakes a faint, falls down the
stairs, and actually injures her ankle (217-18). Presumably,
Christopher and Valentine never get into any bed that
night because, after a long conversation at Mark's and their
separate returns to Christopher's flat, they are soon sum-
moned back by telephone to Mark, now inert in Marie
Léonie's bed (191). Although no blood actually flows,
Mark's face turns "dark purple," and the doctor calls his
attack "fulminant hemiplegia" (190, 29).

The final scene of unconsummated passion occurs at the
very end of this last novel. When Christopher finally returns from Groby, brokenhearted at the destruction of the
great tree and the severe damage to the ancestral house,
Valentine greets him not with kisses but with recrimina-
tions and sends him off again "like a dejected bull-dog"
(291). Now Mark must speak, to try to bring them back together. The result is, of course, his death, presumably
from another infusion of blood. And if no horse imagery
accompanies the two scenes of Mark's strokes in *Last Post*,
Mark is certainly the horse expert of the tetralogy.

Now since these scenes of frustrated passion are some of
the most memorable and enjoyable in *Parade's End*, and
since they seem necessary to keep the work going, one
cannot simply reject them. Nevertheless, they do signalize
a profound thematic inconsistency that really amounts to

unconscious artistic dishonesty. Let us consider for a moment the role of Mark in *Last Post*. Surely Ford and Graham Greene are right that that novel is superfluous to the whole scheme.[20] But it is much worse than superfluous. It exposes Ford's doubts about his entire enterprise. Again and again and again, Ford insists that if Christopher can only get Valentine he will be happy. Yet when he does, presumably, get her, what happens? Christopher essentially disappears from the tetralogy. Ford scarcely ever enters his point of view again. This is, then, our same old Ford, almost totally unable to write from the point of view of a character who is active sexually, the Ford who is at his very best when he observes and speaks through Dowell.[21] Moreover, Christopher is almost never alluded to as a lover. Valentine thinks of him chiefly in relation to their unborn child; Marie Léonie remarks that Christopher certainly conceals any amorous tendencies, and Mark assumes that Christopher ignored Sylvia maritally from the very first (LP, 39, 105). Moreover, *Last Post* is a great esthetic falling off from *A Man Could Stand Up*. Instead of those two superb points of view, Christopher's and Valentine's, we get Mark and Marie Léonie observing in a trivial way such new, trivial characters as Mrs. De Bray Pope, Lord Fittleworth, and the local peasantry. Ford presumably cannot imagine Christopher as happy lover. Indeed, merely trying to be a lover would have unstrung Christopher, like Don Kelleg and Dudley Leicester at the telephone, and incarcerated him in a tiny space, like Lovell. Both these things happen to Mark. Yet, even after shifting Christopher's sexual trauma onto Mark, Ford still cannot specifically imagine Christopher winning Valentine. Many pages must be spent in detailing how their union did not, after all, occur Armistice Night, as the reader of *A Man Could Stand Up* had absolutely assumed. *Last Post* irresponsibly violates the tone of the marvelous last scene of the previous novel, the Armistice Day party.

Indeed, Ford virtually cannot proceed from volume to volume in his tetralogy without discrediting what happened in the previous one. *No More Parades* disregards certain very important facts established by the end of *Some Do Not*. More seriously, *No More Parades* ignores or violates feelings, attitudes, among the characters that are convincingly dramatized in the previous novel. By the end of *Some Do Not*, Christopher has, through careful research, come to the conclusion that the child that Sylvia thought was her lover Drake's is, after all, his own (SDN, 219, 271). Christopher has also discovered beyond doubt and so convinced Mark that Valentine is not, as the Tietjens brothers feared, their own father's illegitimate child and, therefore, that Christopher's love for her is not incestuous (263). Even more important than these rather important facts, however, are the attitudes Ford induces in his readers. We feel at the end of *Some Do Not*, with very good reason, that Christopher and Valentine are irrevocably pledged to one another. When Christopher returns for good from the war, Valentine will become his mistress. Sylvia, out of a newly awakened, selfless love and compassion for Christopher, will permit him to have Valentine without harassment. Sylvia's deep kindness to Mrs. Wannop at the Macmasters' and her heroic backing of Christopher against the bankers, Port Scatho and Brownlie, are high points in the novel, clearly intended to be taken with utmost seriousness. These facts and attitudes are essentially discounted in *No More Parades*. Sylvia's compassion is as if it had never been. Instead, it turns out that Sylvia had only been, Christopher believes, making herself pretend to care for him (NMP, 91). Indeed it emerges that Sylvia struck him in the face his last night in London because he had not slept with Valentine.[22] Now that Christopher is in France, Sylvia is on the warpath again, stripping his bank account, stopping his letters, harrying his commanding officer, and finally pursuing him to France. Meanwhile, Christopher has received no letters from Valentine. Of course, he has not written to her, and she has no military address for him. Her unequivocal pledge to him is also as if it had never happened. Christopher knows he will never see her and credits her with believing that he and she are parting forever (37, 94). He considers himself friendless (28). As for the paternity of Sylvia's child, unquestionably settled in *Some Do Not*, an impenetrable obscurity has settled upon that (23).

Similar inconsistencies obtain between *Last Post* and the previous three novels. Perhaps the most disconcerting is Mark's initial reacceptance of all the old falsehoods he had abandoned in *Some Do Not* and his rejection of the one inference that stands up through three volumes. Having accepted categorically, in a seriously intended scene of fraternal understanding in *Some Do Not*, that Sylvia's son was fathered by Christopher, Mark has to run the whole gamut again: Michael is "Sylvia's by-blow"; the "probability" is that he is "the other fellow's son"; "this boy was probably his brother's son" (LP, 96, 103-104, 107). In that same brotherly conversation in *Some Do Not*, Mark had accepted Christopher's impressive chronological evidence that their father could not be Valentine's also. But now Mark believes that Valentine is Christopher's "half-sister as like as not" (163). On the other hand, Mark begins to question the only event that has never been in doubt before—his father's suicide. Ultimately and in gross violation of the reader's belief, Mark concludes that their father did not commit suicide, hence was not Valentine's father.[23]

Even the delivery of Groby to a Papist is now implausibly motivated. Having long held out against Sylvia's raising their son a Roman Catholic, Christopher suddenly caves in—because, through no fault of his, his check bounces! "It was getting my cheque returned to the club. . . . A fellow who can't do better than that had better let the mother bring up the child" (SDN, 271).[24] Almost as daft is Christopher's reason for not writing to Valentine from the trenches: "by Heavens, he could not write to her! If he stopped one or went dotty. . . . Wouldn't it make it infinitely worse for her to know that his love for her had been profound and immutable?" (MCS, 213).

Ford's imperfect control of his materials makes itself felt in other ways in this, his second-best work of fiction. Ford, the old pro who would roll on the floor in hysteria over Pound's romantic clichés, Ford, the creator of Dowell, whose love of the good soldier includes ironic awareness of his absurdities, Ford at his very best would hardly have perpetrated these: "Their lips met in a passion of pity and tears" (SDN, 129). "She loved him, he knew, with a deep, an unshakable passion, just as his passion for her was a devouring element that covered his whole mind as the atmosphere envelopes the earth. Were they, then, to go down to death separated by years, with no word ever spoken? To what end?" (SDN, 264). What strikes one in these instances, and the next, is not only the staleness of the language but also the banality of the rhythm. "She was then, she knew, so nicely balanced that, had he said, 'Will you to-night be my mistress?' she would have said, 'Yes'; for it was as if they had been, really, at the end of the world" (SDN, 327). "He prized her above money. She thought—ah, she knew—that he prized the child within her above the world" (LP, 247). Three new, recurrent interjections—"oh," "say," "call it"—suggest how impatient Ford has become with the work involved in finding the right word. It is as if he were willing to put down anything in order to get on with his book.

Ford's lapses, inconsistencies, improbabilities, impatiences, the weaknesses, in short, of *Parade's End*, have causes deeper than his carelessness and even his personal responses to his sources. They have to do with the work's fundamental conception. Christopher must from the first be perfect and act perfectly; yet he must develop, grow up somehow, and find happiness. The trouble is that though Ford can see changes in human fortune only too vividly, he at heart believes in neither the development of a character nor happiness. Nevertheless, he would insist upon the perfection of the hero who, despite Ford's protestations, represents Ford himself. To Conrad, he wrote at about the time *Some Do Not* was published: "when I look back on my life I can see nothing to regret except mistaken—or miscalculated, generosities."[25] Christopher and most of the main characters bear witness more than once to Christopher's impeccable behavior. In *Some Do Not*, Christopher knows that he is "spotless," and in *No More Parades* he believes that the course he has taken is "perfectly correct" (98, 107). Christopher is the "most honourable man" Sylvia knows, "perfectly immaculate" (SDN, 207; NMP, 205). Valentine, of course, considers him "innocent as a child" and "always right" in his predictions and pronouncements (SDN, 294; LP, 255). Nevertheless, Christopher is forever being attacked. People like General Campion, Sylvia, Port Scatho, even Colonel Levin, typically confront him with a series of charges or stipulations. Typically, Christopher knows they are false, but still takes "all the blame, sir" (NMP, 290). And typically his accuser, for the time being at least, comes over to Christopher's way of thinking. So Campion thinks: "But he's right to do as he is doing" (NMP, 317). If the recurrent scenes of frustrated passion recall Mr. Sorrell and the Lady Dionissia, these scenes of charges and refutations recall the reversal scene in *The New Humpty-Dumpty* where Macdonald confronts his enemies and the Duke of Kintyre and Lady Aldington back him up munificently.

Besides Ford's perpetual, deeply rooted conviction that passion brings unhappiness and death, and his equally deep need to believe himself innocent of all blame, two episodes occurring during the course of the writing of *Parade's End* may have contributed to the tetralogy's weaknesses. Or perhaps the episodes were an inevitable condition of Ford's getting on at all. I am referring to his affair with Jean Rhys in Paris and his involvement with Rene Wright in New York. The dates of these episodes are particularly significant. The affair with Jean Rhys coincides, according to Mizener, with the beginning of *No More Parades*, October 31, 1924, *Some Do Not* having appeared the previous April. Although Stella later wrote that the Jean Rhys affair "cut the fundamental tie" between them, Ford did disentangle himself and told Stella that "nothing could ever upset us again." She must have believed him, for they tried together to buy a house at Cap Brun, Toulon, in early

1926, when Ford had just begun *A Man Could Stand Up*. He finished it in Paris well before he left for New York the following October. During his four months in America he met Rene Wright, whom he had not seen since their first meeting in New York in that recurrently important year of 1906. Although Ford did not tell Stella about Rene until after his next visit in New York, the winter of 1927-1928, he was writing (incredibly bad!) love poetry to Rene during that first visit of 1926-1927. He wrote *Last Post* between the two visits.[26] The dates of these two extra-Stella affairs of the heart interest me because they coincide with the writing of the second and fourth volumes of the tetralogy. Long before I knew anything about Ford's life, I thought that *Some Do Not* and *A Man Could Stand Up* were much the best of the four, and *Last Post* distinctly the worst. So long as Ford is faithful to Stella, he can render Christopher's and Valentine's delighted pursuit of one another; his usual inability to dramatize a happy union is compounded when he deviates from Stella. Disloyalty to her causes him unconscious self-hatred; the resulting self-pity makes him write sentimentally and drop from the tetralogy either Valentine's consciousness (*No More Parades*) or Christopher's (*Last Post*), with most unfortunate consequences.

A couple of things need to be said in Ford's behalf. He probably sensed that he was not being consistent from volume to volume. He calls *No More Parades* "not so much a continuation as a reinforcement" of *Some Do Not* (NMP, 7). Again, he surely knew that Christopher was impossibly perfect and much of the motivation improbable. In his preface to *Last Post*, he equates, as we have seen, his mental evocation of Marwood with a child asking for a fairy tale. Moreover, he does not even bother to call *Last Post*, like the others, "A Novel."

Despite the relative weakness of *Last Post*, the point of view of the bedridden Mark Tietjens is a useful key to the genuine greatness that *Parade's End* does, after all, possess. Although Mark's impotence recalls Dowell, he differs markedly from his predecessor. Mark *may* be a trickster; he may be a Gubb putting on a great show. Mark himself and his wife think that he is pretending to be ill, that he has deliberately chosen neither to move nor to speak (LP, 288-89, 29). His indignant rejection of a stupid and cruel world is analogous to that conscious act of Ford's, which we have posited, the elimination of Hueffer and the substitution of Marwood. It was a piece of trickery, yes, but perhaps necessary to Ford's survival and whatever sanity he maintained. *Parade's End* succeeds, when it does succeed, not as a deeply moving novel about the sufferings of a good man but as a very good show.

PRE-RAPHAELITE COLORS

The way Ford describes Colonel Levin's narrative really epitomizes what is most memorable about *Parade's End*: "a singular mosaic of extraordinary, bright-coloured and melodramatic statements . . . monstrosities of news . . . without any sequence" (NMP, 84). "Bright-coloured" and "melodramatic"—these qualities characterize the finest scenes in the tetralogy, which succeeds in its bits rather than in its totality. We have already seen how Pre-Raphaelite brilliance of color enhances *The Good Soldier*. Beyond Ford's obvious artistic heritage, his preoccupation with bright colors may have had psychological sources. Although the Pre-Raphaelite colors evoked by Dowell do not seem pathologically based, the green nook and the luminous forehead of the Belgian widow in *No Enemy* do. In *Joseph Conrad*, Ford repeatedly equates remembering with "disordered pictures" of bright colored objects (52, 101, 181). In *Parade's End*, he institutionalizes (or uses conventionally) the previously rare moments of hallucinated brightness. Strange light and bright colors figure in most of the best scenes.

One version of the spot of color remarkably duplicates the parrot-image of Ford's hallucinated moment, noted earlier, and suggests how far from normal realism he has departed. This spot, like the parrot's green, means rest and, though inanimate, recalls a bird. While in the front-line trenches, Christopher becomes fascinated by "a particular splash of purposeless whitewash" situated up above his head. He is convinced that if his head and body were somehow levitated so as to be level with the splash, "he could be in an inviolable sphere." He finds himself "constantly glancing aside and upwards at that splash; it was in the shape of the comb of a healthy rooster; it gleamed, with five serrations, in the just beginning light . . . that cockscomb of phosphorescence" (MCS, 63-64). Christopher is obsessed with the phenomenon.[27] When his knees feel weak, he longs to be levitated so he won't need to use his legs (68). Or, if he "stood in space, his head level with that cockscomb, he would be in an inviolable vacuum—as far as projectiles were concerned!" (71). When Christopher is finally blown up, he remains "suspended in space. As if he were suspended as he had wanted to be in front of that cockscomb in whitewash" (216). The image has, then, a meaning that runs counter to Ford's intended theme. True rest for Christopher means not talking to Valentine but being isolated, encapsulated—or dead, like Mark in his "infinitely . . . extravagantly green" nook (LP, 9, 70).

Whereas here the unhappy mind of Christopher has simply seized upon an actual spot of whiteness and fantasized about it, in other instances he suffers from visual delusions, genuine hallucinations. Upon hearing the name of the private soldier who died so bloodily in his arms, Christopher perceives on a piece of white paper "thin films of reddish purple . . . wavering, then a glutinous surface of gummy scarlet pigment. Moving!" Perhaps to suggest the connection between death and a rural nook, "the glowing image" turns "a faintly luminous green" (NMP, 106, 107). Conversely, Christopher imagines "the embattled world as . . . an embossed map of greenish *papier mâché*. The blood of O Nine Morgan was blurring luminously over it" (NMP, 310). Christopher has a similarly terrifying hallucination of Sylvia. She appears "before him so extraordinarily bright and clear" that he shudders: "Thoroughbred! In a sheath gown of gold tissue, all illuminated, and her mass of hair, like gold tissue too, . . . His eyes, when they were tired, had that trick of reproducing images on their retinas with that extreme clearness . . ." (NMP, 23). The experience ends like a Pre-Raphaelite painting: "The semi-clearness became a luminous blue, like a tiny gothic arch, and passed out of his vision to the right" (NMP, 24). Valentine, however, since she does not yet represent the threat of sexual cruelty, presents herself to his imagination as "a little tranquil, golden spot" (NMP, 38).

Although these hallucinatory moments interest us chiefly as psychic oddities, Ford's vision importantly enhances his best dramatic scenes. Time and again these scenes are rendered memorable by their bright colors, gleaming surfaces, strange light. It is as if Ford were inspired by his infirmity, his longing to escape to the Pre-Raphaelite world of eternal paint. Paradoxically, one effect is to give a youthful, as well as an unearthly, sheen to everything. Even the setting—a "perfectly appointed railway carriage"—of that remarkable first scene has a touch of this quality: "The leather straps . . . were of virgin newness; the mirrors beneath the new luggage racks immaculate as if they had reflected very little; the bulging upholstery in its luxuriant, regulated curves was scarlet and yellow in an intricate, minute dragon pattern" (SDN, 9). But the golf scene a little later with its outdoor light is still more authentically Pre-Raphaelite: "all the distances under the tall sky showed with distinct prismatic outlines." It is "so clear and still in the air" that Christopher, observing the city men with their "red knitted waistcoats," the policeman's "face scarlet like a lobster just boiled," the young woman running "round the corner of a green mound," feels "as if he were in a light museum looking at specimens" (83, 87, 88). The next day, Valentine and Edith Ethel arranging flowers on the breakfast table, with its "congeries of silver largenesses," in the paneled room with its Turners, golden mahogany sideboard, and green silk curtains, are distinctly accessories to a still life (103). Sylvia's "white-enamelled, wickerworked, bemirrored" room in Rouen provides a backdrop for a Pre-Raphaelite subject described by Sylvia herself: "Christopher is playing at being our Lord calling on the woman taken in adultery" (NMP, 141, 143). But the dazzling light belongs to her bedroom where she powders her armpits "in a brilliant illumination from two electric lights," exhibits "her long, shining limbs," her "incredible arms, stretched out amongst a wilderness of besilvered cosmetics" (284). The following day, Christopher awakens when Campion blocks the bar of sunlight on his desk. It is a "bright day . . . full of things with hard edges—a rather cruel definiteness." The Seine is "like an S on fire in an opal," and Christopher recalls another agonizing day that was "a miracle of sunshine" with "a sky that ached for limpidity" in contrast to the "moving slime" that was the German deserters (237, 246, 248, 299).

Ford's abandonment of a personal narrator and his adoption of a point of view free to move among consciousnesses and through space and time enable him to use his spots of color with great effectiveness. Whereas Dowell thinks he needs to justify his scene shifts, Ford does not in *Parade's End*. One of the great moments of *Some Do Not*, and a fine instance of Ford's use of light and color, begins a chapter, with no preparation whatsoever: "Jumping down from the high step of the dog-cart the girl completely disappeared into the silver" (156). Marvelous visual images recur throughout the chapter, but especially interesting are Christopher's thoughts about the scene of early morning Kentish mist. They remind us that Ford is constantly using extreme visual effects. Christopher enjoys "the thought of the grotesque appearance he must present in that imbecile landscape. On his right an immense, improbably brilliant horn of a moon, sending a trail as if down the sea, straight to his neck: beside the moon a grotesquely huge star: in an extravagant position above them the Plough" (157). When Sylvia notices that her face is as white as her teeth and looks like a head on an alabaster tomb, she resists as melodramatic the impulse to slap "an enormous patch of red upon either cheek" (NMP, 178). She would look, presumably, like a clown.

Appropriately, the best two pages of *No More Parades* are the last—a delightful, comic picture of General Lord Edward Campion inspecting Christopher's battalion cookhouse. Everything gleams as it should in a proper military kitchen and as it should in this frequently gleaming novel. Campion looks, as usual, like a "godhead, frail and shining," "brilliantly accompanied by Colonel Levin." The cookhouse is "spotless with limed walls and mirrors that were the tops of camp-cookers. . . . The cook-house was like a cathedral nave. . . . The floor was of coke-brise shining under french polish and turpentine." After briefly addressing the mess sergeant, "with his light step the shining general went swiftly to the varnished panels in the eastern aisle of the cathedral" to inspect spice cabinets. But the scene is even more than a wonderfully bright painting. The cooks, "white tubular beings with global eyes," resemble "the pierrots of a child's Christmas nightmare." When Campion taps the panel marked "PEPPER!" and says to a cook, "Open that, will you, my man?" this is to Christopher "like the sudden bursting out of the regimental quick-step" (318, 319). Thus the scene yokes Ford's shining visual effects with the fun of Christmas pantomimes.

CHRISTMAS PANTOMIME

"Some do not," those very first words of the tetralogy, indicate how closely, from the outset, the Tietjens saga was associated in Ford's mind with popular entertainment, the music hall, and, especially, the pantomime. The phrase comes, we remember, from Ford's 1923 poetic drama, *Mister Bosphorus and the Muses, A Short History of Poetry in Britain*. The rest of the drama's title tells us that Ford is offering a traditional Christmas pantomime: "Variety entertainment in four acts . . . with harlequinade, transformation scene, cinematographic effects, and many other novelties, as well as old and tried favourites."[28] The poem itself beautifully fulfills the title. Like any pantomime, *Mister Bosphorus* has a fairy-tale plot: the apparently ancient, broken-down, mad hero is miraculously transformed by the good fairy into an eternally young lover. In appropriately fairy-tale ritual, the loving young woman, like Cordelia with Lear or Beauty with the Beast, transforms her hero. With "scented soap, white towels, pure water warmed," she washes his feet "in the waters of youth," and dries them with her hair. Bosphorus's "cheeks are no longer sunken; his eyes . . . glow; his shoulders erect themselves! He is a man!" (87, 88). Ford underlines the fairy-tale aspects by questioning the reality of everything that happens. Athis, for example, says she would scream if she thought Cerberus were real: "But we're the creatures of our poet's dreams" (67). Ford mixes up different kinds of entertainment in traditional pantomime fashion. The poet plays the piano and sings. The words of one of his songs are projected on a screen for the audience. (Pantomimes are strong on audience participation.) As is also common, one scene takes place in the nursery, the presence of a great St. Bernard recalling *Peter Pan*. That the dog "is solemnly sick on the hearthrug" (32) suggests Ford is parodying the form—except that pantomimes often include elements of conscious self-parody. With his swiftly changing elaborate sets of many ages and many climes, Ford is simply paying tribute to the gloriously, incredibly elaborate productions of Victorian pantomimes. The heroine, as Columbine, appears in ballet costume, trips along an invisible wire and executes "a mist of entrechats" (106). Her brother as Arlequin appears in a black mask and patchwork clothes. The poet as Pantaloon and the Critic as a clown indulge in slapstick comedy. The wicked Duchess entangles the Policeman in the usual long string of sausages. This scene reaches its climax in the traditional explosion, blowing up Pantaloon, who dies (temporarily) by the traditional blow on the head by a bladder, delivered by his enemy, Clown-Critic-Bulfin.

At the same time that Ford is having fun writing a pantomime he is also playing with the materials he will begin using a few months later in *Parade's End*. As patroness of minor poets and seller of poetic manuscripts, the wicked Northern Muse-Duchess looks forward to Edith Ethel Macmaster; as an invader of, and spy upon, the hero's and heroine's loving privacy in their arbor, she prefigures Sylvia. Bulfin, the hero's best friend become literary critic, establishment figure, and enemy, adumbrates Macmaster of course. The lovely Southern Muse-Clarissa, as companion to her younger brother and rescuer and mistress of the broken-down, forgotten, bankrupt genius, anticipates Valentine. Bosphorus prefigures Christopher in many ways, but particularly in being not the once typical Fordian hero who wishes to pass unnoticed in a crowd, but a living caricature, a "fabulous monster" (to use the memorable phrase from *Parade's End*). On one occasion, Mr. Bosphorus's picture is projected on a screen: "It grins imbecilely; screws up its eyes; starts back as if from a suddenly presented onion; exhibits completely toothless jaws, and vanishes . . ." (40). On another, clad in a long white nightgown, "his face and hair floured chalk-white," Mr. Bosphorus pitches out of an upper window. He lands on a shoulder, bounces on to his feet, leaps high in the air, and comes back down. "He then hobbles, so round-shouldered as to have aspect of a hunchback, peering through enormous spectacles and muttering: 'Ga-ga! Ga-ga!' " (104-105). Just what inspired Ford to write at this time in the vein of popular, music-hall entertainment is unclear. In his London journalist days, he had been an ardent fan of the Shepherd's Bush Empire and had written about ballerinas and music-hall singers.[29] Perhaps the Nighttown section of *Ulysses* with its surreal vaudeville routines was a catalyst.[30]

Whatever the source of Ford's interest in popular entertainment, it persisted through the writing of *Parade's End*. Of course, one cannot at all say (as one can of *Mister Bosphorus*) that the tetralogy "is" a pantomime. Yet the element is sufficiently strong to make the tetralogy different from previous novels and to provide, for me at least, the chief pleasure of the work.[31] The extent of Ford's interest in pantomime and comedy is explicit even in scenes not intended to be close to the popular stage. Christopher's face, for example, when he reads Sylvia's maddening letter, looks to Macmaster like a clown's: "Shapeless! The nose like a pallid triangle on a bladder of lard!" (SDN, 23). Similarly, to Macmaster, Cabinet Minister Waterhouse's features appear "Like an enormous mask of pantomime: shiny, with an immense nose and elongated, Chinese eyes" (SDN, 75). On Armistice Day, Valentine wants to be out "hitting policemen's helmets with bladders" because "that was how Cockney London expressed itself" (MCS, 7, 8). Sylvia thinks of General Lord Edward Campion, likely to be Viceroy, as "this old Pantaloon India" (LP, 195). Sylvia herself looks to Marie Léonie, who once danced for the Paris Opéra *corps de ballet*, "queerly like a pilgrim in a ballet" (LP, 275). As an Anglophobic Frenchwoman with, presumably, no interest in pantomimes, Marie Léonie thinks appropriately of Christopher as "a lumbering character from Molière as presented at the Comédie Francaise; elaborate of phrase and character but protuberant in odd places" (LP, 54).

Mark Schorer's mistaken belief that *The Good Soldier* is primarily a comedy has touched off twenty years of tedious academic controversy, but the question of comic tone in *Parade's End* seems to me far more real. A whole range of passages in the latter work probably strike many readers as quite laughable; indeed, many of the romantic clichés I solemnly listed above (in the second section of this chapter) may seem forgivable precisely because they are funny. Yet the humor was probably at most semi-consciously intended by Ford. Still, many episodes and many declarations by the characters can best be appreciated as high camp. They're so bad they're good, and need to be read in the same spirit in which one listens, say, to Groucho Marx's "You realize, of course, that this means *war*?" Thus Sylvia's: "Oh, *no*, Christopher . . . not from the *club!*" (SDN, 243). (Christopher, having had a check wrongly returned by his club, has just resigned.) Sylvia is an absolute mine of these delights. Upon learning the truth about her husband's shell shock: "But *you*! . . . without a brain! . . ." (SDN, 209). Or, with "emotion . . . going all over" her, she says to herself: "Is this to go on for ever?" (NMP, 172). To her old lover Perowne, she says of Christopher: "If that man would throw his handkerchief to me, I would follow him round the world in my shift!" (NMP, 152).[32] Christopher himself is no mean source of such absurdities. The following is particularly good because the climactic word is so unpronounceable: "Mrs. Wannop, I ought to tell you that your daughter and 1 are being talked about. Uglily!" (SDN, 147). On the occasion of telling Sylvia she may raise their child as a Roman Catholic, he says: "For I must to the greenwood go. Alone a broken man . . ." (SDN, 220).

Christopher, the "fabulous monster" in Sylvia's considered opinion, the "fat golfing idiot with bulging eyes" in Valentine's first impression, is the greatest and most ambiguous source of laughter in the tetralogy (SDN, 209, 106). So many disasters dog him in each volume that a major source of interest lies in wondering, as with Candide, what will hit him next.[33] Christopher's absurdly laconic "conversation" with his father about Sylvia's decampment and his own gentlemanly refusal to divorce her is probably funnier than Ford intended. So, too, his brother Mark's cross-examination, apparently the first serious conversation the two men have ever held: "Christopher said to himself: 'This man has the right to ask these questions!' " (SDN, 251). But Christopher's recurrent quarrels with Campion are almost surely both comically intended and consciously indebted to music-hall routines. Campion, the straight man, always impeccably tailored and respectably outraged, confronts the perpetually disar-

rayed, apparently in the wrong, but always innocent, if ig-
norant, Christopher. Wherever they collide—in the Kentish dawn, a Rouen orderly room, or a trench in Flanders—
Christopher's dubious situation always inspires Campion
to blow up: "No officer could—without being militarily in
the wrong—have a private life that is as incomprehensible
and embarrassing as yours . . ." (NMP, 287). His apt characterization of Christopher recalls Pound's claim that he
"once told Fordie that if he were placed naked and alone in
a room without furniture, I could come back in an hour
and find total confusion."[34] Although Christopher's racier
scenes with Sylvia are a good deal less comic in tone than
his conflicts with Campion, they recall stage comedy and
would be amusing on the stage. Two are pure slapstick:
Sylvia letting fly the whole contents of her plate—salad
and cutlets—at Christopher's head, one oily salad leaf remaining on his shoulder strap, to the puzzlement first of
the maid and then of Port Scatho; and Sylvia causing her
hotel bedroom to be twice invaded and Christopher to hurl
out one invader bodily and to arrest the other, a general.

Christopher himself, at his best, has a good sense of
humor and, like Falstaff, has considerable awareness of
himself as a comic figure. Even his terrific arguments with
Campion, with all their supposed anxieties, seem to be
something of a put-on. Certainly his calling the Liberal
Minister a swine (and then dining happily with him that
night) and his nasty cracks at Sandbach (because Cleveland landownders and Cleveland plutocrats must feud) are
more ritualistic than personal. Christopher—and Ford—
seem quite as aware of the comic as of the pathetic aspects
of all the "money, women, testamentary bothers" afflicting
the soldiers who report to the orderly room to tell their
troubles. These range from claims against the Japanese
government, by a McGill graduate, to bequests to three
mistresses on three continents, by an Inniskilling Canadian. Christopher has his best fun arguing with Valentine
about Latin. But simply striding behind her, on a Kentish
path, admiring her "attractive young woman's back,"

thinking it somehow "Infinitely pathetic!", fantasizing upon their relationship ("Thank God then for the Tory, upright young married man and the suffragette kid. . . . Backbone of England!"), even hearing a musical accompaniment (" 'Land of Hope and Glory!' . . . All absolutely correct! Double basses, 'cellos, all violins: all wood wind: all brass. Full grand organ: all stops: special *vox humana* and key-bugle effect")—all this inspires Christopher and the reader with high good humor (SDN, 134, 136, 135, 133). So, too, does the previous episode on the golf links, when the brightness of Pre-Raphaelite colors joins music-hall slapstick. The "town policeman, silvered helmet and all," looks, to Christopher, "grotesque . . . in the open country." Christopher's mind says to him, "This is an assaulted female" as he runs "rather like a rhinoceros seeing purple." The charming young girls escape, the evil city men are shouted down, the poor policeman gets toppled to his knees. And Christopher is "content" (SDN, 87-90). These two scenes bracket the greatest, and funniest, scene in *Some Do Not*, the celebrated Duchemin breakfast. Here, however, the controlling consciousness belongs to Ford rather than to any single character, or pair of characters. Indeed, one of the best moments comes from a unique shift to mad Mr. Duchemin's point of view as he stands "panting and delighted," free at last to bellow his obscenities: "He surveyed the opulent broadness of his tablecloth; it spread out before his eyes as if it had been a great expanse of meadow in which he could gallop, relaxing his limbs after long captivity" (SDN, 125). But nearly as good is the conclusion of the breakfast, a melodramatic recognition scene, when Mrs. Wannop at last identifies the son of her benefactor. In conversation with a curate, she screams and makes so broad a gesture that her hand almost covers his mouth and her sleeve trails across his plate. She overwhelms Christopher "with vociferous love," tells him how his father saved her life, and moves "off, Tietjens grappled to her, her daughter following as a young swan follows its parents" (SDN, 128).

The novel that Valentine and Christopher particularly dominate, *A Man Could Stand Up*, also contains the most numerous references to pantomime and music-hall comedy. Christopher appears to be really beastly when viewed from Valentine's consciousness in this novel. She constructs her first monstrous portrait of him from memory and from the barely heard details of a confused telephone conversation with Edith Ethel, constantly interrupted by the sounds of Armistice celebration. In Valentine's mind, Christopher has become literally the Beast needing redemption by the Beauty; she remembers a popular, patriotic song of another era:

> "We've fought the Bear before,
> And so we will again!
> The Russians shall not have Constantino . . ."

She knows she will have to contend again with this bear-like man and all his problems. He *needs* her (22, 26). Potentially soppy, the scene is saved like many we have noted in *Some Do Not* by the high good humor of the viewer.[35] At the same time as Valentine's heart aches to rescue her beloved, she can see him and herself as hilariously comic:

> Well, she had had an affair with this honest, simple creature! So good! So unspeakably GOOD. . . . Like the late Albert, prince consort! The very, helpless, immobile sort of creature that she ought not to have tempted. It had been like shooting tame pigeons! . . . So a woman tempted him and he did. . . . No; he didn't quite eat!
> But why? . . . Because he was GOOD?
> Very likely! (36)

Much as she loves him, she sees, like Campion, the *"quality* of his entanglements. . . . He got into appalling messes, unending and unravellable—no, she meant un-unravellable!—messes and other people suffered for him whilst he mooned on—into—more messes!" (34).

If Valentine's point of view gives us Christopher as

fairy-tale hero, a Beast entangled in absurdly exaggerated and complicated messes, Christopher's gives us the Great War as a pantomime. The Germans appropriately play the goblin-like villains. Christopher imagines them mopping and mowing, "fantastically." He thinks of them "engaged in fantastic and horrifying layings out of corpses of vast dimensions" (74). In their gas masks, they look "like goblin pigs with sore eyes, the hood with the askew, blind-looking eyeholes and the mouthpiece or the other nose attachment going down into a box, astonishingly like snouts!" (75). The German who gets into the trench arrives, to Christopher's mind, like the Hero in grand opera. Christopher, knife drawn, tries "to think of the German for *Hands Up*."

> His excursion into a foreign tongue proved supererogatory. The German threw his arms abroad, his —considerably mashed!—face to the sky.
>   Always dramatic, Cousin Fritz! Too dramatic, really. (89)

The sound effects for this dramatic entrance are provided of course by an artillery barrage:

> Noise increased. The orchestra was bringing in *all* the brass, *all* the strings, *all* the wood-wind, all the percussion instruments. The performers threw about biscuit tins filled with horse-shoes; they emptied sacks of coal on cracked gongs, they threw down forty-storey iron houses. It was comic to the extent that an operatic orchestra's crescendo is comic. (88)

Ford renders typographically the pleasurable sound to Christopher's ear of a key-bugle playing to the dawn a seventeenth-century air (97). It is 09 Griffiths practicing for the Divisional Follies and reminding us that the pantomime is not all broad comedy. It always includes beautiful love songs, sweetly played and sung.[36] Not only is the British Expeditionary Force figuratively called a Rag Time Army, but the portion of it under Christopher's command

contains professionals from the field of popular entertainment. Slocombe keeps writing one-act sketches for the
cheap music halls in the suburbs of London, at fifty
pounds each. He is a sloppy soldier but he keeps the other
men entertained, "his mind being a perfect repertoire of
Cockney jests at the expense of Big and Little Willy and
Brother Fritz" (154). Christopher's Company D is "an extraordinary Falstaff's battalion of muddy odd-come shorts
. . . positively, a dwarf concealed under a pudding basin
shuffled a foot-length and a half forward in the mud. . . . It
was like a blurred fairy-tale!" Two of the men "were
music-hall comedians and the whole lot looked as if they
made up a knock-about turn . . ." One of the comedians
actually heard the great Coburn sing "As I wawk erlong
ther Bor dee Berlong / Wiv an indipendent air . . ." while
he himself was being " 'the hind legs of the elephant . . . in
the Old Drury panto!' " And Christopher promises each of
his men a ticket for the pantomime at Drury Lane next December 26. He longs to give his men "a bit of luck" at the
front, "those grimy, shuffling, grouching, dirty-nosed
pantomime-supers" (107, 108, 109, 139, 138).

Whether Christopher indeed took the Other Ranks to
the Christmas Pantomime at the Drury Lane we are never
told, but surely he would have, surely he did. What we do
get to see, though, is the show Christopher and Valentine
put on, on Armistice Day, joined for the grand finale by
the other officers from his line battalion. It is a good show.
Like any respectable pantomime, it has its pathos and its
melodrama. Perhaps the most bathetic line—rivaling Sylvia's, "Oh, *no*, Christopher . . . not from the *club*!"—is Valentine's to Christopher as he is about to tell Mrs. Wannop
over the phone of his determination to make a dishonest
woman of her daughter: "Oh, be kind to her. Be kind to
her . . ." (249). Can Ford be recalling those same awful
words at the end of James's resounding flop, *Guy Domville*?
Wells said that the unhappy actor who had to deliver them
spoke them thus: "Be keynd to Her. . . . *Be* keynd to
Her."[37] What saves the telephone scene is the fact that all
three participants are playing parts and know it, as the

reader knows too. First Valentine tries "to be like a little child trying to get truth home to its mother." Then Mrs. Wannop begins "to talk like a book: an august Victorian book; Morley's *Life of Gladstone*." Then Valentine begins also to talk like a book, and to quote from the Greeks. When she calls Christopher to the phone, she feels "herself to be suddenly a little Cockney shop-girl. A midinette in an imitation Girl Guide's uniform" (242, 244, 246). Christopher observes his own act on the telephone with amazement: "he was astonished at the bitterness of his voice. . . . he was again astonished at the deference in his voice. He was leaning down, positively, as if over a very distinguished, elderly, seated lady" (249).

Still the best part of these wonderful last pages of Ford's third best novel is the series of appearances by the fabulous monster. Steeling herself to becoming the "cold nurse of a shell-shock case," Valentine finds not "a grey badger or a bear," but "a lion." He approaches, "his grey hair . . . shining, charging down the steps. . . . And lopsided." Christopher's "stone-blue eyes" come "fishily into place in his wooden countenance—pink and white." He pants "fiercely beside her. . . . It was infinitely sad to be beside this madman. It was infinitely glad. . . . She might be beside him for long spaces of time with him not recognising her. Like tending your baby!" (230, 229). After opening the door for her and ordering her to wait, he again charges "down the steps. His boots were immense. He lolloped all over on one side because of the piece of furniture he had under his arm. He was grotesque, really" (231). A comic action, if repeated, will be more than twice as funny. And so Christopher, who disappeared clumsily carrying a clumsy object, reappears doing the same thing.

> He was carrying a sack. The sack was the first she saw as he opened the door. . . . He had coal dust on his right forehead. It was a heavy sack. . . . He was panting. He must be stopped carrying heavy sacks. Panting like a fish. A great motionless carp, hung in a tank. (246)

Although these two entrances are the closest things to slapstick we actually get, Valentine does allow herself to think that she could protect herself "against a great carp! She could throw him over her shoulder. She had enough Ju Jitsu for that" (247). And the closest thing we get to a running gag is the reappearance of McKechnie thunderously knocking on the door, then shouting one more time about Christopher's sonnet that he has still not gotten around to translating into Latin. Ford gives McKechnie, seeing Valentine at the door, the same line he gave W. H. Hudson in quest of Conrad: "I must see that fellow Tietjens; you're not Tietjens!" (253).

Christopher's third and final appearance is as mine host, "mooning slowly down the stairs," smiling, and announcing, with "a royal aspect" the availability of prewar "Hooch" (267). A wonderful party ensues, to celebrate not only the Armistice but the union of the happy couple. Like a proper comedy, the book ends with everyone singing and dancing to *"Les petites marionettes."*[38] The heroine of the pantomime rides off on the aforementioned panto elephant: "A dear, meal-sack elephant. She was setting out on . . ." (275). This last mention of Christopher is but one of many allusions to him as a collection of sacks. They link him to his Army cooks, "white tubular beings with global eyes . . . the pierrots of a child's Christmas nightmare" (NMP, 318), to *Mister Bosphorus* with its "two dummies in long flannel night-gowns, peroxide-flaxen curls to waist" and "St. Bernard dog in Berlin wool, life-sized," to puppets, to marionettes, to child-made effigies on Guy Fawkes Day (32).

Christopher at his best, then, is very much a consciously created object rather than a character in a realistic novel. The best scenes are stagey and melodramatic. Sometimes participants in the scenes are even aware that they are watching a show. And so, when Sylvia (generously and dramatically) greets Mrs. Wannop as "The great writer," Valentine feels her "eyes filling with tears. . . . Beautiful! The most beautiful woman she had ever seen! And good!

Kind! You could see it in the lovely way she had given her cheek to that poor old woman's lips" (SDN, 307-308). When Christopher imprudently but humanely gives a Canadian lance corporal a two-hours' pass to see his feeble old mother whom he has not seen in seven years, "There was a mumble like applause and envy of a mate's good luck from a packed audience that had hung on the lips of simple melodrama . . . an audience that seemed to be all enlarged eyes . . ." Christopher is quite aware of the impact that he has made and wonders how Valentine would have viewed it (NMP, 80). Whereas Christopher's battalion commander chooses, among "the various types of Field-Officer" on which to model himself, "that of the genial, rubicund, slightly whiskeyfied C.O. who finishes every sentence with the words: 'Eh, what?' " Christopher consciously plays the nonchalant sort who strolls about casually with his hands in his pockets "Like General Gordon in pictures," and discusses with precision the habits of birds (MCS, 130, 116). At least once Christopher sees himself, comically, as an actual work of art:

> He reclined, on his right shoulder, feeling like some immense and absurd statue: a collection of meal-sacks done in mud: with grotesque shorts revealing his muddy knees. . . . The figure on one of Michael Angelo's Medici tombs. Or perhaps his *Adam*. (MCS, 213)

And once he sees himself as a dramatist, the greatest of them all, in the act of making a masterpiece. Leaning against a shelf in the trench while methodically firing upward Verey lights, Christopher becomes "like a solitary statue of the Bard of Avon . . . like Shakespeare contemplating the creation of, say, Cordelia" (MCS, 88). And once—finally—Ford portrays Christopher as Ford in the act of creating the work in which Christopher plays the largest part. Laying out cards for a game of patience, he tries to plan his life. "Then one half of his mind lost itself in the rearrangement of schedules, and on his brilliant table

his hands set queens on kings and checked their recurrences" (SDN, 102).

Ford's adoption of Marwood's identity would help then
to account for the impressive strengths of *Parade's End*. If
Ford were really no longer Hueffer, the previous marital
and martial agonies, the Army career, and the whole life,
could be seen as a pantomime—hilarious, pathetic, sentimental, but above all unreal and harmless. Ford had always needed a third party to assuage him, whether while
staggering on the Salisbury Plain or while writing *The Good
Soldier*. But if he could *become* that strong third person, his
troubles might be over. The undoubted gain was the ability
to write a sporadically brilliant fairy tale and to rest temporarily in the arms of an understanding woman. The artistic
loss was that epistemological anguish that makes *The Good
Soldier* consistently great; the personal loss was the ability
to commit himself to genuinely loving friendships. Stella
Bowen's doubt that "personal relationships were important at all" to Ford is perhaps especially true of his later relationships and of those with women.[39]

CHAPTER SEVEN

The Double Novels
1928–1934

A LITTLE LESS THAN GODS AND
WHEN THE WICKED MAN[1]

The relative weakness of *Last Post* was an unhappy portent. With the separation from Stella in 1928 came a severe, but temporary, decline in the quality of Ford's fiction. *A Little Less Than Gods* and *When the Wicked Man* are interesting chiefly for biographical reasons and for their connections with Ford's last fictional successes, *The Rash Act* and its sequel, *Henry for Hugh*. *A Little Less Than Gods* is his fictional farewell to Joseph Conrad, *When the Wicked Man* his most explicit experiment with the double motif he subsequently uses for bidding farewell to Marwood.

The immediate source of *A Little Less Than Gods* is, as the preface makes clear, the 1925 posthumous publication of Conrad's unfinished Napoleonic romance *Suspense*. As soon as Ford began to read it, he must have sensed how much the writing of it had been for Conrad an exercise in nostalgia. Ford would have remembered that Conrad contemplated an historical Mediterranean novel as early as February 1905, probably even earlier, at the height of the friendship between the two men.[2] He would have seen, too, that Conrad was harking back one last time to those adventurous days of his late teens in Marseilles which had energized his contributions to *Romance*.[3]

Ford must have found going through *Suspense* a familiar and sentimental journey, perhaps even a painful one. In the preface to *A Little Less Than Gods*, he says that the story was originally to have been written in "collaboration with another writer"; and then that other writer took it on alone, but his "lamented death cut short his story," and Ford felt free to resume work on it himself (vi). At least, Ford would have had the satisfaction of in some sense fulfilling his promise made a quarter of a century earlier to finish *Nostromo* if anything happened to Conrad. *A Little Less Than Gods* does conscientiously follow *Suspense*, and makes explicit what Conrad only hints at in his fragment: that the heroine is the illegitimate daughter of the hero's father and hence the hero's half-sister.[4] In general, Ford's alterations make *A Little Less Than Gods* more of a costume piece than is *Suspense*. Nevertheless, the spirit of the old days with Conrad hovers fitfully over Ford's novel. Some of the phrasing feels like that of *Romance*: "Those following days of still ship gliding in light airs came back to him mostly as memories . . ." (100). George Feilding's trial before a British court-martial for treasonably giving comfort to Napoleon during his hundred days reads like a reworking of John Kemp's trial in *Romance*. George, like Kemp, acts out Ford's persistent longing for a Southern paradise and his equally persistent, guilt-filled, agoraphobic anxieties.

Suspense and *A Little Less Than Gods* look back, then, to the good old days of collaboration; they look back to Arthur Marwood as well. Both novels feature patriotic, eccentric, wealthy Yorkshire squires. Although their ultimate historical source is the *Memoirs of the Comtesse de Boigne*,[5] the two characters exhibit peculiarly Marwoodian physical and psychological traits. Moreover, while their stories are not connected to anything we know of Marwood, they do resemble stories involving two of Ford's Marwoodian characters. That is, in their youths, Conrad's Sir Charles Latham and Ford's Earl Marsden, Mr. Tietjens, and Squire Feilding all went to the Continent to father children. Apparently Ford and Conrad not only possessed a story in common and used it simultaneously, but also imagined Marwood as its hero. Thus, three friends separated in the early twenties by death, water, and conflicting feelings were still coming together, inevitably in Ford's fiction, but in Conrad's last novel, too.[6]

Suspense and *A Little Less Than Gods* are moving chiefly when they remind us of the immediate, suffering lives of their creators. When Cosmo struggles so to write a letter to his sister, Conrad surely is reflecting his own last efforts to write anything at all: "It required all his courage to keep on, piling up words . . . It was like labouring the description of the scenery of a stage after a great play had come to an end." The most memorable passages in *Suspense* have to do with dying old men: Attilio's dreamlike recollection of being adopted on the coast of South America by a wise old hermit on the brink of death; Cosmo's sympathetic observation of an ancient boatman collapsing at his oar, reviving to steer by a star, dying on the last page of the fragment.[7]

A Little Less Than Gods equally, if less movingly, exposes its author's emotional state. Ford was again acutely depressed, needing to be rid of a former love and hoping he had found the right new one. Stella's refusal to be censorious must have exacerbated his guilt. As usual, his fictional hero is blamelessly unhappy. With the heroine aware, as the hero is not, that she is his half-sister, she can be actually guiltless but apparently cruel in persistently rejecting his addresses. In fact, however, Hélène converts into one more Pre-Raphaelite *belle dame sans merci*. Once when George kneels before her, clasping her knees, she catches a glimpse of herself in the mirror. Her face has "the queerest expression—of ecstasy, dread, glee, cruelty, the eyes half closed, the lips rigid. And the whole attitude one of withdrawal . . ." (198). Before she is through, Hélène, like Mrs. Duchemin, is calling the hero an "oaf" and, like Sylvia and Leonora, gesturing with her riding crop (288, 287). George must not only lose the woman he loves but give up both his native England and his adopted France, to settle in America. For Ford, too, success as a writer now depended on America. Perhaps he had as well a premonition that his last love and last home would be American.

When the Wicked Man, Ford's next novel, attempts to fuse

his private myth, expressed to perfection in *The Good Soldier*, with a satire on New York publishing practices and with explicit use of the *doppelgänger*. His experimentation with the double prepares for his final, if modest, fictional triumph in *The Rash Act*. Besides its doubles, *When the Wicked Man* has an unusual, for Ford, point-of-view character: Notterdam, as the title indicates, has really done bad things. Yet despite these interesting departures, the novel vibrates with its author's past fictions and lost loves.

Unsurprisingly, *When the Wicked Man* reflects *The Good Soldier*, for which Ford had just written, in 1927, a special preface. Like *The Good Soldier*, *When the Wicked Man* deals principally with two close friends, and three women.[8] As usual, the resemblances to earlier Fordian fiction are themselves but distorted images of only too familiar happenings from Ford's long, tormented past. Notterdam and Kratch variously recall Ford and Conrad, Ford and Marwood; the women, Ford's women. The length of the friendship, its ups and downs, the habit of talking "like books," these are surely fantasies on the Ford-Conrad relationship. But the joint publishing efforts, Notterdam's steadiness, based on Clifton training, and Kratch's changeableness must mirror the Marwood-Ford friendship. However, when he calls Notterdam a "wife-starver," Kratch is playing Marwood (44). Very much like Elsie, Elspeth refuses a divorce after she catches her husband "creeping" to his "wench" Lola (254). Even the terrible days of 1904 spent at Winterbourne Stoke are echoed in Notterdam's return to his natal village of "Winterbourne Porton . . . where first he had practised fornication" (305).

Even less fortunately, *When the Wicked Man* reflects events of the immediate past. Ford's efforts, through Robert Garnett, to get a divorce so that he might marry Rene Wright, no doubt appear in Notterdam's negotiations with Elspeth's brother Tom. Henrietta Felise surely masks the unyielding Mrs. Wright. But Elspeth's "equable temperament" (61), her brother's name, and the housing arrangements suggest Stella. Lola Porter, the Creole journalist-widow of a young writer and the most extreme departure from *The Good Soldier*, is Ford's revenge on Jean Rhys for putting him in her 1928 novel *Postures*.[9] However, the whole business of Porter's posthumous fame, the publication of his last novel, the issuing of a memorial, collected edition, and his wife's insistence on her rights—all these must reflect the posthumous deification of Conrad in the mid-twenties.

Ford seems to be using his earlier books and his early and recent past in *When the Wicked Man* not so much because he has, for psychological reasons, to justify himself, but because he is desperate for material. The novel probably also fails because to portray a genuinely wicked hero, a seducer of virgins and a blackmailer, is utterly uncongenial to his creativity. And so, despite Notterdam's evil deeds, Ford has to have Henrietta call him "fine . . . generous . . . noble," and Notterdam has to believe himself "perfectly and absolutely guiltless" (213, 255). Similarly, despite a history of innumerable sexual conquests, he finds himself "tongue-tied, like a school boy," "afraid of himself," "shy" in the presence of women (188, 220-21). Internal evidence suggests the fundamental source of the novel's weaknesses—the fatigue and depression of its creator. Unlike the frequently weary Ashburnham and Tietjens, Notterdam is genuinely ill and actually, not metaphorically, old (13, 27, 72). He is "a man going down the slope" (114). He feels "old, heavy, slow. Depressed and depressing!" (296). Like Gringoire in *No Enemy*, Notterdam applies to himself Conrad's epitaph: "Sleep after toil, port after stormy seas . . ." (225). Besides feeling his fifty-five hard-driving, work-filled, frantic years, Ford was surely very lonely. Perhaps he was doubting that he would ever win Mrs. Wright. Moreover, the inferior quality of the poetry he wrote to her suggests that she did not excite him or engage him nearly so deeply as Elsie and Violet and Brigit and Stella had done.[10] Not only had he lost Conrad and Marwood forever, he had no Stella and no genuine prospect of one while writing *When the Wicked Man*.

Yet the good fiction Ford was still to write is manifest, with hindsight, in this novel. Despite his most recent vicissitudes, an earlier, potentially more fructifying, past comes roaring in, through Notterdam. On two occasions, Notterdam is fully conscious of the phenomenon. Driving dead slow in no traffic, he nevertheless has an accident, caused by seeing his face reflected in the windshield. Significantly, he asks: "What was the matter with his youth that it perpetually got between him and his present?" (155). The other occasion for thinking about the power of the past is Notterdam's decision, after all, not to sell the Old Rectory, inhabited by a whole series of Notterdam clerics. Having suddenly recalled his recurring double, he interprets his experience as a warning that if he continues to neglect his ancestral home he will be ruined (177). In short, Notterdam takes the appearances of his double as an admonition to look after his past.

Ford's interest in double stories is hardly surprising. He had written many years before about Rossetti's *doppelgänger* painting *How They Met Themselves*; he had published in the *English Review* James's "The Jolly Corner."[11] But what is most promising about his use of the double in *When the Wicked Man* is its initial quality of authenticity. The double erupts in the kind of intense light that invests the best, hallucinated scenes of *Parade's End*, and even uses the paint of that first strange spot described in *The Heart of the Country*. At the climax of the angry publishers' meeting, when Kratch (as Marwood) calls Notterdam a wifestarver, Notterdam threatens to strike him, and Henrietta interposes, Notterdam experiences strange physiological reactions. His skin feels "frigid and clammy." He sees across the room "himself. Himself at the age of eighteen was standing there in a lozenge green light and boughs. In Goldenfoot Shaw with the catkins out" (46). The place and time are significant. In Goldenfoot Shaw, at eighteen, Notterdam seduced the virginal Lottie, after which they walked in Priory Wood. The double's other four appearances all relate to Notterdam's sexual past and occur, like the first, in the presence of one or another of his women. The last appearance, as in James's story, occurs in the hero's ancestral home. But whereas Spencer Brydon is floored by his double and has to be rescued by his old love, Notterdam, apparently on the brink of raping Lola, pulls out his gun, shoots "His other self . . . a detestable monster: flushed, red-eyed, lecherous, obese" (311), flees Lola, and returns to Henrietta. This deliberate use of doubles suggests that Ford is entering a new phase in which he will once more re-explore his entire past and, for the first time, reveal, in his fiction, how he became Arthur Marwood.

THE LAST REMINISCENCES

Nineteen-thirty witnessed Ford's last great renewal. He was revived in 1909 by the daughter of a Pre-Raphaelite watercolorist, in 1919 by a young Australian painter, and, finally, in 1930 by the young Polish-American painter Janice Biala. He met her on May Day, and his love for her flowered very swiftly into three fine works of art: a charming set of poems called "Buckshee" (1931), one of his most enjoyable autobiographies, *Return to Yesterday* (1931), and one of his most interesting novels, *The Rash Act* (1933). Both prose works had sequels, less effective but still instructive: *It Was the Nightingale* (1933) and *Henry for Hugh* (1934).[12] Unfortunately, enjoyment of the two fictions depends on considerable knowledge of Ford's personal history and familiarity with the autobiographies that immediately preceded them. These four books, the two autobiographies and the two novels, represent the rich development of two subjects ineffectually presented in *When the Wicked Man*: the Americanized Notterdam feels increasingly the need to re-examine his English past; simultaneously he keeps meeting his evil double. Ford's last autobiographies reach clear back to his early childhood and deal at length with the nineties, the *English Review*, and the Great War. As the title *Henry for Hugh* suggests and its dust jacket design of two masks (one green, egg-shaped, and

Fordian, the other pink, angular, and conventionally handsome) indicates, this novel and its predecessor are double stories.[13] However, unlike Notterdam's, Henry Martin's double, the handsome, wealthy, charming, aristocratic Hugh Monckton, represents an idealized self, precisely the person Henry would like to be. But the autobiographies, too, frequently deal with doubling, multiple selves, psychic rapport, mysterious recurrences. And the novels, as usual, hint at events and relationships from his most recent to his most distant past.

Ford's happiness with Janice shines throughout *Return to Yesterday*. Frankly calling the autobiography "a novel," he admits the possibility that he romances. The romancing is almost always benign; as he says toward the end: "I have really nothing against anyone" (387). The only noteworthy expressions of hostility, or hurt feelings, are directed at Wells, Edward Garnett, and Wyndham Lewis. Ford treats them "more . . . in sorrow than in indignation" (251). Toward his young discoveries, who all ultimately kicked him "in the face," he is particularly forgiving: "In the end the young cockerels must bring down the father of their barnyard. Without that the Arts must stand still" (408). Amazingly, Elsie is at last allowed to exist. *Return to Yesterday* begins with that picture of Ford at eighteen on the train, "going courting" (3). Although he of course never calls Elsie by name, he tells how the cumbersome sleeves of the medieval garb of a member of his family got into the baby's milk (56). Naturally, he reserves his most benign statements for Marwood and Conrad. If he had any "personal problems," he would go talk with Marwood "about anything else. Then the clarity of the working of his mind had an effect on mine that made me see if not what was best to do then what would be most true to myself" (375). As for Conrad, "There never was a quarrel. Conrad never in his life addressed an irritated word to me about any personal matter . . ." (190). Of course, there were the "rubs of the game—and what a game for rubs it was!" Nevertheless, their "friendship remained unbroken" (205). Like Marlow about the dead Jim, Ford cannot believe that he will "never drive over to the Pent and ask Conrad some question, or never listen to Marwood encyclopaedically and brilliantly laying down the English Tory law on something or other" (371).

Ford treats himself benignly too in *Return to Yesterday*. All his past troubles had external or physiological causes. The nocturnal terrors of his childhood came as an effect of the stories told by his nurse. Yet Ford "can still see the shadows of wolves if I lie awake in bed with a fire in the room. And indeed I had the fixed belief for years that except for myself the world was peopled with devils" (72). Nor does he deny the misery of the "lost years" of 1904 to 1906. But his pain was exacerbated by incompetent doctoring. Though suffering from depression and agoraphobia, he had no real reason for the depression (266). And though German doctors blamed the agoraphobia on "some sexual disorder or other," Ford now knows that overwork caused a heart flutter which resulted in symptoms resembling agoraphobia "a little" (268). Ford is able to remain at peace with himself and with Elsie, Conrad, Marwood, Violet, Brigit, by the simple act of suppression. He will skip over as too complicated the period from 1911 to 1914 (387). Only in that way can he arrive at so beautiful a celebration of the London of June 1914:

> London was adorable then at four in the morning after a good dance. You walked along the south side of the park in the lovely pearl-grey coolness of the dawn. A sparrow would chirp with a great volume of distinct sound in the silence. Another sparrow, another—a dozen, a hundred, ten thousand. They would be like the violins of an orchestra. . . . Then, as like as not, you turned into the house of someone who had gone before you from the dance to grill sausages and make coffee. There you breakfasted—usually on the lead roof above a smoking room, giving on to a deep garden. There would be birds there too. Those who cannot remember London then do not know what life holds. Alas. . . . (429-30)

Return to Yesterday, like "Buckshee," is obviously the product of a wonderful heightened mood that by its very nature could not last. Its sequel, *It Was the Nightingale*, is distinctly less benign. Surely the menacing international situation contributed: Ford mentions both Hitler and Mussolini. No doubt the subject matter itself and its relative recentness made detachment harder: the letdown after the war, the difficulties in financing the *transatlantic review*, the "dreadful mist of cupidity that burst out before poor Conrad's corpse was cold in its grave" (287). Ford's implicit acceptance of his father's German heritage does not bring about reconciliation. Father still calls son "the patient but extremely stupid Ass!" (249). Ford's family portraits in *It Was the Nightingale* reflect the book's prevailing bitterness. His mother, brother, and even, a little, his grandfather are treated with hostility.

MARWOOD, *THE RASH ACT*, AND *HENRY FOR HUGH*

The Rash Act, however, written immediately after *Return to Yesterday*, partakes of the same sunniness. It begins, indeed, with literal, Pre-Raphaelite brilliance:

> The morning seemed to herald a glorious day. The motionless silver of the sea was ruffled in irregular streaks like watered satin. The light mists were rising from the horizon and the islands. Sunlight from over the stone pines just touched the end of the jetty so that there was a triangle of gold. (9)

The water is so clear that a boat on it seems "suspended in the air." It looks like a "melon slice of incandescent white, a curved stripe of scarlet. Another . . . was of azure." Its sail is "lambent maroon." The scene resembles "a chromolithographic close-up of a prehistoric craft" (9). As we know, when Ford can see colors, he is for the moment secure in the twin illusions of eternally happy romantic love and successfully mastered fictional technique. But he knows, too, that worry makes colors dim (66).

The Rash Act tells of two attempted suicides, one successful, the other not, at the same location on the Mediterranean. An American, Henry Martin Alvin Smith, being divorced by his wife Alice, rejected by his new love Mrs. Percival, abandoned by his wealthy father, and wiped out in the market crash, plans to commit suicide (the "rash act") by stepping off his rented felucca. A sudden, severe storm distracts him.[14] While beaching his ship, he coincidentally saves his life but receives two terrific blows to the head from the ship's yard. At the same time, Henry's distant English cousin, Hugh Monckton Allard Smith, whom Henry has met only twice in his life, also contemplates suicide, despite all his apparent advantages of aristocratic upbringing, physical beauty, and enormous wealth. Subject to recurrent, excruciating physical pain, barred from the pleasures of alcohol and sex, Hugh successfully shoots himself just as Henry, crazed with pain, rushes up the path from the beach. In response to profound longings for rest and a new identity, Henry impulsively substitutes his own passport and suicide note for Hugh's, before passing out. When he comes to, he finds himself, all bandaged up, in Hugh's hotel bedroom, being cared for by Hugh's *maîtresse en titre* Jeanne and her best friend Eudoxie. The blow to Henry's right temple gives him Hugh's sabre-cut scar; the blow to his jaw accounts for Henry's different voice and conceals the lower part of his face. As the novel ends, Henry has successfully fooled Jeanne and the French authorities but not Eudoxie. The sequel, *Henry for Hugh*, works out the complications of the ensuing year, as Henry endeavors faithfully to dispense Hugh's wealth as he would have wished, to deal kindly with Hugh's relatives, especially his old aunt, and to court Eudoxie. When his identity is ultimately unveiled, he is forgiven, proves to be Hugh's legal heir, and wins Eudoxie.

As Ford dramatizes the sexual complications of his fable, he has recourse to the fictional patterns that have served with widely varying success for forty years, and to fantasies upon the events of a long, passion-tossed life. The quartet that Henry escapes by attempting suicide bears resemblances to the four-square coterie of *The Good Soldier*; the trio in which he finds himself looks back to its last pages. Both groups distortedly reflect, sometimes hilariously, sometimes painfully, experiences ranging from Ford's recent past clear back to the 1904 breakdown and even earlier. Ford's ostensible subject is the "Lost Generation" (a phrase he twice uses) and the "want of courage—physical and moral" exhibited by its members in the twenties (48, 190).[15] Thus, in the first quartet, the Henry Martins' best friends are Jack Percival, a tough novelist from South Dakota (Hemingway), and Mrs. Percival, a collector of modern art and a lesbian (Gertrude Stein) in love with Alice Martin. The lesbianism results in a wonderful variation on *The Good Soldier* quartet, with the sexually inactive Henry Martin playing Dowell, his wife, Florence; Mrs. Percival thus plays Edward, and Jack Percival, Leonora! Jack berates Henry for his blindness to their partners' affair the way Leonora explodes to Dowell, but in marvelous Fordian Hemingwayese: "You don't see what's as near to you as your moron's face to your moron's nose!" (142). Thus, Ford, catching Hemingway's childish horror of homosexuality, gains revenge for Hemingway's picture of him as the sexually impotent Henry Braddocks in *The Sun Also Rises*.

Despite Ford's initial hostility to him, the central character as usual owes a great deal to Ford himself. His situation—alone, broke, and suicidal in Carqueiranne in mid-August 1931—corresponds remarkably to Ford's 1928 situation at the same place and season.[16] Again, despite Henry's Ohio past and 1895 birthdate, his heritage and upbringing are a conflation of Ford's and Francis Hueffer's, including German Roman Catholicism, marriage to an Anglo-Saxon, name changes, the son's Germanic schooling in an English-speaking country, the father's contempt for the son, and Henry's service with "Welsh Tommies" (45). Like Ford, Henry has had only one legal marriage, to Alice, but now being dissolved in the courts. Alice, with her intense interest in painting, her "absolute

. . . equanimity," and her role as Henry's wife from the war's end to the late twenties, must owe something to Stella (106). Obviously, Henry's fortunate conclusion, to be installed in a villa with a "great garden" overlooking the Mediterranean and to have as his companion the beautfiul and vital Eudoxie reflects Ford's happy life in the Villa Paul, Cap Brun, with Janice Biala (291).

Still, Henry's love life mainly and inevitably repeats the personal myth that informs virtually all of Ford's fictions. Although Henry's sexual timidity may express Ford's intended theme of the passionlessness of the lost generation, it also follows the revulsion from sex exhibited by so many of Ford's weary young men from 1892 on; Henry's imagination belongs as much to Rossetti as to Hemingway. Henry, believing he is on the point of drowning himself, remembers a picture of a siren diving into the sea, bearing in her arms a youth whose blood she will suck and wearing a "gleeful but aloof" smile (187).

The most truly energized scene involving lovers exhibits the violence and blood that almost always attend the possibility of shared passion. When Eudoxie glimpses Henry's tempest-tossed boat in trouble and sees his red sail like "a gout of flame or of blood whirl away behind him," she frantically waves her fichu to direct him to a safe landing (298). But the storm has come on Henry "with the speed of a racehorse," and the ship is moving with the "gait of the jumping hunter" (196, 200). Although he steers her into the cove and reverses her engines, he nevertheless suffers a terrible blow to the cheek followed by severe pain in his temple. Men on the shore shout: " 'Vous saignez.' . . . 'Mais vous saignez!' . . . 'Saignez' " (203). It comes as no surprise to discover later that Henry's double, Hugh, received his scar on the temple from "a fellow . . . charging down on him on a roan charger" (300).

With the Fordian hero knocked out of commission in the service of love, a reversion to the agonized events of 1904 is inevitable. The shadow of that year is obvious in *Henry for Hugh*, which deals with Henry's long convalescence and interestingly counterpoints Ford's description of his nervous breakdown in *Return to Yesterday*. Whereas Ford's fluttering heart allegedly caused his illness, Henry is simply a victim of nerves (8). The conflicting medical advice that Henry receives recalls Ford's version of his own illness. Whereas the local psychiatrist tells him that if he becomes physically involved with a woman he will go mad, Sir Tresidder attacks *"anti-aphrodisiaques"* and tells him he needs a woman (271, 275). According to *Return to Yesterday*, Ford's German nerve specialists attributed his agoraphobia to "some sexual disorder" and prescribed a diet guaranteed not "to be exciting—sexually," but back in London Conrad's family doctor recommended Ford "ride disagreeable beasts with hard mouths" (268, 269, 306). Finally, the two novels, in depicting the sick hero being cared for by two devoted young women, recall Olive and Elsie ministering to Ford in July, August, and December 1904.

If this were all there was to the double novels, they would remain one last rehashing of Fordian love. But the fact that Henry substitutes himself for Hugh permits Ford to do even more than examine a human relationship like Dowell's with Edward and explore the epistemological problems that so obsessed him in the year of *The Good Soldier*. Henry standing for Hugh shows Ford recognizing that he tried to be Marwood.[17] Hugh Monckton Allard Smith unmistakably reflects Arthur Pierson Marwood. The defining, blighting fact of the brilliant Marwood's life was the chronic illness that cut short his education, denied him a career, and confined him to South Kent. Ford translates this affliction into Hugh's war wound, incurred immediately after Oxford and resulting in permanent, enforced leisure by the Mediterranean Sea, without wine and women. Recurrent terrible pains cause Hugh's incomprehensible exclamations and failure to finish sentences. Like Ford's Marwood, he makes sweeping statements about world affairs and writes brilliantly, unorthodoxly, about economics. Hugh's "paraphernalia of leather goods" recalls recollections about Marwood by Violet and Mar-

wood's family (HH, 105).[18] Presumably, Ford's close attention to Hugh's initial "M" and to the names Monckton and
Martin, reflects the one initial Ford and Marwood shared.
Hugh's family comes originally from Yorkshire. They have
an ancestral country manor, but several of the women, like
the Marwood women, have a London flat which Hugh visits. In *Return to Yesterday*, Ford recalls the endless conversations with Marwood that began as soon as they met (372).
On the occasion of their second meeting, Henry sits up
most of the night with Hugh, Henry being "the first man"
Hugh feels comfortable talking to (RA, 145, 347). All this
recalls Dowell and Edward too, of course. And Henry, like
Dowell, condones his friend's suicide: "There was one in-
controvertible excuse for suicide. To be abandoned by a
woman" (RA, 208).

Although Dowell asserts that Edward "is myself," he
cannot *become* Edward. He does not have the vehicle for it,
as Henry does. Moreover, Henry longs to become someone else far more passionately than does Dowell. Once
when Henry was being manhandled in an Oxford prank,
he "wished intensely to be a certain broad-faced Japanese—a little man with an immense mouth over-filled
with gigantic teeth!" (RA, 31). Subsequently, during times
of intense depression, he wishes to be a policeman, a
newspaper seller, a crossing-sweeper (40, 41). Doubling,
the longing to be someone else, cases of psychic identification, and telepathic rapport recur throughout the autobiographies. The manifestation of doubling most relevant to *The Rash Act* occurs in Ford's account of his mental
breakdown in *Return to Yesterday*. He was in despair, in
Basel, in the autumn of 1904 and used to watch longingly
from his window the nightly return home of a blackened
chimney sweep. The young wife, the baby in its cradle, the
joyousness of the scene made Ford long to project his soul
into "that chimney sweep's body" (267). Here he is talking
only, of course, of the transfer of souls. Indeed the whole
point of the anecdote is the great divergence in appearance
and way of life. Similarly, when Ford identifies with Con-

rad, he insists upon the great differences from himself, differences that make Conrad romantic. "He was dark, black bearded, passionate in the extreme . . . rather small. . . . His gestures were profuse and continuous, his politeness Oriental . . ." (RY, 24, 25). What Ford chiefly remembers of their first meeting is the odd stiffness of his bearing, "his sudden melting into Oriental mannerisms . . ." (RY, 54). Ford's insistence upon Conrad's "Oriental" quality suggests that Henry's first candidate for soul transfer, the little toothy Japanese, is a covert allusion to Conrad.

In contrast to "Conrad's vibrating small figure," Ford emphasizes Marwood's "great shapelessness" and even has Marwood allude to it: "he's like a quivering ant and I'm an elephant built out of mealsacks!" (IWN, 188). Ford also stresses his own physical similarity to Marwood and the fact that one replaced the other in Conrad's life. Ford's value to Conrad, he says, was "perhaps that I was large, blond, phlegmatic on the surface and had a good deal of knowledge of the practical sides of English life . . ." By the summer of 1909 "Marwood had . . . taken my place as general cook and bottle-washer in Conrad's literary establishment. He also was large, blond, outwardly placid . . ." Ford had quickly "become a habit" for Conrad. His "early job was to get Conrad's work over. . . . Later on Marwood was quite as indispensable—quite as much of a habit" (RY, 191, 198, 203).

Whereas the physical similarities between Ford and Marwood are merely hinted at, naturally those between Henry and Hugh are strongly insisted upon, as is Henry's passion to become Hugh. Indeed, it is Hugh who first mentions the resemblance: "Know your face. Because it's damn like my own" (RA, 37). Henry too imagines that they resemble one another, tall, straight, with the same broad brows, brown eyes and hair, and neat brown mustaches (RA, 42). Now Ford and Marwood were both mustached six-footers, but with blond hair and blue eyes. Their photographs do not, however, look very much alike, principally because of Ford's weak chin. Significantly, Henry's account of their resemblances omits any reference to chins. Eudoxie, the only one who pierces Henry's disguise, does so at the moment she sees him without the bandage on his jaws. She does not want him to shave the beard that makes Hugh's Aunt Elizabeth exclaim: "Poor you . . . and I used to be so proud of the angle of your jaw" (RA, 268-70, 314, 305; HH, 12, 14).

Before Hugh speaks to him, Henry has been longing to become that relaxed fellow, to feel as if he had wings, to be sure of a fortunate destiny (RA, 37, 41, 66). Even after his death, Hugh seems "still to stand astride his fabulous grip that was a bursting purse of Fortunatus." But people "were not out for the goods. . . . They desired the companionship, the intimacy, of the god Apollo Fortunatus" (HH, 22, 23). If Hugh can do so much for Henry, what can Henry do for Hugh? "He was at least keeping alive that part of Hugh Monckton that was his name and excited applause. Without that there would be for him, so shortly, nothing but oblivion" (RA, 215). This is, of course, what Ford was doing for Marwood the moment he conceived of Christopher Tietjens:

> And immediately, on that remembrance, I had my central character. Marwood had died before the war, but his knowledge of the world's circumstances had been so vast and so deep that, as it were, to carry on his consciousness through those years seemed hardly to present any difficulties. . . . It was as if he lived again. . . . He died in the fullness of his strength and no death ever seemed to me to be more regrettable. To the best of my ability I gave him life again, and for me he lives still, in Avignon, and I shall have a letter from him to-morrow. (IWN, 202)[19]

This lovely passage, especially the allusion to a letter, is not without its pathos. On Hugh's last night of life, he writes Henry two immensely long, passionately pleading letters essentially delegating to Henry his posthumous reputation and asking him to conceal the suicide (RA, 226,

347). Poor Ford surely knew that he never got, and never would get, any last, long, loving letter from Marwood.[20]

Interesting as are the multiple connections—Henry / Hugh, Dowell / Edward, Ford / Marwood—it is even more interesting to speculate on what the fable meant for Ford as man and writer. To take up a dead person's career and, by acting it out, to continue it and thus make of your own a living novel is a creative venture of some complexity. Envy, exhilaration, responsibility, guilt, epistemological puzzlement are all inextricably involved. One's life becomes a fairy tale, a constant show, that has got, some day, to end. Henry's first thoughts on seeing Hugh's corpse are particularly striking in the light of the fictive Ashburnham's suicide, Ford's metaphorical death, and Marwood's actual death, in probably that order. Envious that Hugh's suicide attempt worked, Henry experiences the same desire to be Hugh that he felt the night before. His next, and most persistent, response is a sense of responsibility. He recoils from the notion of denouncing Hugh Monckton to the police as a suicide (RA, 208). Protecting Hugh's reputation remains a primary motive in both double novels. Eudoxie agrees that Henry can in no better way keep "the suicide secret than by shewing Hugh Monckton as if still alive" (HH, 192). When Henry observes people talking in suspiciously low voices, he fears they are slandering Hugh and wonders "if he ought not to protect Hugh Monckton from the imputation of having led an outrageous life" (RA, 265). He also feels that it is his duty to have a good time for Hugh's sake. After all, Hugh has tried "to create a living novel with a happy ending" (HH, 97).

Becoming Hugh means incurring not only worrisome responsibility but burdensome guilt. Henry writhes when praised for Hugh's war heroism. When somebody says that he saved France, poor Henry recalls his war service in a "canning factory in the Cevennes" and as "Syphilis Inspector" (RA, 212). Henry particularly hates fooling Hugh's dear Aunt Elizabeth, who so desperately wants Hugh "to be alive that she would have denied the evidence

of her senses" (HH, 51). Still, like Ashburnham, Henry
feels obscurely that he cannot help himself, that he has
been handled as if he were "a brown paper parcel" (RA,
221). Moreover, he resists committing any outright crimi-
nal acts: he never really takes anything of Hugh's, never
signs his name, never comes out and says that he is Hugh.

Even more than from guilt, Henry suffers from the
wearying complications attendant upon becoming Hugh.
These recall the epistemological agonies of *The Good Soldier*
year.

> What sort of people was he amongst in this musty and
> mouldering room? He had no sort of clue. They ap-
> peared eccentric but extraordinarily real. And unre-
> lated and unaccountable. . . . A life without recogniz-
> able landmarks. (RA, 276)

Probably the best versions of Henry's complicated dilemma occur during scenes in Eudoxie's presence—not in
the weaker ones in which she is at once avowing and refusing her love, but in the funny ones in which Henry suspects she knows he is not Hugh. And by pretending that
the corpse is himself, Henry lives after his own death and
can, like Tom Sawyer, attend his own funeral, even pay for
it and preside over the ceremonies (RA, 256). Ford wisely
leaves to the reader's imagination the heights to which
Henry rises in attributing to "Henry" all of Hugh's noble
qualities. The greater the complications, the more Henry
feels "coils settling round him," depriving him of "his in-
dividuality" (HH, 62). He feels "tied hand and foot by endless, invisible strings . . . like Gulliver. . . . There were all
these people with feelings to be hurt and all these pre-
tenses to keep up!" (HH, 165). He feels special exaspera-
tion in trying to keep straight Hugh's incredibly complex
genealogy, all the names and dates, even the chronology
of Henry's own life since he became Hugh. So Ford must
have felt as he toiled through volume after volume of the
Tietjens saga!

But Henry's ultimate responsibility is, after all, only to

put on a good show. This he wants to do, even before he becomes Hugh, as he sets out to commit suicide. At the end of the pier, before boarding his ship, he thinks of himself as "a fine fellow," sees himself standing "on high amongst the applause of a world," marching "to his end, Nordic hero. Taking his call. . . . He bowed to the right; to his left; before him. As if he had been an Oriental saluting the sun. His mind was full of sardonic gaiety" (RA, 188). What is intended to be the end of a "tragedy," proves the beginning of a comedy, a fairy tale, a pantomime. When

> the yard of the boat . . . had . . . struck him that cruel blow . . . it was as if the wand of a magician had struck him and the magician, Destiny, had said: "Arise, Sir Hugh Monckton . . ." And there he sat, the young Squire, in Harris tweeds that smelt of peat reek. (HH, 270)

Before he is through, he even intends to play Hugh in a movie (HH, 227).

Happily, Jeanne and Eudoxie prove admirable co-stars, prompters, punsters: "Yes, you! You! You! . . . You've got to be you . . . Hugh," stamps Eudoxie, "violently."[21] "He would have to continue to play that comedy," Eudoxie reiterates (HH, 54, 60). And she helps him, not only by pumping Hugh's aunt for information and studying "every turn of the intricate and tricky game . . . as professionals study . . . chess," but also by putting on, with her friend, a beautiful show (HH, 235). Jeanne, former mistress of the Governor of Cochin-China, has a spectacular wardrobe: a negligée of batik, a robe like a cardinal's, "yards of cream-coloured silk . . . whirling round her silver white person" (RA, 307). Eudoxie, "defiantly rouged" at six a.m., is "got up to resemble southern beauty. A Carmen or, with the wide trousers, a Corsair's bride. . . . Above the immense bell-shaped trousers the top of her bathing-dress was light flame-coloured . . . the belt was emerald green." Even Henry is beautiful in Hugh's pyjamas "of a vivid dark green silk" ; stripped to the waist, he looks like a "Greek athlete. Of the type that saved the world at Marathon." The women talk "familiarly . . . of Cytherea and Circe and Isolde," and the trio bring to mind Lovell's fantasy of Mediterranean bliss among Grecian gods. Eudoxie even juggles oranges, Ford's favorite image for the entertainer: the Roman "boy of Antibes who danced and gave pleasure had probably juggled six oranges in that way" (RA, 259-60, 276, 309).

Still, the comedy must end, and anyway Henry's feelings about Hugh inevitably include hostility. "Damn English gentlemen!" he thinks; and English food gives him insomnia (HH, 268, 78, 84). Above all, he *"wasn't* an English squire. . . . He was a down and out American." He thinks "bitterly" that he has "lost all touch with his own remembrances" and has "been forced to live in the memories of that other man" (HH, 316-17, 64). Through Eudoxie's ingenuity, Henry is at last able to slough off Hugh and become Henry again (HH, 204, 220, 320). As a kind of penance, he revises a manuscript of his own to include ideas Hugh expressed to him that last night. Its preface will really be in Hugh's words, as Hugh has left behind reams of unpublished material about gold. Henry and Eudoxie will splice it together and "at last give poor dear Hughie a chance to express himself" (HH, 320).

Shutting the door on his past in 1909, resolving never to look back in 1919, and starting out anew in 1930, Ford must have felt each time he wrote out his memories that he was writing those of another man. Perhaps that is why he called his autobiographies novels. Certainly his novels, *The Rash Act* and *Henry for Hugh*, contain, if we are reading them rightly, a great deal of autobiographical material. Perhaps all four, the two autobiographies and the two novels, those late, remarkable creations, should be taken as a seamless web, one wonderful fiction. Like Henry and Hugh, the Ford and Marwood of these books are fictional versions of real people. The sympathetic reader should try not to worry that Ford's war experiences in the allegedly autobiographical *It Was the Nightingale* more closely resemble Christopher's than his own, whereas Henry's fictional war experiences are really quite close, in spirit, to Ford's. To protest, as Archibald Marshall did, that getting Marwood's Oxford college wrong and making him Senior Wrangler, in *Return to Yesterday*, is dancing a "mountebank's jig on his grave" is to forget that Ford's Marwood lives on and on as Edward and Christopher.[22]

The autobiographies, like the novels, implicitly signal a separation from Marwood. Ford, though proud to have been a Londoner, now, once again, asserts (surely wrongly) that he is "not really English."[23] He grants that, while in uniform, he had been "as English as it was possible to be" (IWN, 59, 85). His reason for now denying his Englishness is that he has "never had much sense of nationality," and thus he bids farewell to his English face (IWN, 59). That he separates himself completely from the saving figure of Marwood is equally unlikely. Hugh, the apparently tongue-tied Englishman, could, when inspired, make "prophecies" and "let himself go" on questions of war and peace and world finance (HH, 218). Henry, we remember, resolves to make a book blending those ideas with his own. After *Henry for Hugh*, Ford no longer needed Marwood for his novels because he no longer needed to write novels. But in the final flowering of his final phase, Ford would still have use for that "man of infinite benevolence, comprehensions, and knowledges," capable of "taking in not only what was visible, but all the causes and all the motive powers of distant places" (IWN, 188, 202).

Although Ford was to write one more novel, his serious commitment to fiction really ceased with the completion of the books about Henry and Hugh. *Vive Le Roy* (1936) is a very slight mystery story whose only interest lies in the hints it provides as to Ford's state of mind during the last half of his last phase and also as to his final creative interest.[24] Ford's re-use of the substitution theme may suggest the final exhaustion of material. It may also mean that he continues to recognize that during the war he substituted

Marwood for himself and that he continues to long for godlike power in order to do good. The portrait of Penkethman implies an ultimately pessimistic view of the human lot and surely reflects old Ford himself, even to the "large behind" memorialized by William Carlos Williams.[25] He is never more Ford than when he says, "I don't know and ask to be preserved from knowing," unless perhaps during a moment in disguise: "There came gradually through the fantastic mask . . . the profound sadness that was always on the features of the ex Chief Inspector" (264, 294).

CHAPTER EIGHT

Coda

1935–1939

PROVENCE AND *GREAT TRADE ROUTE*[1]

Happily the cessation of fiction writing and the relative inferiority of *It Was the Nightingale* to *Return to Yesterday* did not at all betoken the end to Ford's final renaissance. Rather, his creative fire went wholly into four big works, which combine romantic reminiscence, travel writing, literary criticism, history, and prophecy. It is, of course, impossible to know why Ford had his last renewal and why he stopped producing novels. The triumph of *The Good Soldier* seems to have issued in part out of his belief that he would die soon. His heart attack in December 1930 and the death of Oliver Madox Hueffer the following June would have reminded him forcefully of impending old age and the death that he had feared, and longed for, since childhood.[2] The sense of aging plus the happy, unexpected acquisition of a loving, totally devoted mate must surely have diminished his chronic sexual anxieties. He says in *The English Novel* that you should write about "subjects that spring at your throat" (146). One hopes that Ford's particular beast ceased at last to leap and freed his prose for other than novelistic work. In any case, he turned from Henry and Hugh to write about Provence, about New York and the American South, about peace and understanding, and about the writers whose characters and works meant the most to him.

Now these were hardly new subjects for Ford. Indeed, he touches on most of them in his nonfictional books of the late twenties: *A Mirror to France* (published in 1926, its best chapter written in 1923 along with *Some Do Not*), *New York is Not America* (1927), and *The English Novel* (1929). "The *chose donnée*" of *A Mirror to France* is the same as that of *Provence*, namely, that whatever remnants of chivalry, frugality, intellectuality, and the arts pre-World War I European civilization could show came from the South of France "where flourished the Counts of Toulouse, olive trees, the mistral, the Romance Tradition, Bertran de Born, the Courts of Love and the only really amiable Heresy of which I know" (MF 14-15). *A Mirror to France* contains also the delightful Fordian anecdote of Tarascon that would be the germ of both *Provence* and *Great Trade Route*. An elephant, escaped from a circus, invades the house of a retired West Country merchant. "Mad no doubt with joy at the sight" of his host, the elephant tries to mount the kitchen stairs to embrace him—and brings down the house. The monetary compensation permits the merchant to fulfill his lifelong obsession to follow the European segment of the ancient, "mystic" Great Trade Route of the "sacred" Chinese merchants from Marseilles, "past Beaucaire, up the Rhône, to Cornwall" (119-20). Hearing that story makes Ford realize that Provence alone has been home to him, that he has spent his life following that route, and that he must now leave the world a little bit better by telling this final myth of his life and his ideal. The enemies, in *A Mirror to France*, to the spirit of the Route and to the illusion of a Provence which honors "clearness of Thought and the exactitudes of Art" are the "sentimentalism of the North," the thought of Huxley, Spencer, and Darwin, and the Machine (269, 272). *New York is Not America* similarly prefigures the point of view (that of one who stands "for small, mixed farming") and the theme of the last travel books. Its purpose is to point out "the sameness of humanity in all nations," in the hope that there will "be no more international misunderstandings . . . no more war." "Any hatred of body to body," says Ford, "is a danger to civilisation" (283, xi, 279).[3]

A Mirror to France and *New York is Not America* reflect

Ford's low morale in the late twenties. Familiar and significant images of loneliness and agoraphobia occur in
both books. Furthermore, the Marwood persona that made
possible *Some Do Not* is either inappropriate to the travel
books, or becoming constrictive. As the Marwoodian
clubman in *New York is Not America*, Ford can be really bor-
ing, talking solemnly about what constitutes "Society" in
America, dwelling on the servant problem ("It is all the
bliss of life to have some one fetch a handkerchief for
you"), and revealing that in well-to-do American homes
the cooking is as good as in an English upper-class home
or in "a first-class English club" (131, 184, 204). Still, if
Marwood is yet remembered as snobbish, he is also remembered as saintly and wise, distinguished for the patient acceptance of his invalided state and especially for the
breadth and brilliance of his mind. Ford had come, even in
the twenties, to imagine Marwood in Provence and would
later envision him on a French mountain top, generalizing
about the war. In short, Ford would not have to, and probably did not want to, shed the whole of that saving, Marwoodian self in order to write the last books.

Thus, tacitly acknowledging through *The Rash Act* and
Henry for Hugh that he had once made of Marwood a "solar
myth" and would now try to separate himself from Marwood, Ford proceeded to make a solar myth of himself.
But of what on earth, in the mid-thirties, did that Fordian
self consist? *Provence* and *Great Trade Route* make clear
much that it was not: not Yorkshire, county, or wealthy,
and only fleetingly public school. *Great Trade Route* extolls
the South and damns the North; the "note," he says, of
Yorkshire and the North of England, is "aridity" (279).[4] In
Provence, Ford ridicules the aspiring London literary man
who "must have his thatched cottage . . . his records of
patronizing intimacies with the aborigines. . . . A little
baggage like that is as necessary . . . as a dress-suit. It so
gives you the County Family air . . ." (297-98). Ford makes
no pretensions to a wealthy past, and cheerfully recalls a
time when he could scarcely afford food and clothing

(GTR, 407). If he alludes to himself as a student "of the Great Public School founded by King Alfred," he rightly places it (University College) in the city and proudly proclaims that it was really Elizabeth Praetorius who taught him everything clever he "learned in school, except the writing of Latin verse" in her modern, Germanic, co-educational establishment in Folkestone (GTR, 24, P, 215).

Ford says, early in *Provence*, that all his "travelling has always been one long planning to return" (59). As a Utopian South of France, *Provence* comes out of Dowell's longing for a terrestrial paradise, out of Ford's poetic response to Violet's 1914 wish "for a plan for a working Heaven," and out of Lovell's 1913 dream-vision of the lady with the crooked smile. As a generalized paradise it has affinities with Ford's portrait of *The Heart of the Country* as every Londoner's Isle of the Blest. As an actual place, the South of France is where Ford took Janice in 1930, Stella in 1922, and Violet in 1913. It is the place to which he intended to take the ailing Elsie in 1908 and 1903. But above all, in *Provence*, he associates the place with his father's scholarship and his grandfather's romantic sense of history. Ford's portrait of his father in *Provence* is his most sympathetic recollection of him since that September 1914 evocation of him with Swinburne, and throws a rich, ambiguous light on the book. Ford's memory of his grandfather is even more important, illuminating the whole of Ford's last phase.

When Ford thinks "of the *Sanh del Trobador*—the Provence wine called Troubadour's Blood," he sees "it shining in its chalice in the hand of Bérangère des Baux across the shadows and mysteries of that garden" which the Hueffers had in Hammersmith when Ford was "a little, little boy in London before my father died" (53, 52). Bérangère holds it because, according to one story, her husband, having killed her troubadour Guillem de Cabestanh, makes her unwittingly drink his blood. When she understands, she throws herself from the heights of Les Baux (83). "But sometimes," in Ford's memory, he sees that wine "in the scarlet glass with the emerald green stem from which my father drank" (53), thus suggesting the second version of the legend of Guillem, in which Bérangère's potion makes him sick and eventually mad (83). Anyhow, when "I was not more than twelve . . . my father was dead, and I have never looked at his book . . . the famous one on the Troubadours . . . or the poem of Cabestanh again" (55, 54). In the light of Ford's almost invariably hostile references to his father, the treatment here is striking. The passage expresses, uniquely, a real sense of grief. It moves the death to at least three years earlier than it happened, heightening the pathos and making the loss chronologically close to Conrad's loss, at eleven, of his father. The recollections make clear that Ford's love for Provence and his knowledge of her language and poetry come originally from Francis Hueffer. And the ambiguity of the image—his troubadour-father may be receiving tribute or death from the lady—suggests, in the light of over forty years of wounded Fordian lovers, a profound fellow-feeling between son and father.

Ford's "affectionate admiration for the Albigenses" of Provence, held since early youth, he owes, however, to his grandfather. The latter loved these gentle heretics, and yoked them in his mind and quite against scientific, historical probability, with the martyred Waldenses of Milton's "Avenge, Oh Lord, Thy slaughtered saints!" and with the largely legendary Good King René (133, 136). No sooner was his grandfather dead than Ford was eager "to be at one with his benignant spirit; for I knew then that forty years after that day I should still have to look in vain for a more chivalrous, benevolent and Christian man" (140). He further decides that his grandfather's way "is probably the better way to take one's history" (140). Nowadays, when Ford argues with the young about history, he finds himself responding "with some heat—like my poor grandfather . . . the rhythms of his speech and his characteristic phrases are still singularly familiar to me" (138, 136). Ford had put in nearly a half-century of hard labor as an artist,

and of personal suffering as a lover, in order at last to become his father and his grandfather. Now he would speak
with the assured authority of age.

One of the greatest joys of these last books is just that
newly achieved, old, masculine, authoritative voice.[5] Of
course, Ford had talked like an old man before he was
twenty and had condescended to Conrad and Crane before
he was thirty. But always there had been the undercurrent
of vulnerability, childishness, anxiety, to make the manner
never wholly convincing. Now he lets you see that he really does know what he is doing, that his purpose is quite
serious, that to achieve that purpose he will knowingly ex-
aggerate and knowingly romance, and that, even so, he
does not mind if you laugh a little at his methods.

Early in *Provence* Ford establishes the seriousness of his
travelogue. In Tarascon he patronizes the Café de Paris
rather than the Café du Commerce, not out of snobbish-
ness but because the clients of the former "are professional—and more *rangés*" (58). He goes there in order to
establish himself as *"sérieux"* and thus worthy of being told
the truth. Ford, of course, knows "exactly what to think"
(124). He further insists on his right to experiment: Mistral
may not have been as distinguished a poet as Tennyson
but "if, for the purpose of an argument or to hear what it
may sound like or in furtherance of a train of thought, I
choose to say and, intoxicated by the sun, momentarily to
believe, that Mistral so was, I don't want to be interrupted
in my sermon . . . by someone who will be pained." For
this is "the frame of mind that is Provence" (67). And there
he is the strong old man who goes to bullfights because he
likes to, and needs no justification (347). In that spirit, he
will include precisely what he wants to include in the great
oval that is his Great Trade Route. He will trace the route
across the Atlantic, through southern New Jersey, taking
in Delaware and Maryland, leaving out Pennsylvania. He
will include Princeton, for her spire, Elizabeth, New Jersey
for Stephen Crane's grave, and a "filling-station where the
bus stopped," and, yes, New York. "I for the moment am

bossing this Route" (GTR, 258). And how much it is *his* old Route! The merchants crossed the Seine at Paris (his frequent home with Janice and Stella), crossed the Channel at Dungeness (just below the Hueffers' and the Conrads' Kentish houses), or at Rye (James's town, next to the Martindales' Winchelsea), went along the South Coast to Chichester (site of Violet's Selsey cottage and close to the cottages of Ford and Stella), up, in Roman times, to cross the Thames at London (Ford's birthplace), across the Atlantic to New York (his frequent haven in the twenties), and to the South (of his dear friends Caroline Gordon and Allen Tate).

The American part of the Route, not surprisingly, evokes less good prose than the English and French parts. But Provence (his most nearly permanent, later home) evokes the best of all. "I am giving you my Provence . . . The Roman Province on the Great Trade Route where I have lived for nearly all my spiritual . . . life" (P, 142). "Spiritual" is the key word, and *Provence* is Ford's last picture of Heaven. Everything that he loves and nothing that he hates is in this country of his mind, consisting partly of his impressions of contemporary Provence and partly of his version of the land of the Troubadours. His Provence is an Eden free of evil. The "real Fall" occurred "when man in contagious madness left those regions for the North . . . and . . . what Eve ate sinfully was not an apple but a dish of brussels sprouts" (79, 80). While barbarians raged about in a world gone mad, Provence "evolved the civilization and poetry of the Troubadours, the heresy of the Albigenses and . . . let the legions thunder past" (127). The Albigenses believed in "a theory of two first principles, the one of good, the other of evil" (131). Ford's personal version is to make the first two Persons of the Trinity into these "two first causes, the one vengeful, the other infinitely forgiving; the one Jahweh, the other Elohim; the one creating Provence, the other the rest of the Great Trade Route." (Ford has always had trouble believing in the Holy Ghost anyway, 140.) But because Eve ate that first brussels sprout, we cannot, outside Ford's Provence, get rid of the machine, or war, or private property, or churches, or science, or law, or "the final curse, national patriotism. But all these things must—they will inevitably—be made little . . . the end of humanity is not yet" (320, 333).

In Ford's Provence, as opposed to the world of the Great Trade Route, all these problems have been solved, and Ford's particular curses have been lifted. "It is . . . difficult to sin in Provence." Instead of having to suffer in those "divorce courts that . . . render our Nordic domesticities one long and grinning cacophony," a lady who takes other lovers, in order to assure herself of her lover's perfection by the test of comparison, is paying high tribute to her lover (83, 82). The murderous husband of Bérangère des Baux was an exception. Normally, lords give enthusiastic support to the addresses bards pay to their womankind (176). Provence, naturally, is the only country in the world with a sufficiency of spices,and so "Provençal digestions are tranquillized" (167-68). If Provençal cooking is less glorious than elsewhere in France, it is because of the "frugal, temperate and infinitely industrious strain of mind" that the Romans stamped upon the place (103). Ford in both books stresses the simplicity and hardness of Provençal life. The "dreadful greennesses" of English countrysides "frighten" him:

> I shall suffocate if I cannot get to a hard, hot stone, flat on an iron parched hillside, looking between olive, almond and mulberry trunks over the Mediterranean. . . . There on those stern, baked cliffs I might have a chance of sitting, leaned on my elbow, with leering eyes, sneering at you, the museum visitor. . . . from on top of my baked clay tomb. (P, 295-96)

Ford's Provence is most Fordian, of course, in her art, which includes those qualities of discipline and serenity already suggested. Provence does not partake of the English devotion to "delicacy of colour. . . . We can look with equanimity at pink cliffs, a blaze of purple bougainvilleas, beneath an ultramarine sky, above a vivid emerald sea shot with myriads of scarlet fishes and bottomed with forests of magenta seaweeds" (229, 230). Provence's visual art recalls Ford's own hallucinated imagination. The domestic scenes in the votive pictures of Provence have "that air of super-reality that marionnettes have" (237). Between the picture of a lady caught in the jaws of a crocodile and the picture of her having made her escape, there will be, in the sky, "the image of the saint . . . *within a wavy lozenge of light*" (238, my italics). These paintings go back to the great art of the time of the Avignon Popes, an art inspired by fourteenth-century Italian primitives (239). In short, the art of Provence is intuitively and literally Pre-Raphaelite. But those early painters painted solely "to adorn spaces," "make churches glow and tired eyes be rested." "DEC-ORATION," Ford shouts, "IS THE SOLE . . . REASON . . . FOR . . . ALL . . . THE ARTS" (239, 246). Similarly, the troubadours were strictly entertainers whose job it was to fill the time "between rising from the last meal and going to the practices of love" (190). In the last section of *Provence*, "Mise à Mort*," the matador becomes for a while the type of the artist. Here Ford goes perhaps further than he has ever gone in saying that art is *only* technique. The skill of the troubadour, in rhyme and meter, gave his audi-ence as much pleasure as the actual content of his poems. "Craftsmanship . . . ingenuity . . . patience express . . . the sufferings his passion causes him" (175). The troubadour's subject is the same as Dowell's. But in *Provence* we are a long, long way from Edward's agony and the reality of *The Good Soldier*. We are close in spirit, however, to Ford at his entertaining best in creating Christopher. Still, entertain-ing takes heroism, too, and the matador Lalanda's "tiny steel rod" of a sword looks a great deal like Ford's mighty pen.[6]

MIGHTIER THAN THE SWORD

Mightier Than the Sword is perfectly titled.[7] It is about the power of the pen, the writer as hero, the "strong men who lived before to-day's Agamemnons" (5). Ford's preface uses appropriately forceful language:

> I determined . . . to erect to my—nearly all dead— friends . . . an . . . intimately vignetted representation that should force the public to see that circle of strong personalities as I want them to be seen. I am . . . a novelist, and I want them to be seen pretty much as you see the characters in a novel. . . . As if one should see the frequenters of the Mermaid Tavern in an his- torical romance . . . Ford with his melancholy hat, Jon- son with his learned sock, and the Shakespeare who had once bitten off the the heads of chickens . . . I wanted them to be seen by posterity as I had seen them—the strong, strongly featured men. . . . I have, I repeat, been trying to make you see these people whom I very much loved—as I want them seen. (5, 6)

Four times Ford says, "I want." He wants above all "to make you see." Ford is once again bossing this route or, being now, more precisely, "the *doyen* of English novelists" (145). He intends to force the reader to experi- ence vicariously these "strong . . . strong, strongly fea- tured men," as he experienced them. The experience will be primarily visual as the harping on "see" indicates and the Shakesperian instance insists. But also, *Mightier Than the Sword*, like every impressionistic novel, only more so, will really be about the author. The obsessive use of the first person singular tells us that, and instancing first that other "Ford with his melancholy hat" reinforces the point. For *Mightier Than the Sword* needs to be read ultimately as Ford's last and, in many ways, best portrait of himself as artist and human being. Its eleven chapters on his eleven friends are like a circle of distorting mirrors in a fun house. That one there, see, his body abnormally short, his head magnificently large, he calls "Swinburne."

Mightier Than the Sword is a wonderful book. All the old stories are here—Swinburne dumped drunk into Madox Brown's bath for safety and confinement, Marwood en- raged at *Cornhill Magazine* for turning down Hardy's poem, little Fordie offering a chair to gigantic Turgenev, James talking like a book about his domestic help, shining Galsworthy purveying an English breakfast in solid silver service, Wells baring his amorous life in the London Zoo, Crane writing his life away in a baronial ruin, Hudson bringing the breath of the New Forest into a Soho restaurant. Hearing all those stories one more time, I am, like Richard Aldington's father in Ford's presence, "swimming in bliss."[8] And the anecdotes serve a purpose, to seduce the reader into understanding some central idea about each writer, an idea that is vitally important to Ford's sense of his own career, its trials and triumphs, as well as to his sense of the art of fiction.

As the preface insists, all these writers were powerful men. Indeed, for Ford, the novelist is the hero par excellence. If the world could only really attend to her novelists, wars would cease, peace and understanding prevail. A lot of the best prose in the book is devoted to dramatizing this notion. At the same time, however, Ford is constantly revealing how mysterious, complex, chancy, and vulnerable the creative imagination is. Most of these writers go through phases, sometimes moving on to still higher achievements, but often slipping into serious decline. They contain multiple personalities, usually at war with each other. And although Ford damns official biographers, he clearly believes that a great artist's life and work interpenetrate in complicated, inextricable ways. One last time, either explicitly or through other writers, Ford reveals the importance for his career of his heritage and his childhood terrors. Movingly enough for a man who in his lifetime and ever since has been damned as a liar, Ford convincingly propounds the notion that great writers are great chiefly because of their honesty and integrity.

Many of Ford's supermen-writers are physically strong; most are immensely energetic and productive; most are courageous; some are not really so much superhuman as other than human—animals, fairies, gods. James had the "most amazing vitality, inexhaustible, indefatigable" (20).

Conrad is back to being one of "the great Elizabethans" (289). Improbably, but with the emphasis of a gifted teacher, Ford asserts that Conrad "detested the sea . . . with the hatred of a small man who has had, on freezing nights of gales, to wrestle with immense yards and dripping cordage" (83). Heroically, Conrad "took his courage in both hands" after *Lord Jim*, abandoned the sea as subject, and wrote "*Nostromo*, an immense book," containing "the whole of a vast imagined republic" (269, 92, 96). In 1936, with Conrad in eclipse, Ford still sees him the way he saw him in 1898: "The king shall enjoy his own again" (95). What struck one most about Wells, another little man, was "his tough, as it were Cockney, gallantry of attack." Ford, too, he reminds us, is a Cockney as was Keats (153). About Dreiser, there is nothing little. "We are both big and tempestuous. . . ." (217). When they argue, "Mr. Dreiser hurls gigantic trains of polyphonic, linked insults . . . immense handfuls of Pullman cars" (215). Lawrence reminds Ford of a predator, a fox ready to devour him (105-107). Ford associates Lawrence, like so many of his otherworldly writers, with light and color: "his *panache*, his plume of hair with the sunlight always in it—and his red beard . . . as disturbingly bright as ever" (122). Ford remembers Galsworthy as "radiating bright sunlight," presiding over breakfast, "the sunlight streaming in on the hissing silver entrée dishes, the red tiles of the floor, the bright rugs, the bright screens" (187, 172). The most purely godlike of Ford's writers are Crane and Swinburne. Stephen Crane, "an Apollo with starry eyes, . . . seemed to shine" (41-42). But when Ford was a little boy, Swinburne alone of all those late Victorian greats who frequented the house in Fitzroy Square "was a solar myth with the voice of a Greek god, beautiful and shining and kind so that when *he* came on the scene, drunk or sober, all was gas and gingerbread and joybells and jujubes" (246). Swinburne "will always remain a male creature of a great radiance, chivalry, sweetness of voice, and generous gestures . . ." (263).

Reading all these deifications strung together may give

to those unfamiliar with *Mightier Than the Sword* an unfortunate impression of embarrassing repetitiveness, not to say windiness. But in context, these passages effectively extoll the power of creative artistry. The chapters should be read as inspiriting lectures by a professional writer and great teacher calculated to inspire reverence for the craft of writing and to hammer home his sense of the force of language used artfully.[9] Calling Swinburne a "male creature" underlines how Fordian this book is. Much as Ford has doted all his life on the impossible she and has advocated women artists, his deepest, deepest intellectual and emotional responses are to men. Making so many of his writers otherworldly, godlike, fabulous, this, too, though hardly original, is an authentically Fordian idea. It reflects, of course, his old man's awareness of the strangeness of his own life. But more importantly it reflects Ford's sense of how inexplicable, mysterious, contradictory, incomprehensible is the human act of artistic creation. Virtually every one of his writers possesses a divided or multiple personality. Almost every one of them has experienced some sort of shocking gulf in his career, a change to another phase.

Ford attributes the change in James's writing, his loss of "masculine firmness" and "quiet force," to an entirely new point of view. James "became the creature of infinite precautions. . . . If he was continuously parenthetic, it was in the determination that no word he wrote should ever be misinterpreted" (32, 33, 35). James even changed in physical appearance. Having before looked something like a bearded Prince of Wales, he became clean-shaven; his nervous face gave "the feeling of a forced energy, as if of a man conscious of failure and determined to conceal mortification." The cause of it all was a woman who "let him down mercilessly after a period of years" (33, 34). (Ford's phrasing here, so reminiscent of his own feelings about Brigit, implies that James was rejected in love in the nineties. Although there is no evidence for this, James certainly suffered from the apparent suicide of his old friend

Fenimore Constance Woolson.) It is important to note, however, that Ford never associates with the later James the kind of unconscious dishonesty or disastrous alteration he convincingly attributes to Galsworthy. The periodical version of the James chapter ends in a paean for the last phase: "I shall never write such a wonderful, such a tender and beautiful book" as *The Wings of the Dove*.[10]

Like James, Conrad went through a fundamental change in the orientation of his artistry, but to Ford's mind, the shift was almost wholly to the good: Conrad more and more abandoned the sea, introduced women and landsmen, and turned his attention to politics and revolution (92). Ford is too good a critic to be blind to the flaws in the political novels or to forget that Conrad's "best and, as it were, cleanest work" is to be found in "Youth," "Heart of Darkness," and *The Nigger of the "Narcissus."* Still, Ford rather unfortunately presages F. R. Leavis and forgets his early passion for *Lord Jim* when he says: "it will be rather on account of his land books than on account of his marine tapestries that Conrad will eventually re-emerge and be accounted great. It will be rather *Nostromo* than *Lord Jim*" (87, 97).

The gulf in Swinburne occurred after the poet's death, when Ford could no longer read him (258). Yet he welcomes the possibility of a Swinburne revival because "I loved him and I am none of your incorruptibles" (287). Ford's final image of Swinburne is surely of Ford, too. And it is sheer delight. Calling the highest, snowiest Alpine peaks "the Middle Victorian, tumultuously bearded Great who were a childish nightmare to me," Ford seems "to see Swinburne, poised in the blue empyrean above Mont Blanc, winged, rose-garlanded, and with bow and quiver, aiming an arrow at the heart of Mr. Ruskin" (264, 287-88).

Lawrence and Dreiser are mysterious not because they progress or decline as artists, but because they contain multiple personalities. Precisely like Ford's Henry Martin, Lawrence embodied a "continual fight between the jovial pirate father and the cautious, disapproving, Noncon-

formist, pale mother, going on all the while in the very current of his thought." Ford dismisses any theory of Lawrence's being mother-obsessed. He would rather "explain
him along the lines of Amen-Ra, the Egyptian All-
Father-Mother" who "was at once his own father and
mother and his own wife . . . and husband. And his own
children . . ." (116). How well Ford's new complex applies
to Lawrence is arguable, but it certainly fits Ford—except
that he was also his own grandfather, brother, uncle, and,
according to Olive, great-grandfather. For Ford, Lawrence's greatest gift had nothing to do with his parents. "It
was his passionate—as it were an almost super-sex-
passionate—delight in the opening of flowers and leaves"
(119). Still, that last, familiar sunlit image of Lawrence that
Ford chooses to leave us with is surely that of the
"mother-suppressed child, . . . head slightly bent," standing by "a little impotent," while Mrs. Wells and Mrs. Lawrence fight the Great War in Ford's embarrassed presence
(116, 122).[11]

Dreiser contains many personalities, and his mutiplicity
is precisely his value and his meaning: "It is because he
renders for us this world of fantastic incertitude that
Dreiser's work is of such importance" (234). But much as
Ford enjoys and admires him, Dreiser's lower middle-
class, nonartistic, American origins and his untidy fictional
methods are too alien to Ford for total identification. In
Mightier Than the Sword Ford sees himself at his best as
Ivan Turgenev, the "beautiful genius." Ford's first, childhood memory remains that of a fabulous, aged giant (190).
He most vividly recalls Turgenev in the recumbent position he also so notably attributes to himself in *Provence*:
"reclining on one elbow on a divan, he was a Deity all of
himself" (199). Turgenev's great literary gifts of empathy,
detachment, and acceptance of ambiguity are surely the
ones Ford most hoped that he possessed. He deeply admires Turgenev's talent for identifying completely with
"the passions of his characters" and then being able to look

with detachment at his turbulent creations. "It was perhaps his extreme misfortune . . . but it was certainly his supreme and beautiful gift—that he had the seeing eye to such an extent that he could see that two opposing truths were equally true" (207, 208). Characteristically, Ford puts Turgenev on a railroad train and imagines him identifying with the person sitting opposite (209). Turgenev's ideal combination of gifts enabled him not only to "transfuse himself into all his characters" but to render them "all us" (210).

Besides attributing to Turgenev his own highest artistic ideals, Ford sees Turgenev's life as he would surely, in his cheerful moods, like to see his own, a life of exotic travel, of innumerable casual courtships, effortlessly transformed from time to time into yet another masterpiece (207). Turgenev is never more Fordian than in his friendship for Flaubert. Those two shared, like Conrad and Ford, a hatred for "the manifestations and effects of cruelty produced by want of imagination." In spirit, they were expatriates, as "the great poet is invariably an expatriate, if not invariably in climate, then at least in the regions of the mind" (209). Ford's description begins, precisely, with Turgenev's friendship with Flaubert, in language reminiscent of the way Ford would talk about his love of Conrad: "indulging in night-long verbal pillow fights at Croisset . . . they never went to bed, preferring to talk all night about the assonances of Prosper Mérimée" (213).

If Ford is implicitly omnipresent in *Mightier Than the Sword*, he is also explicitly there, especially in the concluding chapter. Indeed, he touches, one last time, on several of the matters related to his career that have been of recurrent interest. Throughout his life, Ford would keep making the same discovery that, until 1904, or 1909, or 1914, or 1919, he had been utterly naive about himself. But in his old age he came persuasively to see that perpetual naiveté is a good thing and that his favorite writers possessed it. Conrad's naïve astonishment . . . was one of his greatest charms. . . . For it should never be forgotten that an artist or a great man remains great only as long as he can remain naïve and astonished and can examine with a vivid curiosity the minutest, as well as the most enormous, of the workings of nature or of humanity. As soon as he becomes *renfrogné*, conscious of his importance, listless in face of phenomena, grown up . . . the comedy is finished. (91)

In the last chapter Ford observes the strange coincidence that his four favorite authors—Hudson, Conrad, James, Crane—as they wrote about Rima, Rita, and the others, were all really thinking of a Beatrice Portinari (289). Ford is no doubt remembering that in his aching pursuit of the ideal, he always saw it in female form and that Brigit, Stella, and Janice all inspired, pretty directly, his best work. Yet he does not forget in recalling the beneficence of love the terrors of sex either. He especially remembers the occasions when James would make his conversation, for Ford, "really horrific, on the topics of esoteric sin or sexual indulgence. I have attended . . . conversations that made the tall wax candles seem to me to waver in their sockets and the skin of my forehead and hands prickle with sweat" (27).

In this last chapter, Ford also tries to give its due to an approach to art different from that of the great impressionists. He tells once more about Wyndham Lewis's blast at Conrad, James, and himself for wanting ingeniously to make people believe that they are participating in the lives of the characters. Lewis insists that readers want not verisimilitude but entertainment (282). Ford comments on Lewis with venerable mildness: "he expressed no doubt part of a truth. . . . all of us in certain moods like to look at conjuring tricks and performing seals. But not all of us, all the time" (283). These words point forward toward the great mid-century fictional trend, in which Nabokov has been the leader; they point backward as well, it seems to me, to the Ford of *Parade's End*.

But that is not the crucial Ford of *Mightier Than the Sword*.[12] He aligns himself with his heroes, who all "drew out truth from their adventures . . . in the end . . . the true writer . . . has—and oh Great Writer don't you know it!—one thing that is possessed by no other man. That is his integrity . . . of purpose or of achievement" (290). Ford's own purpose, he tells us one last time, was to learn how to create Dowell: "As for me I went on working beside Conrad, trying . . . to evolve for myself a vernacular of an extreme quietness that would suggest someone of refinement talking in a low voice near the ear of someone else he liked a good deal" (278). Ford makes quite clear his awareness of his real, irreducible achievement. He gave up the pen for the sword to protect "the poor shades of Emma and Charles Bovary" after "having just written the only novel of my own that I considered—and indeed consider—at all to count" (280). *The Good Soldier* is enough for him and ought to be enough for us. "What brings back a forgotten artist is what I will call an essential honesty—of writing, of purpose, of selection, of presentation" (288). And no matter what happens to literary reputations, "it is yet sufficient," Ford says, in imagery that resembles Dowell's,

> that somewhere there should exist a fascicle of living words, woven in true thoughts and capturing beauty in its cobwebby net. For the book will live, not the reader, even though all the masonry of a sacked city have fallen on its hiding-place and the ground be buried beneath the dust of vanished civilizations. . . . (290)

Ford Madox Ford died in Deauville in his beloved France, on June 26, 1939. He was not far from Rouen, which he always associated with Conrad. This port, as Ford well knew and often recalled, is where Conrad spent the last weeks of his sailing career, on board the *Adowa*, serving as second officer and working on *Almayer's Folly*, in the winter of 1893-1894.[13] Rouen was dear to Ford also as the home of Flaubert, his and Conrad's idol. And it was from there in 1916 that Ford wrote his war letters to Conrad and received from him the last truly loving responses.

Because of the imminence of a second world war, Ford and Janice had planned to spend that summer in Normandy, near Le Havre, instead of going on, as they would have preferred, to Provence. Still, merely to be in France was to feel close to Avignon. And there, for Ford, would always be, perspiring in his Harris tweeds, Arthur Marwood.

Notes

PREFACE

1. "Hence one of the questions most worth asking about Ford's early career as a novelist is: Why didn't he write *The Good Soldier*, or a novel of comparable stature, before the age of forty?" R. W. Lid, *Ford Madox Ford: The Essence of His Art* (Berkeley: Univ. of California Press, 1964), p. 90. Carol Ohmann asks "the obvious question . . . why did Ford, despite a precocious beginning, require more than two decades to fulfill his promise as a novelist?" *Ford Madox Ford: From Apprentice to Craftsman* (Middletown: Wesleyan Univ. Press, 1964), p. 5. Paul L. Wiley, however, sees Ford's development as consistent and denies that *The Good Soldier* is a "magical feat." *Novelist of Three Worlds: Ford Madox Ford* (Syracuse: Syracuse Univ. Press, 1962), pp. 3-5.

2. Unusual, but not unique. *Manon Lescaut*, for example, is a single gem set in a vast sea of mediocre works by Abbé Prévost.

3. An obvious exception is Arthur Mizener's fine biography, *The Saddest Story* (New York: World, 1971). So, too, are the critical studies by Ohmann and Ambrose Gordon, Jr., *The Invisible Tent* (Austin: Univ. of Texas Press, 1964). Ohmann's book is excellent in showing some of the ways Ford's mind works, but errs seriously, I think, in seeing him as a moralist. Gordon rightly questions previous orderly approaches to the inconsistent Ford. But whereas he finds the key to Ford in World War I, I find it in his personal relations, the most important of which predate the war.

4. Intense as Ford's affection was for Conrad and Marwood, it was surely not homosexual. Indeed, all three men would, I am sure, have been amazed at the notion.

5. Quoted by David Dow Harvey, *Ford Madox Ford, 1873-1939: A Bibliography of Works and Criticism* (Princeton: Princeton Univ. Press, 1962), p. 428.

6. Since Ford's legatee ultimately refused me permission to quote extensively from Ford's works, the liveliness of his prose is, alas, less evident in the present book than in earlier versions.

7. William Faulkner, *Absalom, Absalom!* (New York: Random House, 1936), p. 280.

CHAPTER ONE

1. Quoted by Mizener, p. 1, from Ezra Pound's letter to Stella Bowen of September 16, 1947. Unless otherwise indicated, biographical facts

come from Mizener or from such obvious sources as the D.N.B. and the British Museum Catalogue.

2. Although the year of Oliver's birth is usually given as 1877, the date on the Certificate of Birth in the Public Records Office is January 9, 1876, the place, 5, Fairlawn, Merton (where Ford was born).

3. Olive Garnett's diary belongs to her niece Anne Lee-Michell, daughter of Robert Singleton Garnett. In a book-length typescript, Mrs. Lee-Michell has transcribed a generous selection of diary entries from 1890 to 1906, under the title "A Bloomsbury Girlhood," with an introduction and notes. (A copy is in the University of Texas Library, Austin.) This volume deserves to be published in its entirety. Although I make extensive use of the facts in Mrs. Lee-Michell's introduction, all the entries I quote come directly from the original diary. I am deeply grateful to Mrs. Lee-Michell not only for permission to quote so extensively but also for her warm interest and unstinting assistance.

4. William Michael Rossetti to Catherine Hueffer, January 25, 1889. The Berg Collection, New York Public Library.

5. Beauty, of course, is in the eye of the beholder. Dame Rebecca West remembers Ford as homely, looking "like an egg"; his daughter Katharine remembered him as "quite handsome."

6. According to Mizener (p. 19), Ford instead went to Bonn to receive instruction in the Roman Catholic faith. He did not actually join the Church until November 7, and in Paris.

7. In *Ancient Lights* (1911), Ford tells how a young woman from Hampstead who almost became his first love rejected him for laughing at the pretentiousness of the African novelist Olive Schreiner (228).

8. Mizener, p. 23.

9. Actually, Elsie had had a tubercular gland removed from her neck and an iron wire inserted in a weakened knee. The neck operation confined her to her bed for a year during her teens. Katharine Hueffer Lamb, letter of February 15, 1978.

10. Letters from Ford to Elsie, March 3 and 5, 1894. Quoted by Mizener, p. 23.

11. Olive was apparently unaware that Elsie's initial intention was simply to go and stay with her old aunts in Carlisle until her parents would once again permit her to see Ford. According to Katharine Hueffer Lamb, Elsie did not plan to elope. It was Robert Garnett who persuaded her that she had to get married and told her to say she was of age. Letter of February 15, 1978.

12. Ford's title comes from the title and first line of Franz Schubert's famous *Lied*, "You are Rest and Peace," a setting of Friedrich Rückert's poem, "Come in to Me" ("Kehr ein bei mir"). Ford and Elsie's younger daughter, "handmaiden to the arts" (her phrase), wrote about her father's "love of music, composing, improvising, & the two of them playing & singing together—He had a beautiful touch

on the piano & Mum had a lovely mezzo-soprano voice—I have
never heard anyone with just her timbre. All my knowledge of lieder
came from lying in bed hearing them when I was going to sleep."
(Letter of February 2, 1978.)

13. Juliet M. Soskice, *Chapters from Childhood* (London: Selwyn and
    Blount, 1921), p. 236.
14. Francis Hueffer, *The Troubadours* (London: Chatto and Windus,
    1878), pp. 99, 129, 281.
15. Rossetti's phrase comes from "St. Agnes of Intercession," *The Col-
    lected Works of Dante Gabriel Rossetti*, 2 vols. (London: Ellis and Elvey,
    1890), I, 411. Oswald Doughty uses it as the epigraph to *A Victorian
    Romantic: Dante Gabriel Rossetti*, 2nd ed. (London: Oxford Univ.
    Press, 1960). Unless otherwise indicated, all my information about
    Rossetti comes from this source.
16. Helen Rossetti Angeli, *Dante Gabriel Rossetti: His Friends and Enemies*
    (London: Hamish Hamilton, 1949), p. 260. Arthur Symons, "The
    Rossettis," *Dramatis Personae* (Indianapolis: Bobbs-Merrill, 1923),
    p. 129.
17. Doughty, p. 226.
18. Symons, p. 131.
19. Barbara Charlesworth, *Dark Passages* (Madison: Univ. of Wisconsin
    Press, 1965), pp. 15-16, 20.
20. Quoted by Doughty, p. 225. My italics.
21. *The Works of Dante Gabriel Rossetti*, ed. William M. Rossetti (London:
    Ellis, 1911), p. 100.
22. *The Works of Dante Gabriel Rossetti*, pp. 239-40.
23. Igor Michael Webb, "Sense and Sensibility: A Study of the Influence
    of English Aesthetics from Ruskin to Roger Fry on Ford Madox Ford
    and Virginia Woolf," Ph.D. diss., Stanford, 1971, p. 44. Webb has an
    excellent discussion of the relationship of the Pre-Raphaelite back-
    ground to Ford's creative imagination, pp. 29-50.
24. In his old age, Ford viewed the novel more charitably as an early,
    unnoticed piece of impressionism (*The March of Literature*, p. 766).
25. "It was only a goose walking over my grave" (227) later appears as
    one of Dowell's most striking images and as the title for a fine
    novella by John Hawkes.
26. Frank MacShane praises its "maturity" and "depth of perception,"
    in *The Life and Work of Ford Madox Ford* (New York: Horizon Press,
    1965), pp. 24-25. Lid calls it "more than creditable," p. 92.
27. Quoted by MacShane, *Life and Work of Ford Madox Ford*, p. 87.
28. Erik Erikson, *Young Man Luther* (New York: W. W. Norton, 1958),
    p. 83.
29. Lid comments shrewdly that "Ford did not enjoy being young,"
    p. 11.
30. Mizener, p. 17.

CHAPTER TWO

1. Typically, their times together were concerned with literary and artistic matters, including the quest for *le mot juste*: "As we neared the coast we heard the waves breaking & saw dotted lights. Whistlerish effect. Through the village, & then we sat on a bench facing the sea & drank loveliness. . . . Noise in the rushes behind us. We were silent & then talked . . . & tried to find description for mingling of backward fall of wave with oncoming rush,—in poetry—in music" (November 18, 1894).

2. Although the first known letter from Conrad to Ford is dated September 29, 1898, two Conradian scholars, Eloise Knapp Hay and Raymond T. Brebach, believe they have evidence for a first meeting as early as the previous May. Such a meeting would make Ford a possible inspiration for Conrad's invention of Marlow in "Youth." I myself do not find their evidence persuasive.

3. Thanks to recent scholarship, a good deal is now known about the Conrad-Ford friendship. In the 1960s, Jocelyn Baines's critical biography of Conrad, Frank MacShane's critical biography of Ford, and especially Dr. Bernard C. Meyer's psychoanalytic biography of Conrad provided the first reliable accounts of the friendship. Since then, because of the general availability of a great deal of Conrad's correspondence with and about Ford and the existence of Arthur Mizener's marvelously full biography, we know still more.

4. For an authoritative account of Conrad's depressed personal state at the time, see Zdzisław Najder, "Conrad in 1898," *Studies in Joseph Conrad*, ed. Claude Thomas, Cahiers d'Etudes et de Recherches Victoriennes et Edouardiennes, No. 2 (Montpellier: Univ. Paul-Valéry, 1975), pp. 19-36.

5. Violet Hunt, *I Have This to Say* (New York: Boni and Liveright, 1926), pp. 38, 262.

6. Quoted in Harvey, pp. 251-52.

7. Yale University Library.

8. Zdzisław Najder, "Joseph Conrad: A Selection of Unknown Letters," *Polish Perspectives*, February 1970, p. 39.

9. Conrad to Ford, July 19, 1901. Yale University Library.

10. Conrad to Ford, July 1902, Yale University Library.

11. Bernard C. Meyer, *Joseph Conrad: A Psychoanalytic Biography* (Princeton: Princeton Univ. Press, 1967), pp. 137-38. Conrad to Ford, Sept. 29, 1898. Yale University Library.

12. Conrad to Ford, Oct. 2, 1898. Yale University Library.

13. Conrad to Ford, June 19, 1902. Yale University Library.

14. Conrad to Ford, March 29, 1906. Yale University Library.

15. Conrad's older son, Borys, at the Joseph Conrad Conference, Poland, September 1972.

16. Conrad to H. G. Wells, October 20, 1905, in *Joseph Conrad: Life and*

Letters, ed. G. Jean-Aubry, 2 vols. (New York: Doubleday, Page, 1927), II, 25.

17. Conrad to Elsie, October 1, 1903. Yale University Library.

18. Quoted by Frederick R. Karl, "Conrad, Ford, and the Novel," *Midway*, 10, no. 2 (Autumn 1969), 21 and by MacShane, pp. 40, 49.

19. Mizener, p. 51.

20. See Richard A. Cassell, *Ford Madox Ford: A Study of His Novels* (Baltimore: Johns Hopkins, 1961), pp. 114-25, for a different but reasonable set of early types. Lid sees two women and a man as the characteristic pattern, pp. 21-22. Webb, p. 81, sees the impotent, principled hero, unprincipled new man, vampire, and wholesome heroine as recurrent figures in a cultural melodrama. Caroline Gordon sees the lamia-witch as the most important character-type, in *A Good Soldier*, Chapbook No. 1 (Davis: Univ. of California Library, 1963).

21. H. Robert Huntley's interesting discussion of *The Inheritors* implies a connection between Churchill and Ashburnham, in *The Alien Protagonist of Ford Madox Ford* (Chapel Hill: Univ. of North Carolina Press, 1970), pp. 25-33. For a perceptive analysis of Ford's inept handling of important political ideas in *The Inheritors*, see Robert Green, "Ford Madox Ford's *The Inheritors*: A Conservative Response to Social Imperialism," *English Literature in Transition*, 22, no. 1 (1979), 50-61.

22. See Raymond T. Brebach, "The Making of *Romance*: A Study in Literary Collaboration," Ph.D. diss., University of Illinois at Champaign-Urbana, 1976, for an authoritative history of the extremely complex development of the text. Brebach shows that it is unfair to praise only Conrad for the good and blame Ford for all the bad. Ford's artistry progressed remarkably during the *Romance* years; he was ultimately improving on Conrad's contributions.

23. Conrad was also interested in trials and inquests; he contributed much to the portrait of Kemp as grossly misjudged. Brebach, pp. 35, 65, and JC, 47-48.

24. Brebach, pp. 70, 86, 166.

25. The chief purpose of Conrad and Ford in writing an adventure-romance was to try to capture the audience of the late Robert Louis Stevenson. See David Thorburn, *Conrad's Romanticism* (New Haven: Yale Univ. Press, 1974), pp. 24-26, 32-35. Thorburn's discussion of *Romance* is enlightening.

26. See Samuel Hynes, "Ford and the Spirit of Romance," in *Edwardian Occasions* (New York: Oxford Univ. Press, 1972), pp. 76-77.

27. Mizener connects the Kentish scenes of *Romance* with the Pent Farm and Limpsfield, pp. 40 and 531-32, nn. 16, 17. Ford characterized the voice of the narrator in his original manuscript as the "whisper of a nonagenarian" (JC, 14), underlining his recurrent need to use an asexual point of view.

28. Thorburn finds the impotent l.._ro typically Conradian, pp. 38-39.

29. Aubry, I, 318; Brebach, pp. 143, 145, 146.

30. William Harrison (Harry) Cowlishaw, a young architect, was married to Olive's younger sister Lucy. He designed the Cearne and Gracie's Cottage, at Limpsfield, and Katharine Hueffer Lamb's house in County Galway, Ireland. He also did the book design for *Ford Madox Brown*.

31. Quoted by Mizener, p. 56. See "On Heaven," *Poetry*, 4 (June 1914), 90 and *A House, passim*.

32. See Douglas Goldring, *Trained for Genius* (New York: Dutton, 1949), pp. 103-104, and MacShane, *Life and Work of Ford Madox Ford*, p. 19.

33. Mizener, p. 62. Conversation with Mrs. Lamb, April 26, 1975.

34. Mizener, pp. 89-91.

35. Mizener, p. 93.

36. Yale University Library.

37. Yale University Library. In justice to Conrad, it should be said that his letters to Ford in Germany, infrequent as they were, are full of solicitude as well as offers to help revise and place any articles Ford might be able to write. See Meyer, pp. 210-11, for a discussion of Conrad's characteristic "warding off physical and mental suffering through action."

38. "Author's Note" (1920), *The Secret Agent* (London: John Grant, 1925), pp. ix, xii.

39. Some 63 survive between 1898 and 1903, 29 from 1904 to 1909. Frederick R. Karl, currently editing Conrad's collected letters, has kindly confirmed my census.

40. Mizener, p. 109, believes Elsie discovered Ford's affair with Mary about July 1905. Mrs. Lamb thought the discovery could have been as early as 1903. Letter from Katharine Hueffer Lamb, July 8, 1975.

41. MacShane, *Life and Work of Ford Madox Ford*, p. 70.

42. According to Goldring, p. 64, a wealthy Hueffer uncle died in 1895 and left each of his nephews and nieces over £3,000. Hence Ford once had an inheritance, and spent it.

43. Letter from Ford, from Winterbourne Stoke, near Salisbury, to Dr. Richard Garnett, May or June, 1904. Property of Mrs. Lee-Michell.

44. For two excellent celebrations of *The Fifth Queen*, see Mizener, pp. 133-35, 469-77, and Herbert Howarth, "Hewlett and Ford," *Journal of Modern Literature*, 5, no. 1 (February 1976), 79-88. Serious misgivings are expressed by Ohmann, pp. 23-31, and John A. Meixner, *Ford Madox Ford's Novels* (Minneapolis: Univ. of Minnesota Press, 1962), pp. 44-62. All four critics make intelligent distinctions among the qualities of the different volumes.

45. Elsie herself not only remained a Protestant, but deeply regretted her daughters' conversion to Catholicism. Conversation with

Katharine Hueffer Lamb, January 16, 1978; letter from her January 30, 1977.

46. At his three schools (Aysgarth, Saugeen, and Clifton), Marwood won many prize books for academic excellence in divinity, classics, mathematics, and science. His Form Four prize, *The Life of the Greeks and Romans*, is a translation from the German by Francis Hueffer. Of the time between Cambridge and his marriage, I know only two stories: "that Violet Hunt noted in her Diary as early as Sept. 8, 1890, that 'a man called arthur peason [*sic*] Marwood was [staying at Robin Hood's Bay] with a lady very queer . . .' " (Mizener, p. 553, n. 22); and that Marwood was said to have made a trip to Egypt in hopes of improving his health. He is also said to have owned a large engraving of a battle featuring Major Pierson, presumably the source of his middle name. Lewis Carroll was Arthur Marwood's first cousin.

47. Caroline's father Matthew Cranswick, a farmer and teacher, settled with her mother at Reighton Hall, north of Bridlington, Yorkshire, near the coast. He is now remembered only for owning a racehorse and for fathering ten daughters and seven sons, all of whom did well and most of whom married. Caroline was the third oldest child and the only one of the daughters to leave home for her schooling. She received her nurse's training at the Sunderland Infirmary, run by the "Sisters of Mercy," an order of Anglican nuns, and in 1895 was awarded Sunderland's Hygiene Medal. Later, she became matron of a private nursing home for the distinguished surgeon, Sir Mayo Robsen, in Leeds. He called her his "right hand." There she met, among the patients, Arthur Marwood, and proved herself to be the first person who knew how to take care of him.

48. Caroline and Arthur's marriage is remembered as relatively happy, constantly overshadowed of course by the battle to keep him alive. Sometimes nothing seemed to help him but the sea air, and then they would go sailing off the Channel or Scilly Isles. When Caroline moved them, for Arthur's health, from Winchelsea to the Water Farm, Stowting, she had to take all the responsibility of running the farm. Arthur's eccentricity of liking to take long walks in the middle of the night was probably owing to his tuberculosis of the kidney, which required him to urinate frequently. Although Caroline remembered him as a "saint," her sisters recalled that he was something of a snob who paid a great deal of attention to what was proper, expected you to knock before entering, always dressed for dinner, and would not allow his wife to do any domestic chores or to fraternize with the servants. He was also thought of as a proud, cultured, gentleman farmer. Marwood died May 13, 1916, and Caroline married a neighboring farmer and widower, Walter Pilcher, June 5, 1918. She was widowed again April 11, 1941.

The next generation remembers Caroline well, as she lived until March 31, 1952. For them she is altogether a favorite aunt, a lovely, warm-hearted person, a great cook of country fare who used only the best ingredients, a pretty, smallish woman with light brown hair and gray eyes, who liked to ride about the Winchelsea and Stowting areas in a dogcart, visiting various country houses. The younger generation's impression, I regret to report, of Caroline's impression of Ford is of a "nuisance"; their impression of Caroline's siblings' impression of Conrad is of a "sponge" and of Ford, a "scrounger."

For all this Marwood-Cranswick lore I am deeply indebted to the daughter Caroline adopted during her second marriage, Margery Pilcher, who showed me Marwood's prize books, inscribed books from Ford, and other documents; to Caroline's nephew Henry Bouch, who interviewed his mother, Caroline's last surviving sibling; and to Caroline's niece, Kathleen M. Hill, who allowed me to see the remainder of Marwood's collection of Ford books. I am also indebted to Florence Wynne Finch, to Juliet Wrightson for correspondence with Yorkshireman Ralph Turton, to the Reverend Rex M. Ware of Winchelsea Rectory, and to Borys Conrad.

49. Mizener, pp. 115, 118.

50. Jessie Conrad says Ford first brought Marwood to the Pent "barely a month before my second boy was born." *Joseph Conrad and His Circle* (New York: E. P. Dutton, 1935), p. 116. John Conrad was born August 2, 1906. See Jocelyn Baines, *Joseph Conrad: A Critical Biography*, 2nd ed. (London: Weidenfeld and Nicholson, 1969), p. 329.

51. A letter from Ford to Olive, January 27, 1908, says that he brought Marwood to her place the day before. Ford wants Olive to get to know Marwood because he considers Marwood to have the greatest intellect of anyone alive. Property of Mrs. Lee-Michell.

52. Yale University Library.

53. Jessie Conrad, pp. 112-13.

54. Although *The Nature of a Crime* was not published until the spring of 1909, in the *English Review*, it was finished by July 1906. See Mizener, pp. 118-19, where he dates the work and connects it to *The Good Soldier*. *The Nature of a Crime* was finally published in book form in 1924.

55. Harvey, p. 163. "Views" first appeared in *Songs from London* (1910), pp. vii-ix.

56. See Chapter Three, below.

57. Although *The "Half-Moon"* was finished in June 1907, only a month after *An English Girl*, it was not published until March 1909, some seven months after the publication of *Mr. Apollo*. See Mizener, pp. 126-27, and Harvey, p. 28.

58. Mizener has noted how Ford recurrently follows modern satire with historical romance and celebrates each new romantic relationship in

poetry (pp. 241, 310). Bowen, Pound, Goldring, and many others have commented on Ford's recurrent need for female inspiration.

59. Ford and Elsie can be seen in the names of the hero, Don Collar Kelleg, and his fiancée, Eleanor ("Ellie") Greville; in their ages, early thirties; in his "right great height" and ambiguous foreign heritage. Ford probably named Don's father, John Collar Kelleg, after the infamous promoter of American companies, J. Carling Kelly. See Ernest Terah Hooley, *Hooley's Confessions* (London: Simpkin, Marshall, Hamilton, Kent, n.d.), pp. 232-37. Even Don's fantastic wealth—he is "the richest citizen of the world" (1)—has some biographical basis: Ford dedicated *An English Girl* to his German Aunt Emma, the widow of one of his two wealthy "oncles d'Amérique."

60. Mizener, p. 62.

61. MacShane, *Life and Work of Ford Madox Ford*, p. 93.

62. Jean Rhys, *Postures* (London: Chatto and Windus, 1928), p. 161.

63. Besides portraying Conrad himself, *Mr. Apollo* has interesting affinities with Conrad's newly published novel, *The Secret Agent*. The latter features, for example, the tall, philandering Ossipon, with his "Apollo-like ambrosial head," and his small, nervous, sardonic friend, the Professor. *Mr. Apollo* has a character who resembles Conrad's secret agent, Mr. Verloc.

CHAPTER THREE

1. Mizener, pp. 141-97, *passim*. Ford and Violet being caught by Elsie reminds us that Ford and Mary were similarly "caught" at least twice. Later, Ford was to get into legal trouble by telling a reporter about his "marriage" to Violet much as he had told a reporter in 1894 about his marriage to Elsie. Ford's recurrent bad luck suggests an unconscious wish not only to advertise himself but also to punish himself for falling in love and even to put into jeopardy the new amorous relationship.

2. Lid tentatively connects Pauline Lucas with Turgenev's Pauline Lucca, p. 125. Ford refers to Lucca in *Ancient Lights*, p. 185.

3. Mizener, p. 480.

4. But instead of consistently mirroring Mary Martindale, the sister seems to have figured in Ford's mind as *either* Elsie or Mary. Her name, Ellida, her married state, her habitual mourning attire long after the death of her parents, the way she talks animatedly above the catatonic Dudley, all these suggest Elsie (195). But what of this speech of Ellida's to Robert (added for the book version)? "Katya is a dear, of course, but she's the determination of a tiger . . . and she has meant to have you since you were in your cradles together" (260). Mary could have said this of Elsie, in 1894, or Elsie of Mary in 1909.

5. Mizener, pp. 481; 602, n. 19.

6. See Mizener, p. 262.

7. Quoted by Harvey, p. 303.

8. For Rosamond as Lady Dionissia and as nurse to Ford, see Hunt, pp. 107, 57. Rosamond's surname was Fogg Elliott.

9. Mizener, pp. 215, 482.

10. See Mizener, p. 483.

11. Quoted by Mizener, p. 187.

12. The scene has a further Conradian aspect: it recalls the climax to *The Secret Agent*, when Winnie drives a butcher knife into her husband's bosom. Winnie's blade, however, goes in very neatly, whereas Dionissia makes a bloody mess, typical of feminine Fordian killers (332).

13. Transcribed in full in "Joseph Conrad: A selection of unknown letters," pp. 37-40; Najder dates it "early May 1909" on the basis of references to the May issue of the *English Review*. (The magazine tended, however, to come out late the previous month.) Mizener's date, March 31, 1909, is surely too early in the light of the late April and early May dates of other letters referring to the same incident. See Mizener, pp. 183-85; 554, nn. 30-33.

14. Najder, "Joseph Conrad: A selection of unknown letters," p. 41; Mizener, p. 185.

15. Meyer, pp. 166, 220, and *passim*.

16. Quoted by Baines, p. 372.

17. Hunt, p. 201.

18. Quoted by Karl, p. 32.

19. "Joseph Conrad," *English Reviev* 10 (December 1911), 78.

20. Quoted by Mizener, p. 55.

21. *Lord Jim* (Edinburgh and London: Blackwood, 1900), p. 369.

22. *Some Reminiscences* (London: Eveleigh Nash, 1912), p. 76. (Subsequently titled *A Personal Record*.) Mizener, pp. 155, 166.

23. *Joseph Conrad: Letters to William Blackwood and David S. Meldrum*, ed. William Blackburn (Durham: Duke Univ. Press, 1958), p. 191.

24. Meyer, pp. 154-67.

25. Hunt, pp. 201-202.

26. Quoted by MacShane, *Life and Work of Ford Madox Ford*, p. 87.

27. David Garnett, *The Golden Echo* (London: Chatto and Windus, 1953), p. 51.

28. Hunt, p. 110.

29. Fortunately, I cannot vouch for the accuracy of Ford's picture. A curious comment by Edward Garnett in a letter to Olive may, or may not, be relevant. "You say 'Considering what he MIGHT have said about Conrad.' I suppose you mean about HOUSEHOLD COMPLICATIONS etc. etc. I knew that J. C. did confide in him about a certain delicate matter, and afterwards deeply regretted it" (December 9, 1924). In Anne Lee-Michell's "A Bloomsbury Girlhood," p. 543.

30. Meyer, pp. 164-67.

31. When Olive Garnett termed *The Simple Life Limited* "scandalous," she may have meant something besides Ford's treatment of Conrad, of her brother Edward, and even of herself as the tactless, strident, puritanical, outraged, grey-haired, sturdy-legged Miss Stobhall who visits young revolutionaries in Russia and Italy. Olive would probably have been most angry about Ford's portrait, in Cyril Brandetski, of Sergius Stepniak, the Russian revolutionary and novelist. Her diary confirms that both she and her sister-in-law, Constance Garnett, deeply loved Stepniak and that he probably felt some platonic attraction to them. As a young man, Stepniak had assassinated in St. Petersburg the brutal Czarist bureaucrat General Mezentsev and escaped abroad, coming ultimately to London with his Russian Jewish wife Fanny. In early 1894, Stepniak was severely attacked in a journal by another Russian refugee, "Ivanov." Olive, at first deeply disturbed by the accusations, finally helped Stepniak to write his rebuttal. December 23, 1895, Stepniak was accidentally killed by a train in London under circumstances that suggested suicide to the press, but not to his friends. (Conrad uses this episode at the end of *Under Western Eyes*.) Olive in her grief cut off her hair. Of Constance, David Garnett writes in *The Golden Echo*: "Stepniak's death was a blow from which it took my mother long to recover. But it only cemented more deeply friendship with his widow, Fanny, who came to live at Crockham Hill so as to be near us . . ." (p. 20).

Ford makes Brandetski an utterly despicable double agent (which Stepniak could not have been) of the sort Conrad portrayed in Verloc in *The Secret Agent* and in Razumov and Nikita in *Under Western Eyes*. Predictably Brandetski wreaks havoc among the Colonists. He inspires in Mrs. Lee, a leader of the Colonists, such a passionate devotion that her husband sets detectives on her. Failing in all his plans, he shoots himself. The suicide is hushed up, and Mrs. Lee and Mrs. Brandetski, like Constance Garnett and Fanny Stepniak, are united in grief. The two women devote themselves to "tales of heroic endeavour of the gentleman whom they regarded as a high-souled romanticist, enravelled in the meshes of a gloomy and terrible conspiracy" (372). Thus, in rather good second-hand Conradese, ends Ford's tale of the two Brandetskis.

32. Transcription typed by Violet Hunt. Cornell University Library.

33. Aubry, II, 138.

34. See my "Conrad, Ford, and the Sources of *Chance*," *Conradiana*, 7, no. 3 (September 1976), 207-24.

35. Conrad to Violet, June 2, 1913. Transcription typed by Violet Hunt, Cornell University Library.

36. Jessie Conrad, p. 116. Italics mine.

37. Hunt, p. 195.

38. Mizener, p. 183.
39. Borys Conrad, at the Joseph Conrad Conference in Poland, September 1972.
40. All the quotations are from Mizener's fine account, pp. 180-84.
41. Najder, "Joseph Conrad: A selection of unknown letters," p. 39.
42. Hunt, pp. 61-62.
43. Jessie Conrad, p. 138.
44. On February 9, 1910, Ford inscribed to Marwood a copy of *A Call*, which Caroline kept until her death. The inscription quotes Grimshaw's so Fordian motto: "Do what you want and take what you get for it." It also includes the priest's significant addition: "And God in His mercy pardon the ill we do" (216).
45. Conversation with Borys Conrad, June 15, 1975.
46. In a conversation on February 21, 1975.
47. Hunt, pp. 201, 239.
48. *The New Humpty-Dumpty* is thus indebted not only to Conrad's *Nostromo* but also to his fragmentary manuscript of 1896, *The Sisters*, ultimately published with an introduction by Ford in 1928.
49. Cassell, p. 147, has found it in Turgenev's *Liza*, as translated in 1869 by W.R.S. Ralston, whom Ford as a child knew.
50. See Lionel Trilling, *Sincerity and Authenticity* (Cambridge, Mass.: Harvard Univ. Press, 1973), pp. 106-11, 151-59, and Sondra J. Stang, "A Reading of Ford's *The Good Soldier*," *Modern Language Quarterly*, 30 (1969), 545-63.
51. Hunt, p. 202.
52. Mizener, p. 182.
53. Hunt, p. 24.
54. Mizener, pp. 293-94.
55. Letter from Mrs. Wynne Finch, August 7, 1972.
56. Hunt, p. 238.
57. Ashley Collection, British Museum. Violet says 400 guineas, p. 238. Either Conrad is in error and has left off a zero, or he is talking about an interest payment rather than the entire sum.
58. Arthur Blood's resemblance to Arthur Marwood has been frequently mentioned. See Harvey, p. 180, and Mizener, p. 237.
59. This is a far from universal response. Among the admirers of *The Young Lovell* are MacShane, *Life and Work of Ford Madox Ford*, pp. 107-108, Mizener, pp. 235, 241-42, 485-86, and Sondra J. Stang, *Ford Madox Ford* (New York: Frederick Ungar, 1977), pp. 18, 41, 127. Hynes, however, sees it as a "thin and tedious pastiche of Hewlett," p. 75.
60. Hunt, p. 229. After the 1892 baptism, Ford's full name was Joseph Leopold Ford Hermann Madox Hueffer.
61. Hunt, pp. 234-36.

62. Quoted by Mizener, p. xiv.

63. Hunt, p. 220.

64. Brigit Patmore's history comes from her posthumous autobiography, *My Friends When Young*, edited with an introduction by her older son, Derek Patmore (London: Heineman, 1968), pp. 1-2, 46, 5-7, 49-53. In her book, Violet Hunt calls Brigit "Maleine" and hints at the affair. She describes her as playing secretary to Ford one summer, presumably in 1913, and as appearing on the "Bless" page of the June 1914 issue of *Blast*, which indeed features "Bridgit" at the head of a column of names (pp. 200, 202, 214, 216-20). Dame Rebecca West confirmed, in a conversation on February 21, 1975, Ford's passion for Brigit before the war, but doubted that Brigit cared for him. Brigit's admission to Violet appears in the April 20 entry of Violet's 1917 diary (now at Pennsylvania State University). Edward Naumberg's great Ford collection contains a copy of *The Young Lovell* inscribed "to Bridgit / FMH / October 9th MCMXIII" (Harvey, p. 40).

65. This sentence serves as the epigraph to *The Blood Oranges*, John Hawkes's marvelous 1971 parody of, and tribute to, *The Good Soldier*.

66. See Mizener, p. 123, for the date of the composition of *The Spirit of the People*. Ford's "Dedicatory Letter to Stella Ford," *The Good Soldier*, 2nd ed. (New York: Albert & Charles Boni, 1927), says it was "hatching" for at least a decade before he began writing in 1913, p. vii. In *Thus to Revisit* (1921), Ford says it was "hatching" for a dozen years, p. 140.

67. Graham Greene, "Introduction," *The Bodley Head Ford Madox Ford*, I (London: The Bodley Head, 1962), 12.

68. Letter from Ford to W. A. Bradley, August 13, 1928. *Letters of Ford Madox Ford*, ed. Richard M. Ludwig (Princeton: Princeton Univ. Press, 1965), p. 179.

69. Robert R. Sears in conversation.

70. Rebecca West, letter of April 8, 1975.

71. Letter to Anthony Bertram, September 27, 1934. Ludwig, p. 236.

72. "Dedicatory Letter to Stella Ford," p. vi.

73. "Literary Portraits—XLIII: Mr. Wyndham Lewis and 'Blast,' " *Outlook*, July 4, 1914, p. 16. "On Impressionism," *Critical Writings of Ford Madox Ford*, ed. Frank MacShane (Lincoln: Univ. of Nebraska Press, 1964), pp. 46-47. Hereafter citations to this volume will appear, parenthetically and abbreviated CW, in the text.

74. It is impossible to tell when Ford first looked at the finished book. A few, now very rare, copies of *Chance* were distributed among close friends and reviewers September 18, 1913; the second (trade) issue was published January 15, 1914. See Theodore G. Ehrsam, *A Bibliography of Joseph Conrad* (Metuchen, N.J.: Scarecrow, 1969), p. 264. Ford did not review *Chance* in the *Outlook* until June 20, 1914.

CHAPTER FOUR

1. Mizener, pp. 241; 562, n. 32; 603, n. 32. Ford says he did not begin writing *The Good Soldier* until his fortieth birthday, December 17, 1913. Mizener believes, on the basis of a statement of Violet's, that Ford began dictating it in the summer of 1913. However, during that summer Ford not only wrote the James book, but also made a trip to Germany with Violet and the C.F.G. Mastermans. Since Brigit, the amanuensis for Part I of *The Good Soldier*, stayed with Violet and Ford in London early the following winter, she could have taken dictation on the novel as late as then. See Mizener, pp. 238-39; 243-45; 563, n. 5. See also the fifth section of this chapter, "Final Biographical Speculations."

2. Lydia Rivlin Gabbay, "The Four Square Coterie: A Comparison of Ford Madox Ford and Henry James," *Studies in the Novel*, 6, no. 4 (Winter 1974), 439-53.

3. Henry James, *The Golden Bowl* (London: Methuen, 1905), p. 20. (First published in the U.S. November 10, 1904.)

4. James, p. 535.

5. Lid and Mizener especially stress the importance of Ford's discovering Dowell.

6. See, however, Todd K. Bender, "Conrad and Literary Impressionism," *Conradiana*, 10, no. 3 (1978), 211-24, for a sensible effort to place the movement historically. For penetrating critical discussions of impressionism see Albert J. Guerard, *Conrad the Novelist* (Cambridge, Mass.: Harvard Univ. Press, 1958) and *The Triumph of the Novel: Dickens, Dostoevsky, and Faulkner* (New York: Oxford Univ. Press, 1976), and Ian Watt, *Conrad in the Nineteenth Century* (Berkeley and Los Angeles: Univ. of California Press, 1979).

7. Watt, p. 170.

8. Walter Pater, *Studies in the History of the Renaissance* (London: Macmillan, 1873), p. 209. See Charlesworth for a fine account of the impact of this view on late Victorian writers.

9. See Paul B. Armstrong, "Henry James: Impressionism and Phenomenology," Ph.D. diss., Stanford University, 1976, for a wonderfully clear, thoughtful analysis of James's impressionism. Joseph Conrad, "Henry James: An Appreciation, 1905," *Notes on Life & Letters* (London: J. M. Dent, 1921), p. 21.

10. See Najder, "Conrad in 1898," p. 21.

11. Watt, p. 179.

12. Discussing *The Fifth Queen*, Samuel Hynes says: "Reality is ultimately subjective, life is mirage and Romance and subject to change as the mind changes," p. 76. Besides his "Ford and the Spirit of Romance," pp. 71-79, see also "Conrad and Ford: Two Rye Revolutionists," pp. 48-53.

13. "Literary Portraits—XLIV: Signor Marinetti," *Outlook*, July 11, 1914, p. 46.

14. Joseph Conrad, *The Nigger of the "Narcissus"* (London: John Grant, 1925), p. x. Ford's *Joseph Conrad* seems to me to belong so in spirit to *The Good Soldier* era that I use it in this chapter, though with some reservations.

15. *Stories From De Maupassant*, trans. E[lsie] M[artindale], preface by Ford M. Hueffer (London: Duckworth, 1903), p. xx.

16. Review of *Phineas Finn* and *Phineas Redux, Daily News*, November 1, 1911, p. 4; "The Work of W. H. Hudson," *English Review*, 2 (April 1909), 162.

17. "Literary Portraits—VIII: Mr. Joseph Conrad," *Tribune*, September 14, 1907, p. 2.

18. "Literary Portraits—XXXVI: Les Jeunes and 'Des Imagistes' (Second Notice)," *Outlook*, May 16, 1914, p. 683; "Literary Portraits—LIII: The Muse of War," *Outlook*, September 12, 1914, p. 334.

19. See Ambrose Gordon, p. 66, on Ford as "erring realist."

20. "Joseph Conrad," *English Review*, p. 75.

21. "Literary Portraits—XLVIII: M. Charles-Louis Philippe," *Outlook*, August 8, 1914, p. 174. "Literary Portraits—LII: 'Cedant togae,' " *Outlook*, September 5, 1914, p. 303.

22. "Literary Portraits—XXXII: Mr. Conal O'Riordan," *Outlook*, April 18, 1914, p. 526.

23. "Literary Portraits—XXVIII: Mr. Morley Roberts," *Outlook*, March 21, 1914, p. 390; "Literary Portraits—XLIII: Mr. Wyndham Lewis," p. 16; "Literary Portraits—XLVI: Professor Cowl," *Outlook*, July 25, 1914, p. 110; "Literary Portraits—XLVII: Mr. W. R. Titterton," *Outlook*, August 1, 1914, p. 143; "Literary Portraits—XXV: Monsignor Benson," *Outlook*, February 28, 1914, p. 279.

24. "The Critical Attitude," *Bystander*, December 20, 1911, p. 639. (On the great ballerina Genée. Harvey's splendid bibliography lacks this interesting series of "weekly causeries," November 8, 1911 through March 6, 1912.)

25. "Literary Portraits—XXVI: Miss Amber Reeves," *Outlook*, March 7, 1914, p. 310.

26. "Literary Portraits—XXXI: Lord Dunsany," *Outlook*, April 11, 1914, p. 495.

27. "Literary Portraits—XXIII: Fydor Dostoievsky," *Outlook*, February 14, 1914, pp. 206-207.

28. See Charlesworth, p. 51: "The ultimate dissolution of the self . . . was the threat of skeptical impressionism."

29. See Bruce Johnson, *Conrad's Models of Mind* (Minneapolis: Univ. of Minnesota Press, 1971), pp. 50-52.

30. See Kenneth Fields, "Postures of the Nerves: Reflections of the

Nineteenth Century in the Poems of Wallace Stevens," *Southern Review*, 7 (Summer 1971), 812-14.

31. "Literary Portraits—XLV: Mme. Yoi Pawlowska," *Outlook*, July 18, 1914, p. 80.

32. "Literary Portraits—XLIII: Mr. Wyndham Lewis," p. 15.

33. Isaac M. Marks, *Fears and Phobias* (New York and London: Academic Press, 1969), pp. 119-46.

34. "Literary Portraits—XLV: Mme. Yoi Pawlowska," p. 79.

35. Yale University Library.

36. Ford has Conrad make the statement in French, their private, artist's tongue.

37. "Literary Portraits—VIII: Professor Saintsbury," *Outlook*, November 1, 1913, p. 605.

38. "The Critical Attitude," *Bystander*, December 27, 1911, p. 703.

39. "Literary Portraits—XLVIII: M. Charles-Louis Philippe," p. 174.

40. "Literary Portraits—XXV: Monsignor Benson," p. 278.

41. See George H. Pollock, "On Time and Anniversaries," *The Unconscious Today*, ed. Mark Kanzer (New York: International Univ. Press, 1971): "the 'stood still in time' phenomena, so often described by . . . depressive patients . . . the stoppage of time, the dragging of time, the hesitation of time seem to be manifestations of hopelessness," p. 246.

42. "Literary Portraits—XXXVI: Les Jeunes . . . (Second Notice)," pp. 682-83.

43. Ford first told this story in 1927, no doubt to please his 1906 companion, Rene Wright, whom he was in 1927 trying to make his mistress. See Mizener, pp. 361-62.

44. Katharine Hueffer Lamb recalled her mother's telling how disturbed she was to come upon Mary sitting in Ford's lap. (Letter, July 8, 1975.)

45. *Stories From De Maupassant*, p. xxii.

46. Wiley discusses surprise, pp. 71-74.

47. For a full, intelligent but, to my mind, excessively rational account of Ford's views on impressionism and the theory of the novel, see Cassell, pp. 11-72.

48. *Stories From De Maupassant*, p. xxi; "Joseph Conrad," *English Review*, p. 80.

49. "Literary Portraits—XLVII: Mr. W. R. Titterton," p. 142.

50. Richard Adams calls Conrad's influence "in the whole of Faulkner's work . . . the strongest and most pervasive . . . coming from any writer of prose fiction." ("The Apprenticeship of William Faulkner," *Tulane Studies in English*, 12 [1962], 129.) See also Stephen M. Ross, "Conrad's Influence on Faulkner's *Absalom, Absalom!*" *Studies in American Fiction*, 2 (1974), 199-209. See, *passim*, Albert J. Guerard's *Conrad the Novelist* and *The Triumph of the Novel*, and Joseph L. Blotner's *Faulkner: A Biography* (New York: Random House, 1974).

51. The bulk of *The Critical Attitude* appeared in the *English Review* in 1909, though not in book form until 1911. (Harvey, p. 35.)

52. "Literary Portraits—XXXI: Lord Dunsany," p. 495; "Literary Portraits—XX: Mr. Gilbert Cannan," *Outlook*, January 24, 1914, p. 110.

53. Meixner, p. 17, uses this passage for a different purpose. His whole chapter on Ford's artistry, "Anguish and Cat's Cradle," is very fine.

54. The Affair is a key concept in Wiley, especially pp. 52-57 and Chapter IV.

55. David Garnett, p. 38.

56. "Literary Portraits—XXXIV: Miss May Sinclair," *Outlook*, May 2, 1914, p. 599; "Literary Portraits—XXXVII: Mr. Archibald Marshall," *Outlook*, May 23, 1914, p. 715.

57. Edward Shanks, review of *The Last Pre-Raphaelite, World Review*, June 1948, pp. 58-62.

58. The readings of *The Good Soldier* closest to mine are those of Samuel Hynes in "The Epistemology of *The Good Soldier*," *Edwardian Occasions*, pp. 54-62 (originally published in the *Sewanee Review*, Spring 1961), and Arthur Mizener, pp. 258-77.

59. Joseph Conrad, *Youth and Two Other Stories* (London: Blackwood, 1902), p. 60.

60. Watt, personal communication.

61. *Conrad the Novelist*, pp. 115-17.

62. Charles G. Hoffman, "Ford's Manuscript Revisions of *The Good Soldier*," *English Literature in Transition*, 9, no. 3 (1966), 151. Problems with dates in *The Good Soldier* are discussed at length by Patricia McFate and Bruce Golden, "*The Good Soldier*: A Tragedy of Self Deception," *Modern Fiction Studies*, 9, no. 1 (Spring 1963), 50-60. See also Lid, pp. 63-64.

63. Jessie Conrad, p. 112.

64. Mizener, p. 265.

65. Ohmann says the train window images "might have been taken from a picture book," p. 79.

66. Because of the swans, James T. Cox cites the ending of *Lohengrin*, in "Ford's Passion for Provence," *ELH*, 28 (December 1961), 393.

67. A Freudian would also call Dowell here a fetishist. Dr. Bernard C. Meyer explains: "averting his gaze from the intolerable reality of anatomy," the fetishist "fixes it compulsively upon some contiguous object—garter, girdle, stockings, boots, heels, hair and hair ornaments, or furs—and endows it with the significance of the missing penis." *Houdini: A Mind in Chains* (New York: E. P. Dutton, 1976), pp. 138-39.

68. "Literary Portraits—XLIV: Signor Marinetti," p. 47.

69. "Literary Portraits—XXX: Mrs. Belloc Lowndes," *Outlook*, April 4, 1914, p. 459.

70. In Ford's finest short story, "Riesenberg," *English Review*, 7 (April

1911), 28-29; "The Secret Sharer," *'Twixt Land & Sea* (London: J. M. Dent, 1912), p. 108.

71. "Literary Portraits—XLVIII: M. Charles-Louis Philippe," p. 175.

72. See Hugh Kenner's excellent discussion of Ford's "bewilderment" in *The Good Soldier*, in *Gnomon* (New York: McDowell, Oblensky, 1958), pp. 167-69.

73. "Literary Portraits—XL: Vernon Lee," *Outlook*, June 13, 1914, p. 815.

74. Leonora's final, controlled remark, "don't you know that I'm an Irish Catholic?" is not, *pace* Mark Schorer, anticlimactic. Leonora's religion is one of the great barriers to any possible communication between herself and her husband; Edward's insistence on Protestantism for any sons they may have is a major source of her constant misery. See Mark Schorer, "An Interpretation," *The Good Soldier*, Vintage ed. (New York: Random House, 1951), p. xiv.

75. Mizener discusses the conditioned conscious self versus the passionate unconscious self, pp. 261, 269.

76. Meixner discusses irony as defense, p. 163.

77. Thomas A. Hanzo, in a fine essay, calls Dowell's leaving Edward to the mercy of his penknife an act of kindness: "Down to Darkness," *Southern Review*, 74, no. 4 (Autumn 1966), 832-55.

78. Doubling, like fetishism, is a way of easing castration anxiety. "Doubling, wrote Anna Freud, 'is of course very closely related to the mechanism of denial, namely *turning the dreaded absence into the duplicated presence*' " [italics added], in Meyer, *Houdini*, p. 141.

79. Patmore, p. 53.

80. "The Critical Attitude," *Bystander*, November 22, 1911, p. 398. It was probably Walter Bagehot who first termed the Tories the "stupid party." (Personal communication from John Clive.)

81. "Literary Portraits—XXV: Monsignor Benson," pp. 278-79.

82. Patmore, p. 56.

83. See Mizener, especially, pp. 258-61.

84. See Mizener, pp. 262-63.

85. Mizener, pp. 253; 566, n. 23.

86. "Literary Portraits—XLVII: Mr. W. R. Titterton," p. 142.

87. Mizener suspects that Ford, learning of Violet's syphilis perhaps at the time of *The Good Soldier*, became hostile to her, p. 568, n. 2. Dame Rebecca West distinctly remembers Violet telling her that Ford "was very kind and tender and sympathetic—and was so for some time." Violet later thought, however, that "he had formed a repulsion for her from that time." (Letter, September 4, 1979.)

88. Mizener, p. 102.

89. Hunt, p. 203.

90. Hunt, p. 209.

91. "The Critical Attitude," *Bystander*, November 29, 1911, p. 438; November 22, 1911, p. 397; January 31, 1912, p. 244. (The first two are

Tory pleas for Home Rule; the last is on England as the "land of dys-
pepsia.")

92. "Literary Portraits—XXV: Monsignor Benson," pp. 278-79. Italics
mine.

93. See Mizener, p. 260.

94. "Literary Portraits—XVII: Nineteen-Thirteen," *Outlook*, January 3,
1914, p. 15.

95. In a letter of December 7, 1975, Michael Patmore, Brigit's younger
son, identified the holograph portions of Part I of "The Saddest
Story" (the manuscript of *The Good Soldier*, Cornell University Library) as being unquestionably in his mother's hand. The notes Violet made later on her diary indicate that Brigit first came to stay with
her and Ford on January 7, 1914 and went with them to Selsey. On
February 3, Violet makes a wry comment on Ford's happy countenance when Brigit comes down to breakfast. On February 23 Violet
fears that Brigit's husband Deighton will kill her. On February 24,
Brigit accompanies Ford to town to see his doctor. On March 19, Violet makes a last, obscure reference to Brigit's stay. (Violet Hunt's
notes on her diary. Cornell University Library.)

96. Pennsylvania State University Library. "True Love and a General
Court Martial," manuscript of an unpublished novel, pp. 89, 98,
Cornell University Library. Ford wrote it between September 1918
and spring 1919. Mizener, pp. 300-301.

97. Hunt, p. 202.

98. Patmore, pp. 2-4, 48.

99. "Literary Portraits—XLIX: A Causerie," *Outlook*, August 15, 1914, p.
206.

100. "Literary Portraits—LIII: The Muse of War," p. 335. Mizener, however, connects "That exploit of yours" with the accusations of German sympathy being made against Ford, p. 565, n. 17.

101. Mizener, pp. 252; 565, n. 21. Richard Aldington, *Life for Life's Sake*
(New York: Viking, 1941), pp. 154-55. The first couple of pages of
Part IV, Chapter 5, are in typescript. The remaining pages of that
chapter and all of Chapter 6 are handwritten, almost certainly by
Aldington. (The holograph portion is Part IV, MS pp. 335-68.) Ford
could have delivered in July all of the manuscript except the last two
chapters. I of course accept Mizener's main point that *The Good Soldier* was conceived and essentially finished before war broke out. I
do think it likely that the last two chapters were not written until just
after August 4. Ford thus *could* have introduced the August 4 dates
into the novel as a very belated afterthought. How the mechanics of
such a change could be managed is hard to envision. I am grateful to
my late, dear friend Claude M. Simpson, Jr. for providing me with a
sample from the Huntington Library of Aldington's hand and, in our
last conversation together, strongly supporting my interpretation.

The third hand (for Part III, MS pp. 1-56, 66-78, 85-112) seems to be that of Aldington's wife, H.D. (Julius Barclay of the University of Virginia Library provided me with a sample of her handwriting.) Ford later told how H.D. so suffered from the tragic action of the novel that her husband had to take over as amanuensis (IWN, 241). "The Saddest Story" manuscript (Cornell University Library) thus encompasses another, non-Fordian but very human, drama. During the war years, Brigit had an intimate, intense friendship with H.D. And later, Brigit and Richard Aldington lived together for the happiest decade of Brigit's life. Unfortunately, Aldington ultimately ran off with Brigit's daughter-in-law and broke Brigit's heart. I am indebted to the happily remarried son, Michael Patmore, for this information.

102. "Literary Portraits—LII: 'Cedant togae,' " p. 303.
103. "Literary Portraits—XXII: Mrs. Herbert," *Outlook*, February 7, 1914, p. 174; "Literary Portraits—XXXIV: Miss May Sinclair," p. 600; "Literary Portraits—XXXV: Les Jeunes . . . (First Notice)," *Outlook*, May 9, 1914, p. 636.
104. "Beati Immaculati" is perhaps also an allusion to "Bless Bridgit" in *Blast*, making the novel a love letter to her as well.
105. "Literary Portraits—LV: Trimalchio," *Outlook*, September 26, 1914, p. 399.
106. Hunt, p. 23.
107. From Violet Hunt's transcription of an undated letter, Cornell University Library.

CHAPTER FIVE

1. Although Conrad once promised, comically, not to "spoof old Hueffer," my section title comes from Jessie, who, as early as the teens, frequently expressed her detemination to "hoof out Hueffer." Aubry, I, 313; letter from John Conrad, January 14, 1978.
2. Edwin S. Shneidman, *Perturbation and Lethality as Precursors of Suicide* (Los Angeles: U.C.L.A., n.d.), pp. 32-35.
3. "Literary Portraits—XLVIII: M. Charles-Louis Philippe," p. 174; "Literary Portraits—LI: The Face of Janus," *Outlook*, August 29, 1914, p. 270.
4. Mizener, p. 282.
5. *When Blood is Their Argument* contains five fleeting, vague references to Ford's Germanic past, four of which represent additions to the serial version. He does allude in the preface to his "father's South German Catholic origin" (vii-viii). He lays claim to having many intimate views of the German people (3). He includes himself as spectator at a German military parade (4). He gives two anecdotes involv-

ing two distant female relations, one of the eighteenth century (13). Another anecdote dramatizes once more the muddled Ford-child in all innocence bringing down upon his head the extreme wrath of his elders. Ford, aged twelve, had been taking a walk in Münster when a procession of school children passed, led by a band playing the Prussian National Anthem. Ford took off his hat because the melody was that of "God Save the King." His relatives exploded at this action "with an amount of abuse, of hatred, and of bitterness such as never from my worst enemies have I since received. It was no good my saying that I knew nothing about these matters . . . my relatives retorted that at my age it was monstrous and horrible that I should not have heard of the monstrous, horrible and detestable fate that had overtaken the home of my ancestors" (32). Two anecdotes emphasize the author's separation from Germany. In one he is introduced to an old South German lady "as an Englishman" (39). In the other his father very carefully warns Ford "never to read German prose for any length of time or with any deep attention, for fear of its effects upon my own English" (79-80). I am indebted to John W. Carr for collating the serial with the book version.

6. "Literary Portraits—LVII: Persecution of German Professors," *Outlook*, October 10, 1914, p. 464.
7. "The Critical Attitude," *Bystander*, December 27, 1911, pp. 703, 704.
8. "Literary Portraits—XLI: Mr. Richard Curle," *Outlook*, June 20, 1914, p. 848.
9. Ludwig, p. 269. David Garnett, p. 187. Ford, we recall, made his alter ego Count Macdonald a Russian aristocrat in *The New Humpty-Dumpty*.
10. Mizener, pp. 301; 575, n. 31; Violet Hunt's 1917 Diary, c. October 23, Pennsylvania State University Library.
11. Ambrose Gordon discusses these, for different purposes, pp. 29-37. For a wise appreciation of *No Enemy*, see Stang, *Ford Madox Ford*, pp. 48-54.
12. "Thus to Revisit, III: The Serious Books," *Piccadilly Review*, November 6, 1919, p. 6. Despite the title, this series of five articles has nothing to do with Ford's 1921 book, *Thus to Revisit*.
13. "Thus to Revisit, IV: New Forms for the Old," *Piccadilly Review*, November 13, 1919, p. 6.
14. Ford to Conrad [September 1916], September 6, 1916, September 7, 1916, December 19, 1916, in Ludwig, pp. 71-76, 78-80. Conrad to Ford, August 12, 1915, August 30, 1915, August 15, 1916, August 16, 1916, December 4, 1916, December 24, 1916; the first five are from transcriptions by Violet Hunt, Cornell University Library; the last is in the Berg Collection, New York Public Library. Borys Conrad, *My Father: Joseph Conrad* (New York: Coward-McCann, 1970), p. 31. Conversation with Borys Conrad, June 15, 1975.

15. "Dedicatory Letter to Stella Ford," p. vii. Strangely enough, *Victory*, the novel Conrad wrote while Ford was writing *The Good Soldier*, appears also to be indebted to *Fort Comme La Mort*. See Paul Kirschner, *Conrad: The Psychologist as Artist* (Edinburgh: Oliver and Boyd, 1968), pp. 193-98.

16. Mizener points out a number of biographical elements, pp. 323, 489-94.

17. Harvey, p. 55.

18. Ambrose Gordon's *The Invisible Tent*.

19. Mizener, however, considers that narrator and hero reverse the pattern of *The Good Soldier*, pp. 491-92.

CHAPTER SIX

1. The chief clues to chronology in Part One of *Some Do Not* are the ages of the characters: Christopher is twenty-six, Sylvia thirty; Mrs. Duchemin looks no more than thirty to Macmaster, who is near thirty himself; Valentine Wannop is twenty-two, her mother "forty-fivish" (11, 51, 71, 22, 106, 113). Unfortunately, these facts prove, in the second part, slender reeds upon which to hang a calendar. Whereas Valentine has aged five years to become, in time present of Part Two, twenty-seven, her mother has progressed from forty-fivish clear to sixty (263, 306). On the other hand, Ford provides a couple of apparently consistent keys to time present of both parts. Sylvia recalls that, two or three years before it happened, Christopher predicted, at Lobscheid, the coming of war. Since Christopher goes to Lobscheid immediately after meeting Valentine, Part One must take place about 1912. Between the two parts, Christopher and Valentine have an important, intimate conversation, on a chilly November day (287). They talk about the war and Christopher has not yet joined up, so the year is almost surely 1914. Since this conversation occurs two years before time present of Part Two, that time present must be 1916 (326). (Mizener, however, places this conversation in 1915 and time present of Part Two in 1917, p. 495.) The month is August, "five months exactly" (or four) since the death of Christopher's father in March (262, 251). The dates of the two parts, June 1912 and August 1916, thus square much better with Valentine's aging from twenty-two to twenty-seven than with Mrs. Wannop's forty-fivish to sixty. But two other clues suggest a far longer span than four plus years between the two parts. Sylvia has remained sexually continent for "many years," since, that is, her reunion with Christopher at Lobscheid. And Christopher, in Part Two, recalling his conversation with Macmaster at the beginning of Part One, thinks: "What a long time ago! . . . Ten years . . ." (344).

2. Any hopes that checking subsequent volumes of *Parade's End* will

bring certainty are quickly dashed. Although General Campion in *No More Parades* definitively places the opening of *Some Do Not* in 1912, Christopher places Sylvia's rebetrayal of him "long before the war" (291, 92). Not only is time present of *No More Parades* hard to identify with precision, the novel's chronology muddles the timing of Part Two of *Some Do Not*. Time present of *No More Parades* occurs three months after the end of *Some Do Not*, that is, about November 1916 (23). But this later becomes "three months or so," and by the end, time present of *No More Parades* has become January 17 (91, 315). Moreover, since Christopher, looking back quite a while, recalls an episode in September 1916, and since Mr. Tietjens died five years after Sylvia left Christopher in 1912, time present of *Some Do Not*, Part Two, moves forward a year to August 1917, time present of *No More Parades* thus becoming January 1918 (296, 316).

A Man Could Stand Up appears to be absolute clarity, chronologically speaking. Time present of its first and last parts is indisputably Armistice Day. Time present of the middle section, though never explicitly dated, seems to be early spring 1918. The action occurs some two months after *No More Parades*, it precedes the German spring advance, and a whole American Army corps is now in the line (84, 94). But however clear about itself, *A Man Could Stand Up* confuses over again the chronology of the two preceding novels. Valentine decides, on Armistice Day, that she has not seen Christopher for two years, thus pushing the end of *Some Do Not* back again from 1917 to 1916 (27). This reversion tends to be confirmed by Christopher, who in the spring of 1918, also recalls that he last saw Valentine two years before (204). On the other hand, Valentine recalls first meeting him about July 1, 1912, suggesting the date that *No More Parades* assigns to the beginning of *Some Do Not* (31). Yet, incomprehensibly only two pages earlier, Valentine is thinking that she and Christopher are coming together again "After ten years!" (29). Even stranger, Valentine, who was twenty-two at the beginning of *Some Do Not* and twenty-seven at the end, is now, two years after that, "twenty-threeish: rising twenty-four" (17).

Last Post does nothing to help. Since Mark had planned before his stroke on Armistice Day to go to the next raceweek in Newcastle and also visit Groby, and since he is thinking he would be there now save for his illness, time present of *Last Post* must be 1919—unless Mark plans his racecourse visits improbably far in advance (24). Elsewhere in the novel, however, Mark thinks that he has been playing invalid for "all these years," and Valentine recalls that Christopher has talked dreadfully in his sleep about the war, "for years" (289, 252). Two references to characters' ages act either to push *Last Post* way ahead into the 1920s or to push *Some Do Not* back toward the beginning of the century. Christopher is now, Mark thinks, forty or forty-three; Christopher's son appears to the peasantry to be about eighteen (163, 64).

3. Christopher, Lid points out, is "Dickensian," and "the world he inhabits . . . has conscious overtones of the Dickensian," p. 153.

4. Ambrose Gordon opts for 1912 and 1917 for *Some Do Not* (p. 90); Gerald Levin gives 1912 to 1920 for the tetralogy, "Character and Myth in Ford's *Parade's End*," *Journal of Modern Literature*, 1, no. 2 (1970), 183; Mizener says 1912 to 1926 or 1929, pointing out some but not all of the problems, pp. 372, 510-15; George Core, however, sees the first three novels as spanning "roughly a decade," or 1908-1918, "Ordered Life and the Abysses of Chaos," *Southern Review*, 8, no. 3 (July 1972), 521.

5. The sequel to Christopher's adventures in Rye makes the biographical connection even more persuasive. He goes directly to Germany to join Sylvia, who has met her mother there in order to cover up those months she spent in France with her lover Perowne. Then, to avoid bringing Sylvia directly back to attend his mother's funeral, Christopher takes her first to Russia where he does statistics in Kiev. In March 1906 Ford contemplated taking a trip to Russia with the Soskices, in order to write "a book rather of impressions than statistics." (Quoted by Mizener, p. 116.) Similarly, Elsie went from Italy to Ford's relatives in Germany, where he met her. Instead of returning directly to England, they went first for two months to America where Ford tried to interest publishers in his work.

6. On the level of fantasy, however, Ford may at the time have wished Elsie had a lover to assuage his own guilt. At least, he involved Conrad in *The Nature of a Crime*, with its connections with Elsie in Rome, and he published in 1906 and 1907 two short stories sympathetic to the cuckolded husband, one involving a colonel's shooting gallery that could be Ashburnham's, if not Marwood's. ("Below the Stairs," *Bystander*, August 15, 1906, pp. 337-42; "The Rendezvous," *Bystander*, December 11, 1907, pp. 3-7.) Perhaps, as Christopher first thinks of Valentine as a jolly little mistress for Macmaster and as Macmaster thinks of Mrs. Duchemin as an ideal mate for Christopher, so Ford may have fantasized Conrad and Marwood as consolations for Elsie.

7. Mizener makes all these equations, except the one between Macmaster and Conrad. And he does not tie Mrs. Duchemin's given names to Brigit, pp. 368-70.

8. Mrs. Duchemin's large-shouldered, coarsely woven blue silk dress; her blue-black, regularly waved hair and dark blue eyes; her pomegranate lips—these are not so much Elsie's as Janey Morris's in Rossetti's *Proserpine*. Macmaster calls Mrs. Duchemin "Guggums" as Rossetti called Elizabeth Siddal. Whether Ford so addressed Elsie is unknown, but he certainly wore Rossetti's coat while walking about South Kent with Elsie in her Pre-Raphaelite gown. Ford's recollec-

tion in *Mightier Than the Sword* of his grandfather distracting Ruskin so that Millais could run off with the barbarously used Mrs. Ruskin may have figured in the Duchemin story, with Christopher in Madox Brown's role and Macmaster in Millais's (MTS, 244).

9. Still, Macmaster in his looks and his treatment of Christopher does most importantly reflect Ford's hurt view of Conrad's mistreatment of himself. That first scene of *Some Do Not* is just like one Ford puts in *Joseph Conrad* six months later. Big, blue-eyed, fair, untidy, apparently phlegmatic Christopher sits with "smallish" Macmaster, adorned with his trimmed, pointed black beard and correcting proofs (SDN, 10, 11). Later, the beard develops grayish streaks, and Macmaster adds a single eyeglass "that [gives] him a slightly agonised expression" as well as "the privilege of putting his face very close to" anyone he wishes to impress—all this very like Conrad (SDN, 302). Whereas Christopher is indifferent to professional success, Macmaster is obsessed with it. Conrad, too, was very concerned with the idea of a career (JC, 124). Like Ford for Conrad, Christopher has great affection for Macmaster (SDN, 12). As to its being reciprocated, neither Ford nor Christopher is really sure (JC, 123; SDN, 12). Christopher regards Macmaster condescendingly as Ford would, amazingly, view Conrad (SDN, 85). Sylvia accepts Macmaster as the nervous, mustached, "orientally obsequious protégé" whom her husband "chose to patronize" (NMP, 190). Much as Ford really did help Conrad's writing with subjects, inspiration, and even a little prose, so Christopher characteristically works up Macmaster's statistics for him. Christopher's last meeting with Macmaster, about 1916, is tainted by the knowledge of Macmaster's traitorous appropriation of some statistical methods Christopher has ironically proposed as a way to dish the French if one were so evilly disposed. Not only does Macmaster do it, he conceals his source even from his wife in order to get credit, once in his life, for an original idea (SDN, 350). Christopher, of course, forgives Macmaster, but is so ashamed of him that he cannot look him in the face. Macmaster, "his black, short beard quivering and his wretched eyes turned down," tries to explain. His dishonesty gains him a knighthood and caps his career much as *Chance*, Conrad's last novel to involve Ford, brought fame and fortune to Conrad.

Christopher not only helps Macmaster's career, he lends him two thousand guineas, arguably a fantasy on Ford's hundred-pound loan to Conrad, also secured by a life insurance policy. Christopher's decision, for Valentine's sake, not to remit the debt corresponds roughly with Ford's postwar attempt, presumably for Stella's sake, to get money out of Conrad. (Conrad to Ford, October 16, 1922. Yale University Library.) Ford's portrayal of the Macmasters as having sponged endlessly upon Christopher recalls the irritated recollections of Marwood connections about Conrad's treatment of him and Caroline. Other details of Christopher's relations with the Macmasters probably reflect Ford's sense of neglect, in his time of great adversity, by the now comfortable Conrads of the war years and afterwards. Much as the Conrads expanded their circle during their stay at Capel House from 1910 to 1919, and entertained a good deal at Oswalds between 1919 and 1924 but essentially dropped Ford, so the Macmasters rarely invite Christopher to their famous Friday afternoons, and Mrs. Macmaster vows that Christopher will never set foot in their newly acquired country place in Surrey (SDN, 299). Mrs. Macmaster even alludes to "Capel Court" in a conversation about Christopher (LP, 81). (See Borys Conrad, pp. 69, 158-59.)

Certain aspects of Macmaster reflect not so much Conrad himself as Ford's earlier portrait of him as Bransdon: Macmaster's dangerous weakness for large-bosomed, red-cheeked shopgirls; the Macmasters' lower middle-class origins, which if not true of Conrad are so of Jessie (SDN, 21). Bransdon, however, may indeed be a little Russian Jew. Although Macmaster remains unassailably Scottish, Christopher's business partner, Mr. Schatzweiler, "a little shivering, artistic Jew," reminds Christopher of his former protégé (LP, 142-43).

If Ford, in 1924, makes the bad Conrad into Macmaster, he converts the good Conrad into what he has made of himself—Marwood. No longer the swashbuckling Elizabethan, the Conrad of Ford's personal remembrance wants to be considered an English country gentleman of Lord Palmerston's era (JC, 57). The Korzeniowskis prove to resemble ancient, landholding English county families, "untitled, but aristocrats . . . 'good people' " (JC, 76). Ford and Conrad "met at first as two English gentlemen do in a Club. . . . We took it for granted that each *was* a gentleman, with the feelings, views of the world and composure of a member of the ruling classes . . . tempered of course with such eccentricities as go with the spleen of the *milor anglais*" (JC, 121). (The last phrase Ford uses recurrently also for Earl Marsden.) Ford looked up Conrad in London in February and May 1924, to arrange for publication of *The Nature of a Crime*. Conrad's letters at the time to his agent Eric Pinker indicate that Conrad was only pretending friendship: "I have dissembled my rage . . . the swell-headed creature . . . seems to imagine that he will sweep all Europe and devastate Great Britain with an eventual collected edition of his own works" (February 17 and May 1, 1924; quoted by Mizener, p. 337). It is well to remember, however, that by May 1 Ford had fully recovered his powers, having published *Some Do Not* to rave reviews and being editor of the *transatlantic review* whereas Conrad was old, ill (four months from his death), and unable to write. It is perhaps best to remember only that on May 22, Conrad wrote thus to Ford about *Some Do Not*: "As to the novel, I think that, between us two, if I tell you that I consider it 'tout à fait chic,' you will understand perfectly how much that 'phrase d'atelier' means to the initiated" (quoted by MacShane, *Life and Work of Ford Madox Ford*, p. 165).

Since Macmaster essentially fades out of *Parade's End* after the first volume, Conrad's shade might seem not necessary to Ford's continued creativity. But perhaps it was. Macmaster's nephew, Captain McKechnie, recurs throughout the other volumes and harries Christopher constantly, as if Ford cannot have a Marwoodian figure without a Conradian one. The shell-shocked, unhappily married McKechnie probably reflects Conrad's son Borys, whom Ford looked up a couple of times in France and offered to help in the mid-twenties. Borys suffered severe shell shock at the end of the war; by the time of *Parade's End* he had married, against his father's wishes, and, as it turned out, unhappily. (See Borys Conrad, pp. 133-38, 163. Borys, like Christopher, was partially buried by a shell and, like McKechnie, spent some time at the end of the war in a "shell shock" hospital in London. Ford himself was badly shaken up by the concussion of a shell [Mizener, p. 287]).

10. Mr. Tietjens' death seems to have a specific connection with Marwood: a relation of Caroline Marwood died a similarly inexplicable death, in a shooting accident in Yorkshire, during the war.

11. A segment of Violet Hunt's diary, newly come to light at Pennsylvania State University and running from late February 1917 to late January 1918, confirms the closeness of Sylvia's portrait to Violet. The diary also gives further reasons why Ford would vacillate between 1916 and 1917 for Christopher's wartime relations with Sylvia and Valentine. The diary makes clear that Ford's departure for France in July 1916 was definitive for his relations with Violet; similarly, Christopher's return to France signalized his real break with Sylvia. July 16, 1916 is the last day Ford ever told Violet explicitly that he loved her (Diary, May 9, 1917), and July 1916 is the month when she withdrew from Ford her financial guarantee and thus brought on his indifference (Diary, April 23, 1917). On the other hand, the diary shows that in 1917 Ford spent most of March with Violet in London and Selsey, three days in June with her in London, and three days in October with her in Selsey. (During that last visit Ford first met Stella Bowen, whom Pound introduced to Violet on July 20, 1917.) Also in 1917, Violet spent some ten days with Ford at Whitby, Yorkshire, in late May and early June, and all of August with him at Redcar. Thus 1917 could be for Ford a time frame for the London and Rouen (Army camp) meetings between Christopher and Sylvia and even for the beginning of Christopher's wartime impressions of Valentine.

The diary only too vividly prefigures Sylvia's tortured and tortur-

ing feelings about Christopher. The Violet of the diary is almost totally absorbed in herself and in her feelings about Ford. She still
loves him passionately and wants him to respond sexually. Virtually
every time they meet, they fight, especially on Saturday, the one
night Violet can hope for Ford's sexual attentions. One row, over
another woman, arouses the whole hotel corridor, looking forward
to Christopher's violent night in Rouen. Characteristically, they
quarrel, then she weakens and goes to his bed, or calls him to hers;
and he, not surprisingly, lies cold and unresponsive. Time and again
she notes that she cannot stand it, that it is all over, that she is determined to end all this; and yet until January 1918, she still envi-
sions them as always being together on however unsatisfactory a
footing, and he recurrently insists that he will return to her permanently after the war. In January 1918, however, Violet spends his
week's leave at his mother's while he stays alone at South Lodge.
Violet comments later that her action then finally finished their relationship. (Yet Ford seems not really to have left South Lodge until a
year later. Mizener, p. 306.) As Sylvia, in the manuscript ending to
Some Do Not, strikes Christopher hard in the face, so Violet, on two
or three occasions, reports scratching Ford's face, or pummeling and
punching him; she reviles him for not resisting her physically. Like
Christopher, Ford no longer desires Violet and alludes several times
in their August and October visits together to being impotent at least
so far as she is concerned. (Yet Mizener's hunch, p. 368, is right that
on occasion Violet's old strong physical attractiveness does affect
Ford.) Violet, unlike the Sylvia of the war years, is unfaithful at least
once to Ford. Precisely like Sylvia, however, she exults in pulling
showerbath strings and cultivates male acquaintances in order to
harry Ford. In her rage, she terms Ford various sorts of fish and
animals as well as calling him a baby. Her description of his cold blue
eyes looks forward to Jean Rhys's Hugh Heidler. The truth is that
Violet, so absorbed in her own wrongs, shows, in the diary, virtually
no feeling for Ford as a separate, suffering human being, no appreciation at all of what those so recent months in France must have been.

   The diary's allusions to Brigit illuminate both *The Good Soldier* and
the double novels that follow upon *Parade's End*: Ford and Violet
openly discuss his previous affair with Brigit. Although he asserts in
March that he is still in love with Brigit, Violet believes that it is only
a coverup for his subsequent Cardiff romance. Violet sees Brigit
twice in April, and Brigit tells her that now she does not care for
Ford, though she had previously given in to the flattery of his courtship. The diary, incidentally, implies Violet's clear awareness of
Ford's previous affair with Mary Martindale. Although, in a 1936
addition, Violet makes a remark yoking Ford and the wife of his colonel, the sense of the diary is that Ford has no one at this time really
to love.

As an antidote to Ford's Violet and a reminder of her gifts as a writer, see Marie Secor, "Violet Hunt, Novelist: A Reintroduction," *English Literature in Transition*, 19, no. 1 (1976), 25-34.

12. In her relation almost as ward to the Tietjens family, she recalls Brigit Patmore. Her name echoes Caroline Marwood's. Her role as suffragette daughter of a deceased Oxford don and a well-known novelist recalls Violet Hunt. (Lid points to G.D.H. Cole's father-in-law as a source, on the authority of Stella Bowen, of Professor Wannop, p. 144. Ford later told how kind his father had been to the novelist, Mrs. W. K. Clifford, after the death of her professor-husband [RY, 288]).

The 1906 date of Valentine's and Christopher's mutual attraction is presumably the time of Ford's involvement with Mary Martindale and estrangement from Elsie. In the nineties Ford tramped down Kentish lanes happily discussing serious subjects with vivacious young Elsie much as Christopher walks and talks with Valentine.

13. Ford still has the right college and preparatory school. Besides the obvious connections in family background, physique, and coloring, Christopher parallels Marwood in more substantial ways. Members of Marwood's family have paid tribute to Ford's rendition of Marwood's eccentric manner of catching a train and his traditional Marwood "spleen." (MacShane, *Life and Work of Ford Madox Ford*, p. 173.) Members of Caroline's family recall less engaging characteristics in her husband: his snobbery, his desire to know precisely who someone is before meeting him. Sylvia says Christopher is "so formal he can't do without all the conventions" (SDN, 44). When Christopher blames the golf clubhouse incident on "the times that permitted the introduction into gentlemen's company of such social swipes as Sandbach," he seems to be making an authentically Marwoodian remark (SDN, 98). But it is only fair to Marwood, and to Ford, to say that, like Christopher, he is remembered, on both sides of the family, as "a saint."

14. We have only Ford's evidence for Arthur Marwood's penchant for sweeping statements. Ford, we know, liked in conversation to go to extremes and play with paradoxes; so does Christopher. Christopher and Ford (according to Violet) are both given to getting on their "high-horse" (SDN, 53). Christopher's instinctive knowledge about antiques recalls Ford's uncanny taste in manuscripts by unknown writers. Although tribute has been paid to Mark's stroke as a notable prophecy of the illness of Arthur's older brother William, it also recalls the Ford who, as a child, took to his bed in a rage for a week, who in 1904 lay smiling and limp under Elsie's worried gaze, and who could not speak at all when Violet brought the news of the *Throne* case. (Kenneth Young, *Ford Madox Ford* [London: Longmans, Green, 1956], p. 35.) In *The Heart of the Country*, Ford talks sympathetically of a bedfast countryman who, like Mark, has a mirror put

up so he can look at the countryside (103). Mark's recollection of his little brother as a "rather moony, fair brat . . . with a trick of standing with those goggle eyes gazing bluely at you" recalls Madox Brown's painting of Tell's son (LP, 103).

15. Ford's daughter, Julia Loewe, in "Memories of Ford Madox Ford," a radio broadcast of New York's WBAI, November 5, 1961.

16. Cassell calls Christopher Edward's "later counterpart," p. 157.

17. Ambrose Gordon notes this parallel, and others, between *The Good Soldier* and *Last Post*.

18. See Igor Webb, "Sense and Sensibility," pp. 144-57. See also his "Marriage and Sex in the Novels of Ford Madox Ford," *Modern Fiction Studies*, 23 (Winter, 1977-78), 586-92.

19. There is a second such scene in *No More Parades*, and, interestingly enough, it involves Sylvia. While she and Christopher discuss business affairs in the middle of the night, in her Rouen hotel room, she sits at her brilliantly lit dressing table, her golden gown down around her hips, only a filmy undergarment covering her shining limbs (284, 283). Christopher humanly thinks "Why not have?" Whereupon, the door handle turns; Sylvia's old lover Major Perowne appears, in pyjamas and dressing gown; he makes an immense ruckus after Christopher throws him out so violently his head strikes a wall (258, 261).

20. Mizener discusses the problem, pp. 508-509; 604, n. 60.

21. Ford does enter Mark's point of view briefly in *Some Do Not*, when Mark is still active sexually; but Ford does not dramatize Mark's life with his mistress until it is over.

22. Ford did originally end *Some Do Not* with this episode and Sylvia's promise never to see Christopher again. See Frank MacShane, "Ford Madox Ford's Manuscript Revisions," *Boston University Studies in English*, 5, no. 1 (Spring 1961), 182-84.

23. The instances of amazing, if harmless, inconsistencies in the tetralogy are legion. Sylvia's son is first called Tommie, instead of Michael (SDN, 14). Valentine's brother is first Gilbert, thereafter Edward (SDN, 104, 286). The idea that Mr. Tietjens had two wives and that Mark and Christopher are half-brothers does not emerge until *Last Post* (SDN, 251; LP, 91). Early in the tetralogy there are at least six in the family: two of the four sons are killed in the war (SDN, 261); one daughter, Effie, is married to a vicar; another, Caroline, is a nurse (!) and is also killed in the war (SDN, 14, 212). But later the Red Cross nurse is an only daughter, named Mary (LP, 116). At some point Mr. Tietjens is alleged to have fathered a total of ten children of whom three died young, leaving seven, instead of the six (or five) implied elsewhere. Even the memorably named and memorably killed O Nine Morgan gets reduced, in the subsequent volume, to 09 Evans (MCS, 92). In one novel, Christopher tells Mrs. Wannop on Armistice Day that he has just gotten out of the hospital where he was ill

with pneumonia and mental distress (MCS, 252). In the next volume, he has spent the three weeks prior to Armistice Day doing military duty by day and reading Boswell aloud to his desperately ill brother by night (LP, 151). This last reminds us that Ford said he read Boswell as help against mental depression ("Literary Portraits—IX: Mr. Thomas Hardy," *Outlook*, November 8, 1913, p. 641) and later said his mother had read Boswell to him, in Germany (RY, 270). See Mizener, pp. 509-10; 604, nn. 62, 63, for some of these real and apparent inconsistencies.

24. Mizener, however, finds this episode convincing, p. 303.

25. Quoted by Mizener, p. 337.

26. Stella Bowen, *Drawn from Life* (London: Collins, 1941), pp. 166, 168. Mizener, pp. 345, 334, 347, 350, 352, 361, 357-58.

27. As Ohmann says, p. 157. She takes Christopher's "near insanity" (p. 155) a good deal more solemnly than, say, Ambrose Gordon (pp. 125-28) or I do.

28. However, Ford wrote to Conrad, November 8, 1923, that *Mister Bosphorus* was "inspired by and loosely based on Pope's *Dunciad*." MacShane, *Life and Work of Ford Madox Ford*, pp. 146; 282, n. 66.

29. Ford knew Fred Karno, the music-hall impresario (IWN, 109), and wrote a fine essay on the ballerina, Genée, in the *Bystander*.

30. While writing *Mister Bosphorus*, Ford published an essay defending *Ulysses* against the charge of indecency, and expressing "reverence" for "this incredible genius" who wrote it. Ford is said to have presented Joyce with an inscribed copy of *Mister Bosphorus* when it came out in November 1923. (Harvey, pp. 225-26, 57. Ambrose Gordon yokes *Ulysses, Mister Bosphorus*, and *Parade's End*, pp. 95-96.)

31. Lid describes well the "particular quality" of *Parade's End* as "facetious, whimsical, far-fetched, outrageous, improbable; and ultimately both plausible and real" (p. 146). Although Mizener takes Christopher's suffering seriously, he grants that Christopher's portrait is "not strictly realistic," that Ford is aware of "his comic simplicity," and that Sylvia "is the product of a remarkable and fantastic imagination" (pp. 369-70). For a discussion of how other participants viewed the war as pantomime and music-hall comedy, see Paul Fussell, *The Great War and Modern Memory* (New York: Oxford Univ. Press, 1975), Chapter Six, "The Theatre of War."

32. Ambrose Gordon says that Sylvia has the attributes "of a splendid comic . . . villainess," and calls Ford's depiction of the war "more than anything comic," pp. 111, 113.

33. Alan Kennedy, in "Tietjens Travels: *Parade's End* as Comedy," *Twentieth Century Literature*, 16, no. 2 (April 1970), 85, rightly says that we are not meant to grieve at Christopher's protracted suffering.

34. Elicited and quoted by Cassell, p. 7.

35. I am indebted to Marianne DeKoven for helping me to see the excellence of Ford's portrayal of Valentine Wannop. See "Valentine

Wannop and Thematic Structure in Ford Madox Ford's *Parade's End,*" *English Literature in Transition*, 20, no. 2 (1977), 56-68. Christopher and Valentine will do what they want and take what they get for it, an echo of Ford's inscription in the copy of *A Call* that he gave to the Marwoods, no doubt to indicate why he left Elsie and joined Violet.

36. Ambrose Gordon says, rightly, that "Ford treated the trenches as though they were fairyland," and appropriately terms the bugle episode a "breakthrough into an enchanted realm," pp. 72, 79.

37. H. G. Wells, *Experiment in Autobiography*, 2 vols. (London: Gollancz, 1934), II, 536.

38. The epigraph to Conrad's 1908 book of short stories, *A Set of Six*, is:

> *"Les petites marionettes*
> *Font, font, font,*
> *Trois petits tours*
> *Et puis s'en vont"*
>
> Nursery Rhyme

39. Bowen, p. 165.

CHAPTER SEVEN

1. Although *When the Wicked Man* was finished in 1929, only a year after the publication of *A Little Less Than Gods*, it was not published until 1931. Mizener, p. 389.

2. Aubry, II, 13; Baines, p. 436.

3. From Marseilles Conrad sailed three times to the West Indies. Also, it was in Marseilles that Conrad became, he said, involved in the Carlist revolution in Spain. And finally, in Marseilles Conrad attempted suicide over gambling losses and, perhaps, a woman. In various ways this past of a melancholy, adventurous young stranger in Latin, revolutionary surroundings recurs in Conrad's works, from *The Sisters* of 1896 to such very late novels as *The Arrow of Gold* and *The Rover*, but above all in the Ford-connected *Nostromo* and *Mirror of the Sea*. Innocent of serious political ideas but heavy with suggestions of melodramatic intrigue, *Suspense* is, as Baines says, p. 438, the closest of Conrad's novels, in manner of presentation, to *Romance*.

4. Conrad to Pinker, August 22, 1903 (Berg Collection, New York Public Library). See Ohmann, pp. 176-77.

5. Mildred Atkinson, "Conrad's *Suspense*," *Times Literary Supplement* (London), February 25, 1926, p. 142.

6. An obscure letter of December 15, 1921, from Conrad to Ford, indicates that Ford was worried that their current works in progress might be overlapping. Ford was presumably working on *The*

Marsden Case at the time, Conrad on *Suspense*. Conrad was reassuring: "We can't possibly clash." Yale University Library.

7. Joseph Conrad, *Suspense* (London: J. M. Dent, 1925), pp. 207, 8-10, 271-74. See Guerard, *Conrad the Novelist*, pp. 289-92, and Thomas Moser, *Joseph Conrad: Achievement and Decline* (Cambridge, Mass.: Harvard Univ. Press, 1957), pp. 202-206.

8. Although the allegation of many mistresses of the secretarial sort makes Notterdam promiscuous in a way Ashburnham is not, his explicitly named loves correspond to Ashburnham's: Lottie to the Kilsyte girl; La Buccarino to La Dolciquita; Mrs. Lola Porter, whose husband benefits from her flirtation, roughly to Mrs. Basil; Henrietta to Nancy.

9. Mizener, pp. 345-47.

10. But "Winter Night-Song" is thematically very familiar: "You are my peace . . . my eyes you are." *New Poems*, p. 37.

11. See Wiley, pp. 263-69.

12. The dates of these last two are of the first American editions; the first English edition of *It Was the Nightingale* did not appear until 1934, but is, as usual, the text I use; *Henry for Hugh* was never published in England.

13. Although the artist (Janice Biala) never saw even a photograph of Marwood and had no thought of Marwood, the pink face remarkably resembles his—a tribute to the fictional prose that evoked the portrait.

14. Although Conrad does not appear in *The Rash Act*, his influence persists. "Rash act" is the phrase Conrad uses to describe Captain Brierly's suicide in *Lord Jim*. Moreover, Henry's obsessive tidying up before the act, putting "two heavy pigs of iron ballast" into his pockets, and his intention "to step stiffly" off the boat all precisely follow Brierly's suicide—and recall Captain Whalley's and Decoud's (10, 193, 36). And, naturally, Henry is "at the end of his tether" (156). That "landscape without mercy," "infinitely without the quality of pity," smiling "the heartless smile of syrens" smacks of Conradese (10). The hazardous boat trip through harbor, bay, and cove, including Henry's successful maneuver "to shave the headland" during a driving, blinding, teeth-chattering, shiver-inducing rainstorm, echoes any number of such Ford-connected Conrad books as *The Rescue, Romance, Nostromo,* and *The Mirror of the Sea* (198, 200).

15. Mizener, p. 409.

16. Ludwig, pp. 178-80.

17. Although MacShane and Caroline Gordon eschew biography, they have an interesting argument as to the centrality of the theme of mistaken identity versus Ford's postimpressionist desire to write a book about nothing. MacShane, *Life and Work of Ford Madox Ford*, pp. 217-22.

18. Like Tietjens and Ashburnham, Hugh has a round-backed chair and green-shaded lamp (RA, 125, 245). Hugh's grip has monstrous jaws (RA, 241) recalling Maisie's death. The Marwood of *Return to Yesterday*, like Ashburnham, interests himself in gambling at Monte Carlo (374).

19. Ford says he got Tietjens' dilemma, being tricked into marrying a "bitch" pregnant by another man, from a story Marwood told him, on the train, about "Waring" picking up the woman on the Paris-Calais train (IWN, 209-10). Wherever the story came from (a fantasy on himself and Violet caught by Elsie while getting off the Dover train?), it is another link between Marwood and Ford, as Ford used the name "Waring" in his 1906 account of his own breakdown and in a 1907 short story about adultery. See also Valentine Baker, D.N.B.

20. Hugh's being deeply moved that Henry, a neutral, would volunteer to fight for England suggests that Ford may have hoped his own joining up would have touched the patriotic Marwood, as it unquestionably touched Conrad.

21. No doubt the pun is intentional, just as "Henry" probably refers to Henry Ford. The Monckton fortune Henry inherits comes from a gigantic automobile concern. Ford at this time liked to refer to the American car as being made by his namesake.

22. Archibald Marshall, *Out and About* (London: John Murray, 1933), p. 277.

23. Edward Crankshaw, in the summer of Ford's death, wrote of "his passionate attachment to England." Quoted by MacShane, *Life and Work of Ford Madox Ford*, p. 247.

24. Although *Vive Le Roy* was first published in America in 1936, I quote from the first English edition, of 1937.

25. Mizener equates the two, pp. 433; 522; 605, nn. 72, 73.

CHAPTER EIGHT

1. *Provence* was published first in America in 1935, three years before the English edition used here, and two years before *Great Trade Route*.

2. MacShane says Ford had a mild heart attack in December 1929, *Life and Work of Ford Madox Ford*, p. 206; Mizener puts it a year later, p. 396. Harvey, p. 391.

3. But these ideas appear a decade earlier, too, in *When Blood is Their Argument*.

4. Robert Lowell never forgot Ford's "muffled Yorkshire gasp." Ford Madox Ford, *Buckshee*, with introductions by Robert Lowell and Kenneth Rexroth (Cambridge, Mass.: Pym-Randall Press, 1966), p. xii.

5. Though Wiley praises Ford's "assurance" in the thirties, p. 248, and

MacShane his "serenity," *Life and Work of Ford Madox Ford*, p. 243, Mizener is not persuaded, p. 425.

6. I cannot recommend *Provence* highly enough. It is a beautiful, engaging, noble, and timely book. Ford's devotion to gardening, to eating in moderation natural foods subtly spiced, to folk arts, and to local government; his hostility to technology, his frustration with international politics, and his hatred of hatred seem to me to express the aspirations of recent generations of youths around the world. Although *Great Trade Route* is worth reading and ends hilariously, it works less well. If Ford's celebrations of Washington as leader and Jefferson as artist are convincing, his view of Lincoln as sharp lawyer is not. If Ford could have read Lincoln and looked at Brady's photographs without the southern bias, he would have found a great artist expressing himself in Ford's kind of prose and a truly tragic figure. Had Ford also considered the attitudes of Mark Twain (whom he always praises), he might have seen slavery and the Civil War more deeply and complexly. *Great Trade Route* also reflects uninterestingly Ford's various, physically hard and unpleasant experiences of having to travel, alas, with strict economy. Arthur Mizener properly reminds us that his ideas were common at the time. But it is good to remember, too, that Ford's immediate understanding and loathing of fascism were not exactly common among such conservative, artist friends as Pound and Eliot.

   Provence has been recently re-issued by the Ecco Press.

7. *Mightier Than the Sword* (1938) was first published in America in 1937 under the title *Portraits from Life*.

8. Aldington, p. 137.

9. See Maurice Hungiville, "The Passionate Poets in the Classroom," *The Chronicle of Higher Education*, November 4, 1974, p. 9.

10. Quoted by Harvey, p. 263.

11. Ford's account in *Mightier Than the Sword* of his last view of Lawrence is a classic instance of how Ford distorts in order to express a higher, or at least more personal, truth. He tells how the Minister of Information sent him down to Sussex to make certain D. H. Lawrence was not being persecuted for his pro-German sentiments. Mrs. H. G. Wells drove him the thirty or forty miles. Ford never saw Lawrence again "to talk to" (121).

   The Gods saw otherwise. For the moment we arrived at that pleasant place, Mrs. Wells, who was very small, and Mrs. Lawrence, who resembled the Germania above the Rhine at Rüdesheim—fell into a discussion as to the merits of the Belgians. And, as Mrs. Lawrence saw fit to address, on the side, unfavourable remarks to the uniform I was wearing, I thought it was better—because I *was* there to make a report to Authority—to retire to an outhouse and await the close of the discussion. So that the last image I have of Lawrence is his standing there, a little impotent, his hands hanging at his side, as if he were present at a dog fight in the beautiful, white-walled, shady, aesthetic room of Mrs. Meynell. He was smiling slightly, his head slightly bent. But his *panache*, his plume of hair with the sunlight always in it—and his red beard—were as disturbingly bright as ever. (122)

Violet Hunt, totally absent from Ford's account, previously described the scene: "Mrs. H. G. Wells was staying with us" (presumably at Violet's cottage in Selsey, Sussex); "we all three motored over to see them. And D. H. was not there . . . it was the autumn of 1914," Ford had just written his poem "Antwerp," based on looking at the Belgian women and children refugees pouring into Charing Cross Station, "and we were spilling over with emotion, obviously anti-German." Frieda Lawrence, in a foreign accent, said contemptuously, "Dirty Belgians! Who cares for them!" Whereupon Violet, according to Violet, proceeded to "wipe the floor with her." Ford and Mrs. Wells "retreated to separate corners of the hall to be out of the way" (Hunt, p. 259).

On January 15, 1955, Frieda Lawrence wrote to Harry T. Moore, her husband's biographer:

The Hueffers coming: this is *my* story. When they came, he and Violet Hunt, I said to him: *"Wir sind auch Deutsch?"* That made him squirm and he hummed and hawed. It was wartime. So I did not think much of him. I never said: those "dirty Belgians," I never felt like that! Lawrence was not there, there was no outhouse Ford could have retired to, I made no tirade, he wore no uniform . . .

(*Frieda Lawrence: The Memoirs and Correspondence*, ed. E. W. Tedlock, Jr. [New York: Knopf, 1964], p. 389. See Mizener's comments, pp. 281-82; 569, n. 10. Violet surely gives too early a date for the episode.)

Which version is "true"? Ford's, of course—for Ford. First, for his own artistic reasons, he had to have an intermediate observer (Lawrence) to view the quarrel between the two women. Second, since Ford was personally shattered by the German attack on Belgium and since he immediately began writing anti-German propaganda, he would think of himself as having donned his uniform at the outbreak of war rather than in August 1915 when he got his commission. Third, since Violet Hunt had once been his mistress, she essentially ceased to exist for Ford after he left her in 1919. Fourth, since Mrs. Wells had never been his mistress, had always been kind to him, and now, being safely dead like Conrad and Marwood, could be freely loved by Ford, she, not Violet, represented the perfect advocate of the living truth embodied in

Ford Madox Ford. Fifth, with Lawrence's wife attacking Ford and Ford being characteristically unable to defend himself, Lawrence, had he been there, might well have stood "a little impotent . . . smiling slightly," with "his head slightly bent," might well have looked, that is, precisely the way Ford doubtless realized he himself was looking. Sixth, with Violet fighting like a dog for him, in his presence, Ford must in spirit have been at least in an outhouse, if not in Carcassonne.

Consider Ford's situation. His father's homeland, his own adopted country for the past four years, was making terrible war on his own and his mother's homeland as well as upon France, the land of his happiest dreams. Presumably he was hopelessly in love with Brigit; he was certainly wishing to be free of Violet, upon whom he was financially dependent. Elsie was constantly dragging him into court and causing his name to be besmirched in the daily papers. She had the custody of his two beloved daughters whom he had not seen in years. Among young writers and critics the impressionistic methods he had advocated for over a decade seemed out-of-date, finished. His only really great novel, The Good Soldier, was being ignored or reviled. When you think of all these things and read Ford's version of his last meeting with "Lawrence," you understand why Ford so wanted then to die.

12. Nor really the Ford of The March of Literature (1938). Although he admits there the pull, for the artist, of art as entertainment, or decoration, or pure beauty, his final preference is for realism in its broadest sense. Greek tragedy merits some of his highest praise; he chooses "those who have lived" over "those who have read" (558); although he still loves Christopher's model, Herbert of Bremerton, it is Donne who can speak to man in these "dreadful days" (447).

The gigantic March of Literature, written at high speed at the end of his life, is an incredible achievement. Naturally, it is a literary journey along the Great Trade Route, delighting in coincidence, glorifying Aristotle for his "encyclopaedic" knowledge (154), extolling the "small producer" (84), praising once again the remarkable qualities of the medieval mind. Not surprisingly, the writing itself is sometimes fatigued as Ford, rather mechanically and wearily, brings still another national literature up-to-date and then plods on. But if Mightier Than the Sword treats Conrad inadequately, The March of Literature pays the highest possible tribute this last time to the "most consummate . . . the most common-sensible and the most absolutely passionate man-of-action become conscious man-of-letters that this writer has ever known, read of or conceived of" (763).

13. Baines, pp. 132-33.

Index

Library of Congress Cataloging in Publication Data

Moser, Thomas C
   The life in the fiction of Ford Madox Ford.

   Includes index.
      1. Ford, Ford Madox, 1873-1939—Criticism and
   interpretation.   2. Fiction, Autobiographic.
   I. Title.
   PR6011.053Z795   823'.912   80-7548
   ISBN 0-691-06445-8
   ISBN 0-691-10102-7 (pbk.)